ILLUSTRATED BY

LU YANGUANG

100 Chinese Emperors

WRITTEN BY

WU LUXING

TRANSLATED BY

WANG XUEWEN

&

WANG YANXI

ASIAPAC BOOKS • SINGAPORE

Publisher
ASIAPAC BOOKS PTE LTD
629 Aljunied Road
#04-06 Cititech Industrial Building
Singapore 389838
Tel : 745 3868
Fax: 745 3822
Email: apacbks@singnet.com.sg

Visit us at our Internet home page
http://www.span.com.au//Asiapac.htm

First published May 1996

Designed by Marked Point Design
Body text set in 11 point Garamond 3
Printed in Singapore by Chung Printing

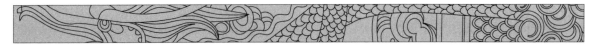

PUBLISHER'S NOTE

*A*s a publisher dedicated to the promotion of works of Chinese philosophy, art and literature, we are pleased to present *100 Chinese Emperors*, the third title in our *100 Series Art Album*.

This volume provides a quick insight into China's monarchy over more than 5,000 years of history, from Yan Di and Huang Di of the Chinese primitive society to the last Qing emperor Puyi. It is a formidable task for any author to compile the records of the many kings and emperors in Chinese history. Lu Yanguang, however, has ingeniously chosen 100 emperors who by their wisdom or folly, turned events and shaped the destiny of the nation. Whether honoured or hated, each of them provides a vital link to understanding the political climate and social mood of their times. The readers would also be able to follow the people's protracted struggles against feudalism, colonialism and imperialism.

In essence, this book is a pictorial outline of the Chinese monarchy, making it very easy for today's readers to appreciate the history of the world's largest nation, who remains unified despite a land area of 9.6 million square kilometres and a composition of 55 nationalities.

We feel honoured to have the artist Lu Yanguang's permission to the translation rights for his art album. Our gratitude, too, to Professor Wang Xuewen and Wang Yanxi for translating this book, and to Pan Shou for his foreword in calligraphy. Last but not least, we would like to thank the production team for putting in their best effort in the publication of this series.

靈迴先生線插繡像申圖一石當那文化悠久民族不惟有

此乎當髡林治中西技法於一爐通古含聲氣孜百生於神上

之繹絀按靈狗花鴻滿兒妝陸雜細針密殊幅圖以一支出百圖石

曲風移雅用兩搃律多異盡懸粉形爭寫競爽辞含人摯音低

潤根索州姬林利圖女士以方以此英術奇能不里畫地為牢出眼

於華文言畧將田共雨姬至之空太圖書号肟弓司出版英譯本以繼

華文言多所分之讀者藉廣添傳淅索一言圖業不菠氣漂筆

題之如左 一九九〇年歲次甲戌之春 唐之溥文 [印][印]

FOREWORD

*T*he line-drawn portraits in the 100 Series Art Album by Mr Lu Yanguang can only be based on the rich cultural heritage of a race with a long history. The portrayal of these figures has been executed with a subtle combination of oriental and western artistic techniques. These beautiful illustrations have been captured in exquisitely refined details. Each picture is like a tune. One hundred pictures, one hundred tunes. They share the same style but each has a rhythm of its own. One just cannot help being overwhelmed by admiration for the artist's creativity in presenting such a wide repertoire of form and posture.

Madam Lim Li Kok feels that such a masterpiece of artistic work should not be confined to the Chinese Language reading public. She has arranged for an English version of the book to be published by her company, Asiapac Books, so that a larger circle of non-Chinese Language readers may also enjoy it.

I have been asked to write a message for this book. Instead, I have chosen to write a few words with my brush.

Calligraphy by Pan Shou
(Poet and Scholar)
Spring, 1994

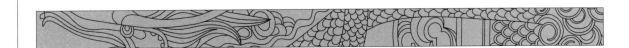

ABOUT THE ILLUSTRATOR

*L*u Yanguang was born in Kaiping, Guangdong Province in 1948. He is presently director of Guangzhou Art Gallery, vice-chairman of Guangzhou Artists' Association and chief editor of *Guangzhou Art Studies*.

His published works since 1985 include *Lu Yanguang's Album of Illustrations, Selected New Works of Lu Yanguang's Illustrations, Album of Lingnan Scenery and Legends, 100 Chinese Women, 100 Chinese Emperors, 100 Chinese Gods, 100 Chinese Scholars* and *100 Chinese Monks*.

A renowned artist, Lu Yanguang started his career by drawing illustrations and cartoons. Instead of the traditional Chinese style of brush painting, each character in this collection is a combination of the old – the dynastic eras of ancient China, and the new – Lu Yanguang's refreshingly artistic technique of *xiuxiang hua* (portraits in decorative style). His illustrations are characterized by a strong sense of speed and rhythm.

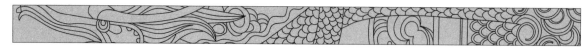

ABOUT THE WRITER

*B*orn in 1944 in Guangzhou, Wu Luxing works as an editor for the *Yang Cheng Wan Bao* in Guangzhou. He is also the writer for the Chinese edition of *100 Chinese Gods*.

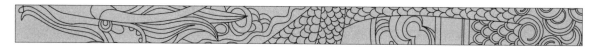

ABOUT THE TRANSLATORS

*P*rofessor Wang Xuewen was born in Hebei Province, China, in 1944. He is professor of English and Dean of the School of International Studies of the University of International Business & Economics, Beijing. He has translated many books and short stories, including *All Creatures Great and Small, James and the Giant Peach* and *Mobi Dick*.

Also an author, he has written several textbooks such as *Business Oral Translation, Practical Written Communication*, and *International Trade English*.

An experienced tutor, he has been a mentor to many MA postgraduates majoring in translation theory and practice.

*W*ang Yanxi was born in Hubei Province, China, in 1964. She earned her BA in Hubei University and her MA in the University of International Business & Economics, majoring in translation theory and practice. Her thesis *On Poem Translation* won favourable comments from experts. She has translated several short stories and articles.

Both of them translated *100 Chinese Gods*, an earlier volume in this series, which won the Silver Prize in the First APPA awards for Fully Translated or Copublished Books organized by the Asian Pacific Publishers Association (APPA) in Tokyo, February 1995.

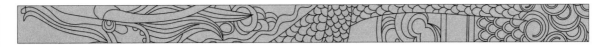

PREFACE

*T*his is an arduous project of art, grand and exquisite, majestic and fine, stately and romantic. The drawings are thought-provoking and of high ornamental value, being as exquisite as ivory carving. Instead of relying on beautiful colours, the drawings have gained their appeal by means of rich imagination, consummate skill, as well as the magnificent style and strength acquired through the meticulously-drawn lines.

This is also a vivid volume of dynastic history depicted in fine lines. Here the figures are kings and emperors. The events they experienced in their times, and the joys and sorrows of the common people cannot be seen directly in the drawings, yet we can faintly perceive the changes and events over the 5,000 years of Chinese history, and the glorious and arduous course our nation has gone through from the 100 portraits of different appearances and airs and from the background with profound connotations.

History is, after all, decided by the people. However, the roles played by the monarchs of each dynasty, either positive or negative, are also an important factor. Otherwise, why should people today still take delight in talking about the "Order and Prosperity of the Zhenguan Period" under the reign of Emperor Tai Zong of the Tang Dynasty and the "Heyday under Emperors Kang Xi and Qian Long of the Qing Dynasty"? It is only natural for people to admire wise and just emperors and condemn tyrants. No monarch can escape the strict and impartial judgement of history, and each of them is either admired or criticized by later generations. (And some of them may be both praised and criticized.) Since ancient times, the common people have had distinct love or hatred towards the all-powerful monarchs since what the latter did was closely related with the weal and woe of the former. The portraits in this collection are no doubt imbued with the artist's mixed feelings towards the wise monarchs and the wicked tyrants. It is only with painstaking efforts that the artist has succeeded in embodying his historical knowledge and feeling in the countless silk-like fine lines. It is no doubt impossible to condense the 5,000-year-long Chinese history in the images of 100 kings and emperors. However, the artist has on the whole succeeded in reflecting in the portraits his basic understanding of the immense time and space and giving expression to his passion arising therefrom. While admitting his general success, I cannot help thinking why he has taken such great pains to undertake this arduous project voluntarily.

I have never asked Lu Yanguang such a question and can only make some supposition. Since ancient times, the common people have always tried to trace the cause of their fate to the supreme rulers either to learn a lesson from the tragic history or to felicitate themselves on the order and prosperity of their times. Therein are embodied their grievances and indignation as well as their memory and gratitude. In case of grievances and indignation, they would condemn tyrants like Jie of the Xia Dynasty and Zhou of the Shang Dynasty; and in case of memory and gratitude, they would admire wise and benevolent monarchs like Yao and Shun. At each turning point in history, people tend to make associations from the bygone great figures or mean ones, which reflects a very natural social psychology. That is why I am of the opinion that the artistic works of historical theme in this collection are in a sense the product of the current social psychology. Whether aware of it or not, Lu Yanguang has offered these significant works in conformity with the sentiments of millions of people.

Being neither a historian nor an artist, it is indeed difficult for me to write a preface for this collection of portraits. I have been willing to do it as I think his efforts are worthy of respect and admiration. We have before us masterpieces by an earnest and honest artist loyal to both life and art who has obviously transcended his past and has shown great potential.

~ Cen Sang

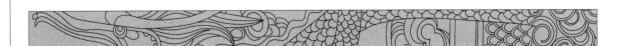

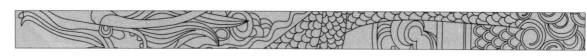

CONTENTS

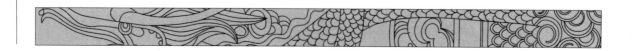

CONTENTS

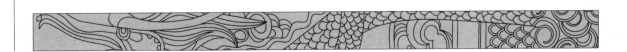

CONTENTS

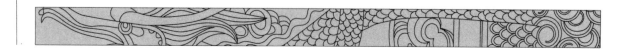

CONTENTS

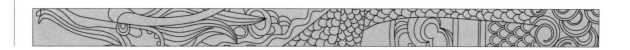

Yan Di

炎帝

Yan Di, together with his brother Huang Di (the Yellow Emperor), was regarded as the ancestor of the Chinese people. Some say he was the Divine Farmer who introduced farming to the country.

Surnamed Jiang, Yan Di was the leader of the Jiang clan that lived around what is today's Shaanxi Province towards the end of the primitive society more than 5,000 - 6,000 years ago.

The Jiangs were a branch of the Xirong nomads that had moved east to the central part of China. For long, they had had conflicts with the Jiuli people headed by Chiyou that lived around the border of present-day Shaanxi, Hebei and Henan Provinces. The Jiangs were driven north to Zhuolu where they formed an alliance with the Ji clan headed by the Yellow Emperor. With the support of the latter, they defeated the Jiuli people and killed Chiyou. Since then Yan Di's clan had settled down in the Central Plains of China.

The low productivity at the time could not satisfy the people's need for food, and Yan Di made great contributions towards the development of agricultural production.

It was said that Yan Di was once pondering over how to teach people the way of farming when a shower of grain seeds fell from the sky. He collected the seeds and had them sown in the cultivated land. And people say that was the beginning of grain farming.

Yan Di also took measures to fight against diseases threatening the people's health. Legend has it that he used to beat on the herbs with a magic whip to reveal their different natures: whether toxic or harmless, and associated with heat or cold. He tasted all the herbs personally to confirm their nature and was one day subjected to poison 12 times. He thus succeeded in distinguishing many poisonous herbs.

In the end, however, he tasted a very poisonous herb for which there was no antidote. He died as a result with his intestines rotted into segments.

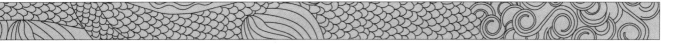

Yan Di

Huang Di

黄帝

Huang Di, or the Yellow Emperor, is referred to as the "Originator of the Chinese Culture", and all people of the Chinese race regard themselves as descendants of Yan Di and Huang Di.

With the original surname of Gongsun (later changed to Ji) and another name Youxiong Shi, Huang Di was also known as Xuanyuan Shi as he lived at the Xuanyuan Hill.

A clan leader towards the end of China's primitive society, Huang Di was the full brother of Yan Di with whom he shared the country. He formed an alliance with Yan Di in later years against the invasion of Chiyou, the chieftain of the Jiuli Tribe. A decisive battle was fought at Zhuolu in the northwest of the present Hebei Province. Legend goes that at the beginning of the battle, Chiyou sneezed out a thick fog all over the place which lasted three days, and the soldiers of Huang Di could not tell their directions. Fortunately Huang Di led his men out of the fog by the "compass chariot" he had invented and won complete victory.

The alliance of Huang Di and Yan Di split after Chiyou was defeated because, it was said, Yan Di intended to infringe upon the various tribes and seize the leading position of the alliance while the chieftains of the tribes preferred to obey Huang Di. As a result the two leaders fought at Banquan. After three fierce battles, Huang Di won victory and was made the "Son of Heaven" by the tribe chieftains.

Strict and impartial, Huang Di was able to get rid of the evil for the people. It was said that Gu, son of the God of Mount Zhongshan named Zhulong, murdered another god at Mount Kunlun in collaboration with a deity called Qinpi. The Yellow Emperor was indignant at their atrocity and immediately had them killed.

The Yellow Emperor was a highly gifted "Son of Heaven". Legend goes that he was the inventor of many things such as making clothes, manufacturing boats and vehicles, building houses and palaces, etc. He also had his court officials Lun Ling make musical instruments, Da Nao compile the Heavenly Stems and the Earthly Branches[1], and Cang Jie invent the Chinese characters. The country was in good order and prosperity and the people lived a happy life.

There were indeed quite a number of wars at the time, which however, broke the narrow limits between the different clans and promoted their merging. The ancient Huaxia nationality was thus gradually formed, being the predecessor of the Han nationality to which the overwhelming majority of the Chinese people belong.

It is said that Yao, Shun and the monarchs of the Xia, Shang and Zhou dynasties were all descendants of the Yellow Emperor. He was thus regarded as the first ancestor of the Chinese nation and to him was attributed the creation of all Chinese cultural institutions.

---

1. *The 10 Heavenly Stems and 12 Earthly Branches are used in combination to designate years, months, days and hours.*

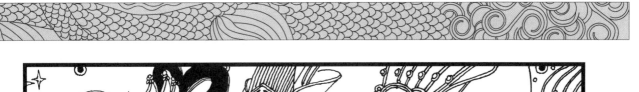

Huang Di

Yao

堯

The first of the three successive sage rulers at the end of the Chinese primitive society, Yao was also known as Taotangshi and Fangrun, and was often referred to in history books as Tang Yao. He was said to be the son of Diku and was five generations away from the Yellow Emperor.

After becoming the "Son of Heaven", Yao named his country Tang with Pingyang (present Linfen County, Shanxi Province) as the capital. He led a frugal life, living in a thatched house, eating coarse rice and drinking wild-herb soup. He put on a deer skin in winter and never made new clothes until his old clothes were worn out. Despite living in such hard conditions, he showed great concern for the welfare of the people. He said that he would be the one to blame if there was a single person suffering from cold and hunger or committing a crime.

Yao was quite democratic. At that time the supreme power of the tribe alliance rested with the Committee of Tribal Chiefs. Once the Committee recommended Gun to take charge of flood control. Yao complied with the decision though he did not agree with the choice.

Following Yao's example, his officials were all devoted to their jobs. Legend goes that his Chief Judge Gao Yao was sagacious and impartial and raised a single-horned divine goat. In cases of disputes and quarrels, the goat would attack the person in the wrong with its horn. Thus the people lived a peaceful and happy life and loved Yao as the sun and the moon.

It was said that Yao had ten sons. But his eldest son Danzhu was far from a qualified successor. As a result, Yao decided to pass on the throne to Shun and meanwhile ordered to have his eldest son banished to the south as an ordinary duke. This decision angered the Sanmiao Tribe in the Central Plain of China, which rose against him. Yao, however, would not change his political decision because of that and sent an army to suppress the revolt instead. The insurgent troops were defeated and their chiefs captured and killed.

Yao has been widely acknowledged as a model monarch in Chinese history. According to *Records of Yao*, people were deeply grieved at the death of Yao as if they had lost their own parents.

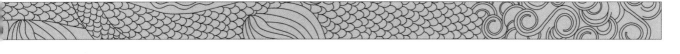

Yao

Shun

舜

The second of the three successive sage rulers at the end of the Chinese primitive society, Shun was also known as Youyushi and Chonghua, and was often referred to in history as Yushun.

He was born in Zhufeng (the present Zhucheng County of Shandong Province). It was said that his mother died not long after he was born. Unable to put up with the maltreatment of his father and stepmother, he fled to the foot of Lishan Mountain near the river Guishui. There he opened up the wasteland and even trained an elephant to help him with farming.

Shun did his best to help others with farming, fishing and pottery making. As a result people kept coming to his place reclaiming the land, and before long, the place became a busy village.

As his son Dan Zhu was worthless, Yao accepted the recommendation of the Committee of Tribe Chiefs and chose Shun as his successor. He put Shun to the test before passing on the throne to him. He had Shun put in the depth of a large forest just before a thunderstorm to see how he would get out of it. It turned out that Shun resourcefully kept away from the wolves, tigers and leopards and got home safe and sound.

The name of Shun's kingdom was Yu. He did a lot of good things for the people during the decades of his reign. As early as in the time of Yao, there had been what people called the "Four Evils", that is, Gun, Gonggong, Huandou, and the riots of Sanmiao. Soon after succeeding to the crown, Shun eliminated the Evils and banished them to the remote border areas.

Shun did farming and fishing himself and he was also fond of playing qin, a kind of stringed musical instrument. When the former monarch Yao married his two daughters to Shun, he also gave him as present a five-stringed qin, which Shun would play in leisure while singing the song *South Wind* composed by himself:

> *Cool wind from the south*
> *Clears away people's worry;*
> *Timely wind from the south*
> *Increases people's wealth.*

It can be seen from the song how Shun loved his people.

When Shun became old, he passed on the throne to Yu who had made great contributions in controlling the flood, instead of his son Shangjun. It was said that he made a tour to the south in spite of his old age and weakness. Unfortunately he died in Cangwu on his way. People said that his remains were put in a pottery coffin and buried in the south of Jiuyi Mountain in Cangwu.

Shun

Yu

禹

The third of the three successive sage rulers at the end of the Chinese primitive society, Yu has been known as Great Yu, the water controller. He is also referred to as Xia Yu or Rong Yu, and was chosen as successor to Shun for his contributions in controlling the flood.

People say that the Yellow River was in flood during the reign of Shun, inundating the fields and washing away the houses. People unanimously recommended Yu, the son of Gun, to take charge of river harnessing. Having taken up the job without hesitation, Yu went about the country with tools in hand and food in haversack surveying the rivers and mountains. He changed the former practice of the different tribes in controlling the flood separately and made a unified plan dividing the country into a number of regions to facilitate the work. For that purpose, he scraped off the bark of the big trees on the borderline to carve marks on. Drawing a lesson from the failure of his father who had for nine years tried to control the flood by "damming", he boldly adopted the practice of "dredging". He first dredged the large rivers to channel the water into the sea before dredging the streams and ditches to channel the water into large rivers. In the 13 years of his hard work, he passed his own home three times without stopping to go in. In the end he got the flood harnessed.

After succeeding to the throne, Yu cast nine huge tripods with the copper contributed by officials from various localities on which were carved pictures of all kinds of poisonous reptiles and harmful beasts as well as ghosts and spirits so that people could recognize them and protect themselves from them. The tripods were placed outside the palace gate for display, and after that "Yu's Tripods" became synonymous with "discerning the evil".

Yu's power was greatly strengthened for his meritorious deeds in harnessing the flood and for the victory against the Sanmiao Tribe achieved under his leadership. When he convened the meeting of state chiefs at Tushan Mountain, there were as many as ten thousand participants and those who were late were put to death. By that time Yu had been a great ruler with authority and power known far and wide. When Yu was old, the Committee of Tribe Chiefs unanimously elected Gao Yao to be his successor. It was believed that Gao Yao was the first to make criminal laws in Chinese history. Unfortunately, he died prematurely before Yu, and people elected Boyi in his place. After Yu's death, however, his son immediately had the chosen successor killed and seized the supreme power. From then on, the system of passing the crown to a chosen person was replaced by inheritance.

Yu

夏・啓

Qi of the Xia Dynasty

Qi was the first king of the Xia Dynasty (21st century to 16th century BC), the first dynasty of the Chinese slave society. His surname was Si, and he was the son of Great Yu.

Qi was able to replace the system of passing the crown to a chosen successor with that of inheritance as history had progressed to the stage where private ownership became predominant.

Qi's succession to the throne met with opposition from the conservative forces. A tribe chief You Hu Shi carrying the same surname as Xia started an armed rebellion and fought against the King's Expedition Army at Gan (the present Huxian County of Shanxi Province). It turned out that You Hu Shi had a disastrous defeat and was reduced to a slave. The suppression of the opposition forces consolidated Qi's position. He twice feasted with chiefs of the subjugated tribes with the purpose of exacting tributes from among them. Thus the primitive tribe alliance was replaced by a power institution oppressing and exploiting the people and the basic form of state power came into being.

Qi was a wilful outrageous ruler. He often went on extravagant feasts in the fields in the company of his favourite officials. In the palace he kept many musicians and girls to perform songs and dances specially for him. Later, he even used the nine copper tripods made by his father for cooking, which met with universal opposition from the people.

His younger brother Wu Guan took the lead in an armed rebellion to seize the throne, which sapped Qi's rule though he was suppressed in the end. After his death, his son Tai Kang who succeeded to the crown was equally dissipated and extravagant and made a mess of the country, which as a result was conquered by Hou Yi of the You Qiongshi Clan.

It was only after decades of twists and turns that Qi's great-grandson Shao Kang regained the crown with the support of his clan. The event is referred to in history as the "Resurgence by Shao Kang".

Qi of the Xia Dynasty

夏 · 桀

Jie of the Xia Dynasty

One of the notorious tyrants in Chinese history, Jie was the last king of the Xia Dynasty who reigned about 3,600 years ago.

Stalwart and dignified in appearance, Jie was exceptionally strong and powerful. He was said to be able to break hard horns with one hand, and straighten crooked metal hooks before twisting them together like twisting fibres into a string. He was even strong enough to fight a beast of prey bare-handed.

In order to tighten his control over the neighbouring states, Jie launched an expedition against Youshishi shortly after his accession to the throne. Unable to resist the attack, Youshishi offered a beautiful girl, Moxi, to the king who doted on the beauty and withdrew his troops. Jie spent all his time in company with his new lady and forced a large number of labourers to build a new palace for her in which were chambers and terraces decorated with jade, pillars made of bronze, corridors ornamented with ivory, and beds carved out of marble. He issued an order to pile up meat into a small hill and to fill in a pond with delicious wine on which there were even small boats. Here, "three thousand people could drink and eat to their heart's content."

His subjects detested him for his extravagance and tyranny, and no one wanted to serve him any more. A virtuous man named Yi Yin was bold enough to remind Jie at a banquet: "The state is going to perish if the monarch refuses to listen to advice." To that Jie replied shamelessly: "I reigning the country am just like the sun shining in the sky. Will it be possible for the sun to perish?" Hearing these remarks, the people cursed, pointing at the sun: "You abominable sun! Why don't you perish earlier? We would rather die together with you."

Later Jie sent an expedition army under a general named Bian against the state of Minshan, whose ruler sent somebody to sue for peace by offering countless treasures and two beautiful girls. At that time, the virtuous Yi Yin who had fled Jie's country and become a senior official in the state of Shang succeeded in getting in touch with Moxi who had lost favour with the King, and got to know a lot of secrets about the country under Jie's rule. Seeing that the opportunity had come, Yi Yin together with Tang, the ruler of the state Shang, led a strong army towards the capital of Xia. After a fierce battle at Mingtiao (east of present Fengqiu of Henan Province), the Xia army was utterly defeated and Jie fled to Nanchao (southeast of present Shouxian County, Anhui Province) where he died later. Thus the Xia Dynasty was replaced by the Shang Dynasty led by Tang.

Jie of the Xia Dynasty

商 • 湯

Tang of the Shang Dynasty

Tang was the founder of the Shang Dynasty, the second dynasty of the Chinese slave society. With the surname Zi and personal name Lu, he was also known in historical records as Tianyi, Chengtang or Wutang.

Shang had been a tribe to the east of Xia, with the swallow as its totem. The first ancestor of the tribe was Qi[1], and Tang was his 14th generation descendant. By this time, Shang, with Bo (north of present Shangqui County, Henan Province) as its capital, had been a rising slave-system state among the vassal states of Xia.

At that time, Tang was a kind and generous ruler. Once he went hunting in the suburbs and saw a man putting up nets in all the four directions to catch birds. He persuaded the man to remove the nets on three directions so as to save some birds from being caught. The other states saw Tang's kindness and leniency in this and some of them broke away from Xia and became Shang's vassal states.

Seeing Shang getting stronger, King Jie of the Xia Dynasty became worried. Following the scheme of a wicked official Zhao Liang, he summoned Tang to the capital on an excuse and imprisoned him at Xiatai (namely Diaotai). Yi Yin, a wise official, contrived to have him set free by bribing the king with treasures and beauties. Tang was thus determined to overthrow the Xia Dynasty.

Following the plan made by Yi Yin, Tang sent troops to attack the three states allied with Xia before invading the suzerain. Yi Yin suggested: "Let's see how Jie will react if we refuse to pay tribute to him." The king of Xia became very angry and mobilized the army of his vassal state Jiuyi against Shang. Yi Yin then said to Tang: "Jie can still call on Jiuyi to send troops against us. Let's refrain from attacking him for the time being." They then apologized to Jie and paid tribute to him. However, when Tang again refused to pay tribute the next year, Jiuyi declined Jie's call to send troops to help him. Seeing that Jie was no longer influential, Yi Yin assisted Tang to organize a military expedition against the Xia Dynasty.

Sitting on a chariot with the army flag and holding a large axe, Tang led his strong army towards the capital of Xia. The two armies met at Mingtiao where Tang declared Jie's crimes to all his troops, who were greatly inspired and defeated the Xia army in only one battle. After the death of Jie, Tang founded the Shang Dynasty and became the king. This event is referred to in history as the "Chengtang Revolution".

---

1. This Qi is a different person from the first king of the Xia Dynasty.

Tang of the Shang Dynasty

Pan Geng of the Shang Dynasty

商
·
盤
庚

Pan Geng, the ninth generation descendant of Tang, was a king of the Shang Dynasty known for his success in moving the capital for the better development of his kingdom.

In the period from Zhongding to Yangjia, the Shang Dynasty was in a state of political chaos and decline with the brothers struggling against each other for the crown, the king bent on building palaces, and the corrupt nobles living in luxury. Pan Geng succeeded to the throne after the death of his elder brother Yangjia.

Seeing the country suffer from years of flood and the people flee their home places, the king intended to move the capital from Yan (modern Qufu of Shandong Province) to Yin (northwest of modern Anyang of Henan Province) so as to change the luxurious ways of the nobles in a new environment and relax the social contradictions of the declining kingdom. This proposal of his, however, met with the opposition of both the officials and the common people. For three times the king called them to the palace, lecturing on his proposal. First he explained to the officials why the capital should be moved. Then he said to the common people: "Your lives have been reserved by me from Heaven. If you fail to obey me, your ancestors will request my predecessors for severe punishment to befall you. Then I shall kill you all, leaving no descendants for you. In that case, you will not be able to go to the new capital even if you wish to. Let's go to the new capital now. Follow me and I shall protect you and your families."

Then again he called members of the ruling group and said: "I am now speaking to you from the bottom of my heart. Your ancestors made contributions to the kingdom. If you act according to my will, the common people will follow us, but if you do not, they will revolt."

Through his repeated mobilizations, his officials and the common people agreed to move the capital. As the new capital was called Yin (modern Xiaotun Village, Anyang), the Dynasty was thereafter called Yin Shang. Pan Geng ordered to build houses with thatch in the new capital. The social order was stabilized as a result of the people's burden being lightened. That paved the way for the development of the kingdom in the later stage of the Dynasty, and Pan Geng was thus regarded as a good king who had revived the Dynasty.

Pan Geng of the Shang Dynasty

Zhou of the Shang Dynasty

商·紂

Zhou, also called Dixin, was the last king of the Shang Dynasty. He was a notorious cruel monarch just like Jie of the Xia Dynasty although he made some contributions to the development of the southeastern part of the country.

The crown of the Shang Dynasty founded by Tang was passed on to Zhou after 31 kings of 17 generations. Strong and powerful, Zhou was said to be able to draw back a carriage pulled by nine cattle. He was also an eloquent person, but he had the vital weakness of being arrogant, conceited, and self-righteous, and always tried to gloss over his mistakes.

Once on the throne, Zhou forced over 10 thousand labourers to build the Lutai Palace in Zhaoge (another capital of the Dynasty, modern Qixian County, Henan Province) where he collected large amounts of treasures. Heavy levies were imposed on the people of his country as well as the dukedoms under his control. In the course of the military invasion of Zhou, a small dukedom Su had to offer to the king a beauty named Daji. Zhou doted on Daji and did everything she wished, giving himself up to pleasure and sensuality. It was said that the king filled the pond with wine and hung meat on the trees in the royal garden. Then he ordered his attendants, either men or women, to strip themselves to the skin, chasing and playing among the trees around the pond, just to please Daji. He invented a variety of cruel instruments of torture for the purpose of muzzling criticism. One of such instruments was a copper grill on which a person to be punished was put with coal fire burning below. Some loyal officials were mutilated and mashed for criticising the king, and even Zhou's uncle was gouged of his heart for remonstrating with him. The tyrannies of the Shang Dynasty accelerated its collapse.

In 1027 BC King Wu of a former vassal state of Shang in its west led an expedition army of 3,000 valiant men and 45,000 armoured soldiers in alliance with 800 small states against Shang. Not until allied troops advanced to the suburbs of Zhaoge did King Zhou despatch his army to Muye (south of modern Qixian County, Henan Province) to meet the attack of the expedition army. At the very beginning of the decisive battle early on the morning of the fourth of the second month of the year, the slave soldiers in the Shang Army revolted and went over to the side of the expedition as they could no longer put up with the oppression of the Shang Dynasty.

Seeing the hopeless situation, Zhou fled into the Lutai Palace, and put on his pearly costume before jumping into the fire. Thus ended the Shang Dynasty.

Zhou of the Shang Dynasty

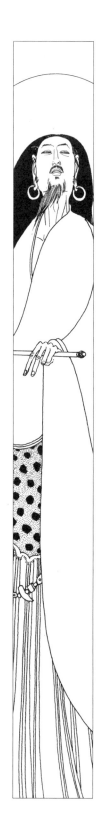

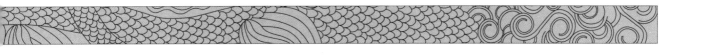

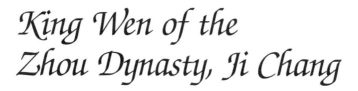

King Wen of the Zhou Dynasty, Ji Chang

周文王·姬昌

With the surname Ji and personal name Chang, King Wen of Zhou was from the place Bin (around the present Xunyi of Bin County, Shanxi Province). He laid the foundation for the Zhou Dynasty and was well known as one of the sage kings in ancient China.

When his father Ji Li was on the throne, Zhou was only a small dependency of Shang. Ji Li led the people of the Zhou Clan eastward along the Wei River and settled down in Zhouyuan to the south of the Qishan Mountain where they built up city walls and laid the basis for marching further east. After his father was put to death by the king of Shang, Ji Chang succeeded to the throne.

Harbouring the idea of avenging his father, Ji Chang was determined to make his state strong so as to overthrow the rule of the Shang. While sending troops to drive away the forces of the neighbouring nationalities, he made a point of straightening out the internal affairs. He was kind and generous to the people and set limits to taxes and levies. Wearing the clothes of the common people, he often went to the fields to supervise the peasants in their cultivation and reclamation, showing great concern for the life of the people, especially old widows and widowers. He issued decrees that when a person committed an offence, his innocent relatives were not to be punished. These policies formed a sharp contrast with the cruel rule of the Shang, and many people came from other states with their families and settled down in the state of Zhou.

To achieve the objective of overthrowing the Shang Dynasty, Ji Chang did everything possible to get talented people. He always treated people of insight, either versed in letters or martial arts, kindly and never neglected to have a cordial chat with them. As a result, qualified people kept coming to serve in his court.

The State of Zhou became a strong power in the west under Ji Chang's wise administration, which alerted King Zhou of the Shang Dynasty. While making Ji Chang "Leader of the Western States", he invited him to Zhaoge, the capital of Shang and had him imprisoned at Youli on a false charge. King Wen was not released until his officials offered beauties and treasures to King Zhou.

After returning to his state, Ji Chang accelerated the pace in his efforts to wipe out the Shang. He led an army across the Yellow River and fought to the central part of the Shang territory, occupying large areas which accounted for two thirds of the whole country. Unfortunately, he died just before launching the final attack, leaving his will to his successor to overthrow the Shang Dynasty without any hesitation. He was granted the posthumous title of King Wen after his son Ji Fa founded the Zhou Dynasty.

King Wen of the Zhou Dynasty, Ji Chang

King Wu of the Zhou Dynasty, Ji Fa

周武王·姬發

King Wu was the founder of the Western Zhou Dynasty, and he succeeded to the crown after the death of his father King Wen.

Determined to realize his father's will to overthrow the Shang Dynasty, King Wu took the strategist Jiang Shang as his teacher and his younger brother Duke Dan as his major assistant in his efforts to found the Zhou Dynasty.

While Ji Fa was engaged in active preparation for the destruction of Shang, King Zhou of the Shang Dynasty was carrying out large-scale wars against the states in the southeast. King Wu decided to take the opportunity to join forces with the minor states for a military manoeuvre so as to test his influence and military strength. It turned out many states responded to his call and led their forces to Mengjin to his assistance, which strengthened King Wu's confidence to wipe out the Shang Dynasty. Nevertheless, they retreated in the end as the opportunity was not yet fully ripe for their efforts. This manoeuvre was referred to in history as "Joining Forces at Mengjin".

In the spring of the fourth year after his accession to the throne, King Wu launched an unprecedented war against the Shang Dynasty. He personally led 300 military chariots, 3,000 valiants, and 45,000 armoured soldiers. And the troops of many states joined the expedition army which had a total of 4,000 chariots, not to mention other forces.

King Wu made a speech for battle mobilization in Muye in the suburbs of the Shang capital. He said: "King Zhou did all kinds of evil against morality and the will of Heaven. Abetted by his concubine, he only indulged in pleasure and practised tyranny over the people, abandoning all the credits and virtues of his ancestors. Acting for Heaven, we are now starting this punitive expedition against this tyrant. Brave men, get ready to charge at the enemy!"

After the mobilization, King Wu ordered his troops to march northward, and thus founded the Western Zhou Dynasty with Haojing (southwest of modern Xi'an of Shaanxi Province) as the capital.

After founding the new dynasty, King Wu created many vassal states in the country to be ruled by members and relatives of the royal family as well as meritorious officials and generals who were vested with hereditary titles and power and were also put under such obligations as making regular contributions to the king. That was referred to as the enfeoffment system.

In the second year after overthrowing the Shang Dynasty, King Wu broke down from overwork in the long years of military life and died in the capital of Haojing.

King Wu of the Zhou Dynasty, Ji Fa

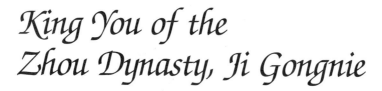

King You of the Zhou Dynasty, Ji Gongnie

周幽王·姬宫涅

Being the last monarch of the Western Zhou Dynasty, King You was notorious for his indulgence in pleasure to the negligence of state affairs.

His father King Xuan (Ji Jing) succeeded to the throne when the state was in peril after the tyrannical reign of King Li. With a view to revitalizing the nation, King Xuan made efforts to "improve domestic affairs and resist foreign aggression" in the 47 years of his reign. This was referred to in history as the "Resurgence of King Xuan" which, however, was only superficial. The acute contradictions in the country formed the basis of the crises for the reign of King You.

In the second year after Ji Gongnie became king, the areas around the capital were stricken by a severe earthquake. "The Qishan Mountain collapsed, and three rivers were drained," causing serious calamity with hundreds of miles of land deserted and countless common people suffering from hunger. The nomadic tribes in the northwest took the chance to invade the kingdom, pushing it onto the verge of collapse. All this, however, did not bring King You to his senses. Greedy and given to sensual pleasures, he trusted wicked officials and favoured flatterers to the negligence of state affairs.

He got a concubine named Bao Si who, though very beautiful, always assumed a serious look. In order to make her smile, King You went so far as to "tease the leaders of the vassal states with beacons" at the cost of the security of the country. He brought the concubine to the beacon tower on one of the fortresses and ordered to light the beacon. At the signal, other beacons were lighted one after another in succession. Heads of the nearby vassal states, as usual, took this as an alarm and immediately led their troops to the capital. Seeing neither any enemy nor any fighting, they retreated in low spirit. The beauty Bao Si could not help laughing at the amusing scene, which made King You feel very much pleased.

King You had a son named Yi Jiu who fled to the State of Shen after his mother the queen was killed by the king for the sake of his concubine. The marquis of the State of Shen was the queen's father. In a rage at the news of his daughter's tragic death, he allied himself with a western nomadic tribe Quanrong to attack King You. At the critical juncture, the king lighted the beacon for help. In view of their past experience of being fooled, no vassal states sent any reinforcements to the king. As a result, the concubine Bao Si was captured by the nomads and King You was killed at the foot of Lishan Mountain (to the southeast of the present Lintong of Shaanxi Province). That marked the end of the Western Zhou Dynasty and the beginning of the Spring and Autumn Period.

King You of the Zhou Dynasty, Ji Gongnie

King Ping of the Zhou Dynasty, Ji Yijiu

周平王·姬宜臼

Ji Yijiu (?–720 BC) was the son of King You and the first king of the Eastern Zhou Dynasty.

He became king with the support of the Marquis of Shen and was known as King Ping. As the former capital Haojing became ruins in the war, the king moved the capital east to Luoyi (present Luoyang of Henan Province) in 770 BC, which marked the beginning of the Eastern Zhou Dynasty.

After moving east, the royal family lost about half of the former territory and population of the country. It had under its control only 500 to 600 square kilometres of land and King Ping was actually reduced to the status of a marquis. As Eastern Zhou was too weak to control the former vassal states, a period of turbulence began in Chinese history, that is, the Spring and Autumn Period. With the support of the states Zheng, Jin and Guo, King Ping managed to sustain his reign. However, he had lost the authority as a king.

Once the Lord of Guo, Jifu, came to Luoyang to have an audience with the king, and the two of them had a congenial talk. It occurred to King Ping that Lord Zhuang Gong of the State Zheng, though a minister of Zhou, had not served in the Zhou Court for a long time. So he mentioned his intention to put Lord Guo in his place for the administration of state affairs. Knowing Lord Zhuang Gong of Zheng was hard to deal with, Lord Guo declined the offer with various kinds of excuses. After learning this, Lord Zhuang Gong of Zheng hurried to the capital Luoyang and took the initiative to present his resignation. King Ping did not dare to offend him and was profuse in his apologies, explaining again and again that he had had no intention to remove the lord. To eliminate his misgivings, the king even offered to send his crown prince to the state of Zheng as a hostage. That was enough to show that the Zhou Dynasty existed only in name from the time of King Ping.

King Ping of the Zhou Dynasty, Ji Yijiu

Lord Zhuang Gong of Zheng, Ji Wusheng

鄭莊公·姬寤生

Lord Zhuang Gong of Zheng (757–701 BC), ruler of the State of Zheng in the Spring and Autumn Period, was from the east of what is today's Huaxian County, Shaanxi Province and was the earliest powerful lord who challenged the authority of the king of the Zhou Dynasty.

His grandfather Lord Huang Gong was made minister of the Eastern Zhou for helping King Ping to suppress the invasion of the Xirong nomads. In addition, King Ping awarded a large area of land east of Luoyang to Huan Gong's son Juetu who later became the ruler of the State of Zheng and was known as Wu Gong. Zhuang Gong was the elder of his two sons, who inherited his position in the state as well as his minister title in the Eastern Zhou.

His mother showed favour to her younger son Duan and secretly gave him support in his plot to replace his elder brother. Learning about the conspiracy, Zhuang Gong sent troops in ambush near the city Jing which had been granted to Duan, and captured the city at one stroke when Duan left it with his troops to seize the supreme power of the state. With his scheme falling through, Duan committed suicide for shame, and Zhuang Gong remained a dutiful son to his mother.

After Zhuang Gong came to power, the State of Zheng became more prosperous and powerful while the Zhou Dynasty went from bad to worse with the position of its king becoming weaker. With a view to curbing the influence of the rising vassal states, King Ping intended to begin his plan with removing Zhuang Gong from the position of minister of Zhou. For that the lord gave tit for tat. He immediately went to Luoyang to tender his resignation, putting the king in an embarrassing position. The two parties then reached an agreement under which Zhou's crown prince Hu shall be sent to Zheng "to study state administration" in exchange for Zhuang Gong's son who was to live in Luoyang. This was actually an exchange of hostages between the two sides, which, contrary to the will of King Ping, promoted the prestige of Zhuang Gong.

In 720 BC, King Ping died and his crown prince Hu also died of excessive sorrow. Hu's son Ji Lin succeeded to the throne, known as King Huan of Zhou. Out of deep hatred for Zhuang Gong, he issued a decree to deprive him of his title as Zhou's minister.

Learning of the news, many senior officials of Zheng favoured an immediate expedition against Zhou. Instead of following their advice, Zhuang Gong sent troops to two small states to plunder their grain just to test the response of the king. As expected, the weak king did not dare to condemn the plunder. Zhuang Gong then decided to have an audience with the king so as to draw in some small states against some others for the purpose of strengthening his position among the states.

Against his expectations, the king gave him a cold shoulder and deliberately offered him ten cartloads of grain by way of blaming him for his failure to pay tribute. Zhuang Gong felt that he had lost face and was worried that the rulers of the states on his way would laugh at him. It so happened that Lord Zhou Heijian gave him as present two cartloads of silk fabric. He then covered the ten grain carts with the silk fabric, trying to create an impression that the king had given him ten cartloads of silk. Sure enough, it spread out around the country that he was favoured by the king, which promoted his prestige even further.

In 712 BC, Zhuang Gong had a large flag made with the words "Punishing Offenders for Heaven" on it. He wiped out the State of Xu with the support of Qi, Lu and other states. Now the King of Zhou finally made up his mind to get rid of this black sheep. In 707 BC, the king personally led the troops of Chen, Cai and Wei in an expedition against Zheng, only to be defeated by the much stronger Zheng army. In the battle, even the king himself was wounded in the shoulder with an arrow shot by a Zheng general Zhu Dan. To avoid being accused of trying to kill the king, Zhuang Gong hypocritically sent people to the king the same night to ask for forgiveness.

In 701 BC Zhuang Gong died of illness at the age of 56 before the realization of his ambition to gain hegemony among the states.

Lord Zhuang Gong of Zheng, Ji Wusheng

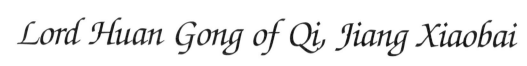

Lord Huan Gong of Qi, Jiang Xiaobai

齊
桓
公
•
姜
小
白

Lord Huan Gong of Qi (?–643 BC) was a ruler of the State of Qi, famous for being the first of the five lords that succeeded in gaining hegemony among the states.

The State of Qi had shown signs of great trouble under the rule of his cruel and dissipated father Lord Xiang Gong. Jiang Xiaobai fled to the State of Lu to avoid imminent disaster. Later Xiang Gong was killed and the officials invited him back to the capital to be his successor. He had intended to appoint Bao Shuya who had once saved his life to be prime minister. Bao Shuya, however, recommended an able man Guan Zhong who had once attempted to kill Huan Gong. Bao went to the State of Lu and contrived to get Guan Zhong back to Qi.

Removing all the previous grudges, Huan Gong appointed Guan Zhong prime minister and respected him as "Father Zhong". Greatly moved, Guan Zhong served the state wholeheartedly. He carried out reforms of the old system for the development of production, levied taxes according to the quality of the land, put mining and salt production under official control, and issued strict orders to officials at all levels to recommend able people. Following the advice of Guan Zhong, Huan Gong acted under the slogan "Venerating the King and Resisting Foreign Aggression". He defeated the Rong Di nomads, saved the State of Xing (the present Xingtai of Hebei Province) and the State of Wei (the present Qixian County of Henan Province), and pacified the internal strife in the royal family of Zhou. In 656 BC, he led the strong allied troops of eight states in an expedition against the southern state Chu and succeeded in curbing Chu's expansion to the central areas of China.

The prestige of Huan Gong became higher and higher. He organized and led alliances of states nine times in his life, and was indeed much more influential than the King of Zhou. In 651 BC, he presided over an alliance meeting of most states at Kuiqui (modern Kaocheng of Henan Province), thus becoming the first lord that gained hegemony among the states. However, he grew complacent afterwards and the lords of the states became disappointed with him.

Huan Gong had five sons each of whom was plotting to gain accession to the lordship. Spotting the hidden crisis, Guan Zhong, on his deathbed in 645 BC, advised the lord to make Zhao the crown prince and to estrange himself from dubious characters. Unfortunately, Huan Gong did not follow his counsel. Wicked officials trusted by the lord ran wild after the death of the minister. That, coupled with the four sons conspiring to seize supreme power, threw the state in chaos.

Two years later Huan Gong was seriously ill and the treacherous officials confined him in a deserted place, passing off their own will as his order while refusing to give him any water to drink. It was only then that he regretted for having failed to listen to Guan Zhong, saying to himself, "How ashamed I would be to face Guan Zhong if the dead did have consciousness!" Thus the once all-powerful overlord declined for being complacent and left the human world in misery. After his death, strife broke out in the State of Qi which was severely weakened and lost its hegemonic position among the states.

Lord Huan Gong of Qi, Jiang Xiaobai

Lord Mu Gong of Qin, Ying Renhao

秦穆公·嬴任好

Lord Mu Gong of Qin (?–621 BC), ruler of the State of Qin, was from the southeast of what is present day's Fengxiang County, Shanxi Province and was famous for being one of the five lords who had gained hegemony among the states in the Spring and Autumn Period of the Chinese history.

After succeeding to the lordship in 659 BC, he made a lot of efforts to carry out reforms of the politics of the State of Qin and promoted able and virtuous people. With his state becoming stronger and stronger, Lord Mu Gong was eager to compete with such states as Qi and Jin in the east and Chu in the south for hegemony in central China.

In 647 BC, the State of Jin suffered from a serious drought and borrowed grain from Qin. Some officials of Qin advised Mu Gong to take the opportunity to launch an expedition against Jin since the Lord of Jin, Yi Wu, had once offended Mu Gong of Qin. However, Qin's senior officials Gongsun Zhi and Baili Xi favoured lending grain to Jin. Baili Xi said to Mu Gong, "Though the Lord of Jin offended you, the common people of Jin are not to blame." After careful consideration, Mu Gong of Qin decided to lend grain to Jin. This was actually an important step taken by him to win popular support.

The next year Qin suffered from famine and tried to borrow grain from Jin. The latter not only refused the request but sent an expedition army against Qin. Having got the news, Qin struck the first blow and the two states fought a severe battle at Hunyuan (between the present Wanrong County and Hejin County of Shanxi Province). Taking advantage of their numbers and strength, the Jin troops surrounded the Qin army, and even Mu Gong himself was wounded. At this critical moment, 300 "wild men" came to their assistance. It turned out that they had once slaughtered Mu Gong's horse for meat on the verge of starvation. And Mu Gong offered them wine instead of punishing them. So they had come today to repay his kindness. As a result, the Qin army defeated the Jin troops, extending the eastern border of the State of Qin to regions along the Yellow River.

In 628 BC, Qin despatched three generals for a surprise attack against the State of Zheng which was friendly with Jin. Learning that Zheng had been well prepared when they marched to Luoyang, the three generals withdrew their troops, only to fall into the ambush of Jin when they retreated to Xiaoshan Mountain (to the northwest of the present Luoning County, Henan Province) and were almost entirely destroyed. This was historically referred to as the "Battle of Xiaoshan".

Realizing his own mistake, Lord Mu Gong of Qin personally went to the suburbs to meet the generals back from defeat and took all the blame on himself. Drawing a lesson from the defeat, the lord made more active efforts to prepare for war so as to take revenge on Jin for the ambush. In 624 BC, Qin launched a large-scale expedition against Jin, dealing the enemy a devastating blow at Wangguan (to the west of the present Wenxi County, Shanxi Province).

The same year, the king of the western state Rong sent You Yu as envoy to Qin. Seeing an able person in the envoy, Lord Mu Gong designed to sow discord between the king of Rong and his envoy. Finally, he succeeded in having You Yu surrender to Qin and help Qin to attack the State of Rong. Since then, the State of Qin had incorporated 12 smaller states, extending its territory by a thousand li[1] and gaining hegemony among the western states. Meanwhile the merging of the Qin people and the Rong tribes were accelerated.

Lord Mu Gong of Qin reigned for 39 years, being one of the five lords who had gained hegemony in the Spring and Autumn Period.

1. One li = 0.5 kilometres.

Lord Mu Gong of Qin, Ying Renhao

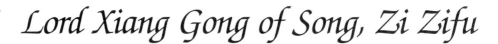

Lord Xiang Gong of Song, Zi Zifu

宋襄公・子兹甫

Lord Xiang Gong of Song (?–637 BC), a ruler of the State of Song in the Spring and Autumn Period, was from what is the border area of today's Henan and Shandong Provinces. He was known as a pedantic advocator of humanity and virtue even in war.

Zi Zifu felt very uneasy when he was made crown prince by his father Lord Huan Gong of Song, and pleaded many times to put his brother Muyi in his place. However, his request met with the flat refusal of his brother. In 650 BC he succeeded to the lordship, appointing his brother Muyi premier in charge of the state affairs. Under their administration, the State of Song was run quite well at the time, and even Lord Huan Gong of Qi who had just gained hegemony among the states entrusted his crown prince Zhao in the care of Xiang Gong of Song.

When Lord Huan Gong of Qi died in 643 BC, a civil strife occurred in the state Qi as his four sons contended for the lordship, and the crown prince Zhao ran to the state Song for protection. The next year Lord Xiang Gong of Song in alliance with some other states defeated the troops under the command of the four Qi princes before putting Zhao on the throne (known as Lord Xiang Gong of Qi). Thus he stabilized the situation in the state Qi, and increased his popularity.

In 639 BC, Xiang Gong of Song intended to become the leader among the lords of states but met with the objection of a strong state Chu. He then invited the king of Chu to the meeting of sovereigns for the alliance so as to get Chu's approval. In the autumn of that year, Xiang Gong left for the meeting in spite of the repeated efforts of his brother to dissuade him from going. As expected, he was put into custody by the troops of Chu in ambush at the place of the meeting Yu (to the northwest of the present Sui County, Henan Province). His brother Muyi hurried back to Song, gathering troops and strengthening the fortifications. The king of Chu sent an envoy to Song threatening, "We shall kill your lord if you do not surrender." The officials of Song replied, "Thanks to the blessings of our ancestors, we have got a new lord." The king of Chu could not do anything but release Lord Xiang Gong of Song.

The next year, the lord of the state Zheng personally went to the state Chu to pay respect to its king. Lord Xiang Gong regarded that as betraying him as the leader of the alliance, and led his troops in an expedition against Zheng. Then the state Chu sent troops against Song in an effort to save Zheng. Turning a deaf ear to the advice of his officials and generals, Xiang Gong led his troops to meet the approaching Chu army, confronting the latter across the Hongshui River (to the northeast of the present Zhecheng, Henan Province).

The Song army had already deployed its troops in battle array on the river bank before the Chu army began to cross the river. A Song general advised, "We are outnumbered by the enemy troops and we should launch the attack when part of them are still in the river." However Xiang Gong refused to follow the advice as he thought an army of humanity and virtue like his should not take advantage of the enemy's precarious position. After the whole army of Chu crossed the river, the general again advised to launch the attack before they deployed into lines of battle. Again Xiang Gong refused to listen. Not until the Chu troops arrayed themselves for battle did the lord give the order for attack. As a result the Song army suffered a crushing defeat and even Lord Xiang Gong himself was seriously wounded in his thigh.

Xiang Gong died of the wound the next year after reigning for a short period of 13 years. Instead of realizing his ambition for hegemony, he made his state suffer from domestic trouble and foreign invasion.

Lord Xiang Gong of Song, Zi Zifu

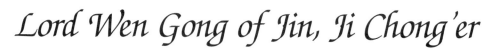

Lord Wen Gong of Jin, Ji Chong'er

晉文公·姬重耳

Lord Wen Gong of Jin (697–628 BC), a ruler of the state Jin, was from the southwest of what is present Shanxi Province. He had been in exile for 19 years before becoming the ruler of Jin and finally winning hegemony among the various states in the Spring and Autumn Period.

Misled by the calumny of a favourite concubine Ji Li, his father Lord Xian Gong of Jin forced the crown prince Shensheng to commit suicide and Chong'er to run away from the state. Lord Hui Gong who succeeded Lord Xian Gong after his death was far from a virtuous ruler who was then succeeded by his even worse son Lord Huai Gong. The important officials of Jin killed Huai Gong as they wished to have Chong'er back as their lord. Under the escort of the troops of the state Qin, Chong'er went back to the state Jin and became the ruler after 19 years in exile, known as Lord Wen Gong of Jin.

Not long after Wen Gong's succession to the lordship, remnants of the former Lord Hui Gong plotted to kill him by burning the palace. A junior court official got to know the intrigue and reported it to Lord Wen Gong who then eliminated the hidden traitors and consolidated his rule.

Wen Gong did a lot in running the state, helping the poor and the needy, and promoting able and virtuous people. As a result the state of Jin soon became strong and prosperous. In the winter of 633BC, King Cheng Wang of Chu led the troops of three states to attack the state Song, that sent people to Jin to ask for emergency help. Xian Zhen, a senior general of Jin, said to the lord, "Here comes the chance to get popular support and gain hegemony." Hu Yan, another important official said, "The states Cao and Wei are Chu's allies. If we attack the two states, Chu is bound to send troops to their support and the state Song will be relieved from the siege." Following their advice, Lord Wen Gong organized three armies (the Upper Army, the Medium Army, and the Lower Army) and sent troops against Cao and Wei the next spring. The people of Wei drove their lord who had thrown in his lot with Chu out of the capital. And the lord was captured by the Jin army.

General Zi Yu, chief commander of the Chu army, was determined to fight against the state Jin and led his troops towards the position of the Jin army. As Wen Gong had received favour from the king of Chu in his exile, he now gave an order to the whole army to retreat 90 li in spite of the objection of his generals. Seeing that, the Chu army marched closely after the Jin troops. In such a life-and-death situation, the Jin army, in alliance with the troops of Song, Qi and Qin fought against the allied forces of Chu, Chen, and Cai at Chengpu (present-day Fanxian County, Shandong Province), and gained a complete victory.

After that, Wen Gong of Jin was formally appointed chief of lords of all the states by the king of the Zhou Dynasty, realizing his ambition for hegemony. In the winter of the year, he sponsored a meeting of alliance among the lords at Jiantu (southwest of the present Yuanyang, Henan Province), and the king of the Zhou Dynasty was also invited to the grand occasion.

Lord Wen Gong of Jin died at the age of 69 in the winter of 628 BC.

Lord Wen Gong of Jin, Ji Chong'er

King Zhuang Wang of Chu, Mi Lü

楚莊王 · 芈侶

Mi Lü was from what is present-day Zigui of Hubei Province. He was a ruler of the state Chu known as Zhuang Wang, and was one of the five lords who won hegemony in the Spring and Autumn Period.

With the Zhou Dynasty becoming weaker and the powerful states contending for hegemony, King Zhuang Wang of Chu gave himself over to feasts and pleasure to the negligence of state affairs in the first three years of his reign, and was not brought around until after repeated remonstrations by his court officials. He removed mediocre officials, promoted able and virtuous people, and streamlined the administration. The political situation soon improved and the state of Chu became strong and prosperous. He sent troops against Jin and Song respectively and won complete victory.

In 606 BC, Zhuang Wang launched an expedition against the Rong tribes in Luhun (north of the present Songxian County, Henan Province). When arriving at Luoshui River, the king deployed his troops in the suburbs of Luoyang within the territory of the Zhou Dynasty for demonstration of strength. The king of the Zhou Dynasty Ding Wang sent Wangsun Man as envoy to the Chu army to express his good wishes, but the first thing Zhuang Wang asked was the weight of the nine tripods which were the symbol of sovereignty. Seeing his ambition to replace the Zhou Dynasty, Wangsun Man told him tactfully that what mattered in running a state was virtue instead of the tripods, whereas Zhuang Wang said contemptuously, "If we dismantle all the spearheads of our soldiers, they will be more than enough for casting nine tripods." Thus he openly showed his disdain for the Zhou Dynasty.

In 598 BC, Zhuang Wang of Chu wiped out the state Chen, making it a county of Chu, on the pretext that an official of Chen had killed its lord Ling Gong. Worrying that this might arouse the dissatisfaction and enmity of the other states, a senior official Shen Shu said to Zhuang Wang, "It is certainly wrong for a person to lead his cattle to trample others' crops. However, isn't it too heavy a punishment to confiscate his cattle just for that? Now it is quite all right for us to send troops against Chen since its official did wrong in killing his lord. But it smacks of rapacity if we make the state Chen a county of Chu. How can we convince the people of other states and make them obey our orders?" Zhuang Wang accepted the advice and restored the position of Chen as a state. In reality, Chen became a vassal of Chu after that.

A year later, Chu defeated the state Zheng, which threw the state Jin into a panic. However, the Jin army was hesitant in action as its generals failed to reach a consensus. As a result, the Jin troops were defeated by Chu. Someone advised Zhuang Wang to use the opportunity to pursue the Jin army for further attack. The king, however, replied, "We never dared to fight against Jin after our defeat at Chengpu. The present grand victory is enough to wipe out our humiliation. There is no point in killing more since both Chu and Jin are large states and will sooner or later come to terms." So he gave an order to withdraw the forces and let the Jin troops go back to their state.

Two years later the Chu army besieged the capital of Song and finally forced Song to surrender.

In 591 BC, King Zhuang Wang of Chu died after reigning for 22 years during which he unified over 20 small states and won hegemony among the existing states at the time.

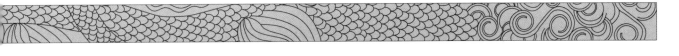

King Zhuang Wang of Chu, Mi Lü

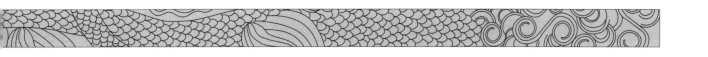

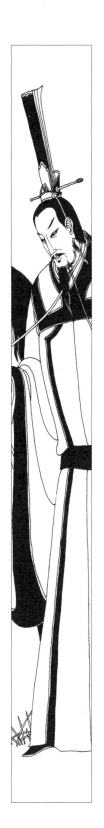

King of Wu, Helü

吳王·闔閭

Helü (?–496 BC), also named Ji Guang, was son of Zhufan and was ruler of the state Wu towards the end of the Spring and Autumn Period.

With the help of a capable general Wu Zixu, the king carried out political and military reforms, building city walls and fortresses, and taking measures to increase the stores. He developed production by means of advanced technology. It was said that when the famous swords "Ganjiang" and "Moyie" were being made, a kind of leather blower was used which was so large that as many as "300 boys and girls were engaged in blasting air and filling coal for the furnace". Meanwhile he promoted the great military strategist Sun Wu for armed expansion of the territory and influence of his state. Later, he moved the capital to Gusu (the present Suzhou of Jiangsu Province).

In 512 BC, the king led an army together with Wu Zixu and Bo Pi against a small state Xu and succeeded in wiping it out. The next target of his military action was the powerful state Chu. For that Wu Zixu said to him that the surest way to victory was to divide the Wu troops into three groups to attack Chu in turn as the power of Chu was in the hands of several people with diversified opinions. Helü followed the advice and sent the three armies in turn into battles with the enemies, leaving the troops of Chu no chance for rest day and night. In 511 BC, the Wu army occupied a part of the Chu territory.

In 506 BC, the king of Wu launched another large-scale attack against Chu in alliance with the armies of Tang and Cai. After arriving at Yuzhang by boat, they landed and marched westwards along the Huaishui River before crossing the Dabie Mountain. His allied troops and the Chu army met at Boju (present Macheng of Hubei Province). The allies won five successive battles, utterly defeating the 200,000 strong Chu army. Finally they captured the Chu capital Yingdu and the king of Chu fled in panic.

The king of Wu became dizzy with success and his troops plundered the Chu capital wantonly. At this time, Wu's neighbour, the state Yue, took advantage of Helü's absence to attack Wu. And fearing that Wu would be getting too strong, the state Qin in the north also sent troops to Chu's assistance. Under the converging attacks of Qin and Yue, Helü still indulged himself in feasts and pleasure at Yingdu. In such a situation his younger brother Fugai stole back to Wu with some troops and spread rumours to the people of Wu: "Helü has already been defeated by Qin and there is no knowing whether he is still alive." Then he declared himself king of Wu. Helü was shocked at the news and the information about the surprise attack against Wu made by the state Yue. Being in no mood for further fighting, he sent people to negotiate peace with the Qin army. Immediately after the withdrawal of the latter, he ordered his troops to hurry back to Wu to suppress his younger brother Fugai and drive away the Yue troops.

In 496 BC, Helü led his troops against the state Yue. Gou Jian, the king of Yue, fought the invaders heroically at Zuili (to the southwest of the present Jiaxing, Zhejiang Province). Helü died of a wound by arrow in the battle and his grandson Fuchai succeeded to the crown.

King of Wu, Helü

越王·勾踐

King of Yue, Goujian

Goujian (?–465 BC), a ruler of the state Yue towards the end of the Spring and Autumn Period, was from what is the present Zhejiang Province. He was well known for undergoing self-imposed hardships such as sleeping on brushwood and tasting the gall every day so as to strengthen his resolve to wipe out the humiliation of defeat.

He became the king of the state Yue after the death of his father Yunchang in 497 BC. Helu, the king of the state Wu, took the chance of the death of his father to attack Yue. Goujian led an army to meet the invading enemies head-on. The Wu troops were defeated with their king Helu killed by an arrow.

In 495 BC, Goujian got information that Fuchai, the new king of Wu, was training his troops day and night so as to avenge the death of the former king. He decided to be the aggressor by attacking Wu first in spite of the objection of his important official Fan Li.

Fuchai sent crack troops to fight back and crushed the Yue army the next year at Fujiao (to the southwest of the present Wuxian County, Jiangsu Province). Goujian retreated with the remnants of his routed army to the Kuaiji Mountain where they were surrounded by the Wu troops. Seeing no way out, Goujian had to send his senior official Wen Zhong to the Wu army for peace. The king of Wu promised peace only on condition that the king and the queen of Yue should be taken to the state Wu in custody. As a result, Goujian and his wife served in humiliation as horse shepherds for three years before they were released and allowed to return to their home state.

Bearing the grudge for the subjugation of his state, Goujian slept on brushwood and would taste a bitter gall before every meal so as to warn himself not to forget the humiliation he had suffered at Kuaiji. He took a series of measures, putting able people in important posts. After seven years of efforts for recovery, the state Yue was becoming strong and powerful.

In 473 BC, the Yue army launched an expedition against Wu which was then controlled by wicked officials with the loyal ministers removed. With its vitality sapped, Wu was routed and its king Fuchai surrounded on the Gusu Hill. He sent an official Gongsun Xiong to sue for peace. Mindful of the shame he suffered, Goujian rejected the request and only promised to send Fuchai to Yongdong (near the present Dinghai County, Zhejian Province) to run a hundred households. Ashamed of himself, Fuchai committed suicide. Later, Yuan Wang, the king of the Zhou Dynasty, appointed Goujian chief of the lords of the eastern states. Thus Goujian gained hegemony in the eastern part of the country.

King of Yue, Goujian

Lord Wen Hou of Wei, Wei Si

魏文侯 · 魏斯

Wei Si (?–396 BC), founder of the state Wei at the beginning of the Warring States Period, was from what is the present Xiaxian County, Shanxi Province.

After the state Jin was divided into the three states of Zhao, Wei and Han, Wen Hou of Wei was a bit complacent with the achievements of his predecessors and was not distinguished in political attitude. Later, with the new landlord class becoming influential in economy and strongly demanding political reforms, Wen Hou began to realize that his state could not get strong unless reforms were carried out. So he did everything possible to recruit qualified people for the reform. Hearing that there was a person named Duangan Mu who was both capable and virtuous, the lord paid him a visit in person to learn from him effective measures of running the state. As Duangan Mu would not accept any offer to become an official, Wen Hou respected him as his teacher. With this information getting around, learned and capable people like the statesman Li Kui and the military strategist Wu Qi came to serve in the state Wei.

Lord Wen Hou appointed Li Kui premier, accepting his advice to put an end to the hereditary system under which titles and emoluments were passed down from generation to generation. The lord also entrusted Li Kui with drawing up laws and regulations to be carried out in the state. Soon after that, he adopted the economic policies put forward by Li Kui meant to stabilize grain prices and bring the initiative of the peasants into better play. He appointed Ximen Bao magistrate of Ye, who undertook the construction of the irrigation system of the Zhanghe River, turning large stretches of saline-alkali soil into fertile fields. The implementation of the new policies enabled the people to enjoy a stable life and the state to have a considerable increase in revenue. With the support of Lord Wen Hou of Wei, Li Kui made a fairly systematic feudal code called *Fa Jing*, the first of its kind in Chinese history.

When the lord planned to attack the state Zhongshan, his official Zhai Huang recommended General Yue Yang to be the commander, who proved worthy of the trust with his valour and strategy and conquered the Zhongshan State.

Then the lord appointed the military strategist Wu Qi as chief commander to lead an army against the state Qin, taking five cities in succession. All the above made Wei the first state to become strong and powerful among the seven powers of the Warring States Period.

Lord Wen Hou of Wei, Wei Si

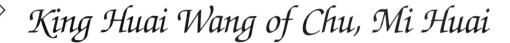

King Huai Wang of Chu, Mi Huai

楚懷王・芈槐

Mi Huai (?–296 BC) was a ruler of the state Chu in the Warring States Period, known as King Huai Wang of Chu.

Huai Wang became the king at a time when the state Qin was getting more and more powerful and kept making expansions eastward in its efforts to contend with the state Qi for hegemony. In order to guard against the invasion of Qin, the six states[1] formed an alliance, with Huai Wang of Chu as the head. However, the troops of the six states retreated after Qin sent an army east of the Hanguguan Pass and defeated the state Han. With a view to disrupting the alliance of Chu and Qi, Qin sent a glib-tongued official Zhang Yi to Chu, who bribed Huai Wang's favourite official Jin Shang, trying to cajole the king out of alliance with Qi. He said, "Qin will return to Chu all the territory it had occupied in the past provided Chu severs relations with Qi."

Misled by calumny and lured by promise of gain, Huai Wang severed relations with Qi irrespective of the objections of his senior official Chen Zhen. He sent an envoy to Qin together with Zhang Yi for the transference of the land promised to him. After the envoy arrived in Qin, however, Zhang Yi denied what he had said in Chu and alleged that he had only promised to give Chu six li of land. It was only by then that Huai Wang realized he had been taken in.

In 312 BC, Huai Wang sent an army of 100,000 under the command of general Qu Gai against the state Qin only to end up in an utter defeat. Instead of gaining any territory, even the 600 sq. li of land of Chu's Hanzhong area was taken by Qin.

Huai Wang put wicked officials in important positions while estranging loyal and virtuous people. Believing the calumny of Jin Shang, his favourite senior official, he estranged the loyal and upright official Qu Yuan, one of the greatest patriotic poets in Chinese history, whom he had trusted very much.

In 304 BC, Qin launched an offensive against Chu in alliance with Chu's former allies Qi, Han and Wei. The next year, Qin launched another offensive, killing 20,000 Chu soldiers. Huai Wang sent people to Qi for emergency help. And Qin coupled military attacks with a promise of peace, inviting Huai Wang to Wuguan (in the southeast of the present Shaanxi Province) for negotiation. The muddle-headed king followed the advice of Jin Shang and went to Qin in spite of the strong objection of Qu Yuan.

As a result, the retreat of Chu army was cut off by Qin, and Huai Wang himself was escorted by the Qin army to Xianyang, the capital of Qin. The king of Qin tried to force Huai Wang to cede territory but was refused. Not until Huai Wang was put under house arrest in Qin did he regret his rejection of Qu Yuan's advice. He tried in vain to escape several times during the three years under house arrest in Xianyang and finally died in the foreign state in 296 BC in remorse and resentment.

---

1. There were altogether seven strong states in the Warring States Period, namely Qin, Qi, Chu, Yan, Zhao, Wei and Han.

King Huai Wang of Chu, Mi Huai

King Wuling Wang of Zhao, Zhao Yong

趙武靈王 • 趙雍

Zhao Yong (?–295 BC), the sixth ruler of the state Zhao in the Warring States Period, was from what is the present Handan, Hebei Province. He was famous for advocating wearing the clothes of the nomads to facilitate actions in fighting.

He became the king of the state Zhao at a time when the various states were engaged in fierce wars in their attempts to annex more territory. Though the state Zhao was able to defeat some small states, it was often invaded by some other small states supported by certain large states. Zhao Yong keenly felt that his state was not strong enough and was determined to carry out reforms.

He saw in battles that the jackets and trousers worn by the nomadic people were very convenient for them to wield arms and shoot arrows on horseback, while the wide sleeves and long robes worn by his own officers and men, mostly infantry and mixture of infantry and chariot troops, were fairly troublesome to wear and inconvenient for the fighters to move in operations. So the king was determined to adopt the garments of the nomads and train his cavalry.

However, his idea met with immediate opposition of the royal family members headed by his uncle Prince Cheng. In order to persuade his uncle, the king went to his home personally, reasoning things out for a whole day before Prince Cheng was convinced of his arguments. While the uncle agreed to his carrying out the reform and was even ready to take the lead in wearing the garments

of the nomads, another prince Zhao Wen persisted in his conservative ideas, saying, "Garments and customs are an important part of the ethics." Wuling Wang retorted, "Ethics and codes should suit specific conditions. If the garments of the nomads are convenient to wear, it is not necessary to stick to the ancient ethics." Zhao Wen and his like could not but comply with the reform.

In 302 BC, Wuling Wang issued a decree for all the people in the state to wear the garments of the nomads, and he personally trained a strong cavalry while improving the equipment of his army. The next year the state Zhao began to grow strong and powerful. It not only defeated the nearby small states that had harassed it, but also expanded its territory northward for a thousand li. In order to deal with the threat from Qin, he abdicated in favour of his younger son Zhao He and appointed some capable officials to help him so that he might be able to gain experience in administration earlier. Zhao Yong himself assumed the title of "Zhufu" meaning in Chinese "father of the king", devoting himself mainly to the major issues and long-term strategies of the state.

Later, a civil riot occurred in the state Zhao as his eldest son Prince Zhang contended with his younger son Zhao He for the crown. In the end, Prince Zhang was killed and Zhao Yong himself was confined to the Shaqiu Palace (to the northeast of the present Pingxiang County, Hebei Province) and starved to death in 295 BC.

King Wuling Wang of Zhao, Zhao Yong

Lord Xiao Gong of Qin, Ying Quliang

秦孝公 • 嬴渠梁

Lord Xiao Gong (381–338 BC), a ruler of the state Qin in the Warring States Period, was a well-known reformer who made vigorous efforts for the prosperity of his state.

When Ying Quliang was born, the state Qin was fairly backward and was held in contempt by the large states east of it. Lord Xiao Gong came to the throne at the age of 21 after the death of Lord Xian Gong. Grieving over the backwardness of his state, he made up his mind to "carry on the cause of his predecessors" to make the state Qin rich and prosperous. He said, "Whoever can come up with good proposals and strategies to make Qin strong, I'll put him in high position and allocate land to him."

Hearing the news, Shang Yang came to Qin from the state Wei. Proceeding from the stand of the rising landlord class, he emphasized that Qin could become strong only through reforms. He pointed out, "It is not neccessary to follow the old practice so long as the state can grow strong, and neither is it necessary to stick to the old rites so long as the people can benefit." From then on, a reform initiated by Shang Yang was carried out in the state Qin under the support of Lord Xiao Gong.

Some members of the nobility tried in every possible means to sabotage the reform which had encroached on their vested interests. They even abetted the crown prince Si in violation of the law. Under the support of Xiao Gong, Shang Yang took resolute action and punished the two teachers of the crown prince as abettors, successfully curbing the attempts of the conservative nobility to sabotage the reform.

After carrying out the new laws and policies in Qin for 10 years under the firm support of Xiao Gong, "the people of Qin were very happy", "towns and villages enjoyed peace and prosperity", and even illiterate women and children were able "to talk about the new laws of Shang Yang". The large states in the east that had looked down upon Qin now began to regard it in a favourable light.

After Xiao Gong's death in 338 BC, his son succeeded to the lordship, and Shang Yang was put to death. However, Shang Yang's new law, championed by Xiao Gong, was still in force and the grand cause thus created was carried forward by the rulers of Qin in later years and laid the foundation for the eventual unification of the other six states by Qin.

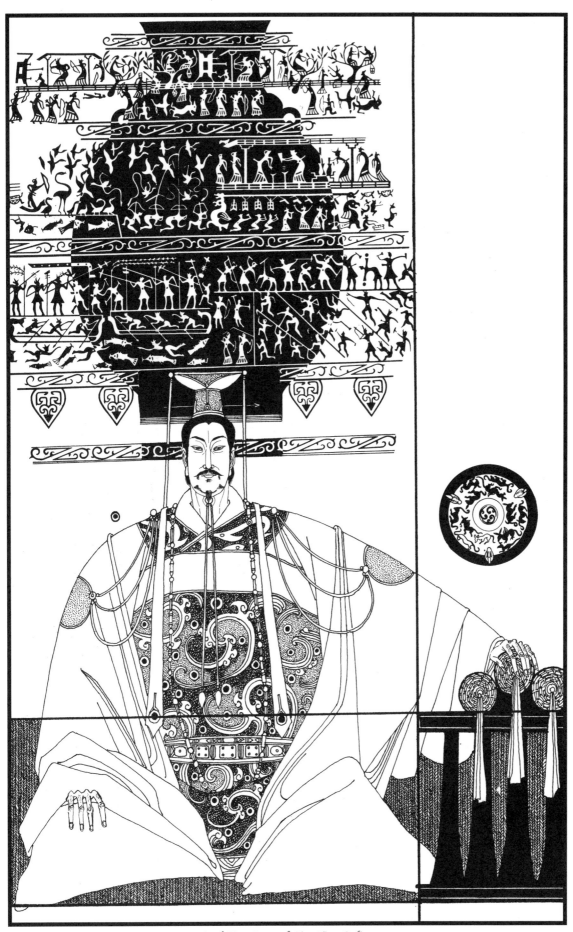

Lord Xiao Gong of Qin, Ying Quliang

Emperor Shi Huang of the Qin Dynasty, Ying Zheng

秦始皇·嬴政

Ying Zheng (259–210 BC), son of King Zhuangxiang of the state Qin, was the founder of the Qin Dynasty, the first centralized autocratic feudal dynasty in Chinese history. He was a household figure for being at once a ruthless tyrant and a monarch of great ability and bold vision who unified the whole country for the first time.

He was only 13 when he became the king and the state affairs were entrusted to senior officials. The premier Lu Buwei and the empress dowager's pet Lao Ai controlled the power beyond their due authority. At the age of 22, Ying Zheng began to run the state affairs personally. Seeing the threat, Lao Ai started a rebellion which was soon suppressed. In July that year Ying Zheng removed Lu Buwei from the premiership.

Now the power of the state Qin was firmly in the hand of Ying Zheng who set about unifying the six states with the help of a capable official named Li Si. Starting from 230 BC, he spent 10 years wiping out the other six states one after another before founding a unified, multi-national, centralized feudal dynasty — the first of its kind in Chinese history.

Ying Zheng was the first to use the title "emperor" and he created a system of bureaucrat institutions compatible with centralized government. Under the emperor there were the "three lords" and "nine ministers" who were to be appointed directly by the emperor and were not to be inherited. And the country was divided into prefectures and counties as units of local administration. To consolidate the centralized system, the emperor issued decrees to unify the varied laws, currencies, characters, and units of length, capacity and weight of the former states. He also ordered to collect the weapons in the country and have them melted and cast into 12 giant bronze men each weighing 100 tonnes. To strengthen his control over the whole country, he issued a decree to dismantle the fortresses, strongholds and defences that had been built by the six former states, and to build main roads radiating from the capital Xianyang. He ordered general Meng Tian to lead an army 300,000 strong northward to fight against the Huns (Xiongnu). To prevent the Hun's invasion, the world famous Great Wall was also constructed under his reign.

In 213 BC, Emperor Shi Huang held a banquet to treat his officials. Chunyu Yue who was from the former state Qi criticized the emperor for his failure to follow the enféoffment system of the previous dynasty. In addition to refuting Chunyu's ideas for restoration of the old system including enféoffment, the premier Li Si proposed that private schools should be banned and Confucian classics and the works of other schools of thought be burned so as to strengthen the ideological control of the people. Following his proposal, the emperor issued a decree to destroy the books by fire. A year later, two necromancers ran away for their failure to get the elixir that they had promised to offer to the emperor. Enraged by their cheating, the emperor ordered to track down and arrest necromancers and Confucian scholars who had spread rumours or slandered the emperor. In the end, over 460 of them were buried alive in the suburbs of the capital Xianyang. That was referred to in history as "burning the books and burying the scholars".

Emperor Shi Huang made five tours around the country after unification during which stone tablets were erected in many places in admiration of his meritorious deeds. He fell ill at Pingyuan Ford (near the present Pingyuan County, Shandong Province) during his last tour. Not until he was dying when they reached what is the present Grand Pingtai to the northwest of Guangzong County of Hebei Province, did he write a letter to his eldest son Fusu who was then supervisor of the army stationed near the northern border, telling him to go back to the capital to preside over his funeral. However, he died en route at the age of 49 before he had time to seal the letter.

Empress Wu Zetian

Emperor Xuan Zong of the Tang Dynasty, Li Longji

唐玄宗・李隆基

Li Longji (685–762), also known as Emperor MingHuang, was the 10th emperor of the Tang Dynasty. He was well known for being an enterprising emperor in the early period of his reign and one indulged in luxury and romance in the later period.

Li Longji was the second son of Emperor Rui Zong Li Dan, and the grandson of Empress Wu Zetian. After her death at Shangyang Palace in 705, her daughter, following her example, plotted rebellion to seize the supreme power. So within eight years, seven coup d'état took place in the imperial court. Later, Li Longji, allied with Princess Taiping, rose to kill Empress Wei and Princess Anle, restoring Emperor Rui Zong to the throne. In 712, Rui Zong abdicated his throne to Li Longji who changed the title of his reign to Kai Yuan the next year. He was known in history as Emperor Xuan Zong of Tang.

At the time of his accession, the new emperor called himself A'Man (the nickname of the household figure Cao Cao of the Three Kingdoms Period), implying his dedication to politics. To consolidate his sovereign power, he took a series of measures, including the relegation of those ministers who had assisted him in seizing the power in case they would be made use of by others to intrigue against himself. On the other hand, he sought for new talented people to aid him. For example, his prime ministers Yao Chong and Song Jing were both capable and qualified. One day, as Xuan Zong looked in the mirror in low spirits, a eunuch tried to soothe him, "Your Majesty look much thinner since Hanlin became prime minister. Why not dismiss him?" Yet he got such a reply, "Though I'm thin, the whole empire must be fat. To select a prime minister is to benefit the people, instead of myself."

Favourable political and economic policies carried out in the early period of his reign brought the dynasty to its zenith. The prosperity was described by the great poet Du Fu as follows:

Rich is the rice and pure the millet,
Overflowing granaries public and private.
And it was known in history as "Peace and
Prosperity of the Reign of Kai Yuan".

In the later years of his reign, the court became more and more corrupt. Later he became infatuated with an imperial concubine Yang and idled time away.

Sleeping till the sun rose high for the
blessed night was short;
From then on the monarch no longer held
morning court.[1]

As a result, the court was dominated by Li Linfu, a hypocritical prime minister and Yang Guozhong, brother of the imperial concubine. Accordingly, a widespread unrest occurred. In 755, the viceroy An Lushan launched a revolt and took Luo Yang. Emperor Xuan Zong fled to Sichuan Province. And his son Li Heng (Emperor Su Zong of Tang) was crowned in Lingwu, announcing Xuan Zong as supersovereign, who did not return to Chang'an until Su Zong recaptured it. The Tang Dynasty never recovered from the consequences of the insurrections. In 762, the distressed emperor died at the age of 77.

---

1. *The two lines are written by the famous Tang Dynasty poet Bai Juyi.*

Emperor Shi Huang of the Qin Dynasty, Ying Zheng

The Overlord of Western Chu, Xiang Yu

西楚霸王·項羽

Xiang Yu (232–202 BC), originally named Xiang Ji, was from Xiaxiang (southwest of the present Suqian County, Jiangsu Province). He had been a leader of the rebellion forces and styled himself Overlord of Western Chu after leading his army into Xianyang, the capital of Qin.

As a child, he lived with his uncle Xiang Liang, who taught him the art of war. One day when Emperor Shi Huang of Qin came to Kuaiji on his tour, Xiang Yu pointed to him in the distance and said, "I can replace him." His uncle immediately stopped him, saying, "Don't talk nonsense! Our whole family and relatives may be ruined for what you have said." From that Xiang Liang felt that his nephew was quite extraordinary.

In July 209 BC, the first peasant uprising in Chinese history broke out at Dazexiang under the leadership of Chen Sheng. In September, Xiang Yu followed his uncle in an armed revolt at Wu (the present Suzhou of Jiangsu Province) in response to the uprising of Chen Sheng. Under the command of Xiang Liang, an army of 8,000 soldiers crossed the river and marched westward. Many rebellion armies including the one led by Liu Bang came to join Xiang Liang, converging into a strong army against the Qin Dynasty. After the death of Chen Sheng, Xiang Liang found a grandson of the former king Huai Wang of Chu and put him on the throne with the same title Huai Wang. After Xiang Liang was killed in a battle, the new king appointed Xiang Yu senior general who immediately led the army northward and crossed the Zhangshui River. After nine fierce battles, he routed the Qin army at Julu and captured its commander Wang Li. Seeing the Qin Dynasty was hopeless, a senior Qin general Zhang Han surrendered to Xiang Yu with 200,000 soldiers. However, Xiang Yu had all the soldiers who had surrendered killed at Xin'an (east of the present Minchi of Henan Province) on their westward march.

Xiang Yu advanced westward on the crest of the victory and reached Hanguguan Pass before long. He ordered to launch an expedition against the army led by Liu Bang hearing that Liu had captured the Qin capital Xianyang. Following the stratagem of his chief adviser Zhang Liang, Liu Bang went to Hongmen (northwest of the present Lintong of Shaanxi Province) personally to attend the banquet by way of making apology to Xiang Yu and finally succeeded in dissuading the latter from attacking him.

A few days later, Xiang Yu led his troops into the Qin capital Xianyang, burning and killing throughout the city, and even putting to death the last Qin monarch Ziying who had already surrendered. Then he sent an envoy to Huai Wang requesting to be made king of Guanzhong. After being refused, he offered Huai Wang an empty title of Emperor Yi Di whereas he created 18 vassal kings in the capacity of Overlord of the Western Chu. Later, he simply had Emperor Yi Di murdered.

The unfair treatment by Xiang Yu caused strong resentment among the meritorious generals and lords. Liu Bang who had been made king of Hanzhong took advantage of the chance to advance to Guanzhong and wiped out the three kings in the area created by Xiang Yu. Then he ordered his troops eastward and started the four-year-long "contention between Chu and Han".

In 202 BC, Liu Bang launched the final attack against Xiang Yu in alliance with the forces of the other local lords and surrounded Xiang Yu at Gaixia (north of the Nantuo River of the present Lingbi County of Anhui Province). The overlord led 800 valiants southward that night trying to break through the ring of encirclement, only to be caught up with by the army of Han by the Wujiang River (northeast of the present Hexian County, Anhui Province). With only 28 followers at the time, Xiang Yu who was at the end of his resources fought with all his might for some time before committing suicide. He was then only 30 years old.

The Overlord of Western Chu, Xiang Yu

Emperor Gao Zu of the Western Han Dynasty, Liu Bang

漢高祖・劉邦

Liu Bang (256–195 BC), also named Ji, was from Pei (the present Pei County of Jiangsu Province). He was the founder of the powerful Western Han Dynasty.

In 209 BC, Chen Sheng led an uprising in Dazexiang, to which Liu Bang responded with his armed forces in Pei County. Hence he was also known as Lord Pei at that time. He fought against the Qin army together with Xiang Yu's insurrectionary army and made contributions to the overthrow of the ruthless Qin Dynasty.

After winning victory over Xiang Yu, Liu Bang came to the throne in 202 BC in the south of Sishui River near Dingtao, founding the Western Han Dynasty. He was historically referred to as Emperor Gao Zu. In May of the same year, the capital was moved to Guanzhong from Luoyang and later to Chang'an (the present Xi'an).

After the founding of the Han Dynasty, Liu Bang practically followed the political system of the Qin Dynasty. In order to restore and develop production, he gave orders as soon as he arrived in Guanzhong that those who had fled from homes because of war should be entitled to regain their lost titles of nobility as well as home and land; those who had been reduced to slavery because of hunger should be given freedom; the demobilized officers and men should be given favourable treatment in terms of land according to their contributions; those soldiers who wanted to stay in Guanzhong should be exempted from corvée for twelve years; and those who returned to their hometowns should be exempted from the same for six years.

At the beginning of his reign, he enfeoffed seven princes who were not members of the royal family, but most of these princes were very ambitious and became a serious threat to the centralized monarchy. Therefore, he later removed six of them for their treasons or on the excuse of their alleged treason and kept only one very unimportant prince of Changsha named Wu Rui. Later, Liu Bang enfeoffed nine princes carrying the royal surname Liu, hoping to strengthen his centralized power through blood ties. However, these princes also constituted a serious threat to the central authority after Liu Bang's death.

Emperor as he was, Liu Bang never forgot his old folks. Stopping over at his hometown Pei County in 195 BC, he held a banquet to treat his old folks. He was so happy after drinking for a while that he even played zhu (a kind of musical instrument at that time) and sang to the music himself.

This is the well-known *Ode to the Gale* he sang at the time:

> *Clouds fly with a rising gale,*
> *I return home in pomp and power,*
> *Valiant men I need to guard the empire.*

Liu Bang made a lot of achievements in his life, but he was also deeply influenced by fatalism. In his later years, he was injured by an arrow on a punitive expedition against his general YingBu. On his way back, he became seriously ill. Empress Lü sent for a doctor, but he refused to have the doctor treat his illness and said rudely: "I am only a common person and have won over the country just with a sword in hand. It is the will of Heaven that determines my fate. It would be useless even if you sent for the famous doctor Bian Que." As he refused to receive any medical treatment, he died in April 195 BC at the age of 61. He was respectfully referred to as "Emperor Gao Zu of Han".

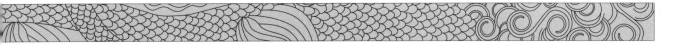

Emperor Gao Zu of the Western Han Dynasty, Liu Bang

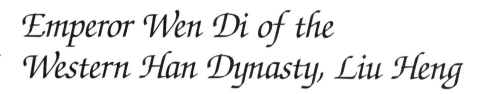

Emperor Wen Di of the Western Han Dynasty, Liu Heng

漢文帝 · 劉恒

Liu Heng (202–157 BC) was the third emperor of the Western Han Dynasty. He was a son of Liu Bang, the first emperor of Han. In 196 BC, after Liu Bang put down a rebellion by Chen Xi, a marquis stationed in Dai, he sent Liu Heng to Dai enfeoffing him Prince of Dai. After Liu Bang's death, Empress Lü usurped the throne. After her death, however, the senior officials headed by General Zhou Bo loyal to Liu seized back the power. Liu Heng was then invited to the capital to be crowned as emperor, known as Emperor Wen Di of Han.

After Liu Heng came to the throne, he ordered an amnesty and even abolished corporal punishment and the punishment of the people related to an offender. There was another law at the time, "Law of Slander and Fallacy", under which whoever criticized the emperor or spread a rumour shall be sentenced to death. On that Emperor Wen Di commented, "With this law, nobody will dare to speak. How can the emperor hear any criticism if he has made a mistake?" So he gave an order to abolish the law.

In 178 BC, a senior official Jia Yi presented a memorial to the emperor to develop production and practise strict economy. Therefore, Wen Di carried out a policy of economic recuperation and development, and reduction of corvée and taxation in the early years of Han. He reduced the tax rate to 1/30 from the original 1/15 stipulated by Liu Bang, and later he simply exempted all the agricultural taxation for twelve years and decreased poll tax and corvée. All this helped promote the development of the social economy.

As the supreme ruler of the whole country, Emperor Wen Di lived a very simple life. The clothes he wore were made of black coarse silk without any embroidery. The curtains used by his most loved concubine Shen was of a plain colour. The people of a place pooled some money and bought him a good horse which could cover a thousand li a day. Emperor Wen Di said, "Where shall I go on a one-thousand-li horse when I only make a tour of 30 li a day?" He told the presenters of the horse to take it back and even gave them their travel expenses. He then issued an edict forbidding the local officials and people to present gifts.

In 157 BC, Emperor Wen Di was seriously ill. Before his death, he made a will that at his funeral no carriages should be used and no guards of honour should be on display. The white mourning belts should be no wider than three inches. And the officials should not forbid the common people to have regular social activities such as weddings, offering sacrifices, drinking wine and eating meat during the mourning period. He also ordered that his tomb should be built against a hill instead of making an artificial hill in order to save labour. At his sickbed, the Crown Prince Liu Qi asked in tears, "What shall we do if Your Majesty leave us?" The emperor said, "In case of a rebellion, just appoint Zhou Yafu to be the general and you don't have to worry too much." After a few days, Emperor Wen Di died at the age of only 45.

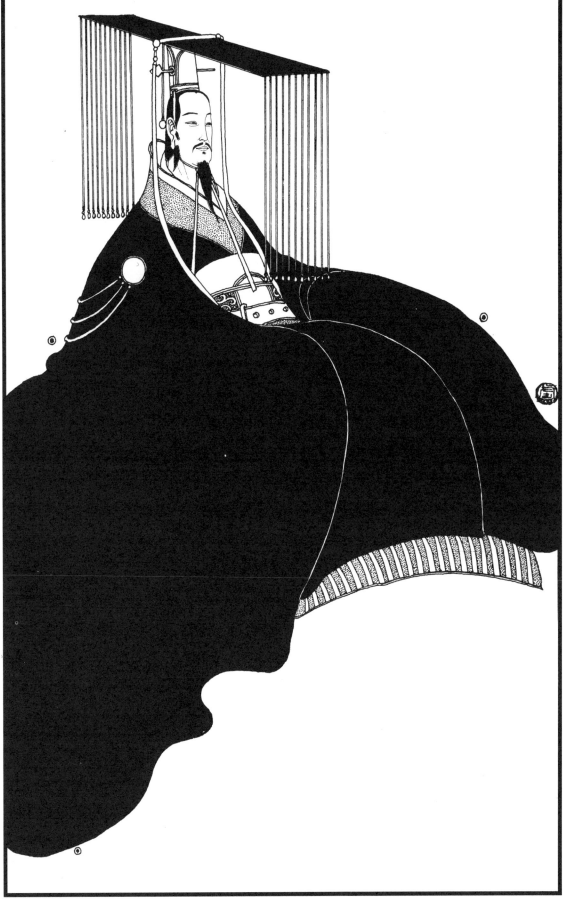

Emperor Wen Di of the Western Han Dynasty, Liu Heng

Emperor Jing Di of the Western Han Dynasty, Liu Qi

漢景帝 • 劉啓

Liu Qi (188–141 BC), known in history as Emperor Jing Di, was the fourth emperor of the Western Han Dynasty. He was the second son of Emperor Wen Di. After ascending the throne, he continued implementing the policy of economic recuperation and development by adopting the same tax rate of 1/30 and constructing irrigation systems with an emphasis on agriculture and a restraint on commerce. Hence, the country was further stabilized. Owing to the implementation of the policy of "economic recuperation and development" for nearly forty years by Emperors Wen Di and Jing Di, the economy had gained unprecedented prosperity since the founding of the Han Dynasty. The period was referred to in history as "Peace and prosperity under Emperors Wen and Jing".

At that time, the repositories of all the prefectures were filled with coins and grain. The money accumulated in the national repositories amounted to several hundred million, even some of the cords used for stringing the coins were rotten, and part of the grain stored became mouldy. Both the royal stables and the stables of the common people were filled with cattle. Due to the well-to-do life, the population increased sharply and in some places, even quadrupled or quintupled.

However, the central power at that time had been constantly threatened by princes carrying the same royal surname Liu. For example, Liu Bi, the Prince of Wu, not only had a large area and powerful troops under his control, but also had his own copper mines to mint coins from, enabling him to be as rich as the emperor. In 154 BC, the 62-year-old Liu Bi allied with seven other princes to stage an armed rebellion against the central government. This event was referred to as the "Rebellion of seven princes in Wu and Chu". As Lord Chao Cuo had long foreseen the rebellion and had made the suggestion to eliminate the princedoms, Liu Bi staged the rebellion with the slogan "Put Chao Cuo to death to rid the emperor of evil officials" so as to cover his ambition to overthrow the central government. Instigated by a spy named Yuan Ang, Emperor Jing Di put Chao Cuo to death. However, his indulgence and yielding did not curb the ambition of Liu Bi, who then assumed the title of Emperor Dong Di. Not until then did Emperor Jing Di fully awaken and order General Zhou Yafu, the son of General Zhou Bo, to go on a punitive expedition to the east against Liu Bi.

Three months later, Zhou Yafu put down the rebellion completely. After that, Jing Di ordered to rid the princes of the power to appoint or remove officials in order to strengthen the central authority, thus putting an end to the enféoffment system adopted since the Western Zhou Dynasty.

In 149 BC, the Prince of Jiaodong Liu Che was made crown prince. In 141 BC, Emperor Jing Di died at the age of 47.

Emperor Jing Di of the Western Han Dynasty, Liu Qi

Emperor Wu Di of the Western Han Dynasty, Liu Che

漢武帝・劉徹

Emperor Wu Di (156–87 BC), the fifth emperor of the Western Han Dynasty, was an outstanding politician of high gifts and bold vision in the feudal society.

After the death of Emperor Jing Di in 141 BC, the 16-year-old Liu Che ascended the throne. Following the period of "Peace and prosperity under Emperors Wen Di and Jing Di", the society at that time was unprecedentedly flourishing. However, Emperor Wu Di was not content with things as they were. He was determined to carry on the policies of Emperor Jing Di and make the Han Dynasty even more prosperous. He summoned all the scholars of the nation, consulting them for ways of successful administration of the country. He adopted the suggestion raised by Dong Zhongshu to "respect only Confucianism", and promoted many talented people.

To weaken the political influence of the princes bearing the royal surname for consolidating the unification of the country and strengthening the power of the central authority, Emperor Wu Di adopted a proposal by Zhufu Yan, that besides the eldest son who was entitled to inherit the title after the death of a prince, the other sons could each get a share of the enfeoffed land to become a marquis.

In 112 BC, Emperor Wu Di removed 106 princes on the excuse that the gold they contributed to the court was of insufficient quantity and inferior quality. In the years of Taichu[1], when there only remained five princes of the early years of the Han Dynasty, Emperor Wu Di still took measures to limit their power to prevent them from ganging up for ulterior purposes.

In 115 BC, Emperor Wu Di implemented a policy throughout the country to regulate transport and control prices so as to prevent the big merchants from hoarding and speculating for huge profits. He also issued a decree to prohibit the prefectures from minting coins and put the printing of money under the exclusive control of the central authorities. At the same time, the emperor also ordered the slave owners in industry and commerce and the usurpers to submit their statement of assets. He also encouraged the people to expose those who failed to submit their statements or made false statements. Thus, the state revenue was greatly increased.

In 109 BC, the emperor enlisted tens of thousands of peasants to repair the Huzi breach in the lower reaches of the Yellow River (southwest of the present Puyang, Henan Province). Since then, there had been no serious floods for 80 years.

In order to ensure the safety along the northern borders, Emperor Wu Di launched wars against the aggressive Huns. He also sent Zhang Qian twice to the Western Regions[2] to ally with Wusun, Dayuezhi and Anxi for common resistance against the Huns. Thus, the security of the country was guaranteed.

However, the excessive consumption of military expenses in the years of wars increased the burden of the people in taxes and corvée. Since the middle years of Emperor Wu Di's reign, the problem of the homeless had been very serious and several uprisings had broken out. The resistance and struggles of the people taught Emperor Wu Di a lesson. He was forced to issue an imperial edict expressing his repentance and declared that he would launch no more wars against the barbarians and would give the people the chance to recuperate. Thus, he eased the once very tense class contradictions.

In 87 BC, the 69-year-old Liu Che died and was granted the posthumous title of Wu Di. In the Chinese history, the Qin Dynasty did not last long although its first emperor unified China. It was under Emperor Wu Di of Han that the unification of China was consolidated and expanded. Due to the powerful Han Empire, the people in Central China were no longer referred to as the "Qins", but the "Hans". And the ancient Chinese people had been called the Hans since then.

---

1. *Taichu: Title of one of the periods of Emperor Wu Di's reign (104–101 BC).*

2. *Western Region: A Han Dynasty term for areas roughly of modern Xinjiang and part of Central Asia.*

Emperor Wu Di of the Western Han Dynasty, Liu Che

Emperor Ai Di of the Western Han Dynasty, Liu Xin

漢哀帝 ● 劉欣

Liu Xin (27–1 BC), known as Emperor Ai Di, was the 10th emperor of the Western Han Dynasty.

Because Emperor Cheng Di had no son, he made his nephew Liu Xin the crown prince. At the time the latter ascended the throne, the imperial in-laws were very influential and Emperor Ai Di had to succumb to them. In view of the serious land annexation at that time, Shi Dan, a senior official, made a proposal to reform the land system. Emperor Ai Di ordered his cabinet to draft an imperial edict for the reform, which, however, was never promulgated, let alone carried out, because of the opposition from the imperial in-laws.

To further expand their power and influence, the imperial in-laws asked Empress Dowager Fu to force his grandson, the emperor, to oust Wang Meng, the advocator of reform. Emperor Ai Di gave Wang 250 kilos of gold and sent him home. Since then, Empress Fu had controlled the imperial power, and the emperor did not dare to concern himself about state affairs.

The year 3 BC saw a serious drought in the Guandong area, and the peasants staged a large-scale rebellion in the name of worshipping Goddess Xiwangmu. The contingents of several thousand peasants marched through 26 prefectures to the capital making a hullabaloo. The upheaval lasted several months. During this period of time, Emperor Ai Di hid in his palace and became ridiculously infatuated with a young man named Dong Xian, living a dissipated life with him.

Later, Emperor Ai Di went even further to get Dong Xian's wife to live in the palace and had sumptuous mansions built for Dong with all the pillars decorated with brocades. Large quantities of silk were also granted to Dong. And on one occasion alone, the emperor granted to Dong 200,000 mu of land, not to mention the countless rare treasures and jewels. What was more, he even had a tomb built for Dong Xian near his own. Once at a banquet, Emperor Ai Di said that he even wanted to give the whole country to this handsome young man. Seeing this, a senior official, Bao Xuan, submitted a statement beseeching him to keep away from the knaves. At first, the emperor was able to listen to his admonition, but later, Bao Xuan offended Premier Kong Guang while performing his duties and was put into prison. Under the pressure from over a thousand imperial students who submitted a petition pleading for Bao, Emperor Ai Di pardoned him from death, but still sent him to Shangdang on exile.

With the loyal and frank Bao Xuan away, the influence of the imperial in-laws became even more rampant. The 22-year-old Dong Xian was promoted to the position of commander-in-chief in charge of military affairs, and even his father, brothers and other relatives were all promoted.

Due to indulgence in excessive sensual pleasures, Emperor Ai Di sat at the throne for only six years and died at the age of only 26. His death signalled the downfall of the Western Han Dynasty.

Emperor Ai Di of the Western Han Dynasty, Liu Xin

The Emperor of the Xin Dynasty, Wang Mang

Wang Mang, founder of the Xin Dynasty between the Western Han and the Eastern Han Dynasties, was notable as one who had usurped the power of the Western Han Dynasty and attempted new laws and regulations. His aunt was the empress of Emperor Yuan Di of the Western Han Dynasty, and for that his uncles had already been in important positions when he was very young. Taking advantage of the favourable conditions, he associated with many influential officials of the court and he himself was also promoted to a high position.

As a result of the social crises caused by the extravagance and dissipation of the nobility and senior officials, the common people and junior officials all wished to have an upright man take up the administration of the state affairs. In view of that, Wang Mang did everything possible to put on an upright and honest appearance to distinguish himself from the corrupt nobility and high-ranking officials.

Once his son Wang Huo killed a servant, and Wang Mang immediately ordered him to commit suicide for that. To gain the support of the royal family members and officials, he granted them large amount of awards. As a result, as many as 480,000 people requested the Empress Dowager to grant him a higher title. He was thus made "Duke Guardian of Han", and the power of the Western Han actually came into his hands.

In 5AD, the 14-year-old Emperor Ping Di was murdered by Wang Mang, who put a two-year-old baby on the throne the next year while proclaiming himself acting emperor. In 8AD, he mounted the throne himself, changing the dynastic title to Xin.

After becoming the emperor, Wang Mang sent people to his aunt, the Empress Dowager, for the imperial jade seal. In a rage, she threw the seal onto the floor, breaking a corner of the seal knob. The surrender of the imperial seal signified the end of the Western Han Dynasty that had lasted 214 years.

In 9AD, Wang Mang decreed to carry out a reform on the basis of the classic system of the ancient times. He promulgated the "royal land system", taking over all the land of the country. However, the system met with strong opposition from the nobility, officials and landlords, and Wang Mang had to cancel it in 12AD.

In February of 10AD, he carried out another new economic measure based on the "Rites of the Zhou Dynasty", taking strong measures against traders and usurpers. But this reform also ended up with strong opposition from those whose interests had been affected.

The failure of the reform aggravated the social crises. And Wang Mang had to resort to launching wars against neighbouring countries, which brought about serious disaster to the people. Unable to endure the hardships, people rose against him across the country. The Green Woodsmen in Hubei and the Red Eyebrows in Shandong were the two largest rebellion forces.

In 23AD, the Green Woodsmen defeated Wang Mang's main forces near Kunyang and advanced straight to the capital Chang'an on the crest of the victory. People in the capital city responded from within and organized attacks on the imperial Weiyang Palace, and set fire on the palace gate. Wang Mang hid himself on the Jiantai Terrace by the side of the Taiye Lake in the palace garden and was killed by Du Wu from Shangxian County. He was 68 years old then, and with his death also came the end of the Xin Dynasty after only 15 years of existence.

新·王莽

The Emperor of the Xin Dynasty, Wang Mang

Emperor Guang Wu of the Eastern Han Dynasty, Liu Xiu

漢光武帝・劉秀

Liu Xiu (6 BC–57 AD), styled Wenshu, was from Caiyang of Nanyang (southwest of modern Zaoyang County, Hubei Province). He was the ninth generation descendant of Emperor Gao Zu and was the founder of the Eastern Han Dynasty.

Towards the end of Wang Mang's Xin Dynasty, peasant uprisings surged with full force across the country. In 22 AD, there was a serious famine around Nanyang which aggravated the plight of the peasants, and the rebellion forces of the Green Woodsmen pressed on towards Nanyang. At that time, Liu Xiu was selling grains around the place so as to buy weapons with the money he made. He then rose in armed rebellion in December the same year before leading his troops to Chongling to join forces with his elder brother Liu Yan against Wang Mang's regime.

In 23 AD, Liu Xiu launched a large-scale attack against Wang Mang's army at Kunyang City and won great victory.

In 25 AD, Liu Xiu assumed the title of emperor at what is the present Boxiang County, Hebei Province, under the same dynastic name of Han. He moved the capital to Luoyang afterwards which was in the east in relation to the capital of the Western Han Chang'an. And Liu Xiu was known in history as Emperor Guang Wu of Han. This was how the dynastic name of the Eastern Han came about.

After coming to the throne, Liu Xiu suppressed the peasant uprisings and the various local armed forces before unifying the country in 37 AD.

In his attempt to solve the problems of land and serfs, Emperor Guang Wu issued decrees on different occasions to set free the serfs of the rich families, and in 39 AD he ordered to check the actual quantity of the land under cultivation as well as the actual number of households and the size of population. With widespread opposition from rich and powerful landlords, however, the emperor had to give up the investigation of the land.

In order to centralize the state power, Liu Xiu did everything to keep the nobility from state administration and made a lot of efforts in advocating the study of Confucian classics and augury. In a discussion with his senior officials for deciding the site of the astrology pavilion, he said to Huan Tan, "I intend to decide the matter by augury. What will you say?" To show his contempt for the superstition, Huan Tan replied, "Your Majesty, I have never read anything about augury." For that the emperor almost put him to death. As a result of the initiation of the emperor, the ideological and cultural field of the Eastern Han Dynasty was enveloped in a superstitious atmosphere.

Liu Xiu was fairly diligent in the administration of state affairs after he unified the country. He worked all day long from dawn to sunset, and often called his officials into the palace even in the evening to discuss the Confucian classics far into the night. When the crown prince advised him to take more rest for the sake of his health, he replied, "I take delight in this and don't feel tired."

In February 57 AD, Liu Xiu died at the age of 63, leaving a will to arrange his funeral "in the simplest possible way."

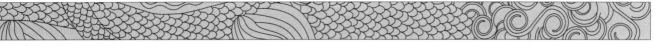

Emperor Guang Wu of the Eastern Han Dynasty, Liu Xiu

Emperor Ling Di of the Eastern Han Dynasty, Liu Hong

漢靈帝・劉宏

Liu Hong (156–189 AD) was the 11th emperor of the Eastern Han Dynasty.

Emperor Huan Di died without a son to succeed him. After consultation with her father Dou Wu, his wife Empress Dou put on the throne the 12-year-old Liu Hong who was a great grandson of Prince Hejian Liu Kai, and was known in history as Emperor Ling Di of Han.

When Emperor Ling Di was 14 years old, the contradictions between the eunuchs and officials intensified, and a eunuch Cao Jie accused the officials of ganging up into a "party" to overthrow the imperial court. Misled by his remarks, the young emperor issued a decree to eliminate the "party elements". As a result, the students, former subordinates, family members, and other relatives of the "party elements" holding official positions were all removed from office and put into prison. Representative figures of the anti-eunuch elements such as Li Yan, a senior official and Dou Wu, father of the Empress Dowager, were put to death. After that the eunuchs were able to do whatever they liked and politics became more corrupt. This event was referred to in history as "the disaster of the imprisonment of the party elements".

After expelling and killing the party elements, the eunuchs still had apprehensions for the scholars and did everything they could to prevent the emperor from appointing them officials. In 178 AD, the emperor set up a new grand school of literature and art to compete against the traditional grand school of Confucian classics. Those who studied in the new school were eligible for official positions after passing the examination.

Thus the opportunities of the traditional school scholars to become officials were taken by graduates educated by eunuchs. Later, Emperor Ling Di simply set up an exchange market openly selling official positions at marked prices so as to further deprive the scholars of their opportunities to become officials.

The muddle-headed emperor put all his trust in the eunuchs while repressing many upright officials. For instance, Yang Qiu, a senior official in charge of the judicial department got evidence that two corrupt officials Wang Pu and Duan Jiong practised extortion and sentenced them to death. But the emperor in another case believed the false accusation of his favourite eunuch Cao Jie and put Yang Qiu to death.

The corruption of the court and the misery of the people led to the Yellow Turban Revolt which broke out in 184 AD. Feeling isolated, the emperor decreed to pardon the party elements and reinstate the scholar officials. These people had a strong hatred for the eunuchs and a stronger hatred for the peasants. Seeing the inevitable fall of the Han Dynasty, they organized their own forces, waiting for the chance to set up their own separatist regimes.

In 189 AD, the 33-year old Emperor Ling Di died. Before long, Yuan Shao who was from an aristocratic family in the north rose in arms and killed all the 2,000 odd eunuchs. With the rise of the various armed cliques across the country, the reign of the Eastern Han Dynasty existed only in name.

Emperor Ling Di of the Eastern Han Dynasty, Liu Hong

Emperor Wu Di of Wei, Cao Cao

Cao Cao (155–220 AD), styled Mengde and with a pet name Aman, was from Qiao of Peiguo (modern Boxian County, Anhui Province). He was a distinguished statesman, military strategist and man of letters in the period of the Three Kingdoms. He became a household figure in China through the classic novel *Romance of the Three Kingdoms* in which he was depicted as a talented but treacherous villain.

At the age of 20, Cao Cao was recommended by his hometown for being "filial and honest" and was appointed magistrate of North Luoyang. He was impartial in enforcing the law and fearless in the face of the influential officials and the nobility. Once the uncle of an influential eunuch Jian Shuo roamed in the city late at night against the regulations in force at the time. Cao Cao had him executed on the strength of the law.

Having suppressed the Yellow Turban Revolt in Yanzhou Prefecture in 192 AD, Cao Cao incorporated over 300,000 rebellion troops in his own army. He chose the crack troops among these and organized his "Qingzhou Corps" which constituted the basic forces in the subsequent wars he waged for the unification of the northern part of the country.

In 196, Cao Cao moved the capital to Xu (east of modern Xuchang of Henan Province) and made arrangements for Emperor Xian Di of Han to settle down in the new capital. He himself took the position of premier, creating a favourable political situation in which he was able to issue orders and decrees in the name of the Han emperor who was then reduced to a mere political instrument in his hand. He promulgated a decree for the garrison troops and peasants to open up land for cultivation, as a result of which "the granaries were full of grain" and "the people were well off", thus laying the material basis for the war of unification.

In 200, another warlord Yuan Shao led a strong army to press on Guandu where Cao Cao's army was stationed. In the face of the enemy forces which were much stronger than his, Cao Cao adopted the strategy of tenacious defence, avoiding large-scale head-on fighting with the enemy. Meanwhile he often sent detachments of crack soldiers to make surprise assaults on Yuan Shao's supply line.

One night, he personally led a cavalry of 5,000 crack horsemen to attack Yuan's army granary at Wuchao, burning up 10,000 carts of grain. Then he took the initiative in launching the general attack, destroying more than 70,000 of Yuan's troops and forcing Yuan Shao to flee northward. After the victory at Guandu, Cao Cao conquered the three prefectures of Wuhuan nomads before unifying the northern part of the country.

In January 208, Cao Cao came back to Yecheng from his northern expedition against Wuhuan. He was already 54 years old then, but still had the ambition to wipe out the southern warlords in the south – Liu Biao, Liu Bei and Sun Quan – without a letup so as to realize the unification of the whole country in his lifetime. However, he ended up being defeated at Chibi (northeast of modern Jiayu, Hubei Province) by the allied forces of Sun Quan and Liu Bei and had to retreat to the north. After that, a situation of tripartite confrontation formed in China between the state Wei in the north, Shu in the southwest and Wu in the southeast.

Cao Cao was granted the title of Prince of Wei by the Han emperor in 216 and died in Luoyang in 220 at the age of 65. In the same year his son Cao Pi assumed the title of emperor, formally making Wei the name of his kingdom and granting his late father the title Emperor Wu Di of Wei.

Cao Cao was also a talented man of letters. Over 20 of his poems and 40 pieces of his prose works are still widely read today.

Emperor Wu Di of Wei, Cao Cao

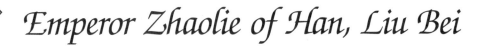

Emperor Zhaolie of Han, Liu Bei

漢昭烈帝 · 劉備

Liu Bei (161–223 AD), styled Xuande, was from Zhuoxian County (modern Zhuoxian County, Hebei Province). He was the founder of the Kingdom Shu in the period of the Three Kingdoms.

Liu Bei was a descendant of Prince Zhongshanjing Liu Sheng who was a son of Emperor Jing Di of the Western Han Dynasty. However, the family was already reduced to poverty when it came to Liu Bei and he had to make a living by making straw shoes and selling straw matresses. He was not exactly diligent with book learning but liked keeping pet dogs and riding horses. He was also fond of enjoying music and was fairly particular with what he wore. What was more, he liked to associate himself with heroes and developed profound friendship with such competent people as Guan Yu and Zhang Fei. He began his career by suppressing the Yellow Turban Revolt and then together with a warlord Gongsun Zan, he joined the expedition against a cruel warlord Dong Zhuo who held the capital and monopolized the power of the court.

When his troops were stationed in Xinyie, Liu Bei made a point of recruiting competent people. Hearing that there was a 27-year-old genius, 20 years his junior, named Zhuge Liang in Longzhong (modern Xiangyang of Hubei Province), Liu went to visit him three times in spite of the long distance. Moved by his sincerity, Zhuge Liang promised to help. In 207, the two of them discussed the situation of the country and Zhuge Liang advised Liu Bei to form an alliance with Sun Quan's Wu in the east, occupy Jing and Yi in the west, maintain peace and friendship with the national minorities in the south, so as to oppose Cao Cao's Wei in the north. His advice was taken by Liu Bei as the guiding strategy in his efforts for the unification of the country.

In 208, Cao Cao led a strong army pressing on Xiakou from Jiangling along the Yangtze River, and Liu Bei sent Zhuge Liang across the river to form an alliance with Sun Quan. After the allied forces routed Cao Cao's army at Chibi by means of fire attack, a situation of tripartite confrontation formed in China. In the next year, 221 AD, after Cao Pi assumed the title of emperor, Liu Bei came to the throne under the same dynastic title of Han (historically referred to as Shu Han), making Chengdu his capital.

Shortly after that, Sun Quan's senior general Lu Meng captured Jingzhou by making a raid and killed Guan Yu. This led to the breakup of the Sun-Liu alliance and resulted in war.

In 222, Liu Bei launched a large-scale expedition against Wu in the name of taking revenge for Guan Yu, only to be utterly defeated by Wu's general Lu Xun in the battle at Yiling. The next year Liu Bei died of illness at the age of 62 in Baidi City (modern Fengjie County, Sichuan Province).

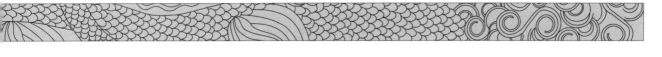

Emperor Zhaolie of Han, Liu Bei

The Great Emperor of Wu, Sun Quan

吳大帝·孫權

Sun Quan (182–252 AD), styled Zhongmou, was from Fuchun of Wujun Prefecture (modern Fuyang of Zhejiang Province). He was the founder of the Kingdom of Wu in the period of the Three Kingdoms.

In the closing years of the Eastern Han Dynasty, his father Sun Jian and elder brother Sun Ce occupied the six prefectures east of the Yangtze River in the tangled battles between the various warlords. Not long after the death of his father, his brother Sun Ce was also mortally wounded by his enemies in a hunting. Before his death, he said to his chief adviser Zhang Zhao and other officials and generals, "Do your best to support my brother after my death!" Thus Sun Quan succeeded his brother and became the supreme ruler of the six prefectures. Thanks to his ability and his efforts to unite the various forces, he soon established his prestige and restabilized the situation in Wu that had once been thrown into confusion.

In 208, after Sun Quan got the information that Cao Cao had fought his way into Jingzhou, he immediately sent his official Lu Su to see the response of Liu Bei in the name of offering condolences for the death of Liu Biao. In Jingzhou, Lu Su had discussions with Liu Bei on forming a united front against Cao Cao. However, when discussions were held later among the officials and generals of Wu, some proposed capitulation as they were awed by the strong military strength of Cao Cao. The capitulationists met with strong opposition from Lu Su and Zhou Yu who resolutely advocated resistance against Cao Cao. Their attitude strengthened the determination of Sun Quan, who drew his sword and cut a corner of his desk, saying sharply, "Whoever mentions capitulation again is to be dealt with like the desk." As a result, the allied forces of Sun Quan and Liu Bei defeated Cao Cao at Chibi. Later Sun Quan's general Lu Meng led an army of 20,000 and captured Jingzhou at one stroke, taking advantage of the absence of Liu Bei's general Guan Yu who had led all the troops from Jingzhou northward in a series of victorious battles against Cao Cao.

In July 221, Sun Quan appointed a young general who was far from a well-known figure in command of the army against the strong invading troops of Liu Bei. In the seven or eight months of confrontation, Lu Sun adopted the tactics of defence by way of fortification and entrenchment without engaging in battles before finally routing Liu Bei's forces at Yiling by fire attack. That showed Sun Quan's vision and boldness in promoting competent people.

In 229, Sun Quan assumed the title of emperor in Wuchang under the dynastic name of Wu. Later he moved the capital to Jianye (modern Nanjing of Jiangsu Province).

In his kingdom Sun Quan practised cruel rule with heavy levies. In reply to the remonstration of one of his officials, he said: "Severe punishment is necessary to rule the base people. It is true our armed forces are sufficient to defend the existing six prefectures. But our present territory is not large enough and to expand it, we must raise a stronger army." For that purpose, Sun Quan made a lot of efforts to expand his land to the southeast. With a view to developing the coastal areas, he sent a large fleet of 10,000 soldiers under the command of General Wei Wen and Zhuge Zhi which reached Yizhou (modern Taiwan). That was the earliest clear record of the contact between Taiwan and the mainland. The advance to the southeast made by Sun Quan promoted the development and the merging of the different Chinese nationalities in the area. The political competence of Sun Quan even won the admiration of Cao Cao who once said, "If only I had a son like Sun Zhongmou."

Sun Quan died in 252 at the age of 70 and was granted the posthumous title of the Great Emperor of Wu.

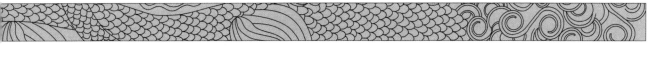

The Great Emperor of Wu, Sun Quan

Emperor Wu Di of the Jin Dynasty, Sima Yan

晉
武
帝
●
司
馬
炎

Sima Yan (236–290 AD), styled Anshi, was from Wenxian of Henei (west of the modern Wenxian County, Henan Province). He was the founder of the Jin Dynasty.

His father Sima Zhao had been the premier of the kingdom of Wei and had all the power of Wei in his hand. After the death of his father in 256, Sima Yan deposed the Wei emperor Cao Huan and assumed the title of emperor under the dynastic name of Jin, making Luoyang the capital of his dynasty which was referred to in history as the Western Jin.

Sima Yan had seized the power with the support of the scholar officials. After the unification of the country, he dismissed the troops of the various prefectures and issued decrees encouraging the prefectures and counties to develop agriculture. These measures brought about a short period of social stability and economic rehabilitation referred to in history as the "Prosperity of Taikang"[1]. Meanwhile, the emperor made some new stipulations in regard to land and taxation, imposing heavier exploitation on the people than the Wei Dynasty. Besides, he restored the enféoffment system of the Zhou Dynasty, creating many princes among the members of the royal family to offset the influence of the scholar officials. Such a policy gave rise to quite a few careerists among the princes.

Sima Yan lived in extreme extravagance and luxury. The total population of the country was about 16 million at that time. But he had in his harem nearly 10 thousand concubines and maids of honour. Nevertheless, he was still not satisfied and issued a decree to select more concubines throughout the country. Each day he would sit in a carriage pulled by sheep, giving free rein to the animals, feasting and sleeping wherever the sheep pulled him.

Sima Yan had a stupid son named Sima Zhong. Although he had worried that the idiot might ruin the dynasty after his death, he failed to put the interests of the country first and preferred to deceive himself as well as others. When he held a banquet at Lingyun Terrace at the beginning of the Taikang Period of his reign, an official named Wei Huan who was already above 60 suddenly knelt down before his imperial seat and said meaningfully while stroking the edge of the seat, "What a grand seat, and what a pity it will be!" Sima Yan feigned ignorance, saying that the official had got drunk, though he understood what he really meant.

In 279, Sima Yan sent 200,000 troops in six routes in an expedition against the kingdom Wu (the kingdom of Shu perished in 262). The Wu army collapsed without a battle. The next year, Jin's navy fought to the Wu capital Jianye and Sun Hao, the king of Wu, surrendered. With the subjugation of Wu, the situation of tangled wars between warlords at the end of the Eastern Han Dynasty and the tripartite confrontation of the three Kingdoms Wei, Shu and Wu came to an end, and the country was unified for a short period of time.

Sima Yan died at the age of 54 with the posthumous title of Wu Di.

---

1. Taikang (280—289 AD) was the name of a period of Sima Yan's reign.

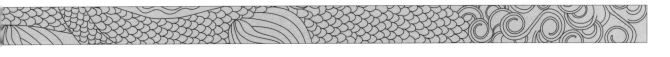

Emperor Wu Di of the Jin Dynasty, Sima Yan

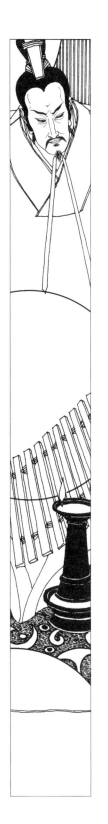

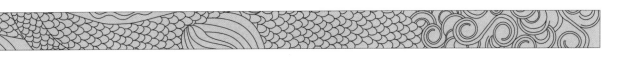

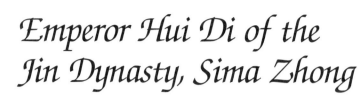

Emperor Hui Di of the Jin Dynasty, Sima Zhong

晋惠帝·司馬衷

Sima Zhong (259–306 AD), second son of Sima Yan, was the second emperor of the Jin Dynasty.

Sima Yan lived in extreme extravagance and luxury after unifying the country. And Sima Zhong who had been brought up in such conditions did not know anything except feasting and pleasure-seeking. Once when playing in the garden with a group of attendants, he asked in all curiosity why there were croaks from the pond. When the attendants told him that it was the frogs, he asked further beyond the expectation of all: "Are they raised by the country or by the common people?" The attendants blurted out an answer just to humour him, "The frogs in the fields belonging to the country are raised by the country, and those in the fields belonging to the common people are raised by the common people." And he kept nodding his appreciation of the answer.

Sima Zhong was made crown prince at the age of nine, but many follies of his caused dissatisfaction among the upright officials. Even his father once had the intention to replace him. He asked his son to make comments and instructions on some reports from the officials just to see whether he had made any progress in his intelligence. Knowing the intention of the emperor, Sima Zhong's wife Jia Nanfeng had someone else write the comments and instructions to be copied on the reports by Sima Zhong. Taken in by the trick, Wu Di was pleased with his son and dismissed the idea of replacing him.

Sima Zhong succeeded to the throne after the death of his father in 289, known in history as Hui Di of Jin. He was already 32 years old, but not a bit wiser than before, neither knowing how to handle state affairs nor able to mediate between the different groups striving for power among the ruling class. Before long, the country was thrown into chaos by frequent wars among eight princes of the royal family, which was referred to in history as the "Riots by the Eight Princes". During this period, Emperor Hui Di was simply a puppet, now in the hands of one prince, then in the hands of another.

In the wars, several hundred thousands of people lost their lives, and in the areas near Luoyang even boys of 13 had to serve in the army, and grain prices were exorbitant. The year 303 saw famine in the area under the control of Prince Hejian Sima Yong and starved bodies were found all across the land. When Emperor Hui Di got report of the situation, he even did not know what was meant by famine and asked, "Why don't the people eat meat porridge if they have no rice?" In 305, Prince Donghai Sima Yue defeated Sima Yong and captured Chang'an the next year. Emperor Hui Di was taken to Luoyang, and was murdered in the same year by Sima Yue with poison meat cake. That ended the life of the 47-year-old muddle-headed emperor.

Emperor Hui Di of the Jin Dynasty, Sima Zhong

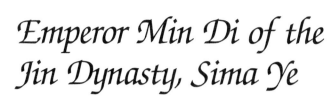

Emperor Min Di of the Jin Dynasty, Sima Ye

晉愍帝 • 司馬鄴

Sima Ye (270–317 AD), styled Yanqi, was the last emperor of the Western Jin Dynasty.

Being a grandson of Emperor Wu Di of Jin, he was made emperor at the age of 43 in Chang'an with the support of senior officials Jia Pi and Ju Yun after the riot of the Yongjia period (307-312).

At that time the Western Jin regime was on the verge of collapse. In the light of the invasion of Chang'an, Luoyang and the Guanzhong area by a Hun general Liu Yao sent by his emperor Liu Cong, Emperor Min Di did everything he could to rope in the landlord forces of the Guanzhong area and managed to shore up the regime for three years. In the wretched circumstances, only one or two percent of the population in fewer than 100 households survived in the former large city of Chang'an, and there were a mere total of four carriages left. The state granary was empty and the only few dozen coarse cakes were consumed by the emperor as imperial food. So when the Hun army pressed on Chang'an, Min Di had to surrender, stripping himself to the waist, leading a sheep in one hand, pulling a coffin in a carriage, and carrying the imperial seal by a string from between his teeth. Thus perished the Western Jin Dynasty.

After surrendering, Emperor Min Di was taken to Pingyang. The Hun emperor Liu Cong ordered him to put on the black clothes of a servant and wait on him at banquets. When the Hun emperor went hunting, he was ordered to run in front of the horse after the game just like a dog.

After all the insults and humiliation he was killed at the age of 47. His posthumous title was Min Di meaning in Chinese "an emperor to be pitied".

Emperor Min Di of the Jin Dynasty, Sima Ye

Emperor Yuan Di of the Jin Dynasty, Sima Rui

晉元帝 • 司馬睿

Sima Rui (276–322 AD), styled Jingwen, was the first emperor of the Eastern Jin Dynasty.

Being a great grandson of Sima Yi, he inherited the title of his father and became Prince Langya at the age of 15, with a position not exactly prominent among the royal family members. During the "Riots of the Eight Princes", he was ordered to defend Jianye (modern Nanjing) by Prince Donghai, Sima Yue, who was then in control of the power of the court. When he first arrived in Jianye, the local influential families in the south referred to him abusively as "the boor from the north", and no one visited him in a whole month. For that he was burdened with worries.

When people swarmed to the Shuibin River offering sacrifices on a festival in mid-spring 307, Sima Rui purposely went to the side of the Shuibin River in a sedan chair in the company of Wang Dao and Wang Dun who were from a renowned influential family that had moved from the north to the south of the Yangtze River, and since then, Sima Rui had got the common support of the rich and powerful families both of the north and south.

Learning about the murder of Emperor Min Di in 318, Sima Rui proclaimed himself emperor in Jianye and founded what was referred to in history as the "Eastern Jin" Dynasty.

The name of the capital Jianye was changed to Jiankang just to avoid the sound of Emperor Min Di's name Ye. On the day of the crowning ceremony, Sima Rui insisted that Wang Dao sit on the throne by his side to share the homage and felicitation of the court officials. The idea was given up only after the polite but resolute declining of Wang Dao. Circulating among the people at the time was such a comment : "The country is shared between Wang and Sima." That showed the regime of the Sima family could not do without the support of the powerful families.

Emperor Yuan Di only promoted people from influential families and never imposed legal sanctions on the powerful and nobility. He granted preferential treatment to these people, allowing them to occupy hills and lakes as well as land, and provided protection to tenants who had illegally attached themselves to them. Needless to say, the emperor showed more favour to the influential families from the north. For instance, when Wang Jiao moved to the south from Taiyuan, the emperor immediately "awarded him 300,000 coins, 300 bolts of silk, about 5,000 kilograms of rice and 20 bodyguards" to help him get reestablished in the south.

As a result of the emperor's connivance, struggles for power and gain took place one after another among the powerful families. In 322, internal dissension occurred between the two brothers of the most influential family that had given the greatest support to Emperor Yuan Di. At that time, Wang Dao had been promoted to premiership, and his brother Wang Dun was stationed in Jiangzhou with a powerful army. The latter started an armed rebellion against the Jin Dynasty and fought his way to the capital Jiankang. Thanks to the resistance by Wang Dao and others, his ambition was frustrated. But the emperor died in worry and indignation in the same year at the age of 46. His posthumous title was Emperor Yuan Di.

Emperor Yuan Di of the Jin Dynasty, Sima Rui

King of the Kingdom of Han, Liu Yuan

漢國王・劉淵

Liu Yuan (?–310 AD), styled Yuanhai, was the founder of the Kingdom of Han during the period of the Sixteen Kingdoms.

Liu Yuan was from the Hun nobility in Xinxing (modern Xin County, Shanxi Province) and was said to be the descendant of the Hun ruler Mao Tun who had married a lady of the imperial family of the Han Dynasty 500 years before during the reign of Emperor Gao Zu of Han, Liu Bang. Just because of that, the Hun ruler had changed his surname to Liu. Liu Yuan lived in Luoyang when he was very young and associated himself with famous scholars and officials. He had studied such books as *The Book of History* and *The History of the Han Dynasty* and was particularly interested in *The Art of War* by Master Sun Zi. Thus he was strongly under the influence of the Han culture.

He was appointed a general and chief commander of the Five Sections of the Hun in the reign of Emperor Hui Di of Jin. During the "Riots of the Eight Princes", he was in the army of General Wang Ying stationed in Chengdu when the vagabonds' uprising broke out in Sichuan. The Left Prince of the Hun, Liu Xuan, called together the members of the Hun nobility for discussion and said, "Since the Wei and Jin Dynasties, we Huns have held a nominal title but are merely common people in reality. Now that the royal family members are engaged in fratricidal fightings, it is a good chance for us to rise in armed rebellion." So they secretly agreed to make Liu Yuan their leader.

In 304, Liu Yuan got away from Chengdu to Lishi (modern Lishi of Shanxi Province) on the excuse of getting recruits for his unit. There he rose in armed rebellion against the Jin Dynasty, assuming at the beginning the title of Great Chanyu and later the title King of Han.

At that time, Liu Yuan was not powerful enough to found a Han Kingdom against the Jin Dynasty. Later, Shi Le of the Jie nationality and Wang Mi of the Han nationality, who had been defeated by the Jin army in the lower reaches of the Yellow River, came to join him and his forces grew in strength and impetus. He sent his troops to attack the prefectures and counties in Hebei and Henan and his army grew to as many as 100,000. In 308, he assumed the title of emperor and moved the capital to Puzi (modern Xixian County of Shanxi Province). The next year he made Pingyang (modern Linfen County of Shanxi Province) the capital of his kingdom. In order to win the support of the Han landlords, he asserted that the Lius of the Hun were the nephew of the royal family Liu of the Western and Eastern Han Dynasties, and he decreed to worship three ancestors (Emperor Gaozu Liu Bang, Emperor Wu Di Liu Che and Emperor Zhaolie Liu Bei) instead of Chanyu of the Hun.

After the founding of the Kingdom of Han, Liu Yuan sent his son Liu Cong, his general Shi Le and Wang Mi, who was from a influential family of the Jin, to attack Luoyang, the capital of the Western Jin, but was defeated. Then Liu Yuan turned out in full force for a second attack, ordering his fourth son Liu Cong to lead 50,000 crack cavalry soldiers as the vanguard that launched a surprise attack, taking advantage of the unpreparedness of the Jin. However, 1,000 valiant Jin warriors under General Jia Yin attacked Liu Cong's army under the cover of night, and 3,000 more crack soliders under the Jin general Sun Hai joined in the attack, putting Liu Yuan's army to rout for a second time.

Liu Yuan died in 310. His Kingdom of Han was the earliest separatist regime founded in the period of the Sixteen Kingdoms. Beginning from this time, China entered a period of disunity and chaos.

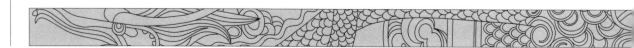

King of the Kingdom of Han, Liu Yuan

King of Zhao, Shi Le

趙
王
·
石
勒

Shi Le (274–333 AD) was of Jie nationality from Wuxiang of Shangdang (north of modern Yushe of Shanxi Province) and was the founder of the Kingdom of Later Zhao in the period of the Sixteen Kingdoms.

His ancestors, probably from the state Shi in ancient middle Asia, were believed to have emigrated to Central China with the Huns and made Shi their surname. As a tenant of a Han landlord, the young Shi Le had a miserable life. Following the armed uprising of Liu Yuan, he started a rebellion together with Ji Sang. After Ji was killed in battle, Shi Le led the troops to join Liu Yuan and was appointed grand general.

Out of extreme hatred for the powerful families of Jin, Shi Le would kill almost all the senior officials of Jin captured in battle. In 311, he surrounded over 100,000 Jin troops, senior officials, and members of the nobility and the royal family, and ordered his cavalry to shoot them all with arrows. And not a single one survived the massacre.

In 318, Shi Le wiped out all the remnant forces of the Western Jin Dynasty in the north. After capturing the Pingyang city in the same year, he said, "It is up to myself whether or not to assume the imperial title. There is no point having anyone else confer a title upon me." So the next year he assumed the title of the King of Zhao, making Xiangguo (modern Xingtai of Hebei Province) the capital.

In 329, he won complete victory at Luoyang in the battle against the Former Zhao, killing its king Liu Yao (the nephew of Liu Yuan). He then captured Chang'an, putting an end to the regime of the Former Zhao. In 330, Shi Le assumed the title of emperor and founded what was referred to in history as the Later Zhao.

At the beginning of his reign, he did everything possible to raise the status of the people of Jie nationality. Meanwhile, he put a Han scholar Zhang Bin in an important position and restored the old system of taxation. He issued a decree for all the prefectures and counties to take a census and for each household to contribute to the state two bolts of silk and two Chinese bushels of grain. Taking advantage of the contradictions between the upper and the lower stratum of scholar officials, Shi Le imprisoned and executed many of the former and succeeded in winning the support of the latter. He took some enlightened measures during his reign such as encouraging honest and upright officials and severely punishing corrupt officials, and the state affair took on a new look as compared with the Western Jin Dynasty.

Shi Le made regulations for the various trades and schools of thoughts, prizing Confucianism, and promoting Buddhism. In 331, a Buddhist monk from India named Futudeng came to see Shi Le and played some magic tricks which thoroughly convinced him. Later, the Indian monk did everything possible to propagate Buddhism by making use of the chances to treat sick officers and men. From then on, Shi Le went in for the construction of Buddhist temples in a big way and even entrusted the temples with the task of raising his own son. And he himself also worshipped the Buddha for his blessing.

Shi Le died of illness in 333 at the age of 59.

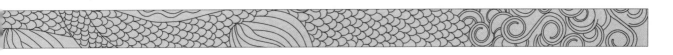

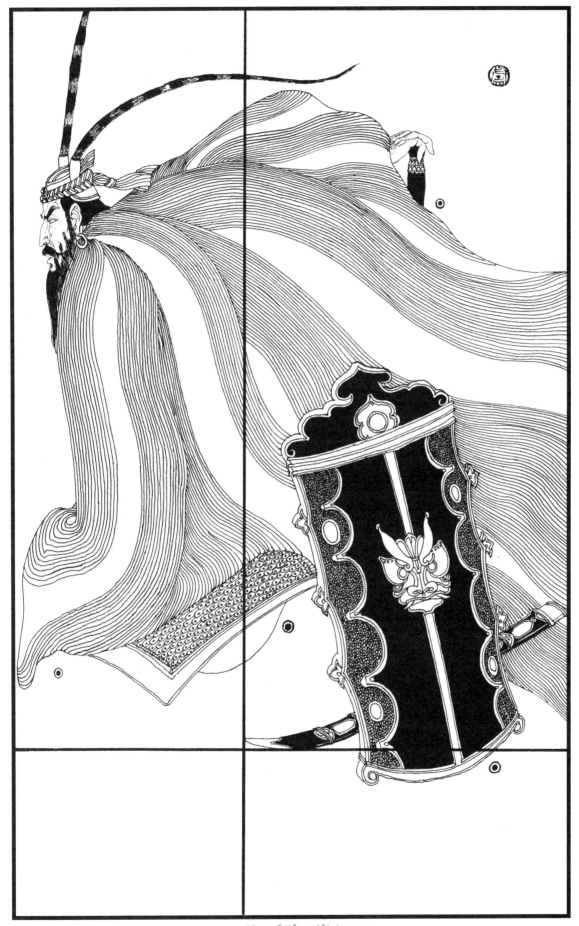

King of Zhao, Shi Le

King of the Former Qin, Fu Jian

秦王·苻堅

Fu Jian (338–385 AD), styled Yonggu, was from Linwei of Lueyang (east of modern Tianshui County, Gansu Province). He was of Di nationality and was a king of the Former Qin in the period of the Sixteen Kingdoms.

His grandfather, Fu Hong, laid the foundation for the Kingdom of the Former Qin and his uncle assumed the title of Heavenly King of Qin after occupying the Guanzhong Area in 351, making Chang'an his capital. The next year his uncle assumed the title of emperor. However, his cousin proved to be a ruthless despot after succeeding to the crown and was killed by Fu Jian in 357, who then proclaimed himself the monarch, assuming the title of "Heavenly King of the Great Qin" instead of emperor.

As a monarch of the Di nationality, Fu Jian accomplished a lot. Unlike Shi Hu of the Later Zhao and Ran Min of Wei who harboured narrow nationalist views, Fu Jian hoped to have a kingdom which cared for its people and in which all the nationalities were united like one big family. He put in important positions not only capable people of such minority nationalities as Xianbi, Qiang, Jie and Hun, but also generals and statesmen of Han nationality.

A typical example was a Han official Wang Meng who was promoted to be the premier and senior general. Within dozen of days after he became the premier, Wang Meng executed over 20 tyrannical and lawless noblemen of the Di nationality and displayed their corpses in public, which made a great impact on the officials and the common people. Fu Jian commented in praise of the premier, "It is only today that I have got to know that a monarch can have true dignity only with the enforcement of law." With the help of Wang Meng, Fu Jian set about rectifying the style of the officials and the ways and customs of the society, started irrigation projects, and took measures to encourage farming and sericulture. As a result, the nation became prosperous and the military forces grew very strong. The people were well-to-do and led a happy life. The King wiped out the kingdoms of Former Yan, Former Liang, and Dai, before unifying the bulk of the northern part of the country and establishing a powerful regime strong enough to contend with the Eastern Jin Dynasty in the south.

In 382, Fu Jian called his officials and generals to his palace hall to discuss his proposal to personally lead the forces southward to wipe out the Eastern Jin for the unification of the country. Despite the objection of many officials, Fu Jian said, "I have an army of almost one million soldiers. And we can stop the flow of the Yangtze River if all the officers and men threw their horse whips into it."

In 383, Fu Jian led an army of 800,000 and left Chang'an in three mighty routes advancing both by land and water towards the Eastern Jin. At the insistence of the premier Xie An, the Eastern Jin Dynasty was determined to put up a resistance, and routed the troops of Qin by the Feishui River with an army only one tenth the number of the enemy. The routed Qin troops retreated in great fright and over 70 percent of them died of cold and hunger. And Fu Jian himself was shot with an arrow before he fled back to the Guanzhong Area.

The Former Qin never recovered from the defeat. Many states that had been exterminated by Fu Jian took the chance to get restored and the northern part of China was again disrupted. In 385, Fu Jian was killed at the age of 47 by one of his generals, Yao Chang, who was of Qiang nationality. And nine years later, the Former Qin was replaced by the Later Qin founded by Yao Chang.

King of the Former Qin, Fu Jian

Emperor Wu Di of Song, Liu Yu

宋武帝 • 劉裕

Liu Yu (363–422 AD), styled Deyu and with a pet style Jinu, was from Jingkou (modern Zhenjiang of Jiangsu Province). He was the founder of the Song Dynasty in the period of the Northern and Southern Dynasties.

When he was young, Liu Yu had been engaged in farming, fishing, and small business before joining the Northern Garrison organized by the Eastern Jin Dynasty to resist the invasion of Fu Jian. In the internal strife of the court, he killed the powerful minister Huan Xuan and seized the political and military power of the Eastern Jin Dynasty. The peasant uprisings led by Sun En and Lu Xun were also put down by Liu Yu.

In order to build up his prestige and authority by way of scoring military achievements, Liu Yu led a strong expedition army against Southern Yan, a kingdom in the north founded by the Xianbei Nationality. At that time, Yao Xing, the monarch of the Later Qin, sent an envoy from his capital Chang'an who said to Liu Yu, "Qin will not sit by doing nothing to see our neighbour Yan being invaded. We have already despatched a strong cavalry of 100,000 horsemen from Chang'an to Luoyang. If you do not withdraw your troops, our cavalry will fight their way directly here." Liu Yu drove away Qin's envoy without hesitation, and comforted his anxiety-ridden subordinates, saying, "If Qin is able to support Yan, it should have sent its troops without delay. What is the point of sending an envoy over such a long distance to give us the message beforehand? That was mere bluff and a deceptive demonstration of strength." Things turned out just as Liu Yu had expected. The Later Qin never dared to send troops while the army of the Eastern Jin led by Liu Yu wiped out the Southern Yan in 410. Seven years later, Liu Yu made a second northward expedition and captured Chang'an. The monarch of the Later Qin, Yao Hong, was escorted to Eastern Jin's capital Jiankang where he was executed.

The two expeditions pushed the northern border of the Eastern Jin to the south bank of the Yellow River. With his prestige reaching an unprecedented height, Liu Yu was made Prince of Song by the Jin emperor.

Under the high pressure of the influence and power of Liu Yu, the last emperor of the Eastern Jin Sima Dewen abdicated in favour of Prince Song in 420. Thus ended the Eastern Jin Dynasty and Liu Yu became the emperor in Jiankang under the dynastic title of Song.

When Liu Yu was in power, he removed the preferential treatment granted by the Eastern Jin court to the influential families that had moved south from the north and let them have the same treatment as enjoyed by the local families in the places where they lived. He cancelled the prefectures and counties set up specially for the northern influential families. This was no doubt beneficial to the unification of administration and the economization of expenditure on the one hand, and weakened the influence of the powerful large families on the other.

Liu Yu was a fairly enlightened emperor. He issued decrees to reduce taxation and corvée and to free household slaves who had joined the army. And he led a relatively simple life for an emperor.

Liu Yu died of illness at the age of 59 in 422 after being on the throne for two years. He was granted the posthumous title of Emperor Wu Di.

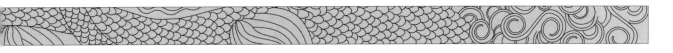

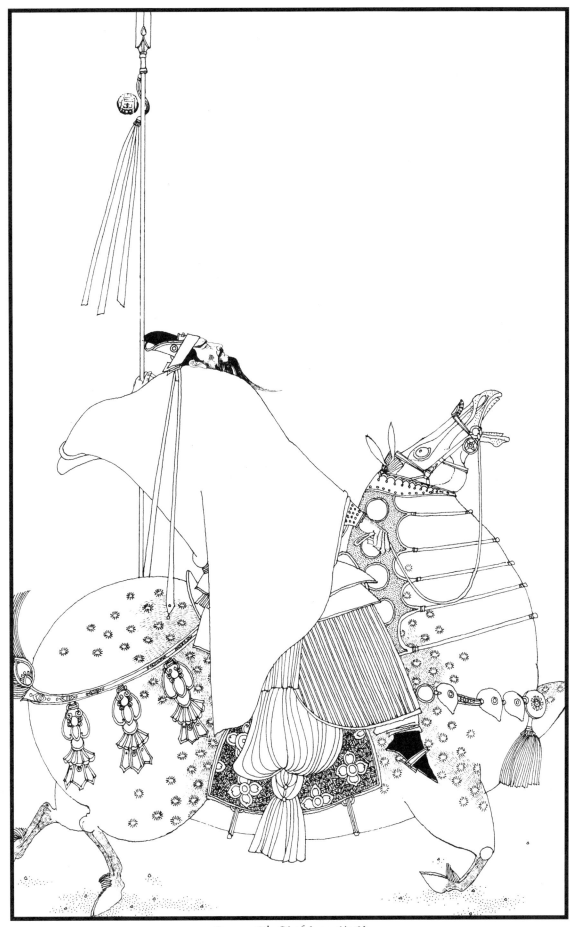

Emperor Wu Di of Song, Liu Yu

Emperor Gao Di of Qi, Xiao Daocheng

齊高帝 • 蕭道成

Xiao Daocheng (427–482 AD), styled Shaobo, was from Lanling (northwest of modern Changzhou of Jiangsu Province) and was the founder of the Qi Dynasty in the period of the Northern and Southern Dynasties.

Born to a poor family, Xiao Daocheng was not ambitious during his childhood. He started his career as a junior staff officer in a local garrison guarding the frontier. Prudent and capable, he was promoted step by step for his achievements in battles. Later, taking advantage of the internecine struggles among members of the Song royal family, he got hold of the important power of commanding the central army.

One day, the last emperor of Song got into his camp without giving any notice. Seeing Xiao Daocheng taking a nap without clothes on, the emperor drew a circle around his navel as the target to shoot arrows at just for pleasure. Fortunately he was dissuaded and only shot at Xiao's navel with an arrow without tip. Worrying about his own safety, Xiao Daocheng made secret arrangements after that for his trusted subordinate Wang Jingze to make friends with the emperor's guard so as to watch for a chance to start a coup.

One night, the emperor threatened to kill the guard. For his own safety, the guard killed the emperor while the latter was fast asleep. He then cut off the head, which was passed on to Xiao Daocheng by Wang Jingze. Early the next morning,

Xiao called a meeting of the senior officials discussing the succession of the throne. As a result, Liu Zhun was made emperor, known in history as Shun Di. And Xiao himself got all the vital power in his own hands.

In 479, Xiao Daocheng proclaimed himself emperor, changing the dynastic title to Qi.

After gaining the crown, Xiao Daocheng consulted a Confucianist scholar Liu Huan for the way the country was run. Liu answered. "Leniency is the key to lasting stability and prosperity. The Song Dynasty perished because its rulers were too cruel. If you can take a lesson from its failure and be generous towards the people, danger will turn into stability."

Thus Xiao Daocheng set about removing the cruel policies of the Song. He advocated frugality and set a grand goal "to make gold cheap as dust after reigning the country for ten years". He made a point of reducing overdue rent and debt and imposing restrictions on the construction of dwelling houses by the princes. He also appointed special officials for strict administration of household registration. However, because of the various abuses in carrying out the policies, there arose a dissatisfaction among the people.

Xiao Daocheng died of illness at the age of 55 in 482. He was granted the posthumous title of Emperor Gao Di.

Emperor Gao Di of Qi, Xiao Daocheng

Emperor Wu Di of Liang, Xiao Yan

梁武帝·蕭衍

Xiao Yan (464–549 AD), styled Shuda, was from Southern Lanling (northwest of modern Changzhou of Jiangsu Province) and was the founder of Liang in the period of the Northern and Southern Dynasties.

Xiao Yan was a distant cousin of Xiao Daocheng, founder of the Qi Dynasty. He had been an ardent lover of reading since his childhood and enjoyed the same popularity as the famous scholar Shen Yue when he was young. In 498, he was appointed governor of Yongzhou entrusted with the defence of Xiangyang. In the closing years of the Southern Qi Dynasty, Xiao Baorong mounted the throne on the strength of the exclusive support of Xiao Yan amidst the fratricidal fightings among the royal family members who simply neglected state affairs. In 501, however, Xiao Yan led his troops and captured the capital Jiankang. He killed Xiao Baorong before assuming the title of emperor and founding the Liang Dynasty.

The new emperor made a lot of efforts to reconcile the relations between the scholar families and the common people, but he connived at the corruption of the royal family members and officials. It was said that he lived a very simple life, eating a simple diet for the three meals of the day, and using the same old quilt for two years on end. That, however, was the deceptive side of this emperor. As a devout believer of Buddhism, he spent large amounts of money building temples and moulding Buddhist statues. There were temples all around the capital extending for 20 kilometres in all directions, with as many as 100,000 monks and nuns. At that time, there were even servants and maids in the temples throughout the country accounting for almost half of the total population. Later, the emperor even declared that he would abdicate to become a Buddhist monk, and for four times he dedicated himself to Tongtai Temple, the largest of its kind in the capital city, but each time he was brought back by the court with a large sum of ransom which totalled 400 million coins, and he was thus called "Emperor Bodhisattva". In addition, the emperor organized some scholars for the composition of 200 volumes of *Notes to the Classics* and 600 volumes of *General History*.

As a result of the various kinds of preferential treatment granted to the temples in Xiao Yan's efforts to advocate Buddhism, there grew up quite a number of rich Buddhist monk landlords as well as very rich royal family members and influential families that formed the ruling class at the time. Once at the sight of his enormous piles of gold, silver and other treasures owned by his younger brother Xiao Hong, he said in praise: "Brother, you are indeed good at arranging your life." In contrast, the common people of the country were reduced to "all skin and bone" under the heavy exploitation of the rich.

In 548, when the rule of the Liang Dynasty was on the verge of collapse, a general Hou Jing, who had betrayed Eastern Wei and surrendered to Liang, started a revolt and captured the capital Jiankang following the besiege of the city for 130 days. And Xiao Yan died of starvation at the age of 85 as his food supply had been cut off. He was later granted the posthumous title of Wu Di.

Emperor Wu Di of Liang, Xiao Yan

Emperor Wu Di of Chen, Chen Baxian

陳武帝·陳霸先

Chen Baxian (503–559), styled Xingguo, was from Changcheng of Wuxing (modern Changxing of Zhejiang Province) and was the founder of Chen in the Northern and Southern Dynasties.

Being from a humble family, Chen Baxian worked as a subordinate of local officials in charge of community affairs, warehouses of vegetable oil, and transmission of orders, before he was gradually promoted to be the magistrate of Gaoyao (modern Zhaoqing of Guangdong Province). It was in this post that he succeeded in suppressing the peasant uprising in Jiaozhou Prefecture and gradually came into prominence. In 549, he rose in Guangzhou in an expedition against the traitor general Hou Jing. He led his army across the Dayu Ridge from Shixing (modern Shaoguan of Guangdong) and advanced northward along the Ganshui River. On his way, people kept joining his troops or supplying grain, and his army soon expanded. At Pencheng (modern Jiujiang of Jiangxi Province), he joined forces with General Wang Sengbian who had revolted against Hou Jing in Jingzhou Prefecture. At the time the morale of the Jingzhou army under Wang Sengbian was shaken for being short of food supply, and Chen Baxian alloted to them roughly 30,000 tonnes of grain out of his own granary of 50,000 tonnes, thus greatly boosting their morale. As a result, the two armies took concerted actions and captured the capital Jiankang in 552, putting Hou Jing's army to rout. And Hou himself was killed by his subordinate on his way in flight.

After the annihilation of Hou Jing, Emperor Yuan Di of Liang, Xiao Yi, appointed Wang Sengbian senior general in command of the garrison troops of the stone-walled capital city of Jiankang, and Chen Baxian senior minister stationed at Jingkou. After the death of Emperor Yuan Di, the 13-year-old Xiao Fangzhi succeeded to the throne,

known in history as Emperor Jing Di. The Northern Qi Dynasty founded by the noblemen of the Xianbei Nationality took the chance and sent their army southward to invade the Liang Dynasty. They roped in General Wang Sengbian who was also of Xianbei Nationality, requesting him to remove Emperor Jing Di and put on the throne a nephew of Emperor Wu Di of Liang, Xiao Yuanming, who had been taken prisoner by the Northern Qi in war. Resenting what Wang Sengbian did, Chen Baxian secretly led his army from Jingkou to the capital and killed Wang in a sudden attack before reinstating Emperor Jing Di.

Learning of the news, the Northern Qi launched a massive attack. When they fought their way to the Zhongshan Hill (modern Zijinshan Hill east of Nanjing), the remaining forces of Wang Sengbian joined them, and Chen Baxian led his army in resistance. Days of incessant heavy rain submerged the ground with a flood of three metres deep, causing great difficulties to both sides. Learning that Chen's army was short of food, the local people prepared at night rice with duck meat wrapped up in lotus leaves and brought the food to the troops. With their support, Chen Baxian succeeded in defeating the Northern Qi army and wiping out the remnant forces of Wang Sengbian. The empire of the Han people in the south was thus saved. In 557, Chen Baxian deposed the Liang emperor Xiao Fangzhi and mounted the throne himself, changing the dynastic title to Chen.

Despite the frequent wars with the opponent states and the domestic insurgences which took place from time to time during the reign of Chen Baxian, economy and culture were gradually restored due to the measures adopted for the benefit of the nation and the people. In 559, Chen Baxian died of illness at the age of 56, and was granted the posthumous title of Wu Di.

Emperor Wu Di of Chen, Chen Baxian

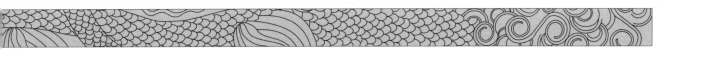

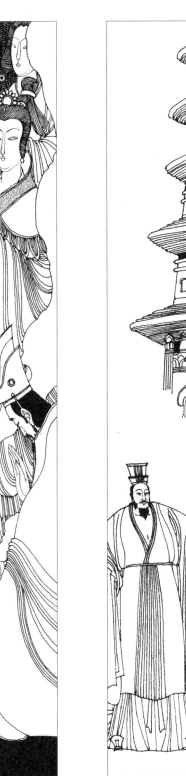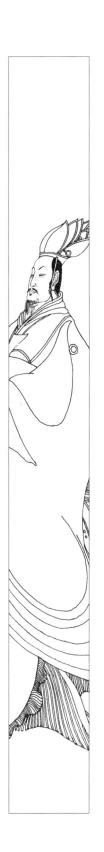

Emperor Dao Wu of the Northern Wei Dynasty, Tuoba Gui

魏
道
武
帝
·
拓
跋
珪

Tuoba Gui (371–409), was from the Tuoba Tribe of the Xianbei Nationality and was the founder of the Northern Wei Dynasty.

Tuoba was one of the nomadic tribes of the Xianbei Nationality moving about the Greater Xing'an Mountains in the northeast of China. With the decline of the Former Qin after the battle by the Feishui River, the national minorities in the north founded their own states one after another. And availing himself of the opportunity, Tuoba Gui, a descendant of the famous tribe chieftain Yilu at the end of the Western Jin Dynasty, united the former followers of the tribe and reassumed the title of "King of Dai" which was then changed to "King of Wei". With his state becoming stronger after wiping out Dugu, Helan and other neighbouring tribes, he assumed the title of emperor in 398, making Pingcheng (northeast of modern Datong of Shanxi Province) his capital.

Tuoba Gui put an end to the organization of tribes after founding the State of Wei, taking measures to realize the transition from the primitive to the feudal society. He appointed the chieftains of the various tribes to be ministers, thus replacing the relations between the head of the tribe alliance and the tribe chieftains with those between the monarch and subjects. Meanwhile he absorbed large numbers of Han landlords for the administration of his monarch, establishing a feudal political system after the model of the Han people.

As a result of the policy he adopted to promote farming and sericulture for the recuperation of the people, agriculture was gradually restored and developed. In 398, he moved 400,000 people of various nationalities to the area of the capital Pingcheng and encouraged them to carry out production by allocating to them land and cattle. He even ploughed the field personally to show the importance he attached to agriculture. The economy of the state Wei thus gained rapid development, which accelerated the pace for the state to unify the northern part of China.

Starting from 388, Tuoba Gui conquered large areas both north and south of the Yellow River. In 395, he routed the army of the Later Yan State at Canhepo (near modern Datong of Shanxi Province), capturing and killing as many as 40 to 50 thousand and getting enormous quantity of arms and other military supplies. And the number of Later Yan officials and officers of different ranks captured in the battle was as large as several thousand. Then he advanced southward on the crest of the victory, taking the important city of the Later Yan, Bingzhou (modern Taiyuan), and its capital Zhongshan (modern Dingzhou of Hebei Province). The regime of the Later Yan thus came to an end.

Unfortunately, Tuoba Gui died in 409 at the age of only 38 before realizing the unification of north China. Nevertheless he had made great contributions to the transition to feudalism of the Xianbei Nationality and laid the foundation for the unification of the northern part of the country. The posthumous title granted to him was Emperor Dao Wu.

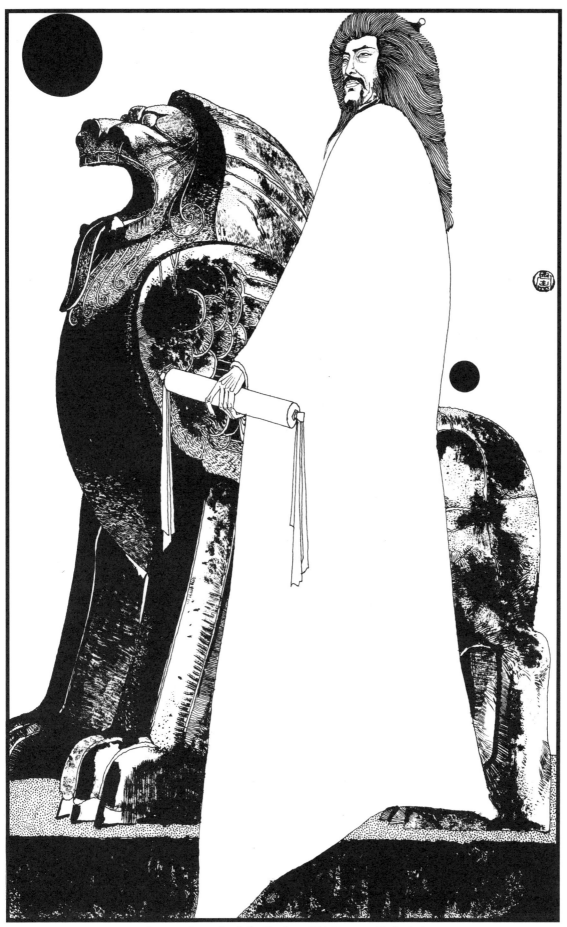

Emperor Dao Wu of the Northern Wei Dynasty, Tuoba Gui

Emperor Xiao Wen of the Northern Wei Dynasty, Tuoba Hong

魏孝文帝·拓跋宏

Tuoba Hong (467–499) was of Xianbei Nationality and was the sixth emperor of the Northern Wei Dynasty after Tuoba Gui.

As a child, he was clever and resourceful and treated his elders with filial piety. At the age of three, he was made the crown prince, and at five he succeeded to the throne which his 18-year-old father Emperor Xian Wen abdicated in his favour. He was deeply grieved when he mounted the throne, saying, "My heart is full of sorrow to replace my father like this."

Eager to control the state affairs, his grandmother the Empress Dowager poisoned his father Emperor Xian Wen when the latter was only 23 years old, as she regarded his presence as an obstacle to achieving her ambition. Not until 490 when his grandmother died did the 14-year-old Tuoba Hong take over the reins of government.

Emperor Xiao Wen was ever ready to follow good advice in handling state affairs. He used to say emperors should guard against being unfair, so he gave instructions to the official historians: "You should record all the important events without reservation and do not cover up the evils of the court."

The greatest contribution of Emperor Xiao Wen was the fundamental reforms he made of the politics, economy, and culture of the Xianbei Nationality. In 484, he issued an imperial edict to carry out the salary system among the officials, stipulating the income of different ranks of officials so as to prevent the corrupt officials from wilfully exploiting the people. Later he promulgated "the system of even allocation of land", and brought a lot of wasteland under cultivation. Meanwhile he reformed the administration structure at the grassroots level with five households organized into a neighbourhood, five neighbourhoods into a community so as to guarantee taxation and corvée according to the actual number of people and quantity of land of each household.

To narrow the gap between the different nationalities, he made a point of implementing the policy for the minorities to learn from the Hans. In 493, he led 200,000 troops southward in the name of attacking the Kingdom of Qi, and declared Luoyang to be his capital. Then he carried out further reforms of the bureaucratic establishment, banned the garments and languages of the minorities, recruited learned people, started schools, adopted the Wuzhu coins which had been in use in the dynasties founded by the Han people and even changed the royal surname to Yuan.

His reforms met with the opposition of a handful of the conservative Tuoba nobles. In 496, his crown prince was put to death as he had attempted to flee back to the former capital Pingcheng to start a rebellion.

The reforms by Tuoba Hong marked the first milestone of the merging of the nationalities after the various minorities from the north and the west moved to Central China, and played a positive role in the formation and development of a unified multi-national country.

Tuoba Hong was only 32 years old when he died, and he was granted the posthumous title of Emperor Xiao Wen.

Emperor Xiao Wen of the Northern Wei Dynasty, Tuoba Hong

Emperor Wen Xuan of the Northern Qi Dynasty, Gao Yang

北齊文宣帝・高洋

Gao Yang (529–559), styled Zijin, was from Tiao of Bohai (east of Jingxian County, Hebei Province), and was the founder of the Northern Qi Dynasty.

His father Gao Huan started his career by relying on the officers of Xianbei Nationality stationed at the norther border towards the end of the Northern Wei Dynasty. He expanded his forces and influence, taking advantage of the decline of the Northern Wei. Unwilling to endure the humiliations, Emperor Wu Di of Wei fled to Chang'an and was poisoned by a senior official named Yuwen Tai. After the destruction of Northern Wei, Gao Huan put emperor Xiao Jing on the throne in Luoyang before moving the capital to Ye. The new dynasty was referred to in history as Eastern Wei in contrast to Western Wei with its capital in Chang'an. Three years after the death of Gao Huan, his second son Gao Yang deposed Emperor Xiao Jing and declared himself emperor, changing the dynastic title to Qi which was known in history as the Northern Qi.

The new emperor promoted to important position a Han scholar official Yang Yin who made reforms of the laws and regulations and took severe measures against corruption. The rich were required to contribute money and the poor to provide labour. In view of the fact that influential families had been establishing provinces, prefectures and counties, forming new separatist forces since the reign of Emperor Xiao Ming of Wei, he issued an edict in 556 eliminating 3 provinces, 153 prefectures and 589 counties. These political measures were conducive to the domestic stability of Northern Qi.

Although he himself is a Han, Emperor Wen Xuan implemented a policy for the Hans to follow the way and culture of the Xianbei Nationality. Among the 100 odd senior officials and generals of his court, 8 or 9 out of 10 were of Xianbei Nationality or identified themselves with the Xianbei Nationality, and Han officials only held secondary positions. Once Gao Yang asked a Han scholar official Du Bi, "Who shall I rely on to run the country?" Du replied, "The Hans should be relied on for the administration of the country, as the Xianbei people are only good at riding horses and sitting in carriages." The emperor resented the reply and before long put Du Bi to death.

Gao Yang selected Xianbei "valiants" to be his guards and sent the Hans to serve in the frontier force. For years on end, he launched one war after another against such nationalities as Rouran, Turks, and Qidan and achieved great victories. In 555, he sent 1.8 million people for the construction of the Great Wall and completed 1,500 kilometres within a year.

Gao Yang was a cruel ruler and very much conceited with his "achievements". Indulging in excessive drinking and lust for women, he died at the age of only 30, and was granted the posthumous title of Emperor Wen Xuan.

Emperor Wen Xuan of the Northern Qi Dynasty, Gao Yang

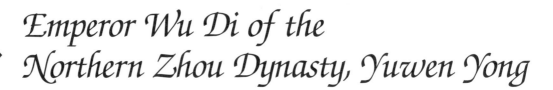

Emperor Wu Di of the Northern Zhou Dynasty, Yuwen Yong

周
武
帝
•
宇
文
邕

Yuwen Yong (543–578), styled Miluotu, was from Wuchuan of Dai Prefecture (west of modern Wuchuan County, Inner Mongolia). He was of Xianbei Nationality and was a distinguished emperor of the Northern Zhou Dynasty who embraced the Han culture.

He was the fourth son of Yuwen Tai, a senior official of Western Wei, whose other son Yuwen Jue overthrew the Western Wei after his death, and founded the Northern Zhou Dynasty. In 560, Yuwen Hu, a nephew of Yuwen Tai, killed Emperor Ming Di of Zhou and made Yuwen Yong emperor known as Emperor Wu Di.

Yuwen Yong was a celebrated feudal emperor who had broken away from the backward ways and customs of the Xianbei Nationality and truly embraced the advanced culture of the Hans. Once he issued a decree to free the slaves in the country, which said: "It was stipulated in the ancient times that if a person committed a crime, his sons were not to be punished. But now once a person is reduced to slavery, his descendants will be slaves generation after generation. That was against the laws as well as the ancient ways." After issuing several decrees, the remnant slave system that had survived for several hundred years since the Wei and Jin Dynasties were practically abolished in the country.

During the Northern and Southern Dynasties, there were a large number of temples and a much larger number of monks across the country, which constituted a sharp contradiction with the sources of troops and the financial income of the government. In view of that Emperor Wu Di of Zhou announced in 574 to abolish Buddhism and Taoism. In 577, he assembled 500 monks in the city of Ye announcing the decision to abolish Buddhism. At the time, a senior Buddhist monk named Huiseng argued against the decision, and threatened that those who advocated the abolition of Buddhism would be condemned to sufferings in Hell after death. To that the emperor replied resolutely, "So long as my people can have a better life, I am willing to go through all the sufferings in Hell." As a result, over 40,000 temples were turned into residences and nearly 3 million monks resumed secular life. This greatly promoted the development of production.

In 577, the emperor promulgated a law, laying down the standard for severe punishment of those who concealed the true quantity of their land or stole what was entrusted to their care. That played a positive role in getting rid of the deep-rooted practice of embezzlement.

In the same year, Yuwen Yong's army wiped out the Northern Qi and unified the northern part of China. Then he promulgated unified units of length, capacity, and weight to be adopted across the country. He also ordered the prefectures east of the Tongguan Pass to recommend virtuous and capable people to the court for discussion of the successes and failures of politics. The northern part of China became gradually stronger under his reign. Unfortunately, Yuwen Yong died of illness at the age of only 35 when he led strong troops in five routes headed northward against the Turks. Emperor Wu Di of Zhou, as was his posthumous title, laid the foundation for the unification of the country, though he did not have the time to realize it himself.

Emperor Wu Di of the Northern Zhou Dynasty, Yuwen Yong

Emperor Wen Di of the Sui Dynasty, Yang Jian

隋文帝 · 楊堅

Yang Jian (541-604), from Huayin of Hong Nong (today's Huayin County of Shaanxi Province), was the founder of the Sui Dynasty.

Yang Jian's father Yang Zhong, one of the 12 great generals of the Western Wei, was conferred the title of Lord of Sui which Yang Jian inherited after his father died. And his daughter became the empress of Emperor Xuan Di of the Northern Zhou Dynasty. When Emperor Xuan Di died, his eight-year-old son Emperor Jing Di reigned under the regency of Yang Jian.

After deposing Jing Di the following year, Yang Jian came to the throne himself, known as Emperor Wen Di of the Sui Dynasty.

Wen Di worked diligently and took a series of measures. He standardized the currency, making the Wuzhu coin the legal tender, formulating codes and laws, reducing conscript labour, relaxing the restriction on liquor and salt, adjusting the administrative divisions, harnessing rivers and setting up public granaries and reconciling with the Turks through marriage. He had once taught the crown prince, "No empire with an extravagant emperor can last long. As the crown prince, you should practise frugality first of all." At that time, the clothes of the ordinary scholars were made of cotton, and their belts were decorated with bronze, iron, animal bone and horn, instead of gold and jade.

The frugality of the emperor was a prerequisite for better government. He rewarded the righteous officials while punishing the corrupt ones. And he was kind to the common people who were allowed when wronged, to appeal directly to the higher authorities, even to the imperial court. Though he dealt severe penalty to officials who had committed crimes, he was lenient to the ordinary criminals. In the year 600, Wang Jia, a junior official of Qizhou was on his way to bring 70 convicts to the capital. Seeing the hardships of the escorting peasants, he dismissed them and the convicts as well and ordered the latter to gather in the capital on a fixed date. As it turned out, all the convicts reported themselves in time. Hearing the news, Emperor Wen Di granted an interview to Wang Jia, speaking highly of his benevolence. The emperor then issued an imperial decree calling on all the officials to follow this good example.

In 588, Emperor Wen Di despatched an army of 500,000 to attack the south. The next year, they captured Chen Shubao—the last ruler of the Chen Dynasty in Jiankang, which put an end to the Southern Chen Dynasty and inaugurated a reunification of the country after 400 years of division. During the 20 years of his reign, the state remained stable and the economy was so prosperous that the grain and cloth in the imperial warehouse alone were enough for the court to use 50 to 60 years.

Wen Di was good at governing his state, but not his family. In 604, the 63-year-old emperor was killed on his sickbed by an assassin sent by his son, Yang Guang, with "his blood splashing on the screen, and bitter cries being heard outside the chamber." From then on, the Sui Dynasty began to go downhill.

Emperor Wen Di of the Sui Dynasty, Yang Jian

Emperor Yang Di of the Sui Dynasty, Yang Guang

隋煬帝・楊廣

Yang Guang (569–618) was the second emperor of the Sui Dynasty and was known as one of the most extravagant and dissipated emperors in Chinese history.

He was the second son and the favourite of his parents, Emperor Wen Di and the empress. During the battle to wipe out the state Chen in 588, Yang Guang displayed outstanding talent and was appointed Governor of Yang Zhou after the war.

Wen Di had five sons among whom the eldest was Yang Yong, the crown prince. In order to replace his brother, Yang Guang tried every means to please his parents. His wish was finally realized in the 20th year of his father's reign when the emperor issued an edict to remove the crown prince Yang Yong and put Yang Guang in his place. When Emperor Wen Di became seriously ill in 604, Yang Guang had his father murdered and usurped the throne. He was known as Emperor Yang Di of the Sui Dynasty.

Shortly after he came to the throne, he issued a decree to carry on large-scale constructions in the eastern capital Luoyang. During the three months, six million peasants were conscripted to build palaces in the city. Fantastic rocks and unusual timber were traced throughout the country. And it would take 2,000 men to carry a single large piece of timber from south of the Yangtze River to Central China. Many people were exhausted and lost their lives on the way.

At the same time, Yang Di assembled a large number of labourers to dig the Grand Canal. The project was completed in six years. With a total length of 2,000 kilometres, it linked up the Haihe, Yellow, Huai, Yangtze and Qiantang Rivers and greatly facilitated north-south transportation. On the other hand, the construction brought great disaster to the people, and places along the canal were strewn with corpses at the time.

For several times, Yang Di had taken pleasure trips around the country. In 605, when travelling to Jiangdu, he rode in a magnificent dragon ship with four decks, two of which in the middle had 120 compartments each. It was escorted by a fleet of thousands of vessels, and 80,000 labourers were required to tow them. In 607, again Yang Di made a tour with his entourage of 500,000 armoured soldiers up to the north frontier, bringing with him a mobile palace which could be dismantled and moved easily on wheels. With a capacity to accommodate several hundred people, it was indeed the earliest grand-size mobile house in the world. Some ministers complained in private about the extravagance of the trip and Yang Di had them all executed on an alleged slander.

Yang Di would not be satisfied with reigning in China proper. In 612, he sent an expedition army against Korea. The army was divided into two routes claiming to have two million soldiers, stretching for 489 kilometres. But the invading army was routed by the Korean people who made heroic resistance. Of the 300,000 vanguard soldiers, only 3,000 survived. Later, the emperor attempted two more raids on Korea, both of which ended in failure. At that time, there were already widespread uprisings against the Sui Dynasty throughout the country.

In 618, realizing that the doom of his dynasty was near, Emperor Yang Di prepared a jug of poisonous liquor for his suicide. Very soon, forces of the peasant uprisings grew stronger and Yang Di was captured by the regal rebels. Afraid to be beheaded, he offered a silk belt to the rebel chief to have himself strangled with. He was then 49 years old and with his death came the end of the Sui Dynasty.

Emperor Yang Di of the Sui Dynasty, Yang Guang

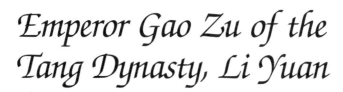

Emperor Gao Zu of the Tang Dynasty, Li Yuan

唐高祖·李淵

Li Yuan (566–635), with another name Shude, was born in Didao of Longxi. He was the first emperor of the Tang Dynasty.

Li Yuan's father, named Li Bing, had been a viceroy of Anzhou in the Northern Zhou Dynasty. And Li Yuan served as governor general stationed in Taiyuan during the reign of Emperor Yang Di of the Sui Dynasty. In 617, the Sui Dynasty was on the verge of collapse, and his second son Li Shimin proposed an uprising. Li Yuan, however, was shocked and intended to have his son sent to the government of Jinyang County to be punished for treason. Actually even the county magistrate was an ally of Shimin. Later, cornered by Emperor Yang Di, Li Yuan had to follow Shimin's advice and revolt in Taiyuan. Two months later, he marched into the Guanzhong area with an army of 30,000 which augmented to 200,000 in another two months and conquered the capital Chang'an. He then made Yang Yu, Yang Di's 13-year-old grandson a puppet emperor with the title of Emperor Gong Di and announced Yang Di who then was touring in Jiangdu far away in the east as supersovereign. By so doing, he was able to bring the remnant of Sui army and officials under his control, and abolish Yang Di's legitimacy, lending no pretext for his opponents to attack him.

In March 618, Yang Di died at Jiangdu. Li Yuan immediately deposed Gong Di and in May, he claimed the throne in Chang'an under the dynastic name of Tang. He was known in history as Tang Gao Zu, the first emperor of the dynasty. And that ushered in the famous Tang Dynasty which lasted 290 years in Chinese history.

In the following years, Li Yuan eliminated various peasant armies and local warlords one after another and reunified the whole country.

But before a ritual was held to celebrate the victory, he had been upset by the vying for power among his sons – the crown prince Li Jiancheng and Prince Qi Li Yuanji on one side and Prince Qin Li Shimin on the other. The muddle-headed Li Yuan came to doubt Shimin's loyalty and even disgusted him, shifting to the side of Li Jiancheng and Li Yuanji. The two brothers made the best use of this, unscrupulously buying up Shimin's subordinates while instigating the emperor to banish Shimin's trusted officials and generals to local positions. The struggles eventually led to the coup d'état at Xuanwu Gate.

In 626, Prince Qin Li Shimin ambushed and killed his two brothers at the palace gate Xuanwumen on their way to the morning court. The emperor was forced to make Li Shimin crown prince, and two months later, he abdicated not without reluctance, claiming himself supersovereign. Li Yuan died of illness at 69.

Emperor Gao Zu of the Tang Dynasty, Li Yuan

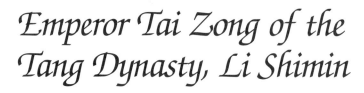

Emperor Tai Zong of the Tang Dynasty, Li Shimin

唐太宗 • 李世民

Li Shimin (599–649), one of the few most admired emperors in Chinese history, was the second son of Li Yuan, the first emperor of the Tang Dynasty.

After his father's abdication in 626, Li Shimin took the throne, making Zhen Guan the title of his reign the following year. He was known as Emperor Tai Zong of the Tang Dynasty.

Twelve days after he was crowned, the Turks, a strong nomadic tribe in the north, launched an assault against Tang, marching to the northern bank of Wei River only 20 kilometres from Tang's capital Chang'an. Tai Zong, with a retinue of six senior officials including Gao Shilian, galloped to the front reproaching the Turks across the river for their breach of the treaty of alliance. Seeing no chances, the Turks had to make peace and withdraw their troops. In 629, Tai Zong sent an army of 100,000 strong under General Li Jing against the Turks. The following year, the Tang army crushed the Turks with 150,000 captives, including their Khan Jieli, which put an end to the Eastern Turks. After that, chiefs of surrounding countries respected Tai Zong as the Khan of Heaven. Good at running the state, Tai Zong carried out various policies to reduce corvée and taxes, which promoted agricultural production. He once said, "The first thing for a wise emperor is to bring his people a better living. An emperor demanding too much from his people is like a man eating his own flesh. When the flesh is all gone, the man dies."

At the beginning of Zhen Guan period, the Guanzhong area suffered a severe famine for three years. Tai Zong then edicted to open the state granaries to feed the hungry. As a result, every household had surplus in grain when the calamity passed. Moreover, the emperor ordered that gold, silver and silk from the imperial treasury be used as ransom for those who had been sold into slavery.

Tai Zong always attached great importance to the selection of able people. Once he found a statement submitted by an official well-written. When learning that the writer Ma Zhou was without any official position, he at once offered a post to him, who eventually got promoted to the position of prime minister. To a prime minister who always sighed for the lack of capable persons, he once said, "Just like using utensils, the key to selecting able people is to bring their strong points into full play. Did ancient rulers have to borrow talents from other times to administrate their country? It is merely because you are unable to find people's advantages."

Tai Zong highly appreciated a remark by Wei Zheng, an important official of his: "Objectivity results from taking opinions of all sides while bias results from taking opinions of one side." Whenever having a discussion with the prime minister, he would ask an adviser to be present. To those who dared to point out the misconduct of the emperor, he would grant special reward or promotion. Once he told senior court officials, "It won't do that you follow my decree without any different opinions. From now on, you should remind me of the improper points in my edict, instead of keeping silent to them."

Tai Zong did devote himself to the administration of the state in the early years of his reign. Yet he began to be indulgent in luxury in his later years, and more and more luxurious construction projects were undertaken. Sometimes he even turned a deaf ear to remonstrations. Actually, he himself was somewhat aware of that. He told the crown prince Li Zhi the very year before his death that though his contributions had exceeded his errors throughout his life, what he had done was "too far from being perfect".

To gain immortality, Tai Zong took some so-called elixir which caused his own death in 649 at the age of 50.

Emperor Tai Zong of the Tang Dynasty, Li Shimin

Empress Wu Zetian

武周皇帝·武則天

Empress Wu Zetian (624–705), with Zhao as her personal name, was from Wenshui County of Bingzhou Prefecture (today's eastern part of Wenshui County, Shanxi Province) and was the only woman sovereign in Chinese history.

Wu Zetian was born in an official-landlord family. At the age of 14, she became a "Cai Ren (rank of concubine of an inferior position) of Emperor Tai Zong of Tang (Li Shimin) and was granted the name Wu Mei (charming) by the emperor. When Emperor Tai Zong died, she was sent away from the palace to Ganye Temple, a convent in Chang'an, and became a Buddhist nun. She was summoned back to the palace and bestowed the title Zhao Yi (a senior title among imperial concubines) when the 22-year-old Li Zhi (Gao Zong of Tang) became emperor. In 655, Gao Zong made her his empress.

In 683, the crown prince Li Xian (Zhong Zong) succeeded to the throne after the death of Emperor Gao Zong. But he was deposed the following year by his mother who made Li Dan, another son of hers, emperor (Rui Zong). Later, the empress put Li Dan under house arrest and got everything under her own direct control.

In 690, the 67-year-old Wu Zetian deposed the puppet emperor, assuming the imperial title of Sage and Divine Empress herself, and changing her name to Zhao—one of the 19 odd characters coined by herself, meaning the sun and the moon shining in the sky.

Wu Zetian made vigorous efforts to achieve prosperity for the country. She had able men collected from all quarters, regardless of their family background and qualifications. Those who passed the imperial examination were assigned official posts. One day, she read a proclamation denouncing herself written in a vigorous style with tremendous force. Learning it was written by Luo Binwang, one of "The Four Talents Of the Early Tang Dynasty", she commented with a sigh, "How can such a genius become a rebel? It must be the fault of the prime minister."

Wu Zetian set great store by agriculture. And she promoted the local officials who had succeeded in bringing wasteland under cultivation and making the peasant households surplus in grain. Otherwise, they would be punished. Besides, she organized scholars to compile a book on agriculture to be issued to the whole country.

In 705, Wu Zetian was seriously ill. The prime minister Zhang Jianzhi staged a palace coup in which Li Dan was restored to the throne under the original dynasty name Tang. The 82-year-old Wu Zetian was forced to abdicate with the title "Saintly Empress Zetian". She died of illness in Shangyang Palace soon after with the posthumous title Empress Zetian.

ASIAPAC COLLECTORS' SERIES

Antique Ceramics

Durable and beautiful, antique ceramics have a timeless appeal. As good pieces become harder to find, being able to differentiate the genuine from the fakes becomes crucial to the collectors.

Written by well-known art critic Lee Ying Ho, the book gives an understanding of the origins and types of porcelain. Readers will also be advised on how to identify porcelain by motifs, marks and other characteristics to enjoy its beauty as well as make a wise investment.

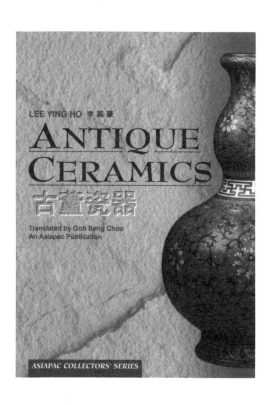

Jadeite

The overwhelming fascination with the gemstone has led to the creation of many beautiful pieces of jadeite jewellery which, with the passage of time, have enjoyed an increase in value and been eagerly traded at auctions.

In this volume, Lee Ying Ho shares with readers the origin, appreciation and worth of jadeite, together with the maintenance of jadeite jewellery, the identification of fakes rampant on the market, and the methods of their production.

《「一百」藝美系列》

中國百帝圖

編文：吳綠星
繪畫：盧延光
翻譯：王學文，王燕希

亞太圖書有限公司出版

THE
COMPETE BOOK
OF
FABRIC PAINTING

REVISED AND EXPANDED

BY LINDA S. KANZINGER

THE ALCOTT PRESS
1993

PORTLAND, OR.

As well, please share with me your experiences of fabric painting. Let me know how the ideas and techniques in this book work for you. Send letters to: The Alcott Press, address as above.

Library of Congress Cataloging in Publication Data
Kanzinger, Linda S. 1951-
  The complete book of fabric painting.
  Bibliography: p.
  Includes indexes.
    1. Textile painting. I. Title
TT851.K36   1986   746.6   85-73432
ISBN: 0-9616180-1-9

Printed in the United States of America

First printing 1986
Second printing 1989
Third printing (revised and expanded) 1993

Permission is gratefully acknowledged for reprinting of the following quotes:
*p.xi, from **THE WELL-BODY BOOK**- Mike Samuels, MD and Hal Bennett. Random House, Copyright 1973.*
*p.xiii, from **THE POEMS OF W.B.YEATS**- edited by Richard J. Finneran, Macmillan Publishing Company, copyright 1983.*
*p.15, from **THE SNOW GOOSE**- Paul Gallico, Alfred A. Knopf, Inc. Copyright 1941.*
*p. 3 , from **KANDINSKY:COMPLETE WRITINGS ON ART**- edited by Kenneth C. Lindsay and Peter Vergo, G.K. Hall and Company, copyright 1982.*
Copyright © is held by each individual artist for work portrayed

Cover illustrations: (left) Lisa Hensley Rector models cotton huiptl painted and drawn with Pelican drawing ink, acrylic paint, Design markers, embroidery paints.(right) "Heart Strings Vest", back view, by Sara Drower. Cotton polyester and textile paint, quilted, with soft-sculpture hearts.

ACKNOWLEDGEMENTS

I want to thank my artist, Phyllis Thompson, for providing so many excellent quality drawings for this book.

Thanks to all the artists who corresponded with me,sending slides and photos of their work.

I appreciate the help of Sue Thompson, Seattle, Washington; Dave Barbara, Cincinnati,Ohio; Jack Straton, Eugene,Oregon; Sarah Chandler, Bellevue, Washington; and Ellen Ross, of Lexington, Kentucky; in photographing a number of items for this book.

Thanks to the people who helped model painted clothing: Beth Brown, Ted Cotrotsos, Ellen Essig Ross, Jennifer Hensley Heller, Lisa Hensley Rector, Douglas Hensley, Judy Hankin, Karen Leeds, Leslie Allen,Carol Petrelli, Patricia Tubb, Laura Dale, Arden Dale, Hope Fox, and Ava Lake.

Every attempt has been made to locate sources for all copyrighted material. If any acknowledgement has been inadvertently omitted, or received after publication of this book, please contact the publisher in order to receive full credit in subsequent printings.

DEDICATION

Most of all, this one goes to Portland, OR. for being such a wonderful place to live,

with open minded friendly and creative people who like to wear wonderful handpainted and dyed clothing,

who understand what I am talking about when I tell them I am a self-publisher and writer,

and finally who, when I tell them I wrote a book on fabric painting, don't immediately ask, "But won't it wash out?"

Also:

To T.T.S. Thanks for keeping me company while I write. My life would be less without all of you.

Thanks to Ted Cotrotsos for his technical support and friendship. Thanks also to Ralph Penunuri for help with computer conundrums.
To Dr. Robert M. Hensley: wihose support helped me get started.
To my mother: Who bought some textile paints many years ago and encouraged me to make things .

And to all small press people everywhere.

Research, Writing, Typing, Editing, Typesetting, Book Production, Proofing, Indexing, Publishing, Advertising, Marketing, Distributing, and Product testing by the Author. This book was revised using a Macintosh LC computer, Microsoft Word 4.0, Pagemaker 4.0, a LightningScan 256 scanner, and Olduvai Optical Character Recognition software.

Note: All painted items or drawings without credit are done by author

TABLE OF CONTENTS

CHAPTER VII

NOTES TO TEXT

Always prewash and preshrink all fabric before painting.

In the interest of avoiding sexism, whether implicit or implied, the pronouns "she" and "he" are used interchangeably.

Anyone wishing to paint immediately can skip to Chapter III, "Simple and Beginning Ideas".

PERSONAL NOTE:

It is personally interesting to me to look back and see how relevant my alternate title for this book is today. **Fabric Painting: a Bridge between Two Worlds,** was one origianl title and it referred to fabric painting as the link between the workds of art and the world of textiles. For, as I study fabric painting today, it is indeed a bridge between these two worlds. A painter decides to paint on unprimed canvas, and goes to the fabric store for some fabric paint and duck canvas. A home sewer sees dimensional paints sold at this same store, and decides to try his hand on some simple decorative ideas. A quilt–maker decides to take a class in drawing , or painting, in order to add painterly aspects to her work, and to include some handpainted or dyed fabrics in her quilts. This is common knowledge now. At the time that I began to research fabric painting, it was not. It was, however, my overriding concept for what could happen with fabric painting, and so it is very gratifying to see the success of fiber art and wearable art today.

HOW THIS BOOK CAME TO BE WRITTEN

This book was written over a number of years. It was first conceived in 1974, during the renewed interest in crafts. I noticed that there were no books on fabric painting, although batik and tie–dye were at the height of fashion. I began to paint, learning not through books or teachers so much as by the slow process of experimentation. Each paint material was tested on a number of fabrics; various ideas were tried out on clothing. The research on fabric painting opened the door for me to the whole art world, and I spent much time in art libraries looking at paintings, thinking about what type of paintings would translate into painted cloth.

In 1977, I began the actual writing of the book and completed it 1 and 1/2 years later. I made the rounds of large publisher, and received a contract from a large publisher who eventually reneged once the entire book was completed! I then decided to do the job myself by becoming a self–publisher. I took classes on layout and paste–up and attended workshops on self–publishing. As well, I read as much as possible on these subjects.

There came a year when the book went into storage, along with all my other possessions, while I searched for a job. When I got resettled, out came the partially pasted–up book. I rewrote parts which had become dated, added the many paint materials now available, and finished the book. This first 1986 edition sold steadily for 5 years, both in the U.S. and abroad.

When the book next sold out, I decided to do a revised and expanded edition. I researched the many new paint products and new processes in 1991-1992. Book production began in November of 1992 and was completed in May of 1993. This edition was typeset on a Macintosh LC computer, using OCR scanning software to scan the original manuscript into the computer. Microsoft Word 4.0 was used to edit and typeset the manuscript. Pagemaker 4.0 created a new page layout.

This is truly a handmade book, from idea to printed page. I've enjoyed every stage of production and learned many new skills. I hope you also enjoying reading and using this book!

■■■

"Clothes can be a way to get yourself into a very high and joyful place. Get in touch with yourself in the most joyful state you can imagine. And then visualize the kind of clothes you'd be wearing at that moment. Remember how the clothes look and feel, and then get yourself real clothes to wear that look and feel like that. You might find it fun to take castaside clothes and cut, dye, and embroider designs on them until they express the feelings you would like them to express."

THE WELL-BODY BOOK
Mike Samuels, MD and Hal Bennett

Had I the Heavens' embroidered cloths,
Enwrought with golden and silver light,
The blue and the dim and the dark cloths
Of night and light and the half-light,
I would spread the cloths under your feet:
But I, being poor, have only my dreams;
I have spread my dreams under your feet;
Tread softly, because you tread on my dreams.

"He wishes for the Cloths of Heaven"
William Butler Yeats

"There is no rest for the messenger until the message is delivered."
Joseph Conrad

1 AN INTRODUCTION TO FABRIC PAINTING

Nothing to do but work,
nothing to eat but food,
nothing to wear but clothes
to keep one from going nude.
"The Pessimist"-Benjamin Franklin King

● ●

When it comes to clothes, some people echo the pessimist. They happily put on their gray business suit every day, or don blue jeans and work shirt, and go off without further thought as to what they are wearing. For other people, however, every day is a show, a chance to be somebody different, to change personality, to express a different mood. Clothes, with their expressive modes of color, texture, form, and movement, amplify these changes.

Fabric painting leans a little more towards the ostentatious than the drab, but it is a matter of choice for the individual painter. For are not the somber hues of Rembrandt far different from Gauguin's bright colors? Yet both are painters and in their difference equal in stature. The range and scope of fabric painting are as wide as that of canvas painting, yet different painting techniques are sometimes used due to the greater permeability of fabric over canvas.

Fabric painting is simply painting on fabric. How and why and what are its implications are far from simple. Fabric painting will be discussed primarily for clothing, both manu-factured and handmade. Examples of other types of fabric painting —such as for wall hangings, quilts and soft sculptures— will be given; but I feel that it is clothing which is the greater challenge in fabric painting.

● ●

GENERAL STATEMENTS ON CLOTHING

Anni Albers speaks of clothing as a habitat which grew out of humans' need for shelter. Clothing is a type of portable environment. We quite literally picked up our tent and put it on. (Witness the simple forms of early garments such as the poncho, the huiptl, the toga.) Clothing is also our closest environment. We carry it on our bodies, we feel it next to our skin. As our bodies identify us, so do our clothes. In our social environment, clothes can be our camouflage or our communication. (Witness the difference in the gray business suit and the blue jeans and T–shirt.)

Clothing is also an industry. Every process of garment making has become mass marketable, beginning with the garment patterns, through the weaving of the cloth, to the dyeing and printing of cloth, and finally to the sewing of the garment. To balance this industrial process, many people design their own patterns, weave their own cloth, print and dye fabric, or sew their own clothes. Fabric painting is but another category of hand expression, yet it is usually overlooked in favor of fabric printing. I suspect one reason for the oversight is the general misconception of what fabric painting is. It is not, although it looks deceptively like, fabric printing, and until it is compared and pulled away from fabric printing, there can be no clear sense of direction as to its development. When people view it as a rudimentary form of fabric printing, fabric printing is seen to be much more efficient as a design technique for lengths of fabric. The approach to painting, however, is quite different from printing, and will be discussed at length.

Fabric painting was relatively little known in the world of crafts until the mid–1970's. Most every art form has received stimulation from our technological society with its rapid communication systems, allowing arts and crafts to be influenced with rich sources of information from variant cultures over the world. It was an oversight and certainly a loss for fabric painting to have received no more than scant attention. Fabric painting books were visible in the 1950's and faded again in the 1960's. A lack of materials plus a lack of understanding of the basic forms underlying the synthesis of clothing design and painting led fabric painting to a dead stop. For those who love painting, this was unfortunate, for past records even show that fabric painting was not as important a method as fabric printing. Until the 1980's, when fabric painting became mainstream and quite popular, many people interested in crafts were not aware of its existence. When told that a piece of clothing has been painted, the question invariably arises, "But won't it wash out?"

And, until the 1970's and 1980's, there were few paints available for fabric painting. With the discovery of fiber–reactive (Procion) dye in England in 1958 and the continuous improvement of acrylic paints and fabric paints since they were first marketed, the technical problems of fabric painting have greatly diminished. In fact, the pendulum has swung the other way, with a plethora of paint materials available. Materials which are available include permanent markers, fabric crayons, embroidery paints, inks, mordants, natural dyes and paints, oil paint with textine, and a multitude of types and brands of fabric paint, which will be discussed in "New Paint Products" in Chapter IV.

DESIGN IDEAS

Simple design ideas can be used, and can be extended in meaning from simplicity to compositional and psychological complexity. Geometric designs have the advantage of being easily drawn. They also have many moods, ranging from the subdued effect and earthern colors of American Indian designs, to the black and white op/pop art style and its variant, psychedelic art. Painted patchwork squares allow one to experiment with different color combinations without the extra complexity of form. Sculpture, calligraphy and drawing, watercolor, abstract and realistic designs, Impressionism, Expressionism, Fauvism, and Surrealism are all sources of design from art history. (Fig.1, Fig. 2)

Through time, art history has shown a loosening of the definition of painting. Classical painting demanded adherence to strict rules of canvas, oil, and brush. Technique no longer need limit new ideas; technique is created to express them. The disciplines of painting and printmaking even overlap so that there is no longer any sense of "pure" painting. This allows many techniques to be combined and new ones invented. If a design idea cannot be expressed through traditional painting, one breaks out and discovers new methods, thankfully so! As Sandra Longmore, a fiber artist from Washougal, WA. succinctly states: "My original training in art was in oils, drawing and painting. I used to feel that I was not an artist if I did not paint on canvas." The combination of canvas painting techniques and ideas, along with clothing and needlework, creates a new method. One can translate ideas from a two–dimensional surface (the painted canvas) and from a static form (a picture hung on a wall), to a three–dimensional form (the body), and to one of movement within the environment (a person wearing clothing.) (Fig.3,Fig.4)

LIMITATIONS OF PRESENT DAY CLOTHING

The combination of painting techniques and ideas with clothing and fabrics is rather exciting in that there are so many possible combinations: patchwork skirts with small paintings on each square; Mexican blouses with painted embroidery alongside thread embroidery, showing differences in texture;

FIG.1:JENNIFER HENSLEY IN MUSLIN SKIRT PAINTED WITH TEXTILE PAINTS AND NATURAL PAINTS.

FIG.2:DYE- PAINTED FLOWER ON VELVETEEN. PORTION OF HANDPAINTED SCREEN BY LENORE DAVIS.

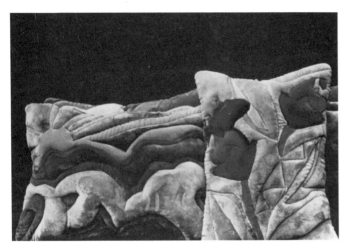

FIG 3: *"TREE FORMS"*–LUGENE BRUNO.
WHITE VELVET PILLOWS PAINTED WITH
PROCION DYE.

FIG. 4: TOP BY PHYLLIS MUFSON. CHINA SILK
WITH DIRECT APPLICATION OF DYE

skirts which remind one of the paintings of Kandinsky or
Modrian or ancient Mayan architecture. If these combinations
seem too ambitious, recall Paul Klee, who was trying to pull
together painting, architecture, music, and poetry, within his
own painting.

To use classical painting as a source for design in fabric
decoration is to approach a fabric surface with a fluidity which
is not to be found with printed fabric. Fabric painting records
the mark of the brush. Painted, as opposed to printed, fabric is
farther from decoration and closer to art when it is a surface that
can only be handpainted. And a fabric surface which can only
be handpainted has as its idea a design which is equally as fluid
as the motion of the brush. This greatly extends the present
limitations of clothing design.

When handmade clothing is limited to the kind of material
which one finds in a store, and what kind of design is printed
on the material, it is nice to have something unique to wear.
And when there are so many of us on this planet, when even a
name does not insure identity, handpainted clothing can be an
expression of one particular person at one particular time.
Sometimes in the daily routine, the days slip by unnoticed
though there are one hundred things worth notice and remem–
brance. With painting, one can record the small occurrences of
a day in design and color, and repeat the mood of that day
whenever wearing the clothing. Since the body is an environ–
ment for design, design a landscape, or figures with backgrounds moving out into their environments, on an arm or leg.

The purpose of this book is to make others aware of the
possibilities inherent in the combination of the world of art and
the world of needlework and clothing. I have tried to express a
variety of moods, sources, interests, and levels of ability. More
a needleworker than a painter, I hope to attract the interest of
painters who can transfer their ideas from canvas to cloth. Just
as the expression of form is inherent in stone, to later be
sculpture, so fabric contains color and form and movement.
Free the painted cloth!

A DEFINITION OF FABRIC PAINTING

Fabric painting may seem to be but a primitive form of fabric
printing. It is, and it is not. Designs created by other fabric
decoration methods can sometimes be painted, but in order to
utilize the unique techniques of painting, it is necessary to
know what type of designs can only be handpainted. It is also
necessary to know what types of designs would be laborious or
repetitious if hand–painted.

A more extensive definition of fabric painting will pull it
away from confusion with other fabric decoration methods.
Fabric painting as fabric decoration emphasizes painting over
other fabric decorative methods, as it is painting rather than
decoration. Yet it differs from two–dimensional canvas painting in that it is painting on fabric, a flexible material which is
both two and three dimensional. Fabric painting combines the
techniques of canvas painting with the function of fabric
decoration methods. To see what this combination forms, it is
best first to look separately at painting and at fabric decoration.

In a painting, many ideas are pulled together and expressed
visually with color, texture, line and spatial composition. Much
of painting is composed mentally before the actual painting is
done, for the idea is directly expressed via the brush, without
the limitations of intermediary devices or tools. The size of a
silkscreen, or the number of blocks needed for a block print,
can limit a design idea. The directness of painting allows the
painter full control and responsibility for the size of the image,

FIG. 5:*"GALAXY"–BY FERNE SIROIS. ACRYLIC STAINING ON RAW CANVAS, OVERPAINTED WITH JAPANESE INK BRUSHES.*

placement of images, and placement of color. The directness of painting also involves making a large number of decisions, because of the wide range of choices to be made. A large painting can be quite complex compositionally as well as taking a long time to complete, whereas with fabric decoration methods, large spaces can be covered in a short time with a repeat motif.

It is not the intention of painting to merely fill up space as quickly as possible. Painting expresses in a visual way what is true for an artist, and in this sense, every painting is unique, rather than a duplication of a former idea. With fabric decoration methods, one design idea can be repeated through space, giving an impression of stasis. As a contrast, painting, due to its vibrancy of color and variance in shape, can come alive and create just the opposite impression from stasis. The concept of painting changes the traditional approach to fabric decoration, with its emphasis on covering a large amount of space with a repeated design and therefore leads to a new method, fabric painting.

FABRIC DECORATION METHODS

Fabric decoration methods include fabric printing, fabric painting, batik, tie–dye, and silkscreen. Most methods approach the large amount of space in a length of fabric by breaking up the space into smaller amounts. The design idea is formed for a smaller space and merely repeated throughout the space of the fabric. Although there are advantages to the idea of the repeat design, the large amounts of space with fabric lengths are not utilized, as they could be in painting.

With the exception of fabric painting, all fabric decoration methods use some intermediary substance to control capillary action. Capillary action is the tendency for paint or dye to spread from fiber to fiber unless blocked by some substance.

Wax, tape, paper, starch resists, wood, and string are some common substances used.(Fig. 7, 11,&12) In fabric painting, capillary action is either used to advantage in the design, or controlled by brush techniques and a thick consistency of paint.

Fabric printing involves transference of a previously formed design via woodblock, linoleum block, silkscreen, to the fabric. In **fabric painting,** however, the design is directly painted onto the fabric. **Batik** is closer in idea to fabric painting in that the design is directly formed on the material rather than being transferred.(Fig.9,10) However, the design is formed in reverse with wax, as the dyebaths form the actual design. Fabric is tied to block out the patterns of the design in tie–dye, a method which also utilizes the three–dimensional aspects of fabric. **Silkscreen** is a method of fabric printing which uses a fabric screen and tusche, a blocking out substance which transfers the design onto the fabric. (Fig.13) In all these fabric decoration methods, with the exception of fabric painting, the design is formed before the interaction of paint and fabric.

Fabric painting omits these intermediary steps and paints the design directly on the fabric. (Fig.5, Fig.6, Fig.8 & Fig.14)

Fabric painting has many effects, techniques, and methods which cannot be created by any other method of fabric decoration. The spontaneity of painting allows for the blending of colors on the fabric, emphasizing the pure color, form, and texture rather than the transference of a preplanned design. The interrelationship between these colors, forms, and textures can intermingle throughout the length of fabric, changing and growing with the flow of the paint brushed, dipped, pushed, and spattered onto the material. (Fig.15) In this way, fabric painting transcends painting a design, and becomes painting, an action.

As Sandra Longmore, a fiber artist from Washougal, WA,

FIG. 6: WRAPAROUND SKIRT BY SUZANNE LARSEN. OFFWHITE INDIA COTTON W/ ACRYLIC PAINTED SUNFACE. OUTLINED WITH INKODYE.

FIG. 7: WALL HANGING BY SHANNA SANTOMIENI. TIE–DYE AND DIRECT PAINTING WITH OILS AND ENAMELS

states, " I paint and create in some way every day. My greatest days are when I feel a sense of accomplished personal rhythm. Every part of my process is a pleasure for me from beginning to end. Almost all artists love the flash or gentle filtering of inspiration for creating as I do."

ADVANTAGES OF FABRIC PAINTING

Painting directly has many advantages. For example, no part of the fabric need be exactly alike, yet all areas can be tied together with a certain theme. (Fig.16) A length of fabric can be painted with flowers, no two alike. A variety of shapes can easily be drawn, whereas in other methods it would be necessary to make different block prints or different screens for various shapes. Also by painting directly, each color can be easily applied. Much preplanning must be done with other methods of fabric decoration; in batik, one must carefully preplan the sequential dyebaths in order to have the correct blending of colors; in silkscreen, separate areas of color must be mapped out. Color applications can also be built up with glazes of underpainting, which is quite different from the flat color of a block–print. With painting, designs and motifs are easily enlarged or reduced; color application is direct.

The use of space is totally open in fabric painting. (Fig.17) This is both exciting and difficult. The large amounts of space in lengths of fabric require that you be somewhat comfortable with composition. It may be helpful at first to limit space the way a silkscreen does (Fig.18) with arbitrary size. Fabric painting involves the use of space both two and three dimensionally. The composition of a canvas painting of various colored abstract shapes must be much tighter than a similar fabric painting, as the three–dimensionality of fabric can change the original composition through draping, gathering, and pleating. A painting which is not extremely well composed when looked at flat could be very interesting when viewed from the various angles at which one can view clothing. There is simply a much greater leeway in the usage of space due to the flexibility of cloth being both two and three–dimensional. At the same time, it is true that composition is more difficult when considering not only the flat plane of a painting, but what happens to the designs when they are molded by the shape and movement of the body. The combination of the free or open use of space in painting, and the restrictions or limitations of space due to the garment form, and some of the problems therein, leads to the necessity for an understanding of holistic design.

HOLISTIC DESIGN

Holistic design refers to wholeness much in the same way as the word gestalt refers to many parts fitting together in a meaningful way. Holistic design in fabric painting refers to the design idea interrelating in a meaningful way, both with the technical processes of fabric painting, and with the design and form of the garment or fabric. Too often, both of these ideas are avoided or ignored, and the resulting painting looks as if it had been laid on, rather than being a part of, the fabric. The design idea must be suitable to the technique of painting, otherwise it would be better to use another fabric decoration method. A repeating shape in the **same** color would best be block–printed while one with **shadings** of color would work efficiently with stenciling.

FIG.8: BETH BROWN MODELS CANVAS BACKPACK PAINTED IN ACRYLICS WITH AFRICAN DESIGNS

FIG.9: "FLORAL GARDEN" BY CAROL RACKLIN. BATIK.

If the design and form of the garment is not considered as well when forming a design idea, the shift of the design from two to three dimensions will be ignored, and therefore what the design really will look like will not even be considered. In some cases, there is not that much difference in a design in its two and three–dimensional state. (Fig. 19) An evenly spaced design, for example, will be less vulnerable to the change in position from two to three dimensions than a design with a delicately balanced composition, since a painting spread out flat will appear radically different from the same in three dimensions.

In order to plan for these two dimensions, one must understand the basics of design and composition for two–dimensional painting, the basics of design and composition in garments, and the successful combination of the two. These are the many parts of holistic design which must be fitted together in a harmonious and meaningful way.

FIG.11: **"STAINED GLASS"**–CAROL RACKLIN.
WAX RESIST WITH DIRECT DYE PAINTING

FIG.10: BATIK WITH DIRECT PAINTING–
SHANNA SANTOMIENI

FIG.12: (BELOW) TIE–DYE WITH DIRECT
PAINTING–JOETTA UMLA.

FIG.13 : "ALHAMBRA WALL" – FRANCES BUTLER. SILKSCREEN.

FIG. 14: BETH BROWN MODELS DIRECT PAINTED T–SHIRT. ACRYLIC AND PROCION DYE.
DESIGN INSPIRED BY KANDINSKY PAINTING.

FIG.15: TED COTROTSOS MODELING
SPATTER–PAINTED T–SHIRT

FIG. 16: HOPE FOX MODELING PAINTED
CAFTAN. EARLY AMERICAN FLORAL DESIGN.

FABRIC PAINTING AS ART AND CRAFT

Fabric painting entails many subdivisions. Do you want to paint on fabrics and hang them—use them in their total space without making them into clothing? Are you interested in costume? clothing? making fabric lengths and letting others use them in clothing? Are you interested in selling what you make? All these need different approaches.

These many subdivisions can be separated into fabric painting as an art, and fabric painting as a craft. As an art, fabric painting emphasizes the uniqueness, rather than the repetition of an image. The painting is a visual idea to be realized, and the process or technique involved is subservient to the idea. A craft, however, stresses technique, and the desired image is shaped through the discipline of the technical process. A roughly formed carved wooden bowl, as an object, reveals the process of its making, records the passage of knife over wood, time over time. As **objects** they are marked: there is the imprint of the potter's hand upon the clay. As a craft, fabric painting concen–trates on repeating a basic form yet amplifying it through individual expression. The potter who specializes in goblets expresses various design ideas through one basic form. By

FIG.19: (RIGHT) PAINTED DOLL BY K. LEE MANUEL

FIG. 17: INSTALLATION AT SEATTLE ART MUSEUM—
PHYLLIS RICHARDSON. (LEFT) DENIM.BLEACHED,
WOVEN. (RIGHT) CANVAS, ACRYLIC.

making fabric yardage, there are ways to paint the material so that it is identifiable as one piece of cloth, yet go beyond the repeat design. The amount of space in a wall hanging makes it ideal for art fabric painting, as one can develop the composition on a two–dimensional space without having to also deal with the three–dimensional. More complex composition similar to canvas painting can be explored. Clothing utilizes fabric painting both as an art and as a craft, ranging from clothing which may take several months to design and paint to a simple border of flowers on a blouse.

Thus far, fabric painting has been discussed primarily as it differs **technically** from other fabric decoration methods or from canvas painting. It is important as well to understand fabric painting as an idea, for the idea of what something is contributes to how it is used. The most important thing that I would stress is that fabric painting is **expression** rather than **decoration.** The design is integrated with the form, rather than being "put on" the form and unrelated to it.

Sandra Longmore, mentioned above, describes very well the expressive qualities of fabric painting. "It's an inner, very deep sensation that can only be satisfied by the process of some kind of mark making, creating. The excitement or best part of doing this is the actual harmony of the work. The day by day companionship of the work. Such a good friend, lover, teacher and wise adviser is the work. It's like when I'm really focused a loop is created between me and the Creator. We communicate through the image making."

She also states the satisfaction of being an artist: "recently the work has taken a new turn, which is another exciting thing about being an artist, there is always another turn in the road, this keeps me curious, alive, and eternally young."

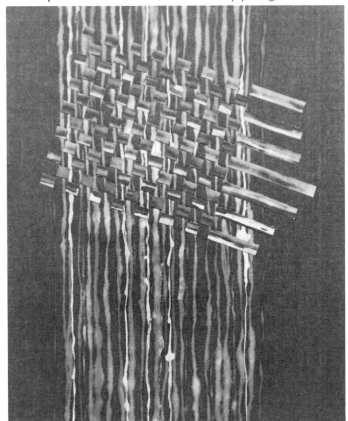

FIG. 18: CLOSE–UP OF ABOVE LEFT. COLOR IS
"SUBTRACTED" BY USING VARIOUS BLEACHES.

approaching fabric painting as a craft, a large number of similarly styled items can be produced—yet retain their individuality. (Fig. 20)

Fabric painting as an art is different in that there is no repetition of a basic form. Five skirts painted in this way are five different works of art, five "moveable paintings". This is important to remember as most clothing is printed and capable for reproduction. Fabric paintings cannot be reproduced. The time necessary for an intricately painted and designed piece of clothing may be many times over that of even a handprinted garment, but then, it is a unique piece of clothing. (Fig. 21; Fig. 22) A painting is not just a representation of some object in reality; but an expression of a feeling, an idea, or a visual representation of an idea.

When is fabric painting best approached as a craft rather than an art? For selling, the repetition of a basic form makes it easier to painting quantity and fill orders on time. If there are variations of a design idea they can be spread out over many different garments, yet retain an identifiable connection. When

To decorate something implies relieving the monotony of a background with ornament or embellishment. Rather than being interrelated, the design and the background are seen as separate entities. Some T–shirts look as if the design were pasted on the shirt in the way one might stick a piece of tape on paper. To express something, on the other hand, is to directly state in a clear manner what one thinks or feels. Expression is a form through which thought, feeling, or the quality of something is manifest. When the fluidity and spontaneity of painting is combined with the form of the garment, the visual idea can be manifest through painting.

Fabric painting as expression rather than decoration echoes holistic design. There is no separation between design and background. There is the interrelationship of paint, cloth, and brush, with the garment form. North American Indian fabric painters were familiar with this idea. In 1880, due to contact with white culture, Indians in the Great Plains began depicting phases of their ceremonial life on muslin and canvas. Many of the Plains Indians' clothing were designed so that when worn, the decorative aspects could be visually appreciated.

DESIGN INTEGRATED WITH FORM

It is very important in painted clothing that design be integral to form. There has to be some meaning to a design idea being expressed through clothing, which relates not only with the body but also with the surrounding environment, and the reactions of other people in that environment. Sandra Longmore has described her process of making painted clothing. "Why do I work on fabric? It's a dynamic connection to the Creator. As an artist friend once said, the first thing that wraps us out of our mother's womb is fabric. And we continue to have this closeness to it...Fabric is like a shield between us and the world. The next step is the imagery on the fabric—that's where I as a fabric artist come in. I get to draw this dynamic imagery. It feeds me...it feeds others, and they buy it and then I get to start all over again." The idea of painted clothing is not to have a design "painted on" a piece of clothing. The idea is to interrelate the paint, cloth, and brush with color, texture, the body, the movement of the body in the environment, and the movement of clothing through the action of the body, as well as the composition of colors, patterns, and textures through various positions of clothing when being worn. (Fig.23, Fig.24) It is reminiscent of the Cubists, who took a variety of subject matter—things such as bottles, winding staircases, paintings or photographs—and unified them into a harmonious whole.

Painted clothing, then, is different from clothing made from woven cloth without a pattern, and even from printed clothing. There needs to be an exploration of what designs on clothing mean, regardless of their technical application. The images created interact, and interact differently, with the environment of the body, the physical environment, and the social environment. Perhaps because of the lack of thought concerning this, there have been, until the late 1970's, very few painted clothes, in comparison to printed clothing. Before then, batik and tie-dye were used in clothing far more frequently than was fabric painting. Susan Springer, an artist from San Francisco, feels that fabric painting "is all very interesting...especially because it is such a unique field to be part of as awareness blossoms." She handpaints silk scarves, as well as creating unique, one–of–a–kind hand–painted garments such as quiana blouses with large floral designs.

Another reason for the scarcity of **painted** clothes stems from the diversity of fabric painting. There are so many different painting techniques—all aimed at so many different levels of skill—that it creates confusion for the beginning fabric painter. And, since fabric painting encompasses the entire spectrum between simplicity and complexity, it becomes necessary to find design ideas inbetween painting the repeat motif, and working in large spaces with highly abstract problems.

FIG 20: (LEFT) QUILTED AND NON–QUILTED SHELL PILLOWS. DIRECT DYE, INKO DYE FOR LINES, ACRYLIC PAINT. (L TO R) COTTON VELVET SUEDE, ANTIQUE SATIN QUILTED SCALLOP IN BACKGROUND. OTHERS, COTTON MUSLIN. ALL BY SUZANNE LARSEN.

*FIG 21: DRAWING– BY PHYLLIS THOMPSON. AFTER MIAO/CHINESE WOMAN'S COSTUME IN **COSTUMES OF THE EAST,** BY W.A.FAIRSERVIS, JR. 1971*

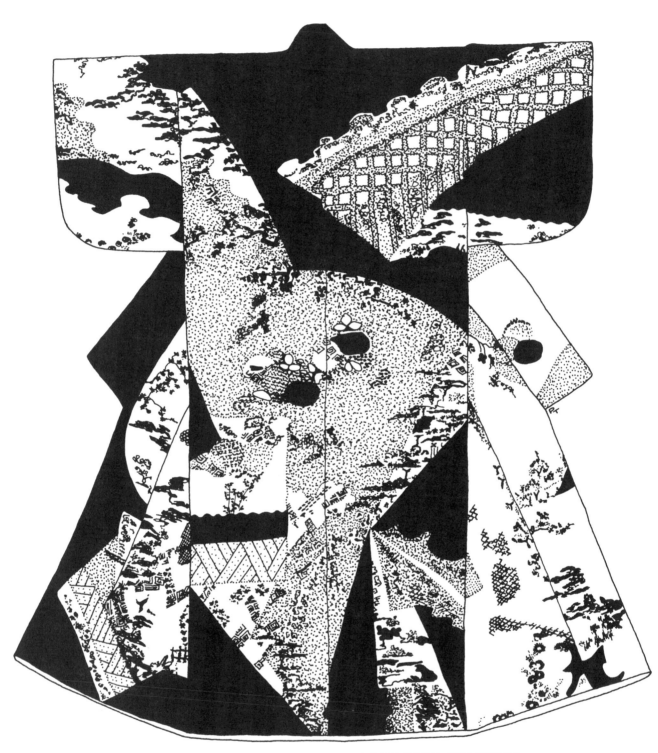

*FIG. 22: DRAWING–BY PHYLLIS THOMPSON. KOSODE IN SATIN (16TH CENTURY JAPANESE-MOMOYAMA) FROM **JAPANESE COSTUME** BY NOMA*

FIG. 23: ELLEN ROSS MODELING PAINTED SKIRT WITH AFRICAN MOTIFS

FABRIC PAINTING AS TECHNIQUE

There are some techniques which are very efficient to fabric painting, and especially fabric painting aimed towards painted clothing. Watercolor, Expressionism, collage, painted squares, and drawing are all suited to fill a variety of needs for the beginning fabric painter. Techniques which can be learned easily are preferred in the beginning as there is, at the same time, much to learn about the interaction of painting materials and clothing composition.

Watercolor is technically simple, and watercolor bands or stripes either on fabric lengths or on clothing, are also compositionally simple. **Expressionism** is well suited for fabric painting as fabric painting emphasizes expression over decoration. Broad splashes of color, and freeform painting maximize the spontaneity of paint and brush. **Collage** is an exciting approach to fabric painting as it divides the space as part of the technique. Torn paper, when used in creating a design, can be utilized to draw a design that would usually be pasted. More durable materials are used for the actual pasting or gluing of collage. **Painted squares** allows one to focus on testing out a wide range of mixed colors as well as the juxtaposition of one color with another. And **drawing** can emphasize the expression or shape and form without totally ignoring color, color shadings, and textures. Drawing is also the basic framework of a large amount of painting, and by focusing on form, one can solve problems that might arise with more complex painting methods.

These techniques work best for beginning fabric painting as they isolate one approach and maximize its efficiency, rather than trying to deal with all possible factors in fabric painting. Watercolor and collage emphasize a practical use of space. Expressionism and drawing are two different ways of painting. Painted squares utilize the possibilities of color.

In all these techniques, the composition mixes unity with diversity, and it is this which is the key to successful fabric painting. Just as in music or literature, painted clothing and painted cloth must have a central theme, a unifying idea, a focal point. At the same time, there must be some diverse elements needing to be drawn together into a unifying idea. Without this interchange, there is neither unity or diversity, there is only sameness. Some examples of this combination could be: random scattering of flowers or starlike shapes with no two alike —leaves, paint splotch clusters, little geometric boxes, motifs both large and small, torn paper strips; African, Indian, Norwegian, preColumbian motifs. Arrange these along a larger gridwork or organic sense of wholeness. The essential unit of cohesiveness is the similar shape or mood of the motif. Try pottery examples, bird tracks, birds flying, pens, alphabets, etc.

Composition which mixes unity with diversity must as well have other characteristics. It must be suited to the technique or painting in terms of the types of effects possible with painting. Therefore the approach to composition must spring from sources other than unilinear repetition of shape. Composition must as well be capable of using the space unique in fabric painting; unique either because through clothing it is a shaped three–dimensional space, or because it is an unlimited amount of space. And last, composition must deal with design in movement and motion as will occur with painted clothing.

THE CLOTHING REVOLUTION

A definition of fabric painting, as can be seen, includes the **technique** of fabric painting, the idea of fabric painting, and efficient **methods** of fabric painting. Perhaps the last question to ask concerning fabric painting is "why do it?" What are its uniquenesses? Perhaps it is simply the expressiveness of painting glazes, scumbling, thick or impenetrably thin colors over yards and yards of cloth. Perhaps it is the love of painting itself.

Artists have viewed painting in a variety of ways. For William de Kooning, painting was "a way of living". He saw that the act of painting, regardless how others reacted to it, was more important than "success". For Adolph Gottlieb, it was necessary to reject established painting styles in order to find his own "voice". What is visually true for an artist is more important than how others react to it. "...Colors of light—, the reel of flight, the push of birds breasting a morning wind bending the tall flag reeds. He painted the loneliness and the smell of the salt–laden cold". The inner vision can be expressed through the media or paint, cloth, brush, body, clothing, and movement; combining and forming new painting in our populated environment.

In the United States, there is a continuous revolution in clothing. What is in style one decade becomes dated the next, and vintage the next. Whether it be punk–inspired, New Wave fashion or romantically inspired ruffled dresses with lace, the techniques of fabric painting can be used with any particular style. Fabric painting, with its multidimensional variety, is yet another dimension to the clothing revolution. I hope that the variety of techniques presented in this book will allow a greater creative expression in the realm of fabric painting, as well as a higher conscious awareness when we pass each other in the street.

*FIG.24: ELLEN ROSS IN KENTUCKY
LANDSCAPE, MODELING HANDPAINTED
SKIRT WITH AFRICAN MOTIFS*

2 *FABRIC PAINTING: A HISTORY*

ANCIENT HISTORY

Fabric is not a durable material. Unlike stone and wood, it is not a predominant artifact gathered from archaeological sites. The record of its passage through time is an irregular one. Histories of fabric are difficult to compile, as the material itself which is to be written about disintegrates after eighty or ninety years, depending upon its condition and where it is stored. The sources that prove to be the most numerous in material are the dry arid deserts and the airtight tombs. The burial tombs in Peru are one of the richest sources for preserved painted cloth, as the pre-Columbian Indians wrapped their dead in clothing and fabric. It would seem that there is as much fabric painting found in the dry Egyptian tombs, and it is known that the Egyptians also wrapped their dead in clothing and fabric, yet they were also known to cremate their dead fully clothed. The Egyptian burial sites are a rich source for decorated pottery and we can only infer that similar designs might be painted on fabric. The dating of these fabrics range from the 4th and 5th century B.C., with few examples, to a high interest from 900–100 B. C.

THE DIFFICULTY OF RESEARCH

To be accurate in describing the history of fabric painting is even more difficult than with other types of fabric decoration. However, there is still a story to tell, though it must be pieced together, like a quilt, from random bits of information gathered from many fields. Anthropology, historical writings of the lives of various peoples, records of the art of different peoples yield various bits of information. Even the history of economics and trade can give one a lead on the history of fabric painting, as various kinds of dyes and paints were traded in different parts of the world at varying times. Piecing together the fragmented history of fabric painting may seem tedious, but it is necessary. The history of something serves not only to tell of its past, it also points to its future. Stimulation occurs when one sees where something has been, and can see where it might go. The lack of a written history in fabric painting may be one reason for its slow evolution beyond the primitive. There are many other reasons for its remaining prehistoric.

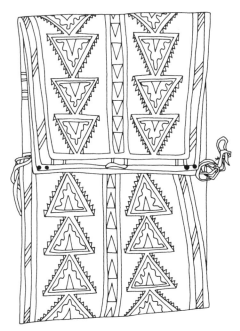

*FIG. 25: PAINTED PARFLECHE (GREAT PLAINS)AFTER **INDIAN ART IN NORTH AMERICA**, BY FREDERICK J.DOCKSTADER. DRAWING BY PHYLLIS THOMPSON.*

It is possible that fabric painting never really caught on due to the disparity in older methods and the methods that we have today at our disposal due to modern technology. The American Indians used earth pigments mixed with a glue which was boiled from the scrapings of the hide used as a canvas. The painting was executed with a sharp stick and was fairly tedious, sometimes taking several weeks. The pioneers and early settlers were busy with more practical matters of survival than decorative clothing. They were also a different kind of people, more interested in the reality of harsh winters and neighboring Indians. The Indians were more involved in mystical and spiritual matters, painting their clothes to protect them from evil influences—as well as the white man's bullets.

The Industrial Revolution, beginning in the 19th century, changed the tenure and tempo of life. Factories could put together garments much more quickly than human beings; factories and technology could also print and dye materials much more effectively than could the individual. It may be a historical leap which caused fabric painting to go from the primitive state to the industrial state, bypassing the hands of the common man and the artist.

A study of modern or industrialized textiles offers some explanation as to this leap, by showing the different types of effects produced by hand and machine printing. By understanding the principles underlying modern textile design, one can also understand the uniqueness of these ancient hand–painted textiles, fragmented and faded but surviving in the museums. (Fig.26, Fig.27)

Archaeological digs largely contribute to our knowledge of ancient textiles. Ancient textiles are valuable to the student of

FIG.26: DRAWING BY AUTHOR OF PRE-COLUMBIAN HANDPAINTED TEXTILE

FIG. 27: DRAWING BY AUTHOR OF PAINTED CLOTH, NORTHERN PERU

textiles as well as to the fabric painter, and yet there are few places where they are known to be found. Until recently, most archaeologists did not consider textiles important enough to be written up, so that which was found was ignored. A large number of accounts of fabric painting comes from pre-Columbian South American sites, many of which have only been excavated and carefully documented in the past.

PRE–COLUMBIAN FABRIC PAINTING

Pre–Columbian Peruvian textiles represent the highest achievement of textile production of the ancient world. Not only was there fabric painting, there were fine examples of weaving, knotting, and knitting. Painted cloth and clothing were used in everyday wear, for the dead, and for spiritual ceremonies. (Fig.34). Many of the patterns of painted clothing were repeated in weavings, and as well it is possible that patterns used for pottery were also used in textiles. Due to a lack of written history, it is difficult to say to what extent fabric painting was used in pre–Columbian societies. With the American Indian culture, the importance of fabric painting can be understood more easily.

AMERICAN INDIAN FABRIC PAINTING

Although all Indian tribes used fabric painting to some extent, the most examples and usage come from the Plains Indians. Fabric painting was used for spiritual power, for healing, as protection from wild animals and white hunters, and for historical purposes such as recording events, counting time, and the identification of clans. (Fig.36)

Painted clothing, as well as painted masks, were worn in spiritual ceremonies, in order to influence the individual towards a certain consciousness. Once a person put on the clothing, he was no longer a person; he became the "power". Dreams and visions seen during quests were painted on clothing. The painting was a symbol through which power flowed. Medicine shirts for healing were similar in that the power came through using certain repeating symbols, although each medicine shirt was unique in appearance. Painted symbols were thought to be powerful on clothing as protection against the enemy, both animal and human. In 1880, the Indians of North Dakota painted their shirts as protection against the white man's bullets. The magic did not work, and the shirts were not worn again.

Painted clothing also had more practical aspects for the Indians. Important events could easily be recorded by painting, as it was a mnenotic device whereby one image would recall a more complex event. As well as clothing, hides, tipis, and saddlebags recorded remarkable events and the passage of time. This type of painting probably evolved from cave painting, where sequenced events were recorded. Another practical aspect of fabric painting by the Plains Indians was for identification purposes. Different clans and peoples used certain symbols on their clothes and tipis as identification with a certain clan.

Plains Indians culture lay great stress on the individual personality, so that much fabric painting could express that individuality. Painted robes have been collected dating well into the second half of the 19th century. The Indians living in the Southwest also did fabric painting, but it was an extension of a social order rather than an individual message, and, except for the Navajo, this painting crumbled when the white man dominated the Indian culture. The need for fabric painting as

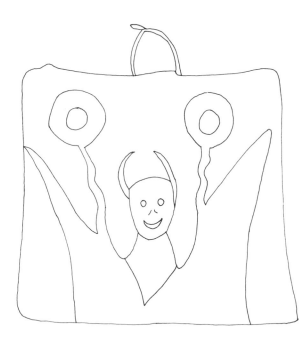

*FIG.28: DRAWING, BY AUTHOR, OF SIOUX SKIN DRUM. AFTER **200 YEARS OF NORTH AMERICAN INDIAN ART**-NORMAN FEDER*

FIG. 29: BETH BROWN MODELING HUIPTL (SHIRT) WITH PAINTED PRE-COLUMBIAN DESIGNS

(ABOVE AND BELOW) FIGS. 31 AND 32: LISA HENSLEY MODELING MEXICAN-STYLE WRAP SKIRT WITH PRE-COLUMBIAN DESIGNS

(LEFT) FIG.30: PATRICIA TUBB MODELING DRESS PAINTED WITH MAYAN DESIGNS

(LEFT)FIG. 36: ARAPAHO *"GHOST SHIRT"* WORN BY PARTICIPANTS IN THE GHOST DANCE RELIGION

FIG.34: MAN'S COTTON SHIRT WITH REPEAT—ING MOTIF. *AFTER INDIAN ART IN SOUTH AMERICA*–F.J.DOCKSTADER # 213

social communication vanished along with that very communication which held the Indians together in a cohesive social unit. Other Indian tribes farther east and north did some fabric painting, but we have little record of it. In 1540, Coronado mentioned painted bison robes of the Zuni of New Mexico. Giovanni da Verrazano mentioned finding painted deerskins in New England in 1524, and in Florida in 1528, Cabeza de Vaca also found painted deerskins. Eskimos used fabric painting rather extensively, on drums and tools, as well as in clothing.

(LEFT) FIG.33: PHOTOGRAPH BY MARTIN CHAMBI JR. OF PERUVIAN INDIAN IN TRADITIONAL GARB (1938)

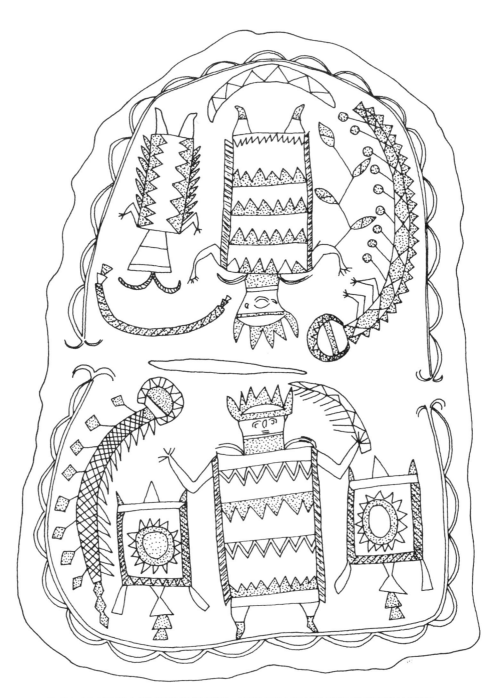

*FIG. 37: DRAWING OF APACHE MEDICINE SHIRT. ALTHOUGH THESE SHIRTS WERE DIFFERENT IN DESIGN, CERTAIN SYMBOLS REAPPEAR: SUN, MOON, STARS, RAINBOWS, SNAKES, TARANTULAS, LIGHTNING, HAIL, AND SMOKE CLOUDS. FROM **AUTHENTIC INDIAN DESIGNS**– MARIA NAYLOR. DRAWING BY PHYLLIS THOMPSON.*

(RIGHT) FIG.39: PAINTED LEATHER HANGING BY K.LEE MANUEL. FEATHERS, BEAD–WORK. THIS IS PAINTED IN A MANNER SIMILAR TO NORTH AMERICAN INDIAN PAINTED HIDES. VERSATEX PAINT.

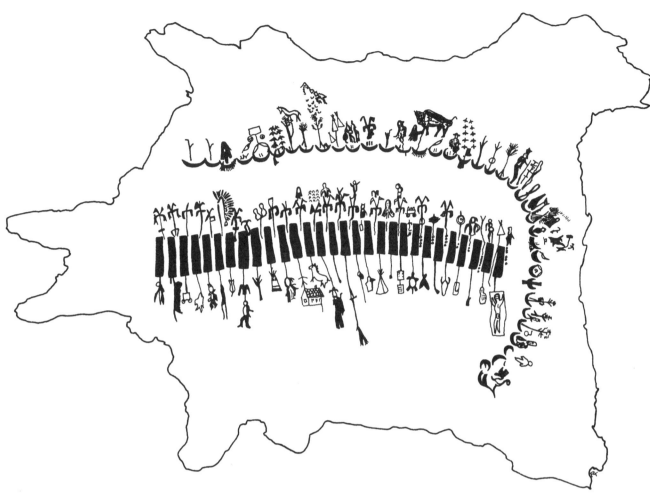

FIG. 38: DRAWING OF PLAINS INDIAN CALENDAR (KIOWA TRIBE) FROM THE 1890'S. A RECORD OF 37 MONTHS IS DEPICTED HERE. FROM **AUTHENTIC INDIAN DESIGNS**– MARIA NAYLOR. DRAWING BY PHYLLIS THOMPSON.

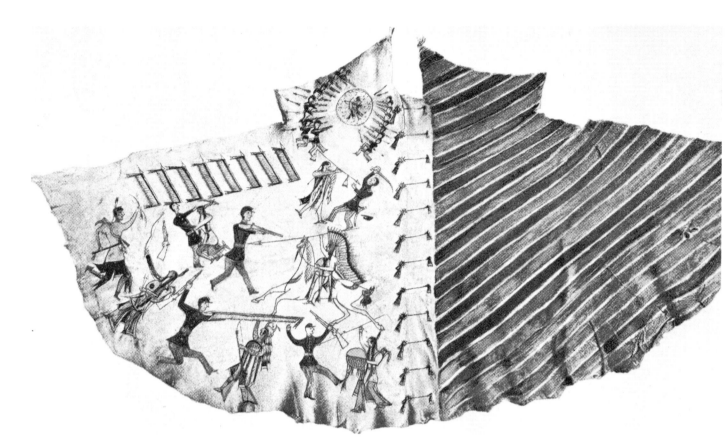

FIG. 41: BATTLE TIPI OF THE KIOWAS.
REPLICA OF HERALDIC TIPI FROM 1872.

FIG.40: PAINTED LEATHER GARMENT
WITH INDIAN DESIGNS. BEADED FRINGE.
ARTIST: K.LEE MANUEL.

FIG. 42: WINTER COAT MADE OF CARIBOU HIDE BY
THE UNGAVA INDIANS OF HUDSON BAY. HAND–
PAINTED BORDER. **AUTHENTIC INDIAN DESIGNS-**
MARIA NAYLOR.

(LEFT) FIG 43: NASKAPI PAINTED BUCKSKIN COAT
FROM THE EASTERN WOODLANDS. GEOMETRIC
AND DOUBLE CURVE MOTIF.

FIG. 44: DETAIL OF FIG. 42

FIG.45: TSIMSHIAN (NORTHWEST COAST
INDIAN) SKIN APRON WITH REALISTIC
DECORATION OF PAINTED ANIMAL
FORMS

FIG.46: AFRICAN PAINTED COSTUME FROM
THE IVORY COAST. FROM **AFRICAN TEXTILES
AND DECORATIVE ARTS** -R. SIEBER. DRAWN BY
PHYLLIS THOMPSON.

AFRICAN FABRIC PAINTING

FIG.47: DRAWING OF AFRICAN PAINTED CLOTH
AFTER BAMBARA, MALI. **AFRICAN TEXTILES
AND DECORATIVE ARTS-** R. SIEBER

Going from the cold to a very warm part of the world, one
finds fabric painting included in African textiles. (Fig.46 ,Fig.47)
They are used in masks and costumes, for cloth lengths to be
used in wrapped clothing, or as fabrics for bedding and drapes.
A lot of fabric painting is done with paste–resists, such as
cassava paste, a substance obtained from a starchy tropical
plant. Although the climate of Africa is hot as is South America,
there is not the aridness and preservative effect of the caves, and
there is dampness which causes mildew and destruction of
some textiles. In general, wood and stone art objects are far
more common in Africa than textiles. Reeds and grasses are also
used in place of other types of fiber constructions. In Oceanic
art, the only examples of fabric painting are on bamboo and
bark, although these are sometimes made into clothing, such as
belts.
African textiles are a rich source of design and technique.
Many dye and resist processes were and still are exten–sively
practiced in Africa, producing beautiful fabrics of high quality.
Tie dye, Indigo dyeing, wax resist printing with a wooden block
called a tampon, cassava resist, and paste–resist, have a long
history in African textiles. Adinkira cloth,which is hand–printed
cloth made with calabash stamps and embroidery, are still a
popular national dress in Ghana, the place of its origins.
Another technique is to apply thickened dyes with a sharpened
stick directly onto cloth.

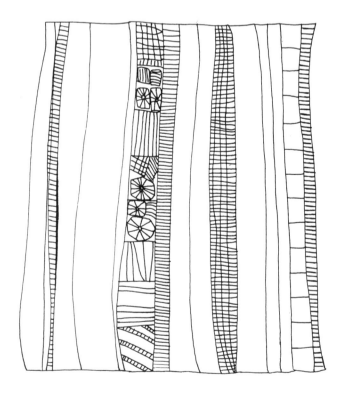

• •

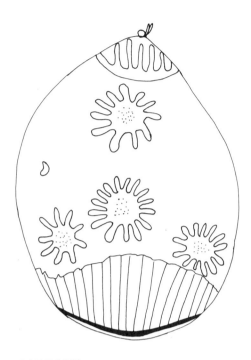

FIG. 48: PAINTED KENYA-TURKANA HEADDRESS.
AFTER PLATE 32, **AFRICAN TEXTILES AND DECO–
RATIVE ARTS-** R. SIEBER. DRAWING BY AUTHOR.

FIG. 50: ANCIENT PETROGLYPHS. DRAWING
BY AUTHOR.

FIG.49:: AFRICAN DESIGNS FROM THE BOOK, **AFRI-
CAN DESIGNS FROM TRADITIONAL SOURCES-**
GEOFFREY WILLIAMS. DRAWING BY AUTHOR.

EASTERN FABRIC PAINTING

■■■■■■■■■■■■■■■■■■■■■■■■■■■■■

Farther east, and farther along in history, are examples of fabric painting from Persia, Arabia, India, China, and Japan. A war dress was found in Senegal with Arabic script on it in 1889. In Persia and India, a number of textiles were painted before hand–printing became more widespread. Hand–stenciling lent itself easily to the repeat motif, but there could be color variation. The textiles of Persia and India became so popular and their use so widespread that they became a threat to the industry of other nations. A decree in Britain was announced in the 18th century which stated that fabrics of Persia, China, and the East Indies such as calicoes, which were painted, dyed, stenciled, printed, or otherwise marked, could not be imported into Great Britain, nor worn, nor otherwise used. The most popular of these textiles that were banned are the now popular India prints used as bedspreads, wallhangings, and for clothing. There are examples of painting on silk in both China and Japan, ranging from the 8th and 9th century, to an account in the 18th century from a Jesuit missionary speaking of painted Oriental textiles. One problem in accounting for examples of fabric painting in China and Japan is the number of paintings on silk. By looking only at a picture, it cannot be always known whether or not the silk was stiffened with glue, as was often the case.

It can be seen that fragmentary examples of fabric painting have been found all over the world. The very earliest fabric painting was found in the 4th century B. C. in Egyptian tombs and in Greek tombs from the Crimea, while the very earliest painting was an Egyptian wall painting in a tomb dating 2500 B.C. Records of fabric painting have been found in a German manuscript from the Monastery of St. Catherine Nurnberg (15th,16th century) in Pliny's writings, and probably in numerous other historical records, as yet undiscovered.

FIG.51: DETAIL OF PAINTED COTTON HANGING FROM INDIA, 18TH CENTURY. MILKMAIDS ARE SHOWN IN A FOREST. GOLD AND SILVER ON BLACK GROUND. AFTER **TEXTILES AND ORNAMENTS OF INDIA**–*ED. BY MONROE WHEELER.*

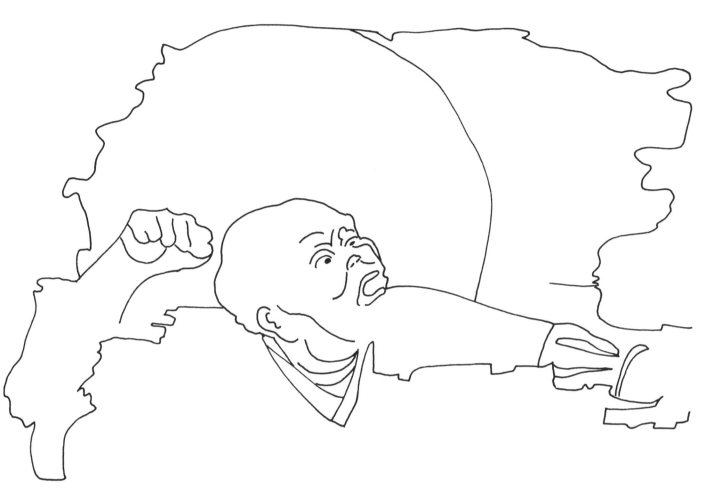

FIG. 52: ONE OF THE EARLIEST RECORDS OF FABRIC PAINTING.
FRAGMENT OF A GESTICULATING MONK, RECOVERED FROM TURFAN,
CENTRAL ASIA, 8TH–9TH CENTURY. PAINTED ON SILK.

MODERN FABRIC PAINTING

There is a large jump from the fabric painting in the tombs of Egypt to what is considered the history of modern fabric painting. Speculation on the gap leads one to consider the advance of industrialization in the 1800's, and the confusion of fabric painting with fabric printing. As well, most paints and dyes used in textile decoration could only be used for industry, not for home use. Materials which could be used at home, such as dyes and natural dyes, were used with hot dyeing, and therefore could not be used very well with fabric painting. Other possibilities for the fading out of fabric painting had to do with the separation of painting and needlework. In the 1600's, the church ruled over painting with an iron hand. During that time as well, it was necessary for a painter to have a patron, as she could not exist on her own. A painter needed the support of the aristocracy or the academy. In the 1800's, the ideas for painting were more influenced by the general public rather than the church. Still, it was not until the 1950's that the definition of painting began to loosen. At that time, the boundaries between painting and printmaking blurred. Picasso and Braque introduced the Cubist movement, combining collage and painting. Pollack moved his canvases to the floor.

THE 1950's – 1980's

By the 1950's, in an attempt to get women back into the home and out of the factories, homemakers were encouraged to learn handicrafts (as contrasted to today's crafts). For fabric painting, that meant booklets on how to decorate curtains and other household accessories with simple stenciled designs. It meant decorating all types of clothing: children's smocks, dresses, aprons, neckties, handkerchief's, scarves, and bedspreads with neatly stenciled designs. A flurry of books appeared, only to go out of print in a few years due to the limited scope of the material presented. The material in these books dealt with design ideas better suited to fabric printing, in my opinion. Hand painting designs which were more easily fabric printed caused the decline and near dead stop of fabric painting by the end of the 1950's.

In the late 60's and early 70's, the design industry turned to the art world for ideas. As well, designers and craftspeople had been incorporating tie–dye and batik in fashion and clothing. New offset printing processes made it possible for anything that could be photographed to be printed, and a wide variety of designs were introduced: photographs of movie stars, political figures, famous buildings, works of art. Textile design was no longer limited to geometrics, floral motifs, and nature scenes.

Much more is being done in fabric painting in the 1980's and 1990's as more is being done in general in the area of individually designed clothing. Fabric painting is now part of the mainstream of the fiber art world. There is a flexibility and diversity in its expression. It is very visible as wearable art, in casual wear, and is used in quiltmaking and also in fine art. Its very definition is coined by a new phrase: surface design.

FABRIC PAINTING IN THE 1980's

Wearable art is a common feature in today's craft shows and fiber conferences. Name artists produce quality work for galleries and high fashion boutiques. In large cities and progressive fashion centers it is pushed to the limit in its definition of art clothing, and is very avant–garde. Wearable art is, indeed, one of the major expressions of fabric painting.

At the same time, there has been a big explosion of casual wear, especially in sweatshirt art and T–shirts. New products such as the Tulip line of fabric paints (slick paint, glitter paint, puffy paint, iridescent sparkle paint, spatter paint, roller paint, and liquid glitter) are popular in decorating sweatshirts.

In the 1980's one began to see a resurgence of tie–dye, mostly among younger people. Tie–dye T–shirts proliferated, along with matching tie–dye shirt and pants or skirt outfits. These outfits have diverged from being loud and wild to include a more subdued and graceful look for a mature clientele.

In the 1980's as well, one saw increasingly more diversity in fabric painting, due to the addition of new product lines of paint and dye, and the re–emergence of the popularity of some standard techniques. Some of the newer products include: opaque fabric paints (Neopaque), more iridescents, metallics, and pearlescent (Lumiere), Jacquard silk paint, Fibracron fiber reactive dye, Telana dyes for silk and wool, synthetic indigo, and Japanese textile pens (Garo). In truth, with so many people working in surface design, there is bound to be a variety and a diversity of technique and idea. It was, and is, an exciting time!

Quiltmaking has also enjoying great popularity, and many quiltmakers, both traditional and contemporary, are finding enjoyment in using hand–painted fabrics as part of their color repertoire. These techniques are being used by a varied group of people. Another area where fabric painting is used in a unique way is by painters and sculptors. They use fabric as their canvas or their form, and paint on it. The result is often a framed piece of art, a combining of fabric and paint.

An Eastern influence affects certain fabric painters of the 1980's and 1990's. Japanese techniques of fabric decoration such as stencil dyeing with paste–resist, nori paste–resist techniques, and shibori (which is a method of shaping cloth by pinching, folding, stitching, pleating, wrapping, or twisting, and then binding it in various fashions), are all popular methods being tried in the U.S. today. Painted weaving is also a popular form of fabric painting, both the technique of warp painting as well as the ikat method. It is inspiring that people are continuing to learn these ancient techniques since they are fast dying out among the indigenous populations.

Silk is another highly visible material being used today in conjunction with fabric painting. Although much of the work being shown in museums, art shows, and fiber magazines is painted silk, remember that many beautiful items can also be made with cotton and muslin. Quilted jackets, wrap jackets, skirts, summer pants, curtains, purses, and quilts all make up beautifully with painted cotton fabrics. Silk is a beautiful fabric and, when painted on by someone with expertise and experience, a truly unique piece of art is created.

FABRIC PAINTING IN THE 1990's

Fabric painting in the 1990's is easier than ever. More is done for you. Many businesses and entrepreneurs have become the intermediary; rather than you cutting and designing the stencil, they have,(with an adhesive backing or tape), and all you do is tape it on your fabric and paint! The rubber stamp is already cut; you get the fun of stamping it on the fabric. Whereas in the past, the information given was "buy some erasers and, using an X–acto knife, cut your own design...etc".

The end result of all this is more quality. You, the fabric painter or designer, are not also expected to be an expert craftsperson at cutting with small knives and making intact designs. This leaves the consumer to be more involved with the creative process of fabric painting. It also speeds up time. Rather than having to make your own garments first and then paint them, there are plenty of diverse garments to choose from. Even T–shirts are being manufactured in more varied styles. With the wealth of diversity of products, there is no end to the kinds of artistic manipulations created from paint onto cloth. I made a charming kitchen towel using a terry cloth towel, a stamp of a bear along with some metallic dimensional paints. It took about 10 minutes to have it finished and ready to use!

All in all, a blossoming has occurred! More than ever, fabric painting is at home in the high school wardrobe, the university art show, the wearable art gallery, and the quilter's guild. One thing that can be said about fabric painting in the 1990's is that it is everywhere! On weekends in the city in which I live, I see a large number of the population wearing surface designed T–shirts, be they tie–dye, direct painting, marbling, wood block print, spatter painting, or a combination of techniques.

Fabric painted clothing is no longer solely the domain of the alternative culture. For better or for worse, it has spread into mainstream society. If people are not themselves painting, perhaps as a "Sunday fabric painter", then they are buying clothing from craftspeople who do. Every summer at the Oregon Country Fair in Veneta, Oregon, almost everyone dresses up in fabric painted and dyed clothing. It is truly a feast

FIG. 53: BATIK SILK SPACE DIVIDERS. FROM ***THE PRINCIPLES OF PATTERN****–RICHARD M. PROC-TOR. DRAWING BY PHYLLIS THOMPSON.*

for the eyes —to see thousands upon thousands of people wearing surface designed fabrics!

LINKING THE OLD WITH THE NEW

Painted clothing can be both a personal aesthetic statement or a social commentary. Just as ancient fabric painting was used in a personally symbolic way, and as a way to establish communication with others, modern fabric painting has the same basis, though disguised and perhaps distorted with time.

An example of ancient fabric painting might be a war dress with special symbols on it, meant as protection to the wearer. In modern terms, this could be a dress with one's favorite images from modern America. Many examples of ancient fabric painting dealt with marking time and telling a series of events. Heroic deeds, journeys, and in general changes through time and space are expressed through fabric painting, both ancient and modern.

By marking time as cyclical rather than linear, it is possible to recycle old clothes as well as old ideas. Many styles of clothing can be combined with many styles of painting. In this way, the concept of clothing can be stretched beyond fashion, with its dictates of time present and time past.

Once clothing is liberated beyond the constricts of fashion, it can be seen as a very flexible environment, lending itself to aesthetic appreciation, costume, social commentary, and social reaction. Clothing is a very personal environment in the sense that any image or symbol in fabric painting is connected not only to the person, but to the body. The meaning of a picture on someone's clothing— and therefore, body, is quite different from the same picture on a wall! Clothing as the most immediate environment relates it ***to*** the environment and breaks down the artificial barriers that keep it ***from*** the environment.

THE AESTHETIC ENVIRONMENT

As an aesthetic environment, painted clothing has no limitations. It becomes a visual pleasure of ones' creative efforts which can cast a spell, create a mood, heighten an effect. There is a ceremony of clothes which is overlooked in the competition of fashion and status. K. Lee Manuel, a fabric painter from San Francisco, sees painted clothing as a way of relating the body to everyday space, and, for this reason, she creates one–of–a–kind clothing. She has painted brightly colored capes, cummerbunds, and dresses. Clothing such as this can be an interference and a distraction; it is not psychologically subdued. It points to who we are. People who wish to be visually or psychologically inconspicuous may prefer mass produced clothing.

Other fabric painters create different effects. Lenore Davis, a fabric artist from New York now living in Kentucky, creates a sculptural effect in painted clothing by padding certain places and then painting them. The clothing becomes very much an environment as it ***extends into*** the environment. Aaron Bartell of Eugene, Oregon, uses fabric painting for optical illusions with the shape of the body being manipulated towards this end. The cloth is the vehicle by which the optical illusion can take place. Painted clothing is an excellent vehicle for games and secret hidden messages, due to the curvatures and hiding places both on the body and with certain designs of clothes.

Costume creates a very definite aesthetic environment and mood as the wearer is transformed into a specific "someone". An Indian dress, a Japanese kimono, a cape like a brightly plumaged bird are close to costume and yet allow the wearer his individual personality. Costume is also a vehicle by which many different cultural and historical motifs and images can be expressed which are not included in modern fashion. As well, ancient images and motifs only to be found in dusty books can be renovated through fabric painting and worn on 20th century streets—an interesting time perspective. In wearing painted motifs of a certain historical period or culture, I find it is as if I have gone to that place, having created that environment. Costume leads to psychological travel, changing the immediate environment from its narrow 20th century slot to a multidimensional view of time/space.

THE SOCIOLOGICAL ENVIRONMENT

FIG.54: A POPULAR SOCIAL ISSUE EXPRESSED ON A PAINTED T–SHIRT. DESIGN AND DRAWING BY AUTHOR.

As well as being an aesthetic environment, painted clothing also creates a sociological environment. It deals with social issues, as well as creating a social commentary and interaction by the use of painted symbols. The sociological perspective of fabric painting is an exciting one, as it deviates far from traditional viewpoints of clothing as "decorative" (The Plains Indians relied on fabric painting as an integral part of social communication, but most clothing lacked a social dimension apart from that of status.)

Painted clothing can be a sounding board for popular social issues. Ecology, nuclear issues, drugs, sexuality, and other political and social issues and persons are popular with modern fabric painting. (see Fig. 54) Fabric painting of this type can be very close to the effect political cartoons have in the newspaper: they are open to and invite social reaction.

One of the more popular mediums open to social reaction which relates to clothing is the button with a message on it. Fabric painting extends the message of the button to a larger ground, such as a T–shirt. The message is echoed back by those who react. Like a bulletin board, painted clothing dealing with social issues is conspicuous and will guarantee an immediate response from others. (As a painter, this can be rather nice, as you need not try and inconspicuously overhear comments made at a museum as to the quality of your work.) Some caution will be advised both in the designing and wearing of clothing which might provoke certain other people. It is not necessary that all socially oriented painting be disruptive, indeed it can be visually aesthetic yet point to a meaning larger than personal aesthetics. The reactions of others to fabric painting leads it to become an open mural. With social intervention in the creative process, one can decide how to develop a painting through the comments and suggestions of others. In the book, ***American Denim, a New Folk Art***– Owens and Lane, Doug Hansen spoke of how he wore his acrylic painted pants through various stages of painting, which then evolved through the reactions and comments of others.

The open mural effect of fabric painting leads to group painting. As well as being an individual artist selecting and choosing from other people's ideas, you can do group work. An autograph shirt is an example of such a combined effort; it has historical value as well. Children's art often is done with groups of children working on a single project. This can be fun for them, and if desired, adults can "edit" the work for a sense of balance and composition.

MODERN FABRIC PAINTERS

Painted clothing can be seen to a variety of meanings, depending upon the type of painting done, its intent, and its reaction in the environment. There are a number of people today experimenting with fabric painting in a variety of ways. Some people paint spontaneously; others sketch and plan. Linda Nelson Bryan, who airbrushes and stuffs soft paintings and sculpture says, "Although my pieces have a traditional quilting basis, in the trapunto work, they are also painted (and sketched many times previous to the painting), so I consider them works of art". She also uses acrylic paint for an unusual reason: to withstand heat in art galleries. Judy Felgar's woven painted surfaces are also preplanned. "All my work is preplanned. After 'getting' an idea, or a new technique suggests a new approach, drawings are made in black and white. Then I continue with color studies, usually felt pens. If I decide to do the piece, the drawing is then transferred to graph paper, then woven and painted."

However, Alan Grinberg, an artist/designer/craftsman who airbrushes with found object stencils, says, "I try not to spend too much time on each piece. It makes me feel freer, and it is easier to take risks without a heavy time investment". Dorothy Caldwell of Canada uses both approaches: "Sometimes a piece is worked out very carefully beforehand through a series of sketches and patterns. Other times, I take a bolt of fabric and just do things to it working completely with what happens and developing something out of it".

Some fabric painters express the practical; others, the abstract. Faith Middendorp, who paints quilt patterns of pillows, says, "In a society where very few people have the opportunity to fashion an object from start to finish in their daily work, I believe there is a profound need for the experiences which would provide a full opportunity to identify in a personal way with the products created by hand, and to give meaning and enduring values to the things we touch and use in our daily lives." Victoria Rivers uses her fabric painted soft three–dimensional wall hangings as abstract statements of sequential movement in time and space. "They reflect my landscape environment which takes on a spiritual rather than physical presence... (they) symbolize the passing of time and experience and the unfolding of knowledge. The rectilinear pieces symbolize collections of personal experiences, thought–forms, or memories that compose the person. These vary in color combinations, often colors remembered from childhood, memories of dresses, packages, etc. that are contained by boundaries symbolizing the physical self."

Many fabric painters make fiber art rather than wearable art. Bill Hinz works with fiber–reactive dyes on white velveteen, as does Lenore Davis. Kathryn Westphal works on fabric with an interaction of "painted, stitched, and imprinted textures in an exciting composition". Judith Stein uses oil–base printing inks and collographs for fabric painted quilts, while Ann Sams works in the hot Florida sun dye–painting hammocks out of heavy canvas.

The 1990's has brought a big change in fabric painters. For one thing, there are hundreds and hundreds of fabric painters working in the U.S. alone. Some of the outstanding names that I am familiar with include: Carter Smith, who has brought shibori (or tie–dye) to an art form as few others. He uses wire, chain, and trees and then wraps around them his pleated, pinched and tucked fabrics. Doing this brings out intricate and precise patternings with an unparalleled excellence of color. Diane Erickson has elevated the simple stencil to an art form, as she creates designs on clothing in very modern ways yet that are reminiscent of stenciled patterns from Asian kimonos and other ethnic design.

Pamela Studstill is a painter who also makes "art quilts". She adds to the precise piecing and color gradations in her work by painting on selected predyed fabric pieces. The result is a precise and joyous celebration of color and texture. Another painter who has translated her skills into wearable art is Sandra Longmore, of Washougal, WA. She likes subjects, lines, forms and colors that are packed with meaning and symbolism, as she responds to the beauty of the world around her. As a multi–media artist, she studies ancient techniques of applying paint to fabric. She often starts with white fabric and creates using fiber–reactive dyes, pigments, and ancient techniques of discharge. For example, first she will discharge dye from an already dyed garment, or one that she dyes herself. Then she will use a screenprint, or airbrush a design, and then finish with some direct painting. She chooses to paint clothing instead of canvas so that her works can envelop those who wear them. The emotions of her work are warm to the touch as well as to the soul, as she depicts flowing forms of nature along with such spiritual symbols as ancient petroglyphs. (Fig.55, Fig. 56)

Despite some differences in appearance, modern fabric painting is based on the techniques used by ancient fabric painters. Although the skill level in fabric painting can vary widely from simple brushstrokes (probably used most frequently by ancient fabric painters), to technically difficult procedures (often used today), one **must** start by learning about three basic elements: the paint, the brush , and the cloth. When these elements are successfully combined, the modern fabric painter can choose to express him or herself in primitive, simple, moderate, or astounding terms!

FIG. 55: ***"THE PEACE COAT"*** *–BY SANDRA LONGMORE. 100% COTTON JACKET. FIBER–REACTIVE DYES, AIRBRUSH PAINTS AND DIMENSIONAL PAINTS.*

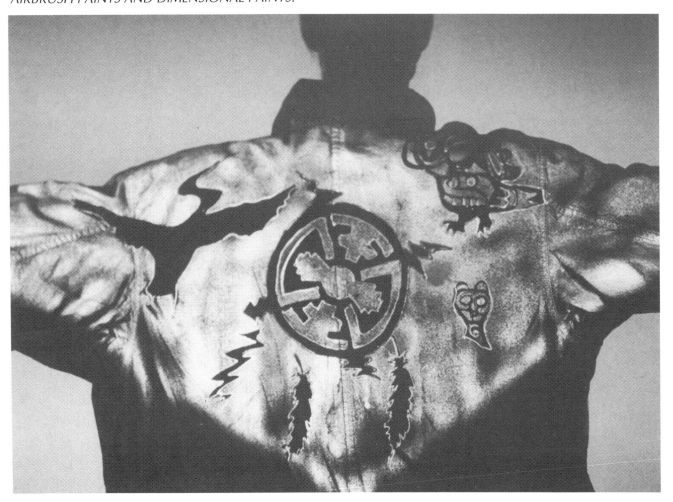

FIG. 56: **"THE ATTITUDE"**– BY SANDRA LONGMORE. 100% COTTON JACKET, FIBER–REACTIVE DYES, CREATEX AIRBRUSH PAINTS, AND DI-MENSIONAL PAINTS. MODEL: NICOLE RAHEY.

3 *FABRIC PAINTING: A BEGINNING*

FIG.57: DRAWING OF PAINT MATERIALS USED IN FABRIC PAINTING–BY KAREN HAMILTON

In its simplest form, fabric painting is an interaction between fabric and paint which is carried out by the use of a tool (the brush). It is a process: the paint is carried by the brush to the fabric. It is a dance and the hand and the eye are a part of the motion. In its simplest form, what is needed for fabric painting is some cloth, a flat surface, a brush, some paint, and at least one idea. In its complex form, fabric painting extends beyond brush painting and into the use of tools such as sponges or spray guns, and embraces different kinds of fabrics which react in different ways. In its complex form, fabric painting uses natural materials such as rocks and clay and wood as well as many synthetics; it utilizes chemical reactions with dyes to produce various effects, even the making of paint itself. (Fig.57)

I shall be using the term painting environment to describe what is necessary and what is useful to the fabric painter. With different kinds of paints and dyes, it is necessary to have different sorts of equipment. It is possible to do some interesting work with a minimum of equipment, just as it is possible to do interesting work with a well stocked studio. What sort of an arrangement you will need depends upon the materials with which you choose to work.

If you think of the paint, the brush, and the cloth as three separate elements forming relationships in various configurations, you may begin to feel the excitement of fabric painting and its range of exploration

THE PAINT

One has so many materials at hand from which to choose. In the category of paint, there is, besides textile paint; acrylic paint with its many accessories (polymer emulsions such as resin, matte and gel mediums, acrylic modeling paste, matte and gel varnish, and gesso), indelible inks such as Pelican and Koh–i–nor, oil paint with textine, oil–base block printing ink, oil–base silk–screen inks, cold water dyes such as Procion, Fibrex, and Dylon with or without thickeners. If you wish to be less reliant upon paint materials found only in stores, natural dyes and paints, mordant painting, and homemade textile paint are all ways to work in a more primitive, less industrial way. Embroidery paints, permanent magic markers and fabric crayons are other materials to use in painting.

These materials can also be mixed with one another or used in combination with each other to create other sources of paint. Cold–water dyes can be used in conjunction with acrylics (with the dye being used in large areas and the paint in smaller, more detailed areas for best effects) as long as the acrylic painting is done after the dye has been set. Jewel–like effects are created with a combination of color crayons, acrylic medium and acrylic color. The contrast between aqueous and graphic sections of a piece of fabric is also seen when drawing with a combination of watercolor, and pen and ink or drawing materials. (Fig.58)

All these materials can be used as traditional painting media, although their effects will be different due to types of cloth used. Watercolor, collage, oil and tempera effects can be had with acrylics. Textile paints have a consistency and effect similar to tempera. Stenciling, marbling, imprinting, fingerpainting, and splattering of paint are other techniques to be used with fabric.

To fully understand the effects of paint, one must form a relationship with color. I would like to refer the reader to other books for the technical explanations on color, the laws of color and the various types of color wheels. I would like to give more intuitive ideas for using color in painting.

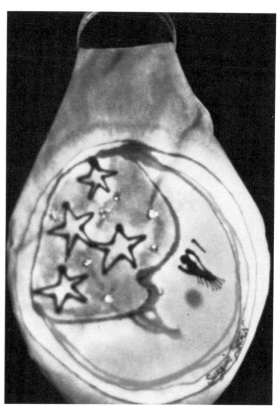

FIG. 58: MOON SIDE OF SUN BRACELET PURSE BY SUZANNE LARSEN. PROCION DYE ON VELVETSUEDE CLOTH. LINE DRAWING IN INKODYE.

Color is an energy source. The Fauvists loved color so much that they used it as the main idea of their art, letting line, shape and form be in supportive roles. They were concerned with the painting of color.

It is a good idea to sometimes limit your palette to one color and experiment with different shades and tones of that color, as well as different shapes which seem to fit the feeling of that color. It is possible in this way to discover a subtle range of effects and materials connected to each color.

Color says different things to different people. Everyone has a favorite color. As you paint, you can begin to form a color language. This can influence the kind of work you do, by building a unity of color within the subject matter. It is helpful to understand a color before working with it, for then there is emotional as well as technical knowledge. As an example, the colors brown and yellow, when used together, make connections in my mind with the smell of dry grass in August, the moist earth, dry autumn leaves on the ground, and the delicate textures of certain grasses.

If color is confusing, there are guides which can help you explore your feelings about various colors and their meanings. Take a painting which you like and copy the general areas of color without copying the entire painting. This is helpful for learning about certain feelings and forms in connection with colors placed next to each other. Take a poem or descriptive passage from a book which you find pleasing and use the colors to form a design (Fig.59) It is not necessary to use a piece of literature to do this, although sometimes it brings up images and associations that a person would not make on his own. Think of some of your favorite images, put them together and notice their colors and use them. Reverse this idea: think of different names of colors, then find design ideas from the objects created from these names. For example, the color crayons bittersweet, mahogany, and apricot are all browns and shades of brown. They call up images of wood and flowering trees and thus form a design through mental imagery.

Hans Hofmann and Josef Albers are two painters who harnessed the power of color in their work. The power of color transcends form. They worked in geometrics, Albers moreso than Hofmann, and the color juxtapositions are what forms the painting. By identifying color with light, Robert Delaunay used color as the fundamental building material of his pictures. In modern art as a whole, the use of color is a direct and independent language of meaning and emotion, and it can be used in this way for fabric painting.

THE BRUSH

The brush is the next element in this configuration of paint, brush, and cloth. The brush is more than a means of transferring the paint onto the fabric, although it does serve the function of intermediary. The brush is a tool; more than that, it is an idea. A machine can print designs onto yards and yards of fabric very efficiently. A machine cannot capture the spontaneity and originality which can happen when a thoughtful person takes up a brush. The brush creates a fabric or garment which is expressive, rather than merely decorative; just as a painting is an expression, rather than a piece of decorated paper.

As well as regular oil brushes to be found in art stores, there are a variety of other brushes to be used —from toothbrushes to house painting brushes, large and small. The brush, as a tool, extends beyond brushlike qualities. It is a connection between the painter and the paint. In this way, tools such as paint rollers, sprayers, squeeze bottles (Fig.61), palette knives, kitchen utensils, pieces of rope and string ("homemade brushes") pine needles, bottles from which to pour paint,and other pieces of cloth, are all brushes. The various types of nibs on drawing pens also function as brushes.

These different types of brushes produce different types of painting effects when used with various types of paint. (Fig.60, Fig.62, Fig.63) It is the interaction between paint and cloth which causes so many different effects, and this interaction comes via the brush. A more static method of fabric decoration, such as block printing has less variety, less confusion, but fewer choices. By learning which types of paint interact best with what kind of cloth via what type brush stroke, there are many more choices for expression.

The handling of the brush ranges from the very controlled to free expression and experimentation. Certain techniques which are established today were yesterdays' experiments. Handling the brush requires using it and observing how certain procedures will create certain effects. Accidental effects become original, controlled brushstrokes. (Fig.64)

There are certain ways of handling the brush which are standard and can be learned. The size of the brush produces certain widths in line; the shape of the brush produces certain standard impressions. These basic brushstrokes, when combined with experimental effects, allow for a flexibility in technique and application. Ideas for brushstrokes should come from sources other than just painting techniques, as the purpose of a technique is to help the artist express her inner vision rather than having the artists' vision be limited by technique.

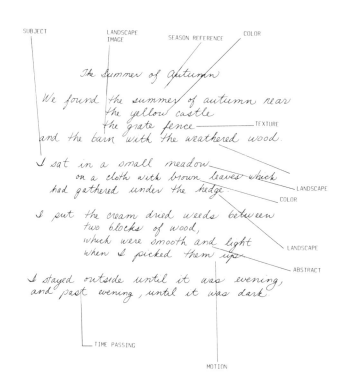

FIG. 59: (ABOVE) POEM BY AUTHOR. (BELOW) FIG 60: PAINTED T–SHIRT BY KIM AND LEIGH LACAVA.

THE CLOTH

Thus far, we have followed fabric painting from its beginning, the paint, to its transition of the paint with the brush. We now come to the end point of the interaction, the cloth. The only difference in fabric painting and canvas painting is the addition of sizing to the canvas in canvas painting. Unprimed canvas is cloth, just as fine drawing paper is finely ground up cloth (rag linen, for example). The connection between the world of traditional painting and the world of fabric design, as well as the separation of these two worlds, is due to one variable: sized or unsized cloth.

It is very important to be able to recognize the fiber content in cloth, so as to know what type of paint or dye will or will not work on the fabric. Knowing this can save you many hours of work, as well as allowing you to use a combination of paints and dyes safely on one type of cloth.

There is a much larger quantity of synthetic fibers on the market today than there were twenty years ago. Many materials which look like natural fibers cotton— linen, wool, and silk— are only blends, and because of this, they react differently than do their pure counterparts. The fiber content of material sold in stores is marked on the bolt, so this is a good way to learn about many fabrics. Random pieces of cloth laying around the house may be more difficult to identify. The burn test for fabrics is helpful; natural fibers, when burned, are reduced to soft ashes, while synthetics smell like chemicals and melt into a lump or hard bead. It is also possible to experiment with fabrics of unknown fiber content by painting them with different types of paint, and recording the effects.

Experimentation, or testing fabrics, is very important in fabric painting. It is a necessary basic rule to avoid wasting time and materials. Most paints or dyes or markers of a certain brand will all react similarly; however, one **could** be the black sheep which could ruin a work of art—if it is not first tested! Testing materials is very simple. Label the type of cloth if it is known. Draw and paint with a variety of materials: acrylics, textile paint, oils, permanent markers, embroidery paints, fabric crayons, dyes. Write the brand and type of material in that material (for example, write Aqua–tec burnt sienna acrylic). Let the cloth dry, then wash it in warm water and soap. Give the material rougher treatment than it would get in normal wear. Nothing is more discouraging than to see a hand–painted garment fading after a few washings because you used certain materials without first testing them. Let the cloth dry and then press it with a medium–hot iron. Again, check the vibrancy of the color and how well the paint or dye has permeated the fabric. Small squares of different types of cloth are good for test pieces, as they can be mounted on cardboard and used for reference. A notebook is also handy in which to keep such information, as it is portable, and could be used for filling special orders in fabric painting.

LISTING AND IDENTIFICATION OF COMMON FABRICS

NATURAL FIBERS

There are hundreds of different kinds of cloth. They can be broken down into the categories of natural and synthetic fibers; natural being cotton, linen, wool, and silk; synthetic being rayons, acetates, triacetates, nylon, polyesters, acrylic, modacrylic, and stretch (made from Spandex or other synthetic elastic fibers) fabrics. Due to the many ways of engineering fibers and yarns, hundreds of different types of fabrics are derived from each of these different fibers.

Cotton, moreso than other natural fibers, is a common fabric and would seem to be easily identifiable. It is, however, more difficult to identify pure cotton due to the creation of polyester cotton blends (65% polyester, 35% cotton), which keep the appearance of pure cotton without being so. The distinctions between these similar looking fabrics must be made, as paint materials will not react similarly. For example, fabric crayons work only on synthetics, and cold–water dyes most always work only on natural fibers.

100% cotton accepts the majority of dyes and paints easily. It perhaps is the only fabric to do so, and so it is a good fabric for beginning fabric painters. Some of the names of cotton fabrics are: unbleached and bleached muslin, batiste, broadcloth, burlap, calico, cambric, canvas, chambray, cheesecloth, chenille, chintz corduroy, cotton knit, crepe, denim, dotted swiss, drill, duck, damask, flannelette, felt, gauze, gabardine, gingham, lawn, madras, monks cloth, needle cord, organdy, oxford cloth, percale, pique, pima, plisse, poplin, sailcloth, sateen, seersucker, shirting, terry cloth, ticking, velour, velvet, velveteen, and voile.

Linen is a very crisp and cool fabric. It is not as commonly used as is cotton, but it is still in demand. It is woven in many weights, from handkerchief through homespun to upholstery. It is a strong fiber, and takes paints and dyes well, with less capillary action due to the strength and stability of the fabric. Cambric, canvas, damask, holland, huck, momie, and sheeting are all made of linen.

Wool is the second most popular of natural fibers, after cotton. The wool fiber is combed and carded in various ways, producing **wool** or **worsted** fabrics. Some of these are: barathea, bengaline, boucle, broadcloth, challis, chenille, Chinchilla cloth, covert cloth, crepe, doeskin, Donegal, double–faced fabrics, doubleknits, felt cloth, fleece, flannel, gabardine, homespun, hopsacking, jersey, lambs wool, merino, mungo, serge, Shetland, Tartan, tweeds, and whipcord. Cashmere, camel cloth, alpaca, and mohair are other, more luxurious woolen fabrics.

Wools are the most difficult fabric to use in fabric painting, as not all wools are washable; the dry–cleaning process may alter the paint, and not all paints and dyes take to wool. Experimentation with different fabrics and dyes is very necessary.

Silk is the last natural fiber to be discussed. Silk is a luxurious fabric, and it is in great use today as a specialty item: fine scarves, kimono–like draped jackets for evening wear or lounging, etc. Cold water dyes which can be used only on natural fibers can be used safely on silk without testing. Silk, produced by the silkworm in spun filaments, has a natural lustre due to the triangular shape of the filament, which reflects light. You can work with or away from this lustre when you are painting. Some names for silk include brocade, broadcloth, chenille, chiffon, China silk, crepe, crepe–back satin, crepe de chine, flat crepe, faille, faissue faille, georgette, habutae, moire, mousseline, organza, ottoman, pongee, satin, shantung, raw silk, silk jacquard, surah, taffeta, and velvet.

(LEFT) FIG. 6l: "LANDSCAPE WITH MOON FIGURE"–LENORE DAVIS. DYE–PAINTED WITH SQUEEZE BOTTLE ON VELVETEEN. DRY BRUSH, BRUSH WASH TECHNIQUE.

(BELOW LEFT) FIG. 62: SILK SCARVES–PHYLLIS MUFSON. DIRECT APPLICATION OF PROCION DYE.

(BELOW) FIG. 63: SILK CHIFFON CAFTAN–SHERRY DE LEON. AIRBRUSH PAINTING USING PLANT SPRAYER, DIRECT APPLICATION WITH PROCION DYES.

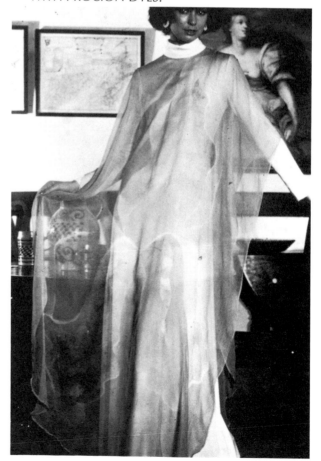

FIG. 64: "THE BRIDGE" –BY FERNE SIROIS. ACRYLIC STAINING. RAW CANVAS IS STAINED USING DILUTED ACRYLIC PAINT AND WATER. IT IS DRIBBLED ACROSS THE CANVAS, WHICH ALLOWS FOR SPONTANEOUS COLOR MIXING. WHEN THE CANVAS DRIES, THE ARTIST EXPANDS THE DESIGN USING AN AIRBRUSH OR JAPANESE INK BRUSHES AND ACRYLIC PAINT.

VISCOSE RAYON

Viscose rayon is a fabric which is neither totally a natural fiber nor a synthetic. It is a man–made fiber but it is made from pure cellulose which is derived from vegetable fibers. Therefore, as far as fabric painting is concerned, it can be considered a natural fiber. Using dyes on viscose rayon will produce brilliant colors. Some of the fabrics made from viscose rayon are: challis, taffeta, twill, satin, shantung and chiffon.

SYNTHETIC FIBERS

These, then, are the natural fibers, blending their colors and weaves in historical time. Synthetic fibers were first created in 1889, with a series of discoveries which led up to the production of rayon. **Rayon, acetate,** and **triacetate** are three cellulosic fibers which means that they use cellulose, the fibrous substance in plants, in their manufacture. The conversion of cellulose to fiber is manmade, and therefore these materials are said to be synthetic. **Viscose rayon,** as has already been mentioned, can be considered a natural fiber when fabric painting, as it has not been chemically altered as has synthetic rayon. Rayon is very receptive to a wide color range of dyes. Rayon is processed to look interchangeably like linen, crepe, or silk. It is also combined with natural fibers. Chenille, damask, knits, ottoman, and tulle can all be made of rayon.

Acetate is another of the cellulosic fibers. It is processed in such a way that acetone will dissolve it. Perfume, nail polish remover, textine, turpentine, and textile paint thinner may eat through the fabric. Acetate takes a wide range of colors, however, and if care is taken in the type of paint or dye, it can be a highly versatile fabric for fabric painting. It is used, and found, as a dressy fabric with a high lustre, and may appear to look like silk. Acetate can rarely be washed, and, if ironed, it should be pressed on the wrong side. Brocade, cire, crepe, damask, doupion, faille, grosgrain, knits, moire, mousseline, satin, sharkskin, and taffeta can all be made of acetate. **Triacetate** is similar to acetate in its production; its properties, however, are quite different. It can withstand heat whereas acetate cannot. It needs little or no ironing, and can be hand or machine washed. Arnel is a familiar brand name of triacetate; surah, taffeta, and blends of knits and woven fabrics are types of triacetate.

Nylon was created in 1938, and announced to the U.S. by Dupont in the form of nylon stockings. Since then, nylon has been used successfully for quick–drying lingerie, crush resistant travel dresses, and numerous other light–weight items. Nylon is receptive to a wide range of colors, but should be separated when washing due to this receptivity to absorbing other colors. It can be either hand or machine washed. Cire, chiffon, knit and woven blends, matelasse, and velvet can be made from nylon.

Polyester and **acrylics** are the next two main synthetic fibers. **Polyesters** are formed from chemical elements derived from petroleum, coal, air, and water. They must be washed in warm water and ironed on low heat. Polyester is often blended with other fibers to increase general strength and stability. Oil and grease stains cling to polyester, so oil–based inks should wear well in fabric painting. Batiste, chiffon, crepe, gabardine, georgette, knit and woven blends, mausseline, satin, terry cloth, velvet, and voile can all be made from polyester. Another popular use of polyester is in a poly–cotton blend. Common poly–cotton blends include broadcloth, corduroy, pinwale corduroy, denim, percale, and sailcloth. **Acrylic** is another synthetic fiber. It is washable, colorfast, and resistant to chemicals and oil Acrilan, Creslan, and Orlon are well–known trade names of acrylics. Boucle, fake fur, less expensive wool–like fabrics, and woven and knit fabrics can all be made of acrylic. **Modacrylic** is a modified acrylic used in fake furs, carpet and other deep–pile fabrics made up into coats and jackets. Modacrylic is also made into children's sleepwear, since its strength lies in its being flame resistance. (Acrylic, on the other hand, is moderately flammable).

Stretch fabrics and **permanent press finishes** are two processes used on both natural and synthetic fibers. The look and feel of the fabric (with the addition of stretchability) will be retained. Spandex and anidex are two synthetic elastic fibers which are used to produce the stretch. When they are spun around the core of elasticity, all the properties of these fibers are retained. T–shirts of 100% cotton are an example of this, as they stretch a little, yet look and feel like cotton. Stretch fabrics should be washed and dried with cool temperatures. Permanent or durable press finishes keep the garment in one shape. This is advantageous for pleated and shaped garments. It is not so advantageous for fabric painting, as dyes cannot be used due to the chemicals used to set the fabric. The dye cannot permeate the finish, and, at best, a rich deep dye will change a white fabric to a very light pastel.These finishes, however, can be removed (See Chapter IV). Acrylics generally work well on permanent press clothes since they do not need to form a chemical bond with the fabrics as does a dye.

Although it is important to experiment with different types of fabric and paint materials, for the beginner, it is best to begin with materials which are already known to work. There are certain types of fabric which are used extensively in fabric painting. They are: cotton muslin (in both the lightweight and heavier weight grades), cotton sheeting (a plain sheet can also be used), cotton broadcloth, white velveteen, cotton percale, cotton poplin, and cotton sateen; rayon chiffon, viscose rayon challis, viscose rayon satin; China silk, silk chiffon, and silk crepe de chine. If you cannot find these fabrics in stores around you, they can be ordered from the following distributors: Testfabrics/ P.O. Drawer "O"/Middlesex, N.J. 08846. For silk: Thai Silks!/ 252 State St. Los Altos, CA. 94022. See also my companion volume, ***1001 PRODUCTS AND RESOURCES FOR THE FABRIC PAINTER AND SURFACE DESIGNER***, for many sources of mail–order fabrics.

TEXTURAL PROPERTIES OF CLOTH

The different types of fibers, as well as fabrics made from them, have textural variety. This variety in textural ground can be well utilized in fabric painting. Dry–brush work picks up the texture of the cloth and emphasizes it, whereas a brush loaded with paint would only clog the interesting texture. In the process of creating a design, learn to observe the texture in

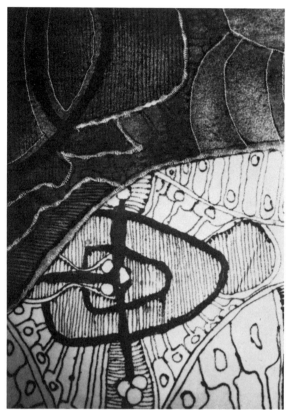

FIG. 65: TIE-DYE AND DIRECT APPLICATION BY JOETTA UMLA. PROCION DYE APPLIED WITH SQUEEZE BOTTLE. THE SMOOTH COTTON ALLOWS FOR VARIATIONS IN METHOD, FROM THE LINEAR DYE TO THE SUBLE SHADINGS OF THE TIE-DYE.

*FIG. 66: (RIGHT) **"NAME SKIRT"**– BY EVE–LYN BYATT. INKODYE ON COTTON. THIS IS AN UNCLUTTERED, ELEGANT DESIGN.*

cloth: muslin as fine–grained as sand, homespun like rough grained wood, silk as lustrous as oil on water. By recognizing the personality of different types of cloth, it is easier to combine the right fabric with the right design. (See Fig.65)

The paint, the brush, the cloth. These have been examined separately in order to understand their function. Fabric painting combines the paint, the brush, and the cloth, in innumerable ways and for many different purposes. But how to sort through all these possibilities? Where to begin? It is best to begin with some "simple and beginning ideas."

SIMPLE AND BEGINNING IDEAS

Simplicity is not necessarily restricted to "simple" designs. Paradoxically, the greater the simplicity, the greater the skill that is needed to separate the necessary elements from those which serve no purpose in the design. It is a good idea for **beginning** painters, designers, and workers with cloth to keep the design or the decoration of the fabric within a realm which is uncomplicated. (Fig.66) New materials and techniques will offer a great enough variety of new and interesting ideas without the added complexity of a complex design. At the same time, I feel that it is necessary for a beginner to be stimulated by a wide range of design ideas so as to not be cramped or uninterested. (Fig.67–70) Also, it is very important to be able to differentiate designs that would be monotonous in hand painting from those which benefit from it. (Fig.71,72)

FIG. 68: *"MONSTER PILLOW"–BY VALERIE GUIGNON. PROCION DYE ON COTTON, STUFFED.*

FIG 67 (ABOVE): PRE–COLUMBIAN BIRDS PAINTED IN ACRYLIC ON CANVAS BAG.

(RIGHT)FIG. 69: LINDA KANZINGER MODELING HANDPAINTED DRESS WITH LACE TOP, TEX–TILE PAINTED FLOWERS, AND EMBROIDERY, ON MUSLIN.

FIG.70 : HANDPAINTED VELVETEEN SCREEN- BY LENORE DAVIS. PROCION DYE IS USED FOR THIS EXAMPLE OF EXQUISITE AND LUXURIOUS FABRIC PAINTING.

FIG. 72: HANDPAINTED T–SHIRT BY LEIGH LACAVA. THIS IS A GOOD EXAMPLE OF A BEGINNING DE- SIGN DUE TO THE SAME SHAPES (BIRDS) WITH VARIATIONS SHOWN BY COLOR.

FIG. 71: **"WOMAN SHAKING QUILT"** –LENORE DAVIS. DYE– PAINTED COTTON VELVETEEN, 20" TALL. THIS DESIGN COULD BE MONOTONOUS TO HANDPAINT EXCEPT IN A SMALL PIECE SUCH AS THIS.

THE LINE

Lines are a simple and effective way to divide space. Paul Klee spoke of taking a walk with a line, to see where it will take you. Lines can be used as simple designs —as stripes, as bands, as borders. Stripes can be used as spacing, for color, with various painting techniques, and to show textured effects. (see Fig.73) Bands and borders are good in beginning painting as there is not as much concern with compositional problems as there can be in painting, due to the restriction of the lines. As well, borders can be placed in many different ways on clothing.

Many different types of designs can be placed within a band or border. Borders using painting techniques, and borders using motifs are two such ideas. **Collage borders** are nice as they utilize a variety of materials within one garment, particularly fabrics that cannot be painted, or look strange when painted. Borders are good for collage as the thickness and or fragileness of the collaged area can be placed in an area of the garment which does not receive heavy wear (for example, the bottom edge of a knee–length skirt). The edges of sleeves and the bottom of a shirt which is not tucked in are other good areas of placement for collage.

Other ideas of painting techniques for bands and borders include adhering natural materials, using lettering as design, and mixed media. Ideas for borders using motifs include African motifs, 17th century American quilt designs, pottery, embroidery, architecture, needlework, and mosaic work. (Fig.74, Fig.75, Fig.76)

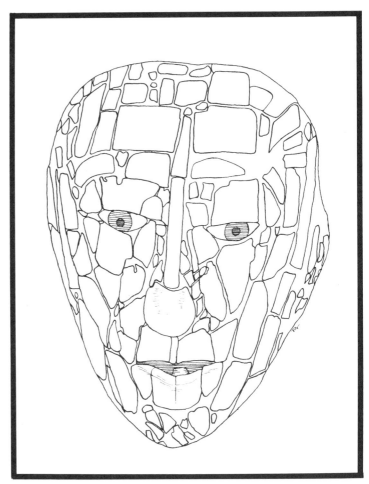

*FIG 64: (ABOVE) LAURA DALE MODELING MOSAIC-BORDERED POLYESTER PANTS.FIG. 65: (RIGHT) DRAWING BY PHYLLIS THOMPSON OF JADE MOSAIC MASK AS USED IN PANTS. AFTER **MEXICAN ART**-JUSTINO FERNANDEZ 1965*

*FIG. 73: **"COLOR STUDY"** – BY DOROTHY CALDWELL OF CONQUEROR WORM CRAFTS. COTTON WITH DYES.*

FIG. 78: SQUARED WORK BY THEODORA ZEHNER.
COTTON VELVETEEN IS SPRAY-DYED WITH PROCION
DYE.STITCHED INTO SPRAY-DYED RICE PAPER. ENTIRE
WORK STITCHED ONTO SPRAY–DYED UNTREAT–ED
CANVAS. 4 AND 1/2 ' BY 4 AND 1/2 '

FIG.76: (ABOVE RIGHT) CAROL PETRELLI MODELS
HALTER DRESS PAINTED WITH COLOR BORDERS.
VERSATEX PAINT ON COTTON.

THE SQUARE

Beyond the line is the square. As a design element, the square offers endless and untold possibilities. As four lines joined together, the square can contain about anything you wish to put in it. (See Fig.77) The square, like the border, reduces compositional problems as there is a defined space within which you may work. As a geometrical shape, the square foretells of the circle, the triangle, and shapes which blend into masses of color,with more specific composition. The square is a common design shape used by modern artists as well as in art history. (Fig.78, Fig.79)

Color squares are a basic design for the square. It is simply a square or squares filled with color. They can be either complementary or analogous colors. Color squares are good ways to practice mixing colors, and seeing the variations in different brands of the same color. You can use a ruler and colored pencils of the same color as the paint, to mark off the lines before painting. Masking tape or stencils could also be used. Color squares allow you to see all the gradations, shadings, and the relationships of different colors to one another. (Fig.80)

Color squares are also good for testing materials. By having a sample of each color with different paint materials, it is easy to see the durability and washability of the different materials. By having this information in one square, it is easy to choose the type paint or dye for a certain project.

Besides color, squares can contain brushstroke techniques, motifs, and simple basic shapes. Squares containing the same design, but drawn with different materials can be compared for clarity and the general effect of the design. Squares in general are simple designs in which to practice other design ideas before transferring them to a larger working space. Patchwork squares are another simple yet fascinating design idea. (Fig.81) Patchwork patterns originate in squares. Intricate samplers in needlepoint, embroidery, and lace are formed in squares. Macrame hangings formed in squares bring but the shape of the individual knots. Almost any design can be "put into" a square.

FIG. 77: "**GOOD EARTH QUILT**"–BY LINDA FISCHER. ACRYLIC TEXTILE PAINT ON COTTON. "EACH SQUARE WAS FIRST DRAWN WITH MACHINE STITCHING, THEN PAINTED TO GIVE IT THE FEELING OF A SOFT, WATERCOLOR PAINTING." (FROM ARTIST'S LETTER). 6 BY 7 FEET.

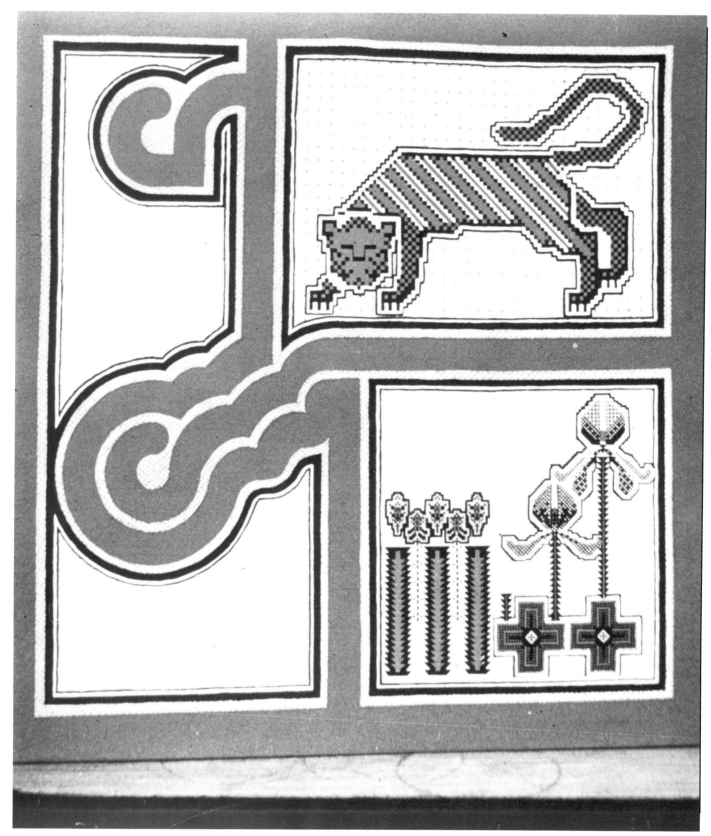

FIG. 79:"**CHINA TIGER**" –BY FRANCES BUTLER. AIRBRUSHED SILKSCREEN.

FIG. 81: "PAINT A QUICK QUILT"– BY FAITH MIDDENDORP. QUILTED COTTON PILLOW PAINTED WITH ACRYLIC PAINT. CIRCULAR SUN FACE.

FIG. 80: PIECED SILK--BY PHYLLIS MUFSON. PROCION DYES SHOW COLOR GRADATIONS.

FIG. 82: DETAIL FROM WRAP SKIRT--BY SUZANNE LARSEN. SUN FACE IN INKO DYE, ACRYLIC PAINT, OFF–WHITE COTTON. A COMMON CIRCLE MOTIF.

FIG. 83: CHAMOIS JACKET AND COTTON CULOTTES– BY K. LEE MANUEL. VERSATEX PAINT. BOTH TRIANGULAR AND CIRCULAR MOTIFS ARE REPRESENTED.

THE CIRCLE AND THE TRIANGLE

The circle and the triangle offer many interesting ideas which are not difficult for the beginning painter. (Fig.82–84) Like the square the circle is a basic form used throughout time. There is an entire philosophy behind these three forms. The circle has no beginning and no end. The circle is very important to the Hopi Indian, as it allows a multiple perspective upon something. (Their sandpaintings reveal this). It is the square which is the foundation for many of our modern cities, perhaps for our modern problem of isolation. Alternative ways of building (the tipi, yurt, igloo, and other circular spaces) change as well the way we relate to each other. The triangle has also come to be seen as more than just three connecting lines. Many books on pyramids explore the power inherent in this shape. The ***connotations*** of these three shapes (the square, circle, and triangle) are many and can be explored and incorporated into fabric painting. It is this connotative meaning which is one of the strengths of fabric painting; it is more than just a decoration of lines, squares, circles, and triangles.

Getting beyond these defined shapes, there are more random divisions of space which evolve in simple and beginning ideas. After you feel comfortable with defined shapes and spaces, it is possible to move on—to the scattered motif, lines across the fabric, general layout compositions from works of art, and freehand painting.

FIG. 84: WALL HANGING--BY K. LEE MANUEL. INKO SILK–SCREEN RESIST IS HANDPAINTED ONTO FABRIC.

THE SCATTERED MOTIF

The scattered motif is an excellent design idea with versatility when used with fabric painting. This is due to the great variety within unity possible with painting. For example, a repeat motif of a flower,when fabric painted, can be many different colors, shapes, and sizes, yet all are considered a flower. Any motif or image which is of one kind or type, that also has great variety **within** the type, can be used in this way. Shells, birds, plants, trees, microscopic animals, bicycles, and boxes are some possible ideas.

LINES ACROSS THE FABRIC

Lines across the fabric is simply carrying a line from one side of the fabric to another, in a creative and interesting way to form a design. Copying composition layouts from works of art is a good way for beginners to learn the basic rules of composition. By using works of art, good combinations of form, shape, and color, can be used. Yet there is no danger of copying, as only the general layout is used as a guideline. Freehand painting lets go of any preconceived idea of a design. One simply begins painting; lines form, colors appear. Freehand painting can be a delightful loosening of the mind, letting the hand supplant the brain.

As has been seen, beyond the square, the circle, and the triangle are less well–defined forms, as well as masses of shape and color which lend themselves well to the movement of cloth. These are painted with more spontaneity of the brush and less mental preparation, and this approaches the mood of fabric painting, the interaction and movement of cloth and brush. But how to approach fabric painting itself? This we shall examine next.

"The creative artist does not need a direct external influence. The work he has created is for him an internal experience—like a natural phenomenon that has made him internally richer, but externally is not necessary for him. If he does not have it, he will still realize his dream in one way or another, as long as the dream remains alive within him." So spoke Kandinsky. People approach painting in different ways. As well as technique, it is a good idea to have some awareness of how you approach painting. Are you calm, excited, sure as to what you will do, uncertain, etc? Being aware of a mood is helpful for deciding what type of painting to approach. Two problems which I have encountered are balancing spontaneity and planning. I need to be sure that I am in the mood for using certain colors, working with certain types of designs. I have struggled with forcing myself to paint, which is not a good idea, as painting is more than good technique, it is expressing feelings and thoughts which form from a certain personal mood. A mood can be harnessed and used, rather than being disciplined into hiding. Another problem which concerns me is dealing with the number of distractions which occur to me while doing a certain painting. One beginning idea inspires many others, and it is difficult to keep a unity about the work. In this case, some planning and discipline is helpful. One practical idea is to do sketches previous to painting. Further ideas can be sketched or jotted down for later paintings.

Being conscious of what you are thinking and feeling while painting allows you to go back to a certain mood if you are in the middle of a large painting. Certain kinds of painting lean more towards definiteness, while others depend upon a fragile equilibrium of mood. Painting, like other art forms, can be approached cognitively or intuitively. As one learns the basics of design and composition, cognitive painting becomes easier; for the beginner, however, an intuitive approach utilizes things already familiar. As well as painting what you feel, you can become aware of certain colors and shapes which are more definite statements of what you ar trying to express. This perception is extremely valuable in painting, and its growth will allow you a more direct expression of your feelings. This evolution of perception accounts for a paintings' change and growth. Fabric painting, unlike fabric printing, is re–evaluated over time: the painting can be changed and developed. It grows in its own time, rather than being "preplanned and pasted" on the material.

Painting from music, and from your dreams, are two good ideas for beginners. This type of painting forms as the imagery and symbolism of the mind is yielded up for examination. The most important thing in an expressive art such as fabric painting is that the artist can constantly be aware of the art as expression of her being. One is painting the inner world, and, as is the inner world, so is the interpretation and expression of the outer reality.

THEME AND VARIATION

Another basic approach for a beginning painter is to paint one idea with variations. "Theme and variation" is a method much used by musicians, and can be a model for fabric painting. For example, one motif could be the theme,with variations in size, shape, color, and placement. This need not be used only on one particular garment: one idea can be explored in one painting, and further varied and expressed in other garments. Sometimes this will form a set of clothes, much like mix–and–match clothing. I find the idea of theme and variation very valuable in fabric painting, as it is possible to keep growing with an idea through various pieces of clothing. For example, in working with a pottery motif, I want to explore it not only on pants and top, but on a skirt, fancy shirt, shorts, etc. As well, I want to experiment with it in various places on the garment to see which gives the best overall effect.

A question which is very important for the beginning fabric painter is "fabric painting for whom? and what?" In Chapter I, we spoke of painting as an art, and as a craft. It is helpful when approaching fabric painting to decide which type you are going to do. As well, a fabric painting could be categorized into fabric painting for general sewing, or for a clothes designer/artisan. Each of these categories emphasizes certain features or fabric painting, and so will be described.

SELLING AS CRAFT

If you wish to paint T–shirts and sell them to friends or at a craft fair, the type of design ideas useful for this would be quite different from a one–of–a–kind garment sold at an exclusive store. Yet both of these could be construed as selling in bulk— in that you are the supplier of painted clothing. It is challenging to sell really complex hand–painted clothing at regular craft fairs, because of the time and cost involved. It is helpful, then, to sort out the type of painting done for crafts and the crafts market, from that which will demand a higher price, and is usually construed as the art (or professional crafts) market.

Painting done for simple craft selling should be able to be executed in a few hours. For some people, this might be brightly striped clothing in watercolor with wide brushes, for others it might be abstract shapes, for others it might be rather intricate drawings. Painting for crafts should be either compositionally simple, or a repetition of one basic type of composition. Again, this does not mean compositionally simplistic design, but rather that the design is independent from the garment form, or less involved with the design of the garment form, and therefore a more simple composition. The repetition of one basic type of composition means that it is easier not to jump around from one type of composition to another. If you are working with intricate designs around the collar and frontispiece, vary the type design from garment to garment, but remain with the basic placement. This is a good learning device as well, for only by painting on different types of garments (shirts, skirts, pants, etc) can the most effective design and garment form be discovered. Other good ideas for crafts painting are the theme and variation, which has been mentioned before, and making fabric yardage.

Fabric yardage entails painting a large piece of fabric which can be cut up into different pattern pieces. It is important that the design idea be such that the material can be identifiable as one piece when it is cut up, without it being as repetitive as a printed piece of material. To do this, similar type designs or certain groups of colors can be used over a large piece of fabric. Think of the characteristics of other types of fabric muslin and cotton, creamy and white like sand, rougher homespun like sand and sawdust, cloth like the bark of trees. Paint is liquid color, and beautiful fabrics can be made, with bright colors, liquid flowers, flowing greens. When considering painting fabrics, think of the relationship of cloth and air; the way air moves across a dress could be painted as the way air moves across a field or wheat. Fabric yardage allows one to concentrate only on design ideas without considering how the design adapts to the garment form. Some themes for fabric yardage could be stained glass window fabric, fabric for earthdresses, circle fabric, wooden fabric.

Special orders are another aspect of crafts selling. If you have difficulty thinking of good ideas for fabric painting, but have good painting technique, special orders can be a good learning experience, as you are executing other peoples' design ideas. However, if you have difficulty in visualizing anothers' idea, special orders may be difficult to execute. One possibility is to have a notebook with samples of designs, which you would be willing to make in a larger or smaller size, or in a different area on someone's clothing. Many people have favorite clothing which they would like to have painted, rather than buying a whole new garment. As well, it is not then necessary that the fabric painter also be a good sewer.

SELLING AS ART

Professionally executed fabric painting is in great contrast to fabric painting for simple crafts. Time, cost, prices, and customer ideas are irrelevant, as the painting is done for the paintings' (and your) sake! Usually this type of fabric painting uses a majority of new and original ideas or combinations of ideas. It means getting the design idea and the design of the garment form as congruent as possible. This type of painting is in total contrast to the squared–off design placed in the middle of a T–shirt.

Fabric painting is also oriented towards those who sew; in fact, sewing is almost as important in fabric painting as is painting, due to the importance of the garment form in the total effect of the painting. Sewing can be divided into general sewing, those who can sew basic and contemporary type clothing; and the designer/artisan of clothing, who does pattern drafting, creating original patterns, and who is capable of sewing intricate and difficult forms. The greater the skill in sewing, the greater the flexibility in fabric painting. People who are limited to T–shirts and manufactured clothing miss the excitement not only of creating original designs in sewing, but in the **combination** of painting and clothing. (One solution to this is if you can't sew, work together with someone who can) Tucks, ruffles, big collars, and pockets all lend themselves to interesting painting ideas due to their shape on the garment. To do this effectively, some knowledge of basic design as it relates to clothing and sewing is helpful.

BASIC DESIGN FOR FABRIC PAINTING

Basic design for fabric painting is different from regular basic design in art. There are a number of reasons for this. First of all, the plane in fabric painting is different from that of both drawing and painting in that it is not always flat due to the movement of fabric. In other words, seeing a design on a piece of cloth is a multi–dimensional experience due to the cloths' flexibility in space. Seeing a design on paper or canvas is usually a one–dimensional experience as it is only in one plane at a time. Also, when fabric painting for clothing, a person is working, simultaneously, on a two and a three dimensional plane. This is due to the fact that, although when painted, the painting is flat, it becomes three dimensional when formed into clothing. This can be a challenging aspect of fabric painting, as it is not always easy to tell what a two–dimensional design will look like in three dimensions. Gathers or pleats also change the two–dimensional flat image in a variety of ways. Lastly, the design elements will be viewed at different angles and distances, due to the form of the body and how close or far the viewer is to the body and the clothing. All of these facets must be considered when learning about regular basic design, and changed or modified for basic fabric painting design. It will first be helpful to understand some beginning ideas in basic design.

When we are first learning to see, we don't see specific objects such as a table, or a house. We learn to attach labels, and see **things,** rather than images. This learning can be replaced with a perceptual sensitivity to elements such as color, shape, texture. The basis for much artistic activity lies in the seeing of images. As well, it is important that ones' painting not be pushed artificially in this direction, but allowed to grow naturally without being overworked. These are two ways in which basic design is used in painting to clarify our perception, to balance our painting Line, shape, space, texture, and color are five basics of design. (Fig.85)

Line can be used as a division of space. Line can be used in and of itself for abstract and representational design. Line can also be used as a space–divider. This is particularly helpful to achieve a better composition on a large piece of fabric. Sometimes it is easier to handle a large area of space by dividing it into smaller areas of space. Line is thin, even at its thickest. Line is thin and running, easily excitable, going places, going through and around and back. Line travels. Travel with a line—see where it takes you !

Shape is not so energetic as line. Shape is slower, bigger. Shape is still movement but it is a more placid movement. Line runs around and where it connects, it becomes shape. Shape is symmetrical or asymmetrical. Line in relation to space is symmetrical or asymmetrical, but of itself it has no symmetry. Shape in relation to space creates more shape.

Space is. It is especially important in fabric painting to have enough space—to spread out and see all the material and all the line and shape at one time. Space connects all the interplay of line and shape; it delineates where there is harmony and balance in this interplay. Space is the invisible material without which there can be no design.

Texture is both one and two–dimensional. Texture can be printed and stamped onto fabric. Networks of line resembling lace, the veins of leaves, molecular structures, are all textural to the eye though they do not rise above one dimension. Texture is: a raised pattern woven in a fabric and sand mixed into the paint and shells glued onto the fabric. When the shells are painted over with blue paint, we may see shells under the ocean or we may see blue shells. When they are only glued on the fabric, their shape, texture, and color become apparent.

Color as we know it is totally dependent upon the light. And with the light there are far more colors than we have names for.

These are the basic elements in design. They mix and intermingle upon the surface upon which they are placed. One sees the different moods of line how line has more energy than shape. Shape moves more slowly through this world of space. Line and shape move horizontally over the fabric, texture stretches upwards, reaches downward, sometimes simultaneously. Color, though on the fabric, exists in another dimension, breathes a more rarified air. Color is white light, the focus of the spectrum, the separation into itself (color), the merging of color into light.

Line, shape, texture, and color can all be used is ways to divide space. Shapes which are interesting in themselves as well as interesting in relation to clothing are good divisions of space. Lines can go from one side of the fabric to the other, or loop continuously around each other. (Fig.86–89)

These are the units of design, and these five elements will be used in various configurations both two and three–dimensionally. It is easiest if they are examined first in a two–dimensional way.

One easy way to learn how to fabric paint is by using already printed fabrics as inspiration. Take samples of some of your favorite fabrics and try hand painting their designs. Then evaluate your work. For example: are the designs too small to be painted neatly? Do they need to be drawn first? Is it difficult to keep the edges from bleeding? Magic markers, pen and ink, or colored drawing pencils could be used to draw the designs. If the paint bleeds, make it thicker by adding a medium. This technical knowledge allows you to paint a design which "works" on fabric and which has further interest by being hand–painted. Some beginning fabric painters' clothes look like they belong in a circus: the colors are garish, the designs, wild. Using already–made fabric as a guideline, there is less guesswork involved in how the two–dimensional fabric will look when made into clothing. Plus, if desired, you can paint something which looks conventional!

The inspiration from printed fabrics can be **direct,** in which case the painting copies the fabric. It is also possible to use the printed fabric as a basic guide, and include variations. The **repeat motif** lends itself well to this, as the gridwork of the repeat motif can be used, but the individual motif can vary. (Fig. 90) Another use of printed material is to actually paint **on** the printed material. The two can complement each other. (Fig. 91) **Modular unit painting** refers to a unit of space which is repeated over the fabric, but which has a larger design than the repeat motif. Fabrics with scenes from rural America, racing horses, or other designs with abstract shapes of various sizes and colors, are examples of what I would call modular unit design. The smaller the modular unit, the greater the freedom in cutting shaped pieces. As the modular unit becomes larger, it becomes more dependent upon its placement in relation to the garment form. For example a large splashy design must harmonize with the lines of the garment in order to be effective. (Fig.92)

Beyond the modular unit is the asymmetrical design. This type or design begins to lean in the direction of composition, as it is less dependent upon one variable for its success. Repeat motifs, modular unit painting, and direct copying from printed materials assume some constancy in the design. An asymmetrical design does not balance and harmonize a design in the way a symmetrical one does. When there are many variables in the creation of a design, there is greater dependence upon the rules of composition. Composition as it applies to fabric painting and especially with consideration of clothing is an important aspect of basic design. There are many things to be considered when designing a garment, as it **becomes** three–dimensional on the body, but is a two–dimensional piece of cloth while painting. The more traditional ways of fabric decoration, with their dependency on the repeat motif, de–emphasize some of the problems encountered when painting asymmetrical non–repeat designs. However, there are ways of designing such a garment so that it remains primarily a two–dimensional surface.

One of the easiest ways to diminish compositional complexities in fabric painting is by keeping the garment form as two–dimensional as possible: in other words, simple, basic forms. Garments which are well–fitted to the body, made with darts and pleats and shaping, may change the design in unexpected ways. Garments which resemble squares, such as

FIG. 85: DRAWING BY JUDY BUSK ILLUSTRATING LINE, SHAPE, SPACE, AND TEXTURE.

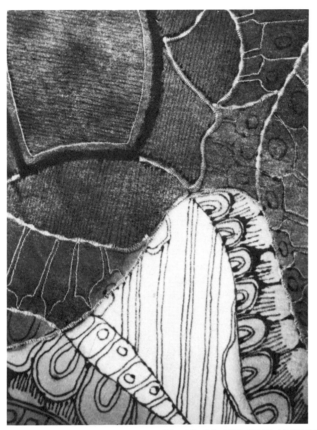

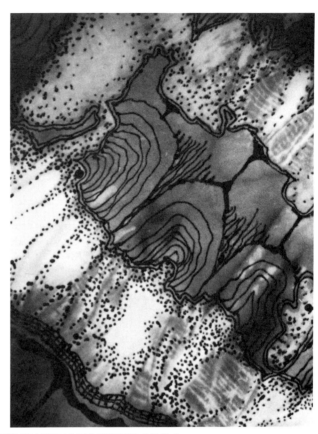

*FIGS. 86–89: TIE–DYE AND DIRECT APPLICATION BY JOETTA UMLA.
THIS IS A WONDERFUL EXAMPLE OF THE CREATIVE USE OF THE LINE.
LOOK HOW JOETTA'S LINE LOOPS AROUND, DOTS, SQUIGGLES, AND
SHADES IN THESE FOUR EXAMPLES.*

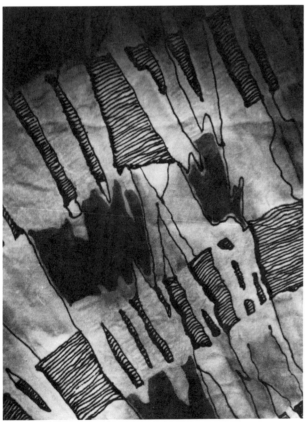

the kimono and the huiptl, are good for compositional painting. Garments which hang two–dimensionally, such as an A–line skirt, an A–line dress, a simple square shirt, a T–shirt, and a straight skirt, are basic conventional garment forms which work well. A gathered skirt, made from a square of material, can be good if the design is not so detailed that it would be lost in the gathers. However, a gathered skirt is a good garment form to experiment with for more complex composition as the gathers sometimes can, in an unexpected way, change the composition for the better. Wrapped clothing is also good in that it is formed from long rectangles of cloth, and how it is wrapped in part determines the design.

Another approach regarding 2/3 dimensionality is for the fabric painter to use flexible compositional approaches. If composition is based on all parts of the design working together in a fixed way, one mistake is disastrous as it alters the total work. Flexible composition allows for the design to be work-able with a greater number or changes, intentional or not. Fabric painting is especially suited to flexible composition, due to the flexibility of fabric and the wide variety in garment forms.

Fabric can be manipulated and its shape be changed by cutting, tearing, and pulling its fibers. Cutting is by far the most common way to shape and form fabric, either by cutting it apart from a length of fabric, or by sewing small pieces together to form a length of fabric. As regards to fabric painting, a length of material can be painted, then cut, either into garment shapes, or into other shapes. These shapes can then be resewn together to form the garment or a length of fabric. If at any point the composition is undesirable, it can be changed by more cutting and more sewing. Fabric can also be cut and glued or sewn over other parts of the fabric if one wishes to change a design. The opposite progression of cutting the fabric, then painting and sewing it, can also be used. In this way, either the garment pattern pieces are cut and painted, or other random shapes are cut and painted. This is much different from painting a large square piece of material, as the design cannot help but be affected by the shape of the material. Sewing is as important a compositional tool as is cutting, and it is as flexible. There is an excitement about taking a group of individually painted pieces, sewing them together, and seeing their effect.

Another flexible compositional approach is taking the gar-ment form and placing other pieces of material on the garment, thus forming a design. This is similar to collage or applique, except that the material is not glued or sewn onto the material. This is a very flexible approach to composition, as you can change the position of the pieces as often as is necessary to create a satisfactory design.

Fabric does not have to be the only material used. Paper is a common and effective design tool. **Torn–paper** designs have an extra spontaneity about them, as the paper is randomly torn and its edges show the result of the tearing. **Cut–paper sym-metry** is best exemplified by the popular cut–paper snowflake. Other shapes and sizes of paper can be used with folded cut–paper designs. For example, take a rectangular piece of paper, fold it four times, then cut designs (slashes, triangles, curved shapes) along the edges and in the folds with scissors. When you unfold the paper, you can trace the designs onto fabric— or paint through them, using the paper as a stencil. As was described above, paper can be used as fabric was, with paper shapes being laid onto the fabric for the design.

Another way paper can be used is as a stencil or template. Randomly cut–paper designs are placed on a large piece of material, and moved around until harmony and balance are seen, and the design is complete. They are then outlined with

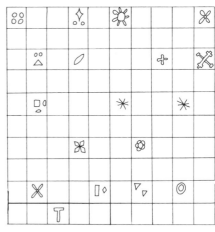

FIG. 90: DRAWING OF THE PRINCIPLE OF GRIDWORK. FIG. 91 (BELOW) KAREN LEEDS MODELING PRINT TOP WITH PAINTED AREAS. FIG. 92: KAREN LEEDS MODELING SKIRT WITH MODULAR UNIT PAINTING.

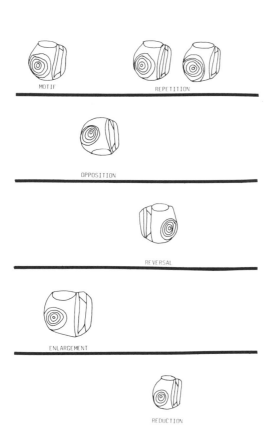

FIG. 93: VARIATIONS OF A DESIGN THEME

colored pencil, removed, and the design is completed by painting or drawing. These cut–paper designs can also be used like a stencil, in which the area **surrounding** the template is painted before removing the template. (This is a type of reverse stencil: regular stenciling will be discussed in Chapter VI)

Regardless of how you approach basic fabric painting design, it is important to understand and remember the principle of organic growth in basic design. Organic, as opposed to synthetic growth, deals with timing. In organic growth there is a regard for the natural evolution of a design. Sometimes you may have the feeling that a design must be completely worked out, under control, before or during painting, in order to be successful. This may be rushing the creative process forming. in your mind—which is creating the design. Allow yourself to leave a painting when it does not feel good to be working on it. Psychologically, you may need time to reorganize, rethink out certain aspects. Don't begin with too rigid of an idea, rather give it room for growth.

By understanding what is the core of the design, it is possible to let that core expand and grow. The core of a design may be a certain horizontal–vertical placement, it may be a certain configuration of lines. The core may be expanded through repetition; variations such as enlargement, reduction, opposition, reversal, are also possible. (Fig. 93) Most of all, organic growth in basic design is a philosophy, letting elements reveal themselves rather than being forced into awareness. And along this same line, it is important that one's inner vision of a painting or design never be subjugated to hard and fast rules of basic design. Basic design is a tool, meant to help the inner vision be revealed. It must always be subordinate to the creative design idea, in order that the design idea evolve naturally rather than being artificially manipulated.

An artist's sketchbook is a good place to jot down design ideas—fragments which are unformed and which can be synthesized over time into workable designs. A sketchbook is also a wonderful place to try out various design ideas, without taking the time to make up the entire garment or object in fabric. I use a hardcover empty book and good quality colored pencils which record my designs neatly and preserve them for future use. If a particular color scheme interests me, I'll sketch it out in various forms without needing to develop it further as a complete design. Later, I'll look back and reflect on which combination is most effective. By working over a design in a sketchbook, the fabric painter can refine her/his design and therein paint more satisfying projects!

THE PAINTING ENVIRONMENT

The last consideration for a fabric painter beginning to paint is the painting environment. The painting environment is where you paint, what you paint with! It is the physical layout of your painting area as well as the containers for paint and where to lay your material. I cannot overemphasize the importance of a well–planned painting environment due to its direct effect upon the type and quality of fabric painting done. For example, if you are painting on a table that is too high or too low, your hand will soon tire and that will effect your painting. Certain painting techniques will not even work without the proper amount of space or a certain kind of table.

There are a number of features in the painting environment: the painting surface, space requirements, the storage of paint, and the permanence of a working space. There are a number of general rules for the painting environment. The painting surface should be flat and sturdy. It can be fixed or movable. Tables of various sizes, drawing boards, large pieces of cardboard boxes (such as those found behind grocery or department stores) work well. I have found that the key to good painting is having a variety of kinds of surfaces. Cardboard which can be leaned against a wall and tilted at various angles works well for certain effects, such as long vertical brushstrokes, dribbling paint, and watercolor, however, it can become tiresome for detailed drawing. Simple arrangements seem to work better than adjustable artist or architect table simply because painting on fabric can become messy, and a flexible working surface will work for different projects.The kitchen table will work well for many beginning projects. A large work table is better when working with big pieces of material. Marking pens, embroidery paints, crayons, and acrylic paints need less working room than dyes, mordants, or oil–based textile paints, since with the latter, there is a greater need for more bottles to mix in, separate containers for chemicals, and in the case of textile paint, a lot of ventilation.

The painting surface should always be covered (preferably with butcher paper or newspaper) so that the paint will not soak through to the table. In fabric printing, many books suggest padding the surface with cloth before putting on the fabric, but I find that this is a hindrance in fabric painting and, especially for drawing, a firm surface is needed to get precise renderings. Newspaper is readily available and works well with all paints except acrylics, which must be watched so that the paint does not dry and stick, along with the newspaper, to the fabric !

Space requirements in fabric painting vary with the type of paint used, the amount of fabric used, and the type of painting technique used. Many things can be made with just small sturdy supports—things such as intricate or small drawings and paintings, with acrylics, marking pens, or fabric crayons, for example. As well, working on small or average sizes of cloth allows one a smaller working space. (Fig. 94)

There are other types of painting, such as spatter painting, painting with large house painting brushes, or painting on hanging lengths of fabric, which need large amounts of room. Painting such as this needs, first of all, a large painting surface, plus room to move around that surface, plus an area to spread out the paint and brushes, as well as areas to lay large amounts of fabric to dry. A garage or basement with a cement floor is good for this, in that nothing can be damaged by paint. In general, there is enough room in the average house to do most fabric painting, but keep in mind what types of painting need what type of room. (Fig. 95)

If you do not specifically plan for it, your paint and equipment can take up more than half of the nice large table you procured from your neighbor for fabric painting ! It is necessary to have your paints close by—for convenience, to avoid having to move around a lot while painting, and to avoid dripping paint or dye on the fabric. As well it is nice to have a variety of brushes at hand. A portable surface, such as a plastic tray, is good for materials and paints, as it can be close to the working area without danger of spilling, and it can be easily moved from one area to another. A moveable cart is nice when working on larger pieces of fabric, fabric which is hanging up to be painted, fabric on an easel, and fabric on any vertical or semi–vertical surface. A moveable cart allows you to move around the area with both hands free for painting.

Areas for drying are important. You may need: large flat areas (basement floors are good) for still–wet dyed fabrics, clotheslines and drying racks for painted clothes and semi–dry dyed fabrics, and grass or cement outdoors for special sun effects with Inkodye. Be sure to use newspaper or plastic sheeting beneath the fabric to avoid dye or paint seepage. It's also a good idea to varithane a drying rack so that dye and paint will not soak into the wood, which can stain wet fabric laid upon it.

Chairs and stools of the correct and comfortable height are important. Please, do not use a chair of incorrect height, as it will cramp your hand, your arm muscles, and surely your painting.

Ventilation and light are the last two physical features of the painting area. Ventilation is especially important when working with textile and oil paints, as turpentine or a turpentine derivative is used with the paint. Always have a source of fresh air when using oil based fabric paints. Natural light, without being bright or glaring, is best for painting. A bright artificial light close to the painting area will also work.

Most of the above requirements are easy enough to plan without a lot of effort. However, the caring and mixing of paint can be more challenging, especially the cold–water dyes. Marking pens, fabric crayons, and embroidery paints need no containers and so there is no problem there. Textile paint, as well, comes mainly in a jar, so there is no problem with paint storage. Oils come in tubes, and should be mixed up separately each time as they are mixed with turpentine or textine for fabric painting, and those materials are too volatile to be left safely sitting around.

Acrylics come in tubes or jars. The tube paints can be stored after mixing in small glass jars. If you mix the colors on a palette,

FIG. 94: DRAWING OF PAINTING ENVIRONMENT IN A SMALL APARTMENT. BY KAREN HAMILTON.

FIG. 95: DRAWING OF THE PAINTING ENVIRONMENT WITH A LARGE AMOUNT OF SPACE. GARAGE AREA WITH LARGE TABLE AND MOVABLE TRAY. BY KAREN HAMILTON.

water can be added to them overnight,and then plastic wrap should be tightly wrapped over the top of the palette. Some people have success when using tube paints with Styrofoam cups and plastic wrap, but I find that the paint dries out in approximately a week. It is best to use the premixed acrylics that come in bottles for any extended use. However, I do like the choice of color mixing possible with tube paints.

It is also very important to have a variety of shapes and sizes of containers for the mixing of paint, so that you are not limited to certain types of painting techniques with certain size brushes. Large and small bowls, cups, plates, sheets of glass, and the traditional palette are all well used in fabric painting. It is, as I said before, important that the paint does not get in the way of the painting. A work space cluttered with bottles and jars of all shapes and sizes does not allow for free spontaneous painting. A moveable tray or cart minimizes this clutter.

Several other topics should be mentioned. There are a number of supplies and tools that can be used in conjunction with fabric painting. Some of these are especially necessary as they will ensure the artists' safety.

Plastic extruders, metal–tipped applicators, and transfer pipettes are all used to make fine lines with dye. You can buy plastic bottles to store dye, plastic beakers to measure chemicals, and an eyedropper to measure small amounts of dye. A balance scale is also useful to measure out dye and chemicals. Transfer pencils and pens are helpful when transferring designs,while a fine–tipped permanent pen is available for signing your work.

There are many types of palettes which can be used. You can buy disposable mixing trays, disposable waxy paper palettes, muffin pans, egg cartons, as well as a regular oil painting palette. Stretchers are available to help keep fabric taut. Bamboo stretchers, called shinshi, wooden batik frames or just wooden frames, embroidery hoops,and Japanese end clamps, called hariki, are all used as stretchers. Steamers are also very important when working with certain types of dyes. You can buy stovetop models that are either horizontal or upright. Upright ones also come with their own electrical element. Steaming paper is also available. A hot–water bath canner can be used as a homemade steamer.

A number of supplies are extremely important in minimizing hazards of art materials. A NIOSH–approved dust mask is available from many suppliers. Goggles protect the eyes from hot liquids and dye particles. Rubber gloves and a plastic apron protect the skin. Hand cleaning pastes will remove any dye accidently spilled onto your skin. Air respirators and window exhaust fans are very important when working with certain dyes and when airbrushing or spray painting.

A thorough listing of these supplies and other tools need for fabric painting are listed, along with their source of supply, in the companion book, ***1001 PRODUCTS AND RESOURCES FOR THE FABRIC PAINTER AND SURFACE DESIGNER–LINDA KANZINGER.***

The last big question about the painting environment is: how hazardous is it? How safe are the paints, dyes, and thinners that you are using? Do you have an adequate ventilation system? This topic is extremely important, primarily because it has only come to light in the past few years due to certain persistent investigators.

A large number of artists have contracted serious diseases such as kidney disease or cancer ***because*** they have been debilitated by the very materials they work with. Many artists are self–employed and therefore are not protected by regulations that protect factory workers using some of the same noxious products. As well, many art materials come under the category of "consumer" goods or professional materials rather than *industrial* materials. Again, industrial materials are, by law, forced to have warnings concerning their use if they are hazardous.

A third major problem is a political one. The art materials industry is balking at proper labeling of art materials, and hide under the excuse that they "need more information". The artists with chronic lead poisoning kidney failure, heart attacks, cancers of the lymph nodes or chest cavity, or mercury poisoning, don't need more information about the *hazards* of working with these material. What has been needed, and is being provided by activists like Michael McCann (see his book, *Artist Beware*–Watson–Guptill, for more information), is educational information so that artists can know what they are working with, whether or not it is hazardous, and how to best minimize the negative effects.

One of the problems with a lot of these materials is that they are not particularly hazardous if the body has a resting period to recuperate from the material ingested or inhaled. When an artist is working not just eight hour days, but sixteen hour days and nights, the body does not have time to "bounce back". It's this maximum exposure to many of the art materials which causes the hazard to one's health. As Sandra Longmore, a fiber artist from Washougal, WA, states, "Artists are athletes. We need to not live *only* in our heads and take care of our bodies— so they can keep going!" She describes a state which is probably common to many artists: that of being so absorbed in your work that you forget everything—including not staying in touch with your body and listening to its needs— needs for rest, for healthy living habits, etc. It's important as creative artists that we not push our bodies past their limit.

Which of this information is applicable for the fabric painter? There are two categories of art materials which are potentially hazardous: dyes, and the pigments in paint. There are problems with **fiber–reactive dyes**. The dye particles can react with the mucous membranes and with lung tissue. Allergies, tightness in the chest, asthma, and other respiratory ailments can occur if the dye molecules are inhaled. They should not be allowed to soak into the skin,either. The **washing soda** (sodium carbonate) which is used with these dyes is also corrosive to the skin and internal organs. **Direct dyes** (also known as household dyes) are very commonly used. They can be used with a thickener for fabric painting,and some of the colors are highly toxic. The darker shades contain benzidine or benzidene derivatives, which is a known carcinogen. Bladder cancer has been correlated to benzidine. **Acid dyes,** which can be used on silk and wool with a thickener for fabric painting, are also hazardous. They are a suspected carcinogen as liver cancer has occurred in tests on lab animals. **Vat dyes** and **basic dyes** have lesser risks involved, as they only seem to cause skin irritation. **Naphthol dyes** will cause severe skin irritation; other possible hazards of this dye are not yet known. **Pre–metalized** and **disperse dyes** should also be approached with caution, though I do not have specific information on them.

As well as the dye itself, the various chemicals used with the dyes can be harmful. **Lye** is used with Naphthol dyes with thickener. It is highly corrosive to skin and internal organs. **Glauber's salts,** which are used with thickened household dyes, is mildly harmful in that it causes diarrhea. **Glacial acetic acid** is used in the thickener for basic dyes. It is highly corrosive by skin absorption, inhalation, or ingestion. Vinegar is an acceptable substitute. **Gum tragacanth,** a popular thickener, may cause allergies, but is not nearly as harmful as **gum arabic (gum acacia)**. Inhaling gum arabic can cause asthma, other respiratory allergies, as well as skin allergies. Other chemicals, such as glycerin, tartaric acid, urea, sodium nitrate, ammonium sulfate, sodium alginate, and disodium hydrogen phosphate are also used with dyes, and they should be checked out as well for their comparative safety.

Paint pigments and thinners must also be examined regarding their potential hazards to the artist. **Mineral spirits** and **tupentine** are moderately toxic by skin contact and inhalation. Turpentine is fatal if ingested, and it can cause skin allergies. **Paint thinners** used with fabric paint and **textine** (used with oil paint) are particularly hazardous. If they contain either toluene or xylene, they are highly toxic. Proper ventilation is essential with their use.

Some pigments are suspected carcinogens. (See **Artist Beware** for a listing of safe and hazardous pigments). It is also important to realize that the so–called organic pigments can be as hazardous as the synthetic ones, as many organic pigments are now made in the laboratory from petroleum derivatives and are therefore suspicious It should also be remembered that many of the problems are caused by *chronic* ingestion of very small amounts of pigments. It is the ingestion of materials which causes most cancers and poisoning.

Use rubber gloves and a dust mask when dealing with dyes. A large plastic apron will protect your clothes and you might wish to wear a protective cap on your hair when working with dyes. Goggles will protect your eyes when working around dye powders or when airbrushing. A hand cleanser can be used to remove any dye or paint that gets on your skin, and a barrier cream can be used on your hands to protect them. For spray painting, a fume hood and a window exhaust fan are important because the pigments can remain suspended in the air for up to two hours, and chronic poisoning can occur.

Other important guidelines to follow are: don't eat or drink while working with paints and dyes. Don't let paint get in sores or cuts on your skin. Remember to wash your hands thoroughly after painting. Don't use kitchen utensils for painting and then use them again for food. And certainly don't ingest paint materials! *Do* use common sense while in your painting envi– ronment !

Another question to be asked in considering the features of a painting environment is, shall it be permanent or imperma– nent? Shall I paint on the dining room table, only to clean it off every night or should a special place be made only for fabric painting? If you plan to do a lot of fabric painting, the latter is probably a better idea, as dismantling a painting environment takes a lot of time. As well, a painting, in contrast with a design, is usually worked on over a period of time, and in this time, the artist re–evaluates the work, letting it grow and evolve. By having a place set aside, it is possible to let the paintings grow slowly. Then the artist need not feel rushed to finish them. Once the painting environment is understood and planned, it is easier to get involved in a greater variety of fabric painting, both in terms of kinds of paints and types of designs. These will be discussed in the following chapters, Chapter IV and Chapter V.

FABRIC PAINTING AND CONSUMERISM

■■

One of the things I've noticed lately is how consumeristic fabric painting has become. This is not good or bad, but I do want to make a few comments about it. A lot of the advertising about fabric painting and certainly the products advertising that I read about says that everything is so easy to do, all you need to do is to buy this or that and then you will have a finished product.

I've been painting for a long time. When I first started out, I always had a fear of that white fabric, particularly if it was a piece of clothing, because I knew that I had "one shot" to do it right. (Later I learned that pieces can be reworked by using discharge pastes, and dyes which strip or remove color from fabrics) It wasn't like drawing, where one could do seven rough sketches and work up to a finished drawing by the tenth. One could do that with ten silk scarves, but I think that is rather wasteful. So, as I started again with a number of these new products, I found that the first time I do something it doesn't necessarily come out where it is wearable art and I am going to show it to people. Instead, I have to toss it.

I ask myself how can I avoid this? My recommendation would be to use some old T–shirts and practice on these. When you get a design that you like buy a new T–shirt and paint on it. By then you will have practiced enough to be comfortable with the design. (The same end result can occur by practicing on old sheets or muslin fabric).

The second thing is to expect some loss. If you are buying a lot of new wearables and printables and new products and you have not painted very much, then you are going to have to expect some loss.

Another method is to **applique** a design painted onto cotton fabric onto a good T–shirt. In other words, cut the design after it has been painted and applique it onto your shirt. You can even shape the applique as a square and then just pop it onto the middle of your T–shirt. It will look very similar to popular silk–screened artwork that appears on T–shirts today. For the same reason, iron–on transfers are very practical, in that you can choose a design that you like, iron it onto a design that you like, and then "paint by number" and you are more than likely to get a pleasing result. That's a really good place to start for the beginning fabric painter who wants to begin wearing their beginning fabric painted creations!

■■

CONCLUSIONS

1) It is wonderful to have the choice of fabric painting products to use in fabric painting. Remember, however, not to get caught up in products alone, but remember also that pleasing techniques can be had with a small amount of paints and white cotton fabric.

2) When using printables or blanks or wearables, expect some loss, particularly if you are not already a practicing artist. If you are, then the chances are that you will already know more of what you are doing. However, for the non–artist, remember that it takes some time and practice to learn techniques for fabric painting. It is recommended that you practice first on old cotton sheeting and then when you are comfortable with certain techniques and designs paint them on wearables. Remember that the advertisers who say that "it's easy" don't at all mind if you have to keep coming back and buying more products— before you get that finished result! Do what works best for you.

4

MATERIALS- AND THEIR MESSAGES

"Each artist who is driven to express and create visual forms realizes the importance that his material has upon his response and his product. Identifying with a material enables him to create those forms with which he is involved. Some artists often feel it necessary to change from one media to another to complete an idea. Other artists, feeling an allegiance to their material, reject ideas that will not comply." **Bill Farrell**
AESTHETICS AND HISTORY OF ART

"I like to switch mediums. Each one has a totally different feel."
Mary Frank, sculptor
"Crafts Horizons"

Materials produce a variety of responses among its users. The importance of knowing the variety of effects of different materials in fabric painting cannot be overstated. Learning how paint materials react with various types of cloth is rather like learning a language; you are learning a "language" of materials. It is possible to have, after a period of time, a certain fluency in this language and you will know what types of effects are possible with a particular paint material.

There are a number of ways in which paint materials can be classified. Many of these classifications have polarities: from most popular and versatile, to limited use and limited exposure; or, high quality and expensive materials versus budget materials producing lesser quality. Materials can be categorized as those which are simple to use versus those which are complex.

Some of the more popular paint materials used in fabric painting are textile paints, acrylics, and the many fiber–reactive cold water dyes. Dye pastels and fabric markers are also popular. There are other paint products and regular art materials which can also be used. In some ways they are marginal and limited in use, yet they can be perfected within the limits of their usage. These include inks, marking pens, embroidery paints, natural dyes and paints, mordants, fabric crayons, silkscreen inks, linoleum block print inks, and latex or enamel paints.

High quality paint materials, such as some of the textile paints and silk dyes, produce excellent results. Especially when they are used in combination with high quality fabrics, such as silk or some of the mail–order cotton fabrics, it is hard **not** to create something beautiful. Since the quality of material used affects the result, it is true that using inexpensive materials will sometimes create slightly lower quality effects. What is important about this is to not expect "designer" effects when using muslin and acrylic paint. Nevertheless, many fine, practical items can be made with these materials.

Paint materials also vary in their complexity or simplicity of use. Fabric crayons, dye pastels, acrylic paints, and some textile paints are relatively easy to use. Dyes, on the other hand, are quite complicated in their usage. There are many chemicals which must be used with dyes, and care must be taken in the handling of these dyes and chemicals.

Some paint materials are used exclusively for fabric or surface design. They include textile paint, fabric crayons, embroidery paints, fiber–reactive dyes, silk dyes, starch and wax resists, mordants, natural paints, silkscreen textile inks, and other printing textile inks. Other paint materials are regularly used in "art" painting, but can also be used for fabric painting. These include markers, drawing inks, pastels and craypas, acrylics, and oil paints.

There are so many types of paint materials for fabric painting that, rather than generalizing, I feel it will be more useful to walk you through each type and give you specifics of each particular brand. There are a number of issues that can be discussed with each paint material. Besides the issues mentioned previously (popular or varied use/limited use; high quality (expensive) / low quality ("budget"); and simplicity/complexity of use) there are other factors to consider. How does the paint material affect the hand, or feel, of the fabric? How washable is it? Is it best used for clothing or other items? What types of fabrics are best used with it? Is it slow, or fast, to use? Can one be productive and efficient using the paint material? What kinds of uses are there for the material? What kinds of things can be made with it? How lightfast is the material? How available is it? What are its weaknesses and strengths? Are there any special uses or special effects? And most importantly, how does one use it?

There are so many different kinds of paint materials for fabric painting that it is not possible for the fabric artist to gain expertise with all of them at once. Most artists experiment with them, and then choose several which fit their present needs. Remember also that what the advertisers say about a product is not always true. It helps to experiment with a new paint material to learn what it can do, as well as what it is promised to do!

NEW PAINT PRODUCTS:INTRODUCTION

With the new paint products available today, fabric painting has exploded in popularity. It is now very mainstream, and hand–painted and dyed clothing pieces are found in the malls, the shopping centers, the hobby shops, as well as in the wearable art galleries and boutiques. It is to the credit of the *diversity* and availability of the new fabric paints that this has come about.

There are a number of things to say about the New "1990's models" of fabric paints and dimensional paints. For one thing, almost all the products are nontoxic. They are safe for children. They are waterbase. They are heat set by aircure; no more ironing or baking in the oven! And many of them can be used on all types of fabrics, thus eliminating the need to differentiate between natural fibers and synthetics. Many manufacturers as well are offering lines of fabric paint and dimensional paint simultaneously, all in matching or compatible colors.

Technology is making possible many effects that were not previously possible. This includes metallic paints, puff paints, shiny paints. These new paints paint practically paint themselves! It is possible to make an effective looking design as a beginner, especially when working with sportswear and sweatshirts. The new paints, however, are more expensive. They come in small bottles with bigger prices but they do many wonderful things.

There are several broad categories of new paint products. **Dimensional paints,** one of the new categories, include paints such as **shiny;** (hard paint that dries and looks like a bead), **puff** (when heat–set, the paint "puffs" up); as well as a multitude of **glittery, iridescent, pearlescent, opalescent, metallic, matte, neon and fluorescent** paints. Dimensional paints come in a small squeeze bottle with a pointy tip on the end. They come out in a fine line which has enough consistency to stand "up" on the fabric, thus the name "dimensional paints".

Other new paints have been developed and marketed for specific needs, be they a select group of people, a certain technique, or a particular fabric. Certain paints have been created for specific types of fabrics. **Stretch paint** was developed specifically for use on fabrics such as Lycra and other sportswear fabric. Certain fabric paints, often with the word "Bright" in their name, are marketed for **dark fabrics.** An entire line of paint products has been marketed for **home decor and home interiors.** These include stencil paints, stencil tape, fabric paints, marbling paints, sponge painting, spray painting with dyes, and lacquer paints for floor cloths. **Paints for kids** are a big market, and there are many kits as well as specific paints for younger people.

Another big change in fabric painting products has to do with the creation of many new accessory items. **Printables,** or **blanks,** as they are sometimes called, are simply manufactured items of clothing ready to paint. These include a wide variety of sportswear without sizing or permanent press finishes that impede the painting process. **Sweatshirt art,** which utilizes many of the new dimensional paints, also includes the use of applique, foil art, as well as using glues, glitters, rhinestones and a myriad of other new items to be used with fabric painting.

Lastly, there is more sophistication in fabric painting, and the brushes, applicators, and accessory items for techniques such as **silk painting, marbling, stenciling, and rubber stamping** as well as just regular fabric painting have grown ever more wonderfully diverse. For this reason, I am adding in these new paint products, by type, *after* each regular section. For example, the new fabric paints can be found under "New Fabric Paints" following the discussion of other fabric paints. In cases where entirely new categories of products have been created, they will go under a separate heading. For example, "Dimensional Paints" follows "New Fabric Paints" and has its own separate section, since it is a new type of fabric paint.

PRODUCT TESTING

I have tried to test as many new paint products as possible. However, there were a small number of companies who did not respond to my request for a sampling of their new paint products. Weekly there are new products and I was not able to obtain all of them to put in this revised edition. In my companion publication, *1001 PRODUCTS AND RESOURCES FOR THE FABRIC PAINTER AND SURFACE DESIGNER* (The Alcott Press) I list *all* the paint products and accessories (including printables and blanks, and fabrics) that I am aware of that are used in fabric painting, as well as where to obtain them. I also list books, magazines, videos, schools & classes on fabric painting and surface design. As I obtain more new products and test them, they will first be added to additions of this new book under "New Products".

CATEGORIES OF NEW PAINT PRODUCTS

The following categories of paint products were tested and are described in Chapt.IV under New Products: **acrylic paints, fabric paints and dyes,** (many with lines of **iridescent, pearlescent, glittery, metallic, and shiny paint** as well as paints for **dark fabrics**), **paints manufactured for certain types of fabric,** including **fabric dyes for shoes and leather, accessory products (handbags, belts, etc); paints marketed for certain markets,** such as **paints for kids and products for home interiors; specialty paints** such as **fabric painting sprays and paints which change color, dimensional paints, dyes, dyes used in the microwave, silk dyes or paints, textile inks, and fabric markers.** Paints marketed for particular painting *techniques* such as **stencil paints and accessories, iron–on transfers, transfer paints and inks, rubber stamps, sponge paints and sponges, marbling dyes and materials,** will be covered in Chapter VI, under each technique.

Also there are new **brushes and applicators,** as well as there being the new category of **"printables" or blanks:** manufactured clothing for hand painting and wearable art. There is the category of **sweatshirt art.** As well, I am including non–paint items used in wearable art, such as **glues** and **glitters, rhinestones, beads, applique, foil art,** and other decorative items often used in conjunction with fabric painting.

ACRYLICS

Compared to oils, acrylic paint is a fairly new substance, coming on the market in the 1950's. At first painters who were used to the slow application and drying time of oils found that acrylics dried too quickly and thus upset their painting habits. As well, some of these painters did not like the brighter colors of acrylic paint as compared with oils. The industry responded by creating an acrylic retarder, which can slow down the drying time, and by marketing brands of acrylics that had resin bases, dried more slowly, and had colors closer to oils. Today, there is a new type of paint, called alkyds, which combines the smooth, creamy texture of oils with the quick drying time of acrylics.

Acrylic paint is a polymer tempers. Acrylics are waterbase

FIG. 96: DOUGLAS HENSLEY MODELS PAINTED T–SHIRT. ACRYLIC PAINT OVERDYED WITH PROCION.

BRANDS AND ACCESSORIES

There are a number of brands of acrylics out today. They include **Liquitex, Hyplar, Shiva, Aquatec, Permalba, and Atelier.** Shiva produces a resin–based acrylic called Signa–Tex, while Bocour produces another resin–based acrylic called Magna. They are sold in either tubes or jars. In tubes, they are concentrated, and last through many paintings, but you must spend time mixing each color batch. The jar colors are about the same consistency as textile paint, thick and creamy.

As well as the acrylic colors, you will find many other acrylic materials in the store. There is: **acrylic retarder,** which retards the drying time of the paint, **modeling paste,** for sculptural effects, **gloss medium** for gloss effects, **matte medium**, for matte effects, **gesso,** for application to canvas or wood surfaces, **acrylic resin,** which can be shaped into mosaic or sculptural pieces, and **gel medium,** a heavy bodied transparent gloss medium used in impasto work, for better mixture of colors, and for its adhesive properties. Many of these materials can be used in conjunction with fabric painting.

NEW ACRYLIC PAINTS

The newer acrylic paints are marketed either for regular artwork or for fabrics. This is why so many fabric paints are called "fabric acrylics" or "acrylic fabric colors". This merely designates that these *fabric* paints have an acrylic base. In general, if a paint is called a "fabric craft" paint, most likely it is an acrylic paint to be used on both fabrics and other surfaces.

I find that the new acrylics are a real pleasure to use in fabric painting. With the variety of brands of pre–mixed colors plus the addition of fabric mediums and extenders, acrylic fabric painting is easier than ever! While stiffness of hand is still an issue, practice with the paints and fabrics used can diminish this.

Accent Elegance manufactures **Country Colors Acrylic Paint,** and it is often used in fabric painting for stenciling, as well as decorative and folk painting. It is available in a 2 oz plastic bottle, as are all the below–mentioned acrylics. Because it does dry a little on the stiff side, it is best used for these techniques where small amounts of paint will be used. When thinned with water, however, it softens, and therefore can also be used with watercolor techniques. Along with **Accent Acrylic Essential Colors,** there are 99 colors, plus 13 metallics. Some of the colors include Sunkiss Yellow, Light Iced Tea, Purple Canyon, and Avon–on–the–Green. Like other acrylic paints, these paints are waterbase. They are available in most craft and art stores, and are moderately priced. Although acrylic paints do not need to be heat–set, it helps to press with a warm iron just to "finish" the piece. Look for **Judy Martin's Textile Medium** to be used with these Accent Acrylic Products.

Apple Barrel Colors Acrylic Paint from Plaid Enterprises is another popular acrylic paint which can be used on fabrics by adding the **Apple Barrel Fabric Medium.** However, these acrylic paints by themselves are sturdy paints that do not wash out. I like this paint very much. It is creamy in consistency, and is clear and crisp for different techniques. For opaque painting, the shapes are clear and crisp. When using a watercolor wash, the wash is even and smooth. Dry brush or stippling techniques are clear and precise when applied to fabric. In other words, there are a variety of techniques which work successfully with this acrylic paint. It is a waterbase paint, and only needs to dry overnight. It is readily available though Plaid Enterprises, as

and water repellant, which means that they are mixed with water before using, and, when dry, are waterproof. It is a plastic–base paint. It may crack or fleck off if twisted, which is why some T–shirts painted with acrylic paint do not last. When painting on knits, test first, and do not paint too thickly.(Fig. 96)

Acrylic paint is a wonderful material for the fabric painter! Especially for the beginning painter, acrylics are simple and easy to use with good results. The fact that they are waterbase is important, for solvents and thinners which can be dangerous, needing good ventilation, are not a consideration here. Since they are waterproof when dry,whatever you paint with acrylics will last for years and years. (The first skirt I ever made with acrylics is still in the same condition ten years later.) Acrylics are relatively inexpensive, and they are easily available in art stores. One can buy a wide range of colors without spending a lot of money. Since they are quick drying, painting experiments and products can be finished in a short range of time. Since beginners have a tendency to be impatient, wanting to see the results of their work, acrylics are a good beginner's paint material.

The basic drawback of using acrylic paint in fabric painting is that this plastic based paint does alter the hand of the fabric substantially. Depending on the brand that is used, acrylic can slightly stiffen or greatly stiffen the fabric used. Thinner fabric is prone to greater stiffening. As one learns how to more effectively use the paint, this problem can be lessened, but never altogether eradicated.

I have found that Aquatec acrylic paint is the least stiffening, Liquitex the most.(Fig. 97) As one learns to paint just the correct amount—not too thin, not too thick, the acrylic paint will not stiffen the fabric as much. As well, if you first paint, and then overdye with a fiber–reactive dye, the stiffening effect seems to lessen.

FIG. 97 : PAINTED BACKPACKS. SEWN BY BETH
BROWN. ACRYLIC ON CANVAS.

well as craft and art stores, and is inexpensive in price. Ther e are a variety of colors, including English Lace, Black, and Light Pink.

Ceramcoat by Delta: This is a very nice creamy pre–mixed acrylic paint in a bottle. It dries a little stiff but smooth on the fabric. It can be much improved by adding **Delta's Textile Medium,** which also makes the colors more transparent. It is a nice paint, with a good choice of colors. I suggest that you use it on casual clothing, such as T–shirts, as well as on heavier fabrics. When using it on more delicate fabrics, use lots of the medium to soften the paint and do not try to cover large areas. This paint is good for opaque work, as well as for stenciling.

Delta Gleams Ceramcoat: Gleams is the metallic line of Ceramcoat, and comes in silver, gold, bronze, etc. However, it is also very scratchy to the touch unless used with the **Textile Medium.**

Deco–Art Americana Acrylics: This paint is very nice and creamy, with good colors and good for stenciling. While not soft to the touch, it dries smooth on the fabric. I find it comparable to Ceramcoat by Delta. **Deco–Art Americana Dazzling Metallics** is also a nice metallic acrylic paint.

Folk Art Acrylics and Metallics: The colors are beautiful, the consistency is nice and creamy; therefore easy to work with. Folk Art acrylics can dry quite stiff and scratchy unless used with the **FolkArt Textile Medium.** I would suggest painting on fabric only when using this medium. Extra enhancement occurs when also using the **FolkArt Extender,** which softens the paints and makes them more transparent. The **Metallics,** when used by themselves only will dry quite stiff and scratchy. With these two mediums added to the paint, they can be painted on silk and will dry very soft and smooth. I especially would recommend the colors in the Metallic line. They are exceptionally full bodied and beautiful.

Duncan Decorator Acrylic Paints are also very nice. They are creamy and smooth, and dry without scratchiness. They blend well into the fabric. They come in Opaque, Pearl, and Metallic, in a variety of colors, including Christmas Red, Sunshine Yellow, and Cinnamon Stick.

Jo Sonja's Artist's Acrylic Gouache is a good paint for fabric painting, with the addition of her **Textile Medium**. It dries flat and fairly soft on the fabric.

Liquitex now markets pre—mixed concentrated **"Artist Color"** in regular shades, metallics, and even a small selection of dimensional paints, for painting on fabric as well as other surfaces. This is a very *nice,* soft acrylic paint. Their **metallic** colors are rich in color with a deep sheen. They also have **fluorescent** and **opalescent** colors.

Maxwell's MaxiColors Acrylic Craft Paint is another paint available for fabrics. It dries quite soft and smooth. On fabrics, the colors will be lighter than in the bottle, as they suggest using 1–2 coats. They come in 4 oz. bottles, and are quite economical.

Other new acrylic paints that I am aware of for fabric

painting but do not have include: **Wally R Premium Acrylic Artists Paint; Carnival Arts Haute Colors (fluorescent acrylics); Palmer Christmas Glitter Craft Paint; Palmer's Paint Pots (Glow–in–the Dark, "Neon", Fluorescent, Luminous, Permanent Acrylic, Fluorescent, & Metallic); Duncan Precious Metals Acrylic Craft Paint, Palmer Creative Touch Fabri–Acrylic Acrylic Paints, and Createx Acrylic Fabric Paints.**

ACRYLIC PAINTING TECHNIQUES

One of the most exciting aspects of using acrylics in fabric painting is the many types of painting techniques that can be used with acrylic paints and their accessories.

They can be used as an *ink,* for watercolor effects, as tempera, as impasto, as oil, in indirect painting, for many of the direct painting techniques, and for collage and other adhesive effects. To make an ink, polymer gel is mixed with water, and then the color is added until the right consistency is reached. A regular fountain pen with various ink tips works quite well. Paint that is the consistency of thin cream works well on smooth medium–weight materials. However, painting or drawing on a thin fabric will not make the design diffuse if the ink is made thick enough. The versatility of acrylic paint makes it easy to adjust the consistency of the ink to various types of fabric. In general, the thicker the fabric, the thinner the ink, and vice versa. A wash made from matte or gel medium can be laid down on the fabric (using water to thin it) before using the ink. This will stabilize the fabric and control capillary action.

The basic technique of *watercolor* is well used in paintings as the medium of water makes it easier to paint large areas of fabric. As well, watercolor techniques with acrylics produce fabrics that keep a fairly soft hand. Acrylic paint is also a good type of paint material to use with watercolor because the paint can be thinned with water to any consistency.

To get ideas for watercolor fabric painting, look at watercolors done on paper. Watercolor is nice on fabrics also because of the melting of one color into another, and the soft, shaded effects of color and tone. Watercolor washes can be used as backgrounds upon which you can draw. The backgrounds can suggest simple drawings such as birds flying over mountains, subtle landscapes. Watercolor stripes are another easy way to maximize blending of colors.

By adding less water and more paint, acrylics can be mixed to the consistency of *tempera;* by adding a greater amount of a medium, especially gel medium, it can become very thick and used as an *impasto.* Acrylic in jars is the consistency of tempera, and you can use it like tempera paint to get flat, smooth paint surfaces. Impasto can be created by building up layers of paint with a brush, by using a palette knife to slab on the color, or by carrying the paint in thick brushfuls to the cloth. *Modeling paste* can also be added to acrylic color for a very thick impasto.

Some *oil* effects can be used with acrylics, especially the resin–based acrylics such as Magna and Signa–Tex. However, this type of acrylic has a limited use with fabric painting. Drybrush effects work best, as the paint is thick and viscous.

Acrylics are unmatched for their *adhesive properties.* The gel medium can be used as a glue and will adhere to any surface other than an oily one. Fabric, paper, beads, seeds, lace, knitted and crocheted pieces, small pieces of fired clay (to produce mosaic–like structures), wood, bark, twigs, small stones and shells, yarns, buttons, and small beads and sculptures made from acrylic modeling paste can be glued to the fabric. (Fig. 98)

The adhesive quality of the gel allows one many possibilities in the area of collage. *Collage,* coming from the French word, collere, meaning "to glue", is a good source of inspiration for the fabric painter. Fabrics can be glued to other fabrics and used in wall hangings, curtains, and drapes. The gel can also be used to lift pictures from paper (slick magazine ads on heavy paper transfer well) onto cloth. The adhesive properties of acrylics make it easy to mix many small things into the paint. Sand, shredded paper or fabric, small rocks, crushed clay or leaves can be mixed with the paint. These ideas are better used for wall hangings than for clothing, as most of these mixtures cannot be washed. However, small beads or buttons made from acrylic modeling paste could be glued onto certain areas of clothing, such as the frontispiece of a dress.

Acrylic resin, like **acrylic modeling paste,** can be molded into small shapes and glued onto fabric. Acrylic resin needs to be poured into a pre–formed shape and left to dry. Regular modeling clay can be pressed into shapes on Saran wrap, then the clear resin, mixed with acrylic color, can be poured into these molds. These small plastic pieces are reminiscent of modern jewelry. Jewelry, stained glass, work with precious metals, and stonework in architecture could be inspirations for these techniques.

FABRICS USED

All of the above techniques show the many advantages of acrylic paint. The basic disadvantage, as mentioned before, is that acrylics will stiffen certain fabrics. The worst types of fabrics for this are stretchy knits, polyesters, lightweight cotton and other gauzy or thin fabrics, and fabrics with a heavy finish. As well, napped fabrics, such as corduroy, velvet, or wool, should not be used. Muslin canvas, poly–cotton, blue jean fabric, cotton duck, sailcloth, and canvas work well with acrylic paint. Plain white fabric works better than already dyed, or colored fabric. Close weave fabrics also work better than stretchy fabrics.

HOW TO USE

There are several other basic instructions needed for working with acrylic paint. It is very important to keep brushes in water at all times; otherwise the paint will harden and ruin the brushes. A friend of mine calls acrylic paint the insidious brush eater! Watercolor or sable brushes can be used for watercolor and light washes, as well as the lightweight Japanese brushes. All other painting can be done with oil or bristle brushes, and big household or housepainting brushes. Always wash your brushes in soap and water after using them.

Acrylic paint dries quickly; use a palette with a cover, or put Saran wrap over your palette to keep the paint from drying out while you are painting.

Acrylics do not need any setting to make them permanent. However, I like to iron the painted cloth with a warm or hot iron; this often smooths the paint onto the fabric. Acrylic painted fabrics should not be exposed to high temperatures nor rough handling. They can be washed in a washer and dryer, but I would suggest that all hand–painted clothing be handwashed.

Acrylics are a popular, flexible medium for fabric painting. They are especially good when painting very large projects, as they are economical and easy to use. There are no fumes, no complex heat setting, and they are waterbased, so that you just have to wash your hands after painting. To sum up their qualities, look at the chart below:

FIG.98: WALL HANGING WITH NATURE SCENE. PEN WITH ACRYLIC INK. ATTACHED ROCKS. SAND MIXED WITH PAINT FOR THE "RIVERBED".

Use: popular and flexible with versatile uses

Quality: medium quality art material

Price: economical

Ease of use: simple to use

Hand: fair to poor, depending on fabric used and skill of painting

Washability: excellent

Usage: for clothing and many other items—wall hangings, pillows, sheets, backpacks, quilts, toys, etc.

Fabrics used: Cotton, muslin, cotton blends, canvas, sailcloth, denim,duck

Productivity: Fast results,with good productivity possible

Availability: in art stores, hobby shops, fabric stores; readily available

Lightfastness: Excellent

How set?: no setting needed

STENCIL PAINTS AND ACCESSORIES

Stencil paints include acrylic and craft paint, but specific stencil paints are also manufactured. **Accent's Acrylic Country Colors, Accent Fabric Colors, and Folkart Acrylic paints** are some familiar and popular acrylic paints which can be used for stenciling. **Adele Bishop's Water Base Stenciling Fabric Paint** is a good consistency stencil paint with 23 different colors, including Pewter Blue, Flag Red, and Burgundy. These paints give a "soft" appearance to the work. They can be used on all fabrics except wool and fabrics treated with a finish. They are heat–set by ironing with a dry iron for three minutes and are moderately priced.

Stencil brushes are available at most art supply stores. Some brands are **Loew–Cornell Jo Sonja Stenciler brush, Loew–Cornell Jackie Shaw Liner #2, and Adele Bishop Golden Stencil Brushes** Also important in making your own stencils is the **Hot Knife Stencil Cutter,** from Adele Bishop. A good stencil brush will offer firm enough bristles for control yet enough flexibility to maneuver into small spaces.

Delta Stencil Dye is a thicker dye product especially made for stenciling. It comes in 22 different colors. These waterbase textile paints are colorfast and all are intermixable.

Heat Setting: Most solvent based stencil paints will be heat set, by ironing with a dry iron, usually for 10–15 minutes. Waterbase acrylic paints do not need heat setting.

There are a number of other stencil paints available which

I have not yet tested. These include: **Delta Stencil Paint Creme (and Magic Stencils) Gick Stencils and brushes, Adele Bishop Japan paint, and Stencil Decor Stencil Paint.**

FABRIC PAINTS AND FABRIC DYES

Fabric, or textile, paint is the next paint material to be discussed. As the name clearly states, fabric paint is made especially for use on fabrics. Today there are many brands of fabric paint on the market, possibly due to the rise in popularity of fabric painting and other methods of surface decoration.

Some fabric paints are called *paints,* and others are called *dyes.* What is the difference? A fabric or textile paint is made with a paint pigment which is larger than a dye particle, and therefore stays on the *surface* of the fabric. However, a dye particle, or molecule, can penetrate the fibers of the fabric. Premixed fabric dyes are of the same consistency as fabric paint, but they chemically interact in a different way. Sometimes companies sidestep the whole issue and call their paints "fabric colors".

There are a number of brand names of fabric paint. These can be divided into waterbase paints and solvent based paints. Waterbase paints include: **Versatex textile paint, Deka Permanent fabric paint, Createx Poster/Fabric colors and Createx Textile Pigments, Eurotex Permanent Fabric color, Sennelier Texticolor, Lefranc and Bourgeois textile paint, Gold Label Magic Touch all–purpose paint (including fabrics), Dylon textile paint, Badger Air–Tex Textile Color, and Colortex Fabric paint. The solvent–based paints include Prang Textile colors, Bishop and Lord, Flopaque, and Inmont Textile colors.** Both of these types also carry metallics, fluorescents, pearlescents, and day–glo colors. The variety of fabric and textile paint available today is a wonderful contrast to the situation ten years ago. For many years, fabric paint was limited to stenciling projects advertised in women's magazines. The crafts movement of the 70's expanded the interest in creativity, and thus, in fabric painting and surface design. We are lucky today to have so much from which to choose.

The greatest advantage of fabric paints is that it can be used on a wide range of fabrics with guaranteed permanency. Unlike acrylics, they do not stiffen or change the fabric upon which they are painted. Fabric paint will not wash out or run, although it does fade a little over the years. The colors are comparable to, though a little less bright, than acrylics. In the jar or tube, many fabric paints have a consistency similar to acrylics.

Since fabric paint is made specifically for fabrics, its wash–fastness and colorfastness is good. There are some disadvantages, however. Unless you are doing small amounts of painting, fabric paints can become expensive to use. Certain brands are more economical than others. Also, the solvent–based brands are used with a turpentine derivative; therefore, one must deal with the inevitable fumes. Working outdoors or in a special painting area is needed.

Because there are so many different brands of textile paint, as well as accessories, each brand will be described individually. Descriptions of new fabric paints, as well as dimensional paints, will follow this next section.

KINDS OF FABRIC PAINT

Prang Textile Colors is one of the oldest fabric paints around. It has now been reissued as a water–base, rather than a solvent based paint, and is called Prang Fabric Paint. The Textile Color is used with an extender, and a penetrator–thinner (a turpentine derivative). Both types are moderately priced, with a range of the basic colors: red through violet, with black, brown, and white. The colors can be easily mixed. With the new water–base colors, one does not have the problems of strong smelling fumes. They are manufactured by the American Crayon Company. (Fig.99)

Prang Fabric Paints are of a medium consistency, much like tempera paint. They can be used on both natural fibers, such as cotton, muslin, linen, and silk; and on some synthetics, such as acetates and organdy. The colors are heat–set by ironing with a dry iron for three minutes on a cotton setting, or five minutes on a synthetic setting. They can be used on colored fabrics as well as on whites; mix more white with the various hues to make the paint more opaque, if necessary. To achieve a more transparent effect, thin with water.

Versatex textile paint is a popular water–base textile paint that first appeared on the market in the 1970's. Versatex is a more full-bodied paint than is Prang. It comes in a range of 28 different colors. It is manufactured by Siphon Art, in Ignacio, California, and can be ordered through Dharma Trading Company. Versatex can be used on white or colored fabrics. Mix colors with white to produce an opaque color. The paint can be mixed with an extender to produce more transparent colors, or to merely "extend" the paint. Versatex also carries a **binder,** which is used with the paint when painting on 100% synthetics. Versatex can be used on a variety of both natural and synthetic fibers, including cotton, poly–cotton, muslin, linen, silk, rayon, nylon, acetate, and polyester. When painting on 100% synthetic, add 1 part binder to 9 parts color.

Versatex textile paint is heat–set similar to other textile paints. Iron on the back of the fabric with a cotton setting. It is a popularly used textile paint, although I personally find the density of the paint difficult to work with. It is moderately priced, with versatile uses.

Deka Permanent Colors or Deka Fabric Paints are another fabric paint which are very popular with fabric artists (it happens to be one of my favorite fabric paints). The Permanent Colors were manufactured in Germany and exported to this country; at the present time, they are no longer allowed over U.S. borders. The American version, Deka Permanent Fabric Paint, is almost equal to the quality of the Permanent colors. Besides carrying a variety of colors—from lemon and golden yellow through the reds, burgundys, and violets, to blue, green, olive, ginger, and white and black. Deka carries a diverse line of paints including opaques, fluorescents, and metallics.

Deka paints are waterbase. They are flowing in consistency, neither being too thick nor too thin. They can be used on both white and colored fabric Mix Covering White (a particular white shade) with other colors when painting on colored fabric. Deka can be used on both natural and synthetic fabrics. Deka Permanent Fabric Paint is now manufactured by Decart, Inc. in Morrisville, Vermont. The paint is available in some art supply stores; and some can be ordered through Dharma Trading Co. in San Rafael, CA. Besides manufacturing the basic shades, Deka carries a nice line of sparkling metallics, called **Deka Permanent Metallics.** They are available in gold, silver, yellow, red, blue, green, and copper. Also, you can mix Pearl White Metallic with the basic shades for other metallic colors.

Fluorescents are also available —in yellow, orange, pink, red, blue, and green. The fluorescents are very bright, with blacklight tendencies. Deka paints are heat–set by ironing on the wrong side of the fabric after it has completely dried. Make sure that the heat is dry heat, and use a setting comparable to

FIG. 99: STENCILED LEAVES ON ROCKS. PRANG TEXTILE PAINT ON MUSLIN.

the fabric. Deka paints are moderately priced and I find them to be one of the most versatile textile paints available.

Sennelier Texticolor is another nontoxic, waterbase textile paint which has been on the market for a number of years. It is about the same consistency as Deka and a very nice paint, but slightly expensive if you are painting in any great quantity. At present time, the most popularly stocked Texticolor paints are the Iridescent or Pearlized colors. They are available in turquoise, lemon, yellow, dark brown, pale green, emerald green, carmin, light blue, gold, black, white, violet, and ultramarine.

Texticolor is manufactured in Paris, by the Sennelier Company. It is non–toxic, appropriate for all types of fabrics, and is heat set with a warm iron.

Another exciting new line of fabric paints is available to the fabric artist. Color Craft, Ltd., in Avon, CT. is manufacturing a number of different types of textile paint, including **Poster/Fab–ric Colors, Textile Pigment Colors, Metallic colors, Hi–Lite Colors, and Pearlescent Colors.** They are all water base, with a large variety of colors. The Poster/Fabric Colors are opaque pigments, while the Textile Pigment colors are transparent. They can be intermixed with each other. You can add an **Opacifier** to these pigments to make them easier to use on dark fabrics.

These colors can be used on all natural or synthetic fibers, both white and colored. The consistency of the paint is such that it is nonspreading, yet it is not too thick. I find that these paints equal Deka in their consistency and variety of effects.

They are somewhat expensive compared to other fabric paints, but they are also a quality product

You can use an **Opaque Extender** for the Poster/Fabric Colors and a **Transparent Extender** for the textile pigment colors. Both extenders will "extend" the paint without thinning the viscosity. The extender will also lighten these colors, something other extenders do not do. The Metallic colors include pearl white, silver, satin gold, and copper. The pearlescent colors are a new product, and they are *very* nice. They are similar to the Texticolor Pearlized Colors. They are available in such exotic colors as teal luster, jade green, plum wine, lilac, apricot, electric blue, dusty rose, brown berry, pink gold, candy apple red, and champagne beige. Hi–Lite Colors are very opaque paints with a iridescent base. They will cover colors better than the Poster/Fabric.

Color Craft also markets a number of accessory materials to be used with the fabric paints. They include a catalyst, a bond–all, a thinner, a thickener, a binder, a permaseal, and a softener. The **catalyst** allows colors to become washfast at a lower temperature. The **bond–all** can be used on knits or loosely woven fabrics to insure wash–fastness. It also helps in alleviating problems caused by fabrics with sizing in them. The **thickener,** of course, will thicken the paint, while the **thinner** thins them; the thinner will not cause loss of color, but too much will delay drying time. The **perma seal** is similar to a Scotchguard type sealed coating; it supposedly does not alter the hand of the fabric. The **binder** will protect the pigmentation of watered–

down paint. And the **softener** will help soften the hand of the fabric.

After painting with any of these colors, let the fabric dry for 24 hours. Then iron on the reverse side at cotton setting with dry heat. Color Craft products are extremely versatile. When I first began painting on fabric, I used to fantasize that there would be a paint that came straight from the bottle, very vivid, bright, and ready to use, with wonderful results. Color Craft paints can fulfill that fantasy!

Eurotex Permanent Fabric Colors are another fine, waterbase fabric paint. They are similar in consistency to Deka and Createx (Color Craft),and are a semi–transparent paint. They come in 18 different colors; a standard range and three fluorescent colors. There are several accessory products. **Extender base** extends the paint when light, transparent values are desired. **Eurotex thickener** is used to thicken the paint, especially desirable when stenciling. The **Eurotex retarder** can be used if you are painting large areas of color and want to slow down the drying time so that your brushstrokes don't show.

Eurotex can be used on most natural and synthetic fabrics, such as cotton, muslin, rayon, linen, wool, silk, polyester, and other synthetics. Eurotex, unlike other fabric paints, does not have to be heat-set. It can be air–set in five to seven days. (However, I have found that the fabric is not harmed if ironed with a dry iron like other heat–setting procedures). It can be used with white or colored fabrics; mix opaque white to the various colors to use with colored fabrics. Its price is moderate, and it is also a flexible, versatile fabric paint that is easy to use with good results.

Gold Label Magic Touch Paint is manufactured for a number of surfaces other than just fabrics, but it can also be used *for* fabrics. It is also a very nice opaque, waterbase paint. It has a range of colors unequaled by other paints: 48 colors, black, white, 17 greys and 11 fluorescents. The only problem I've had with this paint is that it dries slightly scratchy to the touch and a bit stiff. Painting on small areas, rather than trying to cover large areas of fabric, would help alleviate this problem. They are somewhat expensive if you intend to do a lot of painting, but the color range is excellent among the choices of fabric paint.

Gold Label Artist Color, as the paint is also called, is manufactured by Magic Touch of Anaheim, CA. It can be found in art stores, or ordered through them. They are of a medium consistency. They dry quickly and do not have to be heat set. They can be thinned with water for watercolor effects and for use with an airbrush. They can be used on a variety of fabrics; I have had more luck using medium to heavy weight cottons— such as canvas, duck, sailcloth. They are the best paint to use for colored fabric, as they are truly opaque.

Flopaque Art, Hobby and Craft Colors are another type of paint which can be used for other materials as well as fabrics. They carry a variety of colors: **Flopaque Colors, Flo–Metallic colors, Lustre Glaze colors, and Flo–Glo Fluorescent Colors.** It is a solvent based textile paint, and uses **Dio–Sol,** a thinner, rather than being mixed with water. There are altogether 61 different, intermixable colors; 38 are the regular colors with a flat sheen, the others are metallics and fluorescents.

Flopaque is a very thin textile paint. For this reason, I find it has limited use, and is not as versatile as other paints mentioned. It is hard to control the capillary action, and since it is not a waterbase paint, watercolor effects do not work in the same way. Some practice is needed to maximize its benefits. It is good with dry–brush, and it can be used on a variety of fabrics. The manufacturers say that it can be used on all fabrics, but I have found that it dries very stiff on polyesters and synthetics, especially knits. This is a good paint, however, for heavy fabric such as canvas and duck, and for projects such as floorcloths, outdoor furniture made of canvas or sailcloth, or canvas backpacks. As stated before, Flopaque can be used on a variety of fabrics (cotton, linen, muslin, nylon, etc) but its hand is very bad. It dries stiffly even on muslin painted with a "light touch". Therefore, it is best used for wall hangings and other items where the soft drape of the fabric is not crucial (as is the case with clothing).

Flopaque has some unusual colors. They include: rose, coral, flesh, dresdan, chartreuse, Paris green, olive, lilac, magenta, maroon, burnt umber, terra cotta, henna, buff, samoa, and sandstone. Flopaque soaks into the fabric, so it is not very satisfactory for painting on dark fabrics. It does not have to be heat set, and it is important not to iron with anything hotter than a warm iron. Flopaque is a moderately priced textile paint.

There are quite a few other textile paints available on the market. Some of them I have used, others I have not. There are also textile paints that are a combination of oil paint and turpentine, or oil paint, enamel paint, and turpentine. (This last method is used by Marge Wing in her book, *How to Paint on Fabric).* **Bishop and Lord** is a solvent based textile paint I used a number of year ago. I have not seen it on the market recently. **Dylon textile paint (Color–fun)** is a waterbase paint with very good hand. It is manufactured by Dylon International Limited in London, England, and can be found in some art stores. It is heat set with a hot iron, and can be used on a variety of fabrics. It comes in regular and fluorescent colors.

Other fabric paints have been used by other fabric painters: these include Colortex, Inmont Textile colors, Delta Fabric Dye, and Water–Tex textile paint. **Colortex** is a waterbase paint, with a base, pigments, and a binder that you mix together. It is heat set with an iron. It is moderately priced. **Inmont Textile Colors** are highly recommended by Patricia E. Gaines, author of *The Fabric Decoration Book.* They are available through the Inmont Corporation in Clifton, New Jersey. **Delta Fabric Dye** is used by Serene Miller, author of *Painting on Fabric.* (see New Paints section for discussion). **Rosco–Haussmann products** are recommended by Deborah Dryden, who wrote *Fabric Painting and Dyeing for the Theatre.* There are several available fabric paints : **B–2 Latex Colors, Sprila Glazing Colors, Fabric Colors, and Polydyes.** B–2 Latex Colors are waterbase, can be used on cotton and viscose rayon, as well as other fabrics. By using the **Latex Fabric Color, Extra White Opaque** with the other pigments, one can paint on dark fabrics. Sprila Glazing Colors are solvent based; a thinner is used with the colors, and alcohol is used for cleanup. There are nineteen colors in the Sprila Colors. The fabric colors are waterbase,with 25 colors. A thickener and a resist are available. Fabric colors can be used on silk,wool, and stretch synthetics. Polydyes are used on polyesters and synthetics. They do not need steam–setting. The basic problem for these products is that, unless you would be using them in large quantities (such as is possible in theater work) they are not available any other way.

Speedball Textile, Britex,Good stuffs, Aqua–set, and Fashion Paints are other textile paints which I have read about, but have not been able to locate.

AIRBRUSH FABRIC PAINTS

Another category of textile paints are airbrush textile paints. They include **Versatex Airbrush paint, Deka PermAir, Air Waves Airbrush Fabric Paints, Badger Air–Tex Opaque Textile Colors, and Hot Air Textile Artist Pigments.** All the airbrush paints are naturally thinner than some of the textile paints. **Versatex airbrush paint** comes in a range of 22 colors and includes a binder. This allows one to paint on 100% polyesters and synthetics. The paint is heat set by ironing on the back of the fabric at a cotton setting. **Deka PermAir** is waterbase, with 30 different shades. They include metallics and covering white, for use on dark fabrics. **Air Waves** is also waterbase, with 12 colors, plus a covering white. **Badger Air–Tex** has 12 opaque colors also and is waterbase. It is heat–set by ironing. It can also be used in marbling, as it has the right viscosity. **Hot Air Textile Pigments** have 11 colors, and opaque white for covering dark fabrics. As well, it has a **binder**, which helps the pigment adhere to the fabric, and a thickener, **CP–X Printing Clear**. You always use the binder and the color in equal amounts. Cotton, muslin, cotton blends, silk, rayon, and acetate can also be used with Hot Air Colors. For handpainting, add 60% of the Printing Clear to 20% of the Binder, then add 20% of color. Watercolor effects can be achieved by working on slightly damp fabric. Hot Air paints are very versatile, and a good airbrush paint to use for fabric painting. Most all airbrush paints come in smaller amounts than other fabric paints; they are not as cost effective as other fabric paints.

There are several other materials that I am going to mention here. While they are not called fabric paints, technically they are closer to fabric paints than any other paint category mentioned. One such material is Aritex Mineral Dyes, the next is Caran D'Ache Gouache, and the third is Pentel Watercolor Dyes. **Aritex Mineral Dyes** are a very nice product. They come in tubes, and can either be used like a liquid embroidery paint, or they can be used with a brush. I prefer the latter, as the paint flows out of the tube fairly quickly. Aritex is water soluble, with 11 bright vivid colors. Aritex can be used on cotton, linen, silk, nylon, and synthetics. It does not need to be heat set. It can be thinned if desired, or used as it comes out of the tube. I find Aritex a high–quality product that is easy to use. They are reasonably priced.

Another very similar textile paint is **Pentel Water Color Dyes.** There are 12 colors which come in a tube, just like Aritex. They can only be used with natural fibers, however. A handy plastic palette comes with the set. They are a waterbase paint, with no heat setting required.

Caran D'Ache Gouache, a Swiss product available through art stores, can be used in fabric painting. It is advertised as being used as a batik dye. The watercolors are available in sets of 8 or 15 colors. They are waterbase paints, and work very well with watercolor techniques. They can be heat set with an iron and are washable, although since they are not technically a fabric paint, it is best to gently wash them in water with little soap. One of the best aspects of Caran D'Ache Gouaches is that they in no way alter the hand of the fabric. They can be used on both natural and synthetic fibers. Although these paints are limited in their use, they are a very nice material, being both delicate with vivid colors. They can also be used in conjunction with the Caran D'Ache Neocolor sticks, which will be discussed later under fabric markers.

Another possibility with fabric paint is to make your own. Some artists still like to practice the traditional craft of mixing their own paints. This can be done with fabric paints as well. Dry pigment powder is mixed with glycerine, a thickening agent such as tragacanth gum, a binder or varnish, and oil of wintergreen. Mineral spirits are added as a thinner.

Making your own paint is an adventure. Patience, experimentation, and careful record keeping are important. Check **The Textile Arts**– Vera Berril for more specific instructions for textile paints.

NEW FABRIC PAINTS

WALLY R PAINTS: GRUMBACHER

Grumbacher manufactures Wally R paints, which is certainly one of my favorites of the new fabric paints. They offer two basic types of paint with nine further categories. What is actually their regular fabric paint is called a fabric painting dye. They also manufacture a permanent fabric paint, which is a dimensional paint. (Please refer to next section) Both products are waterbased. The fabric dyes are: **Designer Colors, Fluorescents, and Galaxy.**

These paints are an excellent choice for beginners and experts alike. There is a wide range of color choice, and the colors are very vivid and pure. It is a high quality paint of reasonable price. It is easy to switch between the dyes and paints and use them together for varying effects. With such a variety of types of paints (the glitters, metallics, fluorescents, matte colors, etc) there's a lot to play with and it is very convenient to line up some colors and experiment. I really like this paint: it is easy to use, there are lots of choices, and the bottles are small and convenient to lay out, even in a small area.

The **Permanent Fabric Dyes** come in small plastic bottles and are primarily used with a brush, although they can be squeezed out. Designer Colors is the name for the regular dyes. They include colors such as: carmine, pink, sap green, violet, tropical, iris petal, India green, lemon, light red, light brown, wine red, mauvelous, orange sherbet, pinkie, teddy bear, koala, sunkist, golden yellow, coral reef, harbor blue, and dark brown, among others. Be sure and mix the Designer Colors well. Sometimes the paint is rather gelatinous and the colors do not blend well. These paints are very nice and are especially nice when used as a background color laid down, with the dimensional paints drawn on top.

The **Fluorescents** are similar to other brands of fluorescent colors, and include blue, pink, orange, and green. Just as with the other Permanent Fabric Dye colors, the Fluorescents need to be mixed well; if you just dip your brush into the bottle, it will come up gelatenous. Subtle blended colors worked well for me; otherwise, I found this dye rather challenging. I did make some nice highlights with a fan brush, both dry–brush technique and with water.

Galaxy Permanent Fabric Dye is the last type of dye in this line. The colors include: milkyway, papaya, Irish green, neptune green, green olive, comet blue, black, valentine, uranus violet, gold, tulip yellow, silver, starwhite, ginger, moonlite yellow, pewter. These colors are metallic or glittery in effect. Most of them have a perfect consistency. A few of them need mixing to achieve a good consistency. Unlike the fluoresecents, when Galaxy is used on dark fabrics the paint does not soak in but lays more on top of the fabric.

COLORTEX: DIZZLE DIZZLE FABRIC PAINTS

Another one of my favorite new fabric paints is called **Dizzle Dizzle Fabric Paints.** (made by **Colortex**) These are some of the most pleasant and high–quality paints that I have worked with. They are also waterbase paints, and can be used on all fabrics. They come in 1 oz tubes, some of which are brushed on the fabric and others which are dimensional paints. (See next section) The **Brush–on Soft Paint** is your basic fabric paint in this line. It comes in 25 colors, including Periwinkle, Crimson, and Peach. The colors can be intermixed, blended on a palette, and they work well on silk as well as cotton. They come with an **Extender,** which allows you to create pastel shades. **Dizzle Glo–in–the–Dark** is a true fluorescent; it can be used with a brush or as a dimensional paint. **Dizzle Tint Brush–On Paint** is advertised to be used with Dizzle Pre–Shaded transfers, in that it is an iridescent paint, and can be painted over the shaded design. I find it very nice when used together with a brush, and as a dimensional paint. The iridescence will lie on the top and the color shows from below. It is a lighter "glittery" than the Dizzle Glitter, more iridescent.

Dizzle paints do not need to be heatset. Let the fabric dry overnight, and wait one week before washing. However, on some fabrics, washability is improved by briefly ironing the fabric on a hot, dry setting.

Like the previously described Wally R paints, I like these Dizzle paints because they can be easily interchanged, from fabric paint to dimensional paint and back. They are easy to hold, reasonable in cost, and an all around high quality fabric paint. There are many color choices, and the colors are strong and vibrant.

DUNCAN PAINT PRODUCTS: SCRIBBLES FASHION PAINTS

Both Scribbles fabric paints and Scribbles dimensional paints (see next section) are waterbase. They can be used on a variety of fabrics, and are washable. They do not need to be heat set; merely let dry for 4–6 hours flat and 24 hours for complete setting. Do not wash until 3 days (72 hours) have passed. They are moderately priced.

Scribbles Soft Fashion Paints come in the following lines: **Matte, Iridescent, Glittering, and Crystal** in 72 colors, including: Apricot, Butterscotch (Matte); Watermelon, Golden brown (iridescent); Glittering Gold, Violet flash, Lemon Drop. The **Matte** is a very nice paint. The Matte is a *very* soft paint—it is pleasant to work with and just glides on. It has a creamy consistency, with vibrant colors. It is easily to control by the brush, and produces a neat finished look. The **Iridescent**, also is a fine quality paint. It is well mixed, unlike some other iridescent brands. The glitter is very fine and when applying this paint, it goes on very smooth. The Iridescent is more viscuous. I used a water undercoat before painting lines since the paint was so thick. Both of these paints are highly recommended. The **Scribbles Soft Fabric Paint Matchables Glittering** is less mixed, meaning that you have to mix more with the brush after you apply it. It works well over dark fabrics and also over underlying layers of paint, since it is translucent. Glittering is used with a brush. It is fairly viscuous. It can be painted on as a watercolor wash, but best used in small areas. You can paint over it with the Dimensional paints. The **Crystal** also has a viscuous consistency but is well mixed. It has a nice light tint with sparkles added to the paint, which gives a light touch but with the refractory element of the sparkles, thus, the origin of the name!

ACCENT ELEGANCE FABRIC PAINTING DYES

Accent Elegance manufactures fabric paints as well as an acrylic and a dimensional line (see above section and next section). **Country Colors Fabric Painting Dye** is a fabric paint–ing dye, which simply means it comes in bottle and can be used with a brush. **Soft'N'Silky Water–Based Fabric Painting Dye** has a very nice hand. The colors are vibrant. They can be used on muslin, silk, sweatshirt fabric, and all synthetic fabrics. They are waterbase paints. The regular colors do not need heat–

setting (unless you are painting on 100% cotton), merely let dry for 5 hours. When using the Pearlizer colors, or the Gold and Silver Liner, or when painting on 100% cotton, you will need to heatset your project. Simply iron on the wrong side of the fabric for several minutes, using the appropriate setting for the fabric. Along with 21 regular colors, there are also 4 enhancers: Pearlizer, Pastelizer and Extender, and the Gold and Silver Liner. Their prices are moderate, and these paints can be found at many craft, hobby, art and fiber art suppliers. In general, Accent Elegance Soft'N'Silky Water–Based Fabric Painting Dye has replaced the older line of Country Colors Fabric Painting Dye.

CARNIVAL ARTS FABRIC PAINTING DYE

Carnival arts manufactures a unique fabric paint, called **"Just Enough" Fabric Painting Dyes.** This is because they come in a small cup container, and you can just snip off one little paint pot of color at a time. This makes painting easy and convenient, and they do offer quite a range of colors, including: Merry Red, Amethyst, Aquamarine, Orange Blossom, Cotton Candy, Sea-shell Pink, Merry Geen, Wedgewood blue, Natural Linen, Electric Blue, Periwinkle Blue, Candy Mint, Simply Olive, Sherry Red, Silk Blue, French Poppy, and Dusty rose. Fabric paint colors seem to have taken a tip from the fashion designer's language; every color has the fashion world's colorful language rather than just the straight basics of color language! This paint is fluid and smooth on fabric. It works nice with watercolor techniques. It would be good for stenciling, and for small images and detailed work, since these paint pots are *little !* This is a concentrated fabric paint; it can be diluted with water for extended usage. Carnival also offers this paint in 2 oz bottles for larger projects. It works on both natural fibers and synthetics, as well as blends. Heat set with an iron.

Carnival Arts also carries a number of textile mediums which can change the effect of the fabric painting dye. **Dye*namite Radiance** is a spray glow–in–the–dark coating for use with clothing; **Ultra Haute Radiance,** another glow–in–the–dark medium, **Spray Glitter,** and **Webbing** (a textural medium).

DECART'S DEKA FABRIC PAINT

Deka Permanent Fabric Paint has two new color lines: **Southwestern Colors** (such as Desert Yellow, Misson Gold, Pepper Red, Santa Fe Aqua, Cactus Green, and Sandstone Brown). The other is the **Harvest Collection,** with Colonial colors such as Maize, Ginger, Dusty rose, Brick, Commonwealth Green, and Porcelain Blue. By creating lines such as the SW Colors and the Harvest Collection, it is easy to paint images reminiscent of the color schemes. Even easier is to match these paints with an iron–on transfer with a compatible theme (such as a SW theme). Deka also carries metallics, opaques, and regular colors. This is a good quality paint, and has stood the test of time. The new color lines come in plastic squeeze bottles, rather than the glass jars.

DECO–ART FABRIC PAINTS

Deco–Art carries a number of fabric paints, among them **DecoArt Shimmering Pearls Fabric Acrylic Paints, DecoArt So–Soft Fabric Acrylics, DecoArt Heavy Metals,** all of which I have tested. Other fabric paints they carry are the **Christmas Collection Fabric Paints; Dazzling Metallics (pearlescent), Deco–Art's Liquid Sequins,** a brush–on glitter paint, **Heavy**

Metals Light (for light fabrics), **Glo–It Luminescent Paint, Hot Shots,** (neons), and **Snow–tex** (a textural paint which simulates snow). They all come in 2 or 4 oz plastic bottles.

Shimmering Pearls is a very nice iridescent fabric paint which is easy to apply. 23 colors include Apricot, Magenta, and Grape Purple. It has a soft hand with a creamy consistency. The **So–Soft Fabric Acrylics** are an opaque paint, and they also have a soft hand, although they are a slightly thinner paint. They come in 35 colors, including Peaches and Cream, Terra Cotta, and Dark Teal. This paint can be thinned with a **Transparent Medium** and used as a tint with shaded iron–on transfer patterns. **Heavy Metals** is a non–toxic liquid glitter paint which can be mixed with other paints to achieve a glittery effect. They are especially effective when painted on dark fabrics, but can be used on all colors of fabric and with other paints. It is recommended that two coats be used on fabric. Paint the second coat within an hour of applying the first. They also have a soft hand, and come in 12 colors, including Autumn Glo, Glimmer, and Satellite Blue. All of these paints can be air–set; they need no heat–setting.

DELTA/SHIVA

Delta manufactures **Delta Fabric Dyes**, a regular dye, as well as **Starlite Fabric Dye,** a metallic dye. These Delta products are heat–set with a dry iron. The regular dyes (or paints) have 38 colors; the Starlites have 33. The Starlite colors are especially good when painted on dark fabrics. They dry clear and with a vibrant color. There are now also 12 new colors of **Delta Starlite Fabric Dyes for Dark Fabrics. Delta Fabric Dye Extendor** can be used instead of water for a slightly thicker paint. The extendor also acts as a retarder, allowing the paint to dry more slowly.

FASHION SHOW FABRIC PAINTS

Fashion Show manufactures **Fabric Soft Paint** as well as **Fashion Show Jazz–it Dimensional Paint** and **Fashion Show Dimensional Paints** (see following section). The fabric paints come in the following categories: **Sparkle**, Glitter, (with reflective crystals); **Jewel, Metallic, Pearl,** (shimmery); **Sheer Tint, (clear and glossy); Neon,** (with fluorescent pigment); **Pastel, Country, and Basic** (with vibrant colors).

The Fabric Soft Paint has 89 colors, including Ice, Raspberry (Sparkles); African Violet, Midnight Star (Glitter); Garnet Red, Emerald Green (Jewel); Sequin Black, Antique Gold (Metallic); Champagne Pearl, Rose Pearl, Pearl Hot Magenta (Neon); Porcelain Rose (Pastel); Homestead Brown, Denim Blue (Country); Nautical Blue, Real Red (Basic).

There is a good diversity of types and colors of this paint. I find the Jewel sample that I received a very nice color. The **Basic Soft Fabric Paint** has a soft hand, with a matte color that is rather "flat". The **Jewel Soft Fabric Paint** is very, very nice with a soft hand, and a vibrant and shimmery color. Fashion Show paints are waterbased and need to dry for 72 hours before washing. They can be used on a variety of fabrics.

TULIP FABRIC PAINTS

In spite of the numerous Tulip products manufactured, I was only able to test a few for this edition. Unfortunately, Tulip was the only manufacturer whom I contacted who was unwilling to send a small sampling of products for testing. Craft stores vary in the brands and quantities of fabric paints that they carry, since there is now such a large selection. Perhaps in a future edition, I will be able to locate more Tulip products. Their fabric paints include the following products: **Brush–Top Applicator and Paint All–In–One, Fiber Fun** (Metallic fibers), **Designer Metallics, Fashion Tints, Liquid Glitter, Fashion Glitter, Fashion Suede Fabric Paint, Soft Metallics, Easy Tie–Dye Colors, Designer Dyes, and Spatter Paints,**.

Tulip Lite Soft Metallics is a fabric paint marketed for use with pre–shaded tranfers. The color and iridescence is very nice; however the paint dries stiff and scratchy. It is best used on sweatshirts or other heavyweight fabrics as opposed to lightweight fabrics.

Tulip Brush–Top Applicator and Paint All–in–One is like a liquid fabric dye. It comes out very fast from the bottle, but with the brush right on top, one has control. Both dry–brush effects and watercolor washes are equally nice with this product. Its hand is soft, and it does not need heat setting.

Tulip paints are more expensive than other comparable fabric paints. They come in small bottles with high prices. Although Tulip has breadth in their product line, there are many other similar fabric paints of equal quality available today. Tulip also carries many kits and boxed sets aimed for kids. (See section on "Paints for Kids") Tulip paints do not have to be heat set. Wait 72 hours before washing.

Other new fabric paints which I do not presently have and therefore have not yet tested include **Crayola Craft and Fabric Paint, which comes in Pearl, Glitter, Glo–in–the–Dark, Glossy, Metallic, Neon, & Tie–dye Effect; Jones Tones Fabric Paint by Brewer; Delta /Shiva Glo–up, a luminous fabric paint which comes in both brush–on and dimensional form; Delta's Liquid stars and Liquid Hearts fabric paint (a glitter paint with iridescent stars/hearts); IVY Craft's Fabric–Arts Paint; Deka's PermGlitter Fabric Paint, Doodad's Brand "X" Professional Fabric Paint, Jacquard Permanent Textile Colours, (in Traditional shades, Metallics, Fluorescents, Opaques, Starbright Jewel Collection, & Starbright Pastel Collection); Mayco/ Image's Brushable Fabric Paints; Cerulean Blue's Lumiere Fabric Paints; Primal Glow Fabric Paints; Cloud Cover Fabric Paints; Neopaque Fabric Paint; Pebeo's Setacolor Transparent, Opaque, & Pearl** fabric paint; and **Dizzle Magic Sticker Paints.**

CATEGORIES OF FABRIC PAINT

There are so many new paints available! Besides the regular lines of fabric paint, there are what I call specialty paints. Often, these paints are are targeted or marketed specifically. I have divided them into the following categories: *paints designed for specific fabrics; paints designed for particular markets; specialty paints (paints which change color with heat, fabric spray paints), and paints designed for specific techniques.*

PAINTS FOR SPECIFIC FABRICS

Stretch Paints: Stretch paints are a type of paint manufactured for particular types of fabric. **Tulip Stretch Flexible Fabric Paint** is one brand I tested. The paint stretches with the fabric. This paint is best used with fabrics such as Lycra, cotton knit jersey, polyester knit stretch fabric, as well as clothing such as stretchy tops, socks, tights, swimwear, and workout clothes. It is best used with lines and small areas. Dots work real well. The paint comes out in big blobs but can be controlled with a brush. Lines aren't particularly even and squarish; they are more rounded.

When the paint dries, it really is pretty interesting, because you can pull and stretch it and actually *see* the paint stretch!

However, when it dries, it dries a little bit sticky, as it is a viscous paint. Use it on such clothing items as tights, socks, for sort of fun type wearables, silly kooky looking bright colored items! It can also be used in conjunction with regular fabric paints. Another brand is **DecoArt's Dimensions Dimensional Paints,** which has a rubber–like paint resin base causing the paint to be stretchy.

Painting On Dark Fabrics: Many of the new fabric paints have manufactured specific fabric paints for use with dark fabrics. In the older fabric paints, most suggest mixing more white with the regular colors to make the paint more opaque. Prang Fabric Paints and Versatex Fabric paints suggest this technique. In my experience, painting with some of the older fabric paints on dark fabrics did not always give good results. Many times it was preferable to paint on white fabric, and then overdye. Hi–Lite Textile Colors, by Createx (Color Craft, Ltd) is one of the the best overall older fabric paints for use with dark colors. Caran D'Ache Gouaches are also good, although they are not very washable.

Another option is to first lay down an undercoat of the opaque white, and then paint over it with the regular color. For example, if your end result is a pastel color, first paint with a pure color mixed with the opaque white. Then lightly paint over the design with just the pure color.

Eurotex fabric paints carry an **Opaque White** to add to the various colors, as does **Hot Air Airbrush Textile Pigments.** Both **Deka Fabric Paints** and **AirWaves** airbrush fabric paint have a **"Covering White",** which is mixed with the regular colors. **Color Craft's Textile Pigment Colors** comes with an **Opacifier** to make them more opaque, whereas their **Poster/Fabric Colors** and **Hi–Lite Colors** are already opaque. **Delta's Starlite Fabric Dye** works well on dark fabrics, with a pure rich deep color.

The newer paints either follow this procedure, with some kind of an opaque white paint, or a specific *opaque* line of fabric paints in all colors. The following companies make paints specifically for dark fabrics.

Dizzle Brush–On Brights is an excellent paint for dark fabrics. It covers the fabric completely and is very shimmery and shiny. It also works nicely on light–colored fabrics, although it was not manufactured for that purpose. It has a good consistency (not too thin, not too thick). Tulip manufactures **Brite Ideas,** for use on dark fabric. Many metallic, iridescent, opalescent, glitter, fluorescent, and neon regular and dimensional fabric paints and acrylic paints also work well on dark fabrics. Some of these include: **Delta Gleams Acrylic Paint; FolkArt Metallic Acrylics; DecoArt Heavy Metals fabric paint; Tulip Polymark Iridescent Dimensional Paint; Wally R's Dimensional Galaxy Dyes, Wally R's Fluorescent Paint, Delta Glitter Stuff (dimensional paint); Fashion Show Jewel Fabric Soft Paint; and Createx's Acrylic Fabric Paints with Pearlescent colors.**

Painting On Denim: Tulip carries a specific paint for painting on denim, called **Jumpin' Jeans Denim Paint.** It is marketed for kids, but could be used by anyone to paint on denim.

Painting On Leather, Canvas and Vinyl Shoes And Accessories: Dylon manufactures a product called **Dylon Shoe Color.** It can be used for shoes and accessories such as purses, and belts. One simply uses an abrasive pad to prepare the surface, then a stiff brush is used to apply the color. This is easy to use, with good results. However, be careful when working around the heels and sides of the shoe, so that the dye does not bleed into these areas. Plaid also carries a fabric paint for shoes and accessories called **"Color Steps",** Dharma Trading Company carries **Dharma Leather** paint for leather and vinyl, although I

have not tried these products.

Painting On Silk: Most silk paints are listed under the section on silk painting and silk dyes. In general, we use a fabric painting product for the specific fabric that it is marketed for. We use opaque paints for dark fabrics on dark fabrics, just as we use a silk dye for silk, not for another kind of fabric. However, this idea that was challenged in the booklet **Lynn Paulin's Wearable Art 2** wherein she was using silk dyes on cotton and poly–cotton T–shirts. The results are a beautiful watercolor rendering of images with soft blendings. This is an important concept to remember in using the myriad of fabric paints and dyes available to us today. While it is important to learn the technique that is described, do not hesitate to experiment and step outside the accepted conceptual framework. In this way, new discoveries are made, products have multiple uses, and you too can write booklets on your newly discovered technique!

PAINTS FOR SPECIFIC MARKETS

Paints for Kids: A number of manufacturer's of fabric paints are now marketing them especially for kids. Do products for kids differ any from other fabric paints? I have found that paints for kids tend to be highly packaged, in the format of kits. Also, they emphasize safety features, such as non–toxic paints, and ease of use. There are even fabric paints which wash out, which I suppose are good for very little kids, (but it seems to me to defeat the purpose of fabric painting!) Also, kid's paints often feature themes, especially holiday themes, such as Halloween and Christmas.

The following paints are manufactured especially for kids: **Binney and Smith's Crayola Craft Paint; Capri Arts "Just Enough" fabric painting dyes; CCA Cousin Corporation of America Chalk Talk Transfers; Colortex's Dizzle fabric painting kits; Kids do it, Fun Fashions for Kids, Halloween; Delta/Shiva's Little Squirts, Skwoosh Fabric paint, Twinkle Glitter, Peek–a–boo transparent paint, Rainbow painting glue, Kaleido–whirl kit.Gick's booklets for kids include Jumpin Jeans Denim for Kids. Tulip offers Happy Chalk,(an iron–on design with a chalkboard which can be written on), Candi Crystal Colors (dimensional glitter paint,) Jumpin Jeans Denim Paint Glitter Glue Pen (for sneakers); and the following kits: Jumpin Jeans Denim Paint Box Kit, Neon Easy Feet Sneaker Painting Fun Kit, Jim Henson's Muppets Paint–a Patch Kit, Glowild, and Supersparkle Box Kit.** They also carry: **Tulip for Kids Paint Sets** (Glitter, Spatter mania, Easy Tie–dye, Puffy Paint, Neon Nite Lites) and **Tulip for Kids Color Switch** (9 colors and 9 switches).

At the present time, I have not tested any of these kits, but I believe they are worth your while especially when doing beginning fabric painting with small ones. The fabric paint is packaged in smaller bottles and overall the scale of the projects are appropriate for young children.

Also, the magazine **Crafts and Needlework Age** has a Kid's Review of products, written by Jim Lamancusa. He tests out various products and comments on their appropriateness for kids. It is a nice column.

Paints For Home Interiors: Several companies market fabric paints and materials for home interior decorating. Home decor as it relates to fabric painting includes projects such as painted curtains, sheets, pillowcases, pillows, quilts, comforters, tablecloths with matching napkins, painted lampshades and roller blinds, floorcloths, cloth woven or knit rugs, bathtowels, kitchen towels, tea towels, napkins, placemats, potholders, deck chairs, hammocks, and any canvas or heavy fabric used in upholstery work.

As well, there is a type of fabric painting for interiors which is a cross–over between textiles and fine arts. Besides making banners, painted screens, wall hangings, and fabrics for interior decorating, some artists are making "one–offs". These are one of a kind unique textile pieces similar to regular paintings, shown in art galleries, in public spaces, and as commissioned pieces for clients such as designers and architects.

Two companies, Duncan Enterprises and Gick Publishing, have teamed up together to produce the Creative Home Center. Their products include: **Duncan's Decorator Acrylic Paints, Duncan Decorator Acrylics Dimensional Writer, and Gick's Decorator Sponges, Iron–On Fashion Transfers, Iron–on Decorator Borders, Iron–on transfer books and Non–stick transfer paper.** These are marketed together which makes for easy shopping decisions.

Accent Products carries a number of products in their home decorating line. Their **Country Manor spray paint** (good for stenciling and spray painting) in 8 colors coordinates with their Country Colors Acrylics. Add to this **Judy Martin's Fabric Painting Medium,** which can be added to the Country Colors acrylics for use on fabrics. They also advertise a Country Colors Home Decorating System, with **Faux Finish Decorating Glaze,** to be used for texture painting and marbling. This can be used for floorcloths and on other canvas material.

Delta/Shiva carries **Fashion Tape,** a designer stencil tape used in fabric and craft painting to create easy to do borders on fabric surfaces. Because the tape "sticks" to an upright surface, it is easy to use in home decor projects. And Plaid Products carries a new book applicable to home decor, called *Home En–chantments,* for decorative painters.

Stenciling is one of the strongest fabric painting techniques used with home decor, so many of the stencil paints, stencils, stencil tape, and acrylic paints manufactured by various companies can be used in home decor work. Gick also has a booklet, "A Beginner's Guide to Stenciling", to use along with their laser cut stencils. All these products are useful for the fabric painter interested in home decor.

SPECIALTY FABRIC PAINTS

Paints That Change Color. A most interesting specialty fabric paint is a paint which is heat sensitive, and changes color when one touches it, or irons it, or exposes it to heat of any kind. **Chameleon Color Change Paint,** by Timberline Design, is one such paint. There are 12 paints, which change from one color to another, so they offer a total of 24 colors. Some of the color changes include: Sky Blue to Purple, or Pink to Indigo, or even Light Blue to Deep Plum. With a slight change in temperature from 87 degrees Fahrenheit or above, down to 71 degrees or below, the colors change! This is a dimensional paint. Tulip Paints also puts out a **Tulip for Kids Color Switch fabric paint.** There are 9 paints with a switch, for a total of 18 colors. Some of the color switches include Black to Bright Orange, & Turquoise to Soft Yellow. Truly amazing things are happening in the chemist's labs who specialize in fabric paint!

Spray Fabric Paints are another specialty paint. I have not seen too many of them, but **Carnival Art** produces **Jewels and Jazz,** a spray fabric paint that is metallic and pearlescent. This is an interesting concept, and we may see more of this in the future.

QUALITIES OF FABRIC PAINT

As can be seen, there are a great variety of fabric paints available today. They range in consistency, use, and price. Many are waterbase, a few are solvent based. Most are heat set by a dry iron, some need only overnight drying to be set. They are all washable, especially those truly classified as **fabric** paints. Those that are available in larger quantities are best used when one is painting a lot. Those manufactured in small quantities can be very good when one is painting small motifs. Most can be used on dark fabrics, with the addition of an opaque white pigment.

Many of the new fabric paints, such as the iridescent/glitter paints, encourage the use of decorative motifs because the paint itself has so much character. It leads to glitz, glitter, fanciful designs rather than using the paint to create an image. This limits the usage of these colors, but at the same time makes them very easy to use. For example, you would not necessary try to paint a picture—such as Van Gogh's "Sunflowers" with this type of paint. On the other hand, simple lines, squiggles, and shapes are very interesting looking because of the color and "look" of the paint. This paint essentially "paints itself"—which is why it has become so popular with the general public. One does not have to have artistic talent to create a pleasing work of art.

When I reflect over the many years that I have collected and tested fabric paints, I am pleasantly impressed with the improvement in quality and ease of use. As I reread some of the older fabric paints with their binders and pigments and bases which had to be mixed together in certain percentages, I think about how easy it is today. Also, when I remember mixing lots of colors of acrylic paint, as well as trying to keep them from drying up, it is such a pleasure to use the fabric acrylics of today, with premixed colors. I also love the opportunities provided by the various lines of fabric paint: the iridescents and metallics that seem to paint themselves, the puff paints, and the fun to be had from all the dimensional paints.

To sum up the qualities of fabric paints, refer to the chart below:

Use: very popular, flexible with versatile uses for most brands. Some brands have limited use.

Quality: a medium to excellent range quality material

Price: Varies from moderately priced to some expensive, high quality textile paints

Ease of Use: Very easy to use

Hand: very good for most all brands.

Washability: good to excellent, especially with the technically true fabric paint

Usage: especially good for clothing and other wearable items. Excellent for delicate fabrics, high quality items.

Fabrics used: All cottons, linen, silk, rayon, acetate, synthetics, polyesters, blends, knits, canvas.

Productivity: Fair to good. Some fabric paints require a long drying time.

Availability: Good to excellent in art, craft, and fabric stores. Best to mail–order through a surface design or fabric decoration supply house for specific items

Lightfastness: Good to excellent.

How set?: Most heat set with a dry iron, some are air set.

DIMENSIONAL PAINTS

The prototype of dimensional paints are the Tulip line, and many other companies have followed in their path to make similar types of paints. Dimensional paints come in a squeeze bottle, so no brushes or water are needed. The squeeze bottle becomes the brush. The squeeze bottle produces the various width of line, and by manipulation, you can make the line wider. Also, most dimensional paints are opened by using a pin, but you can also cut the top of the squeeze bottle and that will produce a thicker line. Dimensional paints are thick, hold their shape on top of the fabric, so that they create a sculptural effect on the fabric. They are often used for *outlining* (such as on a sweatshirt with an applique), and in designs with small dots, squiggles, and small shapes.

When they start getting old, you can tell because they will become drier, harder to squeeze out of the bottle and will begin to "ball up". You can still use them for awhile, but use both hands to squeeze them out. Also, you'll want to use them on top of another paint, a brushed on paint, while still wet, so that the dimensional paint will stick. If you just squeeze it on directly to fabric, the chances are good that your older dimensional paint won't have the sticking power and will drop off after several washings!

Dimensional paints come in various types. The same type may be called a different name depending on the brand. In general, the lines are: **Regular (or Matte), Shiny (or Slick,) Pearl (or Pearlescent,) Opalescent, Iridescent, Glitter(or Glittering or Glittery), Metallic, Fluorescent, Neon (or Glo–In–The–Dark), and Swell (or Puff, or Puffy)** . Most of the names are self–explanatory. This last category of paints SWELL up when heat is applied. **Shiny Dimensional Paints,** sometimes called **Slick,** dry hard, slick, and shiny. They are good for outlines and for making "liquid beads" (see Chapter VI under Needlepainting, Colorpainting, and Liquid Beading). There are even being developed right now new dimensional paints with double and triple colors. Who knows what I'll discover for you in the coming years!

WALLY R DIMENSIONAL PAINTS

Wally R paints, by Grumbacher, manufacture two basic types of paint with nine further categories. They produce a permanent fabric paint, which is a dimensional paint. (They also make a fabric paint: see above section) Both products are waterbased. There are six different types of dimensional paints, **Sunbeams, Raindrops, Moondust, Moonbeams, Fluorescents and Meteorites.**

The **Sunbeam** is a very freeflowing dimensional paint, good for writing, squiggly lines, etc. It comes in the following colors: red, peach, light beige, kahlua and cream, icy lime, black, holly green, white, yellow, tea rose, navy blue, orchid, india green, verona brown, king's violet, violet, iris petal, baby blue, among others. It can be used from a brush but works particularly well squeezed from the bottle.

Raindrops is a dimensional paint which works well as drops, hence the name. It dries hard and shiny. It can also be used with a brush, and dries flat and shiny, like a sidewalk after rain. It is similar to "shiny stuff" made by other companies. Raindrops comes in the following colors: red, pink, yellow, clear, green, blue, lilac, as well as others.

Moonbeams is another dimensional paint which is iridescent and comes in many beautiful colors. Some of these include: Aquarius, red, conch pink, bronze, pearl white, salmon, amber, rain cloud, fuchsia, topaz, juniper, turquoise, almond, glacier blue, indigo, and purplescent, among others. (Be careful when you set it by ironing with an iron—the dimensional paint can flatten and stick on your protective ironing paper.) Moonbeams flows well from the tube.

Moondust is another sparkly, glittery dimensional paint. It is very nice to use over the designer dye, the underlying colors come through with an added extra sparkle. Moondust has interesting and fun colors: some of which are tangerine, pavo green, sea green, nile green, kelly green, baby blue, lunar lites, purple icing, poppy pink, bronzetone, empire blue, mitis green, praline, hot pink, juniper, key lime, coal grey, and red rubies.

Fluorescents are another type of dimensional paint. Included are the colors: pink, orange, yellow, green, and blue. These are very nice paints; they really make a splash, especially on dark fabrics. You can really let go in squiggly lines with these glo–in–the–dark colors! They are best used from the squeeze bottle; if you use a brush, they just soak into the fabric and disappear.

Meteorites are the last type of dimensional fabric paint in the Wally R. paints. Meteorite is a dimensional paint with both iridescent and sparkle in it. It has a lot of white paint in it which streaks through the glitter part of the paint, hence the name. When used with a squeeze bottle, the white paint predominates, as it is the heavier paint. I prefer using it with a brush, as the white and iridescent aspects of the paint can blend. It is an interesting concept in fabric paint. It comes in aquamarine, black, silver, red, gold, green, copper, crystalina, and mauve, as well as other colors.

This particular brand of dimensional paint does not have to be heat–set. It is simply left to air dry. All the dimensional paints can be applied with a brush as well as being squeezed from the bottle. This adds to the variety of effects possible. This is a moderately priced fabric paint.

COLORTEX: DIZZLE DIZZLE DIMENSIONAL FABRIC PAINTS

Another one of my favorite new dimensional paints are made by Colortex and are called **Dizzle Dimensional Fabric Paints.** These are some of the most pleasant and high–quality paints that I have worked with. They are also waterbase paints, and can be used on all fabrics. They come in 1 oz tubes, some of which are dimensional paints and others which are brushed on the fabric. (See above section) Because this dimensional paints' design is long and slim, it is easier to hold in the hand and maneuver. The *flow* of paint also is excellent, whereas with some dimensional paints, it is difficult to get the paint really flowing easily. **Dizzle Iridescent Dimensional Paint** is a very nice paint. The color is rich, the iridescence is of high quality. I have also found that the iridescent paint can be brushed on as well. It comes in 22 colors, and is also available in a 4 oz squeeze bottle. **Dizzle Glitter Dimensional Paint** has a good consistency of medium and glitter; it is not spotty, as are some glitters. There are 18 glitter colors. **Dizzle Slick Dimensional Paint** is very easy to apply. It is similar to other dimensional slick or shiny paints in that it is very shiny, slick, and plastic–like; also it glows in the dark. There are 15 shades, with 5 Neons included in this line. Dizzle Slick paint can also be used to make "Slickle" art by painting a design on plastic wrap, and letting it dry overnight. The "Slickle" will then adhere to smooth hard surfaces. **Dizzle Puff Dimensional Paint** is a puff paint which needs to be heat set in order for it to puff up. Let dry from between 5–48 hours, then iron on a low setting (dry) with the wrong side of the fabric touching the iron's surface, for about 1 minute. The heat from the iron will "puff" the paint up. Also, you can use a hair dryer to heat–set the paint. Additionally, the clothing item can be put in a clothes dryer for 5–10 minutes which will further heat–set the paint. **Dizzle Glo–in–the–Dark** is a true fluorescent; it can be used with a brush or as a dimensional paint. **Dizzle Tint Brush–On Paint** is advertised to be used with Dizzle Pre–Shaded transfers, in that it is an iridescent paint, and can be painted over the shaded design. I find it very nice as both a dimensional paint, where the iridescence lies on the top and the color shows from below when applied with a brush. It is a lighter "glittery" than the Dizzle Glitter, more iridescent. **Dizzle Brush–On Brights** is an excellent paint. It is designed for painting on dark fabrics, and on them it is very shimmery and shiny and covers completely. However, I've also found it can be used as a dimensional paint. There is no need for any undercoat of an opaque white, as is common with many other fabric paints when painting on dark fabrics. It also works nicely on light–colored fabrics, although it was not manufactured for that purpose. It has a good consistency (not too thin, not too thick).

Dizzle paints do not need to be heat–set. Let the fabric dry overnight, and wait one week before washing. However, on some fabrics, washability is improved by briefly ironing the fabric on a hot, dry setting.

Like the previously described Wally R paints, I like these Dizzle paints because they can be easily interchanged, from fabric paint to dimensional paint and back. They are easy to hold, reasonable in cost, and an all around high quality fabric paint. There are many color choices, and the colors are strong and vibrant.

DELTA/SHIVA: DELTA DIMENSIONAL PAINTS

Delta offers in dimensional paints Shiny stuff, Glitter Stuff, Cool Stuff, and Swell Stuff. **Shiny Stuff** is very nice—very shiny. It flows easily from the tube. Some colors are more liquid than others, so it is a good idea to sample test it before starting a project. **Glitter Stuff** is pretty. It also is well mixed and comes out with an even consistency. It "doodles" and "scribbles" real easily—you can draw fast with these dimensional paints! Shiny Stuff is both regular and Opalescent. **Regular Shiny Stuff** is shiny, flows well from the tube and dries hard and clear. **Opalescent Shiny Stuff** is similar except it has a slight pearlescent type of glow. It's easy to make wavy lines and writer–type doodles with Shiny stuff. **Delta Cool Stuff** is a very "plasticy" paint which dries very clearly and shiny. It can also be used with the Kaleido–Whirl to make shirt designs. Since Cool Stuff is transparent, it's fun to use one color over another, making snake–like lines of colors which wrap over each other on the fabric, in a dimensional way! **Delta Swell Stuff** is a puff paint. It is a very nice full–bodied paint and puffs up real nice and smooth. It is heat–set by air drying for 12 hours, then, using a steam iron for 10–15 seconds, let the steam puff up the paint.

It is one of the more full–bodied puff paints, and I would recommend it.

All these paints are heat–set by air drying, just like the previous ones. Air dry 4–6 hours. Do not wash for a period up to five days. Handwashing is always preferable, especially with dimensional paints. They are non–toxic, waterbase, and reasonably priced.

DUNCAN PAINT PRODUCTS: SCRIBBLES DIMENSIONAL FASHION WRITERS

Scribbles dimensional paints are waterbase. They can be used on a variety of fabrics, and are washable. They do not need to be heat set; merely let dry for 4–6 hours flat and 24 hours for complete setting. Do not wash until 3 days (72 hours) has passed. They are moderately priced.

Scribbles Dimensional Fashion Writers come in 1 oz squeeze bottles. They include **Matte, Shiny, Iridescent, Glittering, Crystal Gel, Fluorescent and Glow–in–the–Dark.** There are a total of 84 colors, many which match the Soft Fashion Paint colors. Some of the sole colors in the Fashion Writers are Gold, Silver (Iridescent); Ruby, Amethyst (Glittering); and Ginger Peach, Medium Green (Matte/Shiny). Fluorescent colors include Neon pink, orange, green and yellow; Glow–in–the–dark include Orange, Pink, Green, Yellow, Glittering, and Ghostly Glo. Scribbles Dimensional Paint also comes in a larger 4.5 oz size, for multiple projects, or use with spin art machines.

The Fashion Writer has a very fine line. It is dimensional enough to use in a circular motion to fill in a small area. The flow from the Fashion Writer generally is good, unless you get a defective bottle of paint. In that case, cut off the tip and sometimes that will get the flow going. When using the larger 4.5 oz squeeze bottle, there are two line lengths you can use: thick or thin. Use a pin for a thin line; cut off the top with scissors for a thick line. The flow is good from the squeeze bottle, and control is good, even with thick lines.

Scribbles Double Color Fabric Writer: This dimensional fabric paint is made with two colors that write simultaneously. In general, they come out as a double line, although sometimes one color predominates and there are times when the colors mix and muddy. However, in general, this is a wonderful invention with many interesting results.

Scribbles Snow Writers is an exciting new product! It replicates the look of snow, and is easy to use on wearables with Christmas or snow sport designs. It is a dimensional paint but doubles as a brush–on. As a dimensional writer, the "snow" comes out hard and a bit crusty—very realistic! When smoothed by a brush, all the blue, green, purple, and mauve sparkles appear. This product is really easy to use with successful results.

Duncan Decorator Acrylics Dimensional Writer: I find the Dimensional paint extremely easy to use with very good results. It has an excellent flow and is easily manageable on the fabric. It dries flat and hard as it lays on top of the fabric, but since it is a dimensional paint, this is not a problem. These paints come in Opaque, Pearl, and Metallic, and in a total of 36 colors.

DUPEY'S U–TEE–IT DIMENSIONAL PAINTS

This is a very nice paint which keeps its flexibility for many years. I have had some of these paints for 4–5 years and they come out of the bottle as easily as when I first bought them! They come in Glitz, Gloss, and Pearlescent, in a variety of colors. Their flexible squeeze bottle is easy on the hands.

FASHION SHOW DIMENSIONAL PAINTS

Fashion Show's Jazz–It Dimensional Paints as well as its companion **Fashion Show Soft Fabric Paints** (see above section) are offered, in the following categories: **Sparkle, Glitter,** (with reflective crystals); **Jewel, Metallic, Pearl,**(shimmery); **Sheer Tint,** (clear and glossy); **Neon,** (fluorescent); **Pastel, Country, and Basic** (with vibrant colors). The Jazz–it Dimensional paint category has 60 colors, including Citron, Jade (Sparkle); Night Star, Rainbow (Glitter); Aquamarine (Jewel); Silver Sterling (Metallic); Ice Blue, Plum (Pearl)and Clear. Kelly Green (Sheer Tints).

There is a good diversity of colors in this paint. However,the **Jazz–it Dimensional Paint** I found unsatisfactory. The bottle was hard to use. They instruct you to use a heat source to open the tip of the bottle. This is awkward. As well, they advertise a scotch tape tapered tip for variety in width of line, but this too is awkward. I found the paint was not well blended, the bottle was hard to control and the lines were thick and "blobby". More recently, in connection with their promotion of "Liquid Beads", Fashion Show offers **Fashion Show Dimensional Paints in Shiny, Pearl, Metallic, Jewel,** among others. This paint is of very good quality, and also quite economical in the 4 oz squeeze bottles.(1 oz bottles are also available). Whether used for beads or for linear painting, this dimensional paint comes out smooth and creamy. This product is of much higher quality than their previous dimensional paints. Fashion Show paints are waterbased and need to dry for 72 hours before washing. They can be used on a variety of fabrics.

LIQUITEX DIMENSIONAL PAINTS

Liquitex offers their **Concentrated Artist's Colors** in a dimensional line as well. It is a glitter paint called Liqui–gems. This is, in my opinion, the best brand of dimensional paints for the "glitter" line. The bottle is bigger than most glitter dimensional paints; therefore the paint flows out easily. The glitter is especially fine, with a deep rich color.

MAXWELL'S MAXICOLORS DIMENSIONAL FABRIC PAINT

This is another new paint, very economically priced of good quality. It flows well, and dries very shiny. It also makes good "liquid beads" (see Chapter VI on Needlepainting, Liquid Beads, and Colorpainting)

TULIP DIMENSIONAL PAINTS

In spite of the numerous Tulip products manufactured, I was only able to test a few for this edition. Unfortunately, Tulip was the only manufacturer whom I contacted who was unwilling to send a small sampling of products for testing. Craft stores vary in the brands and quantities of fabric paints that they carry, since there is now such a large selection. Perhaps in a future edition, I will be able to locate more Tulip products. Their dimensional line of paints includes: **Puffy Paints, Nite Lites (Glow–in–the–Dark Fabric and Fun Paint), Neon Nite Lite Paints, Soft Nite Lites (Fluorescent), Candi Crystals Dimensional Fabric and Craft Paints, and Designer Dimensional Paint Pens (in Slick, Glitter, Puffy and Iridescent).**

Tulip was the first company to manufacture dimensional paints. In 1968, their parent company, Polymerics developed Puff Paint (the first dimensional paint) and Glitter Paint. By 1983 they had added Slick paint to their line, and this is when Tulip Productions was created. For many people new to the field of fabric painting in the 1980's, their only knowledge of fabric paints begins with Tulip paints. Tulip is also, to my knowledge, the first and only company to advertise fabric painting on television.

The **Tulip Polymark Dimensional Fabric and Craft Paint Pen** is very nice. It is easy to draw on fabric with this pen, as the flow of the paint is good. It's easy to draw fast, and with good control with this paint pen. The colors are vibrant. **Tulip Slick Dimensional Paint** is very nice, it dries nice. It is good for making liquid beads. **Tulip Pearl Dimensional Paint** also is very nice, and also dries hard and is good for liquid beads. I found the **Tulip Glitter Dimensional Paint** hard to get out of the squeeze bottle. I have also had this problem with other glitter dimensional paints. The white part of the paint comes out but the actual glitters remain stuck inside the tube!

In general, Tulip products are in the high price range, and are marketed in small bottles. The Polymark Dimensional Pen is more moderately priced. Tulip paints do not have to be heat set. Wait 72 hours before washing.

Other dimensional paints of which I am aware but do not yet have include: **Deka Flair Dimensional Paint, Deka Fun Sparkling Outliners, DecoArt's Dimensions, Duncan's Glo–up dimensional fabric paint (luminous), Duncan Scribbles WideLiner (for calligraphy and wide lines), Duncan's Scribbles TriLiner, Decart's Deka–Fun sparking outliners; and Image's Dimensional Paints; Maxwell's Maxi Colors Dimensional Fabric Paint in Solids, Metallics and Glitters; Gala–craft's Galacolors (Crystal, Glitter, Pearlescent, Neon–Pearl, Plexi, Neon, and Gala–fetti), NW Fabrics & Crafts Mega– Colors; & Fashion Show's Shiny Fine Line Writer Tip Dimensional Paint.**

To sum up qualities of dimensional paints:

Use: extremely popular

Quality: high quality art material; only a few brands have less than quality product

Price: reasonable

Ease of use: fairly easy to use; some bottles are stiffer and harder on the hand with extended use

Hand: Dimensional paints lay on top of the fabric

Washability: Fair to good; handwashing is recommended. Do not wring.

Usage: Sweatshirts, T–shirts, other clothing and accessory items; quilts, backpacks, toys;

Fabrics used: All kinds of fabrics

Productivity: Fast results, with good productivity possible

Availability: Very available, in craft/art stores, toy stores, dime stores, etc

Lightfastness: Excellent

How set?: Air dries

OIL PAINT

Oil paints can be used as a kind of textile paint. They can be mixed with a number of different thinners and materials. In the older books and pamphlets on fabric painting, oil paint is a major paint material. Some books recommend squeezing the oil onto a glass palette to drain off the oil, then adding turpentine to the paint before using. Another product which can be mixed with oil paints is textine, a thinner specifically manufactured by Grumbacher for use with oils on fabrics. In her book, **How To Paint on Fabric,** Marge Wing uses a mixture of oil paint, enamel paint, and mineral spirits.

When oils are mixed with any of these other substances, a type of textile paint is created. The colors blend easily, and Impressionistic types of work can be easily achieved. Anyone who has already worked in oils would find it easy to transfer their skills to this technique. However, this type of textile paint needs good ventilation, for there are a lot of fumes with either the turpentine, and especially the textine. It is not a good paint material for children.

HOW OILS ARE USED

Any type of oil paint can be used: Shiva, Grumbacher, Permanent Pigments,etc. **Turpentine, mineral spirits (or turpenoid) and textine** can all be added to the oils. Working with oils and turpentine or mineral spirits works well on small areas or for detail work. Colors blend well when using oils. They also appear. "soft" on the fabric, and do not disturb the hand of the fabric. I have painted successfully with them on a variety of polyester blends, textured fabrics, cotton knits, as well as cotton and muslin. Some cottons will stiffen a little when painted with oils, but the synthetics don't.

Don't thin the paint down too much or the turpentine will stain the fabric. On the other hand, too much overpainting or painting with thick paint is not desired either.

Use a disposable waxy palette, and dab a bunch of different colors on your palette. Thin them with either turpentine or mineral spirits. Then begin painting, using a firm brush, such as one used for oils. You can blend such minute amounts of color that your painting can have many many different tones very easily. The oils contrast most with the flat areas of color of some textile paints. Try flowers, landscapes, using a variety of colors. Stenciling also works well with oils, as the edges come out sharp and clean with the paint.

The main problem when using oil paints with thinners is the fumes. Textine, mentioned above, contains xylene, a very dangerous chemical. Heart problems and menstrual problems can occur if one ingests this chemical. You need a good ventilating system such as a window exhaust fan. If this is not possible, at least use a face mask and work outdoors, if possible.

Oils can be used on dark or colored fabrics. A method is used similar to that described with textile paints. Opaque white is mixed with a color and applied. Then, if desired, the same hue without the white can be added, lightly though, so as to not stiffen the fabric. A variety of fabrics can be used, but do not try to cover large areas of fabric with oil paint. Use it for small designs.

Oils can be mixed with enamel paints, with turpentine or mineral spirits added. **How to Paint on Fabric,** by Marge Wing, gives a thorough explanation of this process. Generally speaking, the same methods are used as mentioned earlier. You can paint with just enamels and turpentine, as well.

Working with oils and thinners is moderately expensive. It depends,of course, on how much you paint. The following chart enumerates the various qualities of painting with oil and turpentine, textine, or oil with enamel paint and turpentine:

Use: not well–known except among certain craftspeople. Limited use, yet good effects within limits

Quality: medium to good quality

Price: moderately expensive

Hand: good to very good,depending upon the technique of painting used

Washability: good

Usage: can be used on clothing if small painted areas are used rather than trying to cover fabric. Good for curtains, lampshades, wall hangings

Fabrics used: cotton, muslin, cotton knits, polyester blends, synthetics, canvas, and denim

Productivity: Good to very good. Oils do take some time to dry, however

Availability: Excellent. All paint materials can be purchased at art stores and the enamels can be purchased at hardware or department stores

Lightfastness: good to very good

How set?: heat set with a dry iron, for oils with turpentine; also oil with textine; with enamels additional air dry is sufficient

NATURAL DYES

The above fabric paints, acrylics, and oils, are all manufactured paints. The next group of paint materials are made from the raw materials of paint ingredients and include natural dyes, natural paints, and mordant paints.

Natural dyes have been used for many hundreds of years. The American Indians and other indigenous cultures used natural materials in the form of dyes, paints, and inks for coloring matter. Chemical substances in the earth, in plants, and in some animals can be used for dyes. Today natural dyes can be found in the trees, flowers, and plants which grow in the city or the country. They can also be found in your flower or vegetable garden, as well, and some of them can be found in the grocery store. For example, coffee, tea, tumeric, curry, paprika, and wine can all be used for natural dyeing. Vegetables such as the peelings from eggplants, tomato vines, carrot tops, red cabbage leaves, red onion skins, and pickle juice can also produce colors such as silver blue, yellow–green, and purple. Edible berries, such as the blackberry, huckleberry, blueberry, and elderberry are potential dyes, and the nonedible pokeberry is an excellent dye. Potter's clay becomes a dye; so does clay from the earth. Wood ash, when combined with lye, forms a soft black dye. Mushrooms, lichens, dandelions, grass, rose hips, and sunflower seeds are other surprising sources of dyes. And there are many more.

In the woods, one finds roots, twigs leaves, and bark of many trees which can become dyes. Madrone bark produces a dark brown, as does walnut bark or hulls. Apple, alder, birch, hemlock, maple, pear, sassafras, white oak, and willow bark can be used. The roots of the osage orange, bloodroot, beet, and waterlily can be used. Goldenrod, morning glory blossoms, marigolds, sunflowers, and cotton flowers all produce a dye when boiled. Among hundreds of other possible dyestuffs there are mullein leaves, wild mustard, seaweed, sagebrush, horsetails, cedar berries, dock, sumac leaves, pricklypear cactus, the Oregon grape, and mistletoe. These are all substances which have been tested and written up in books. To discover other dye–producing substances, when you are gathering known materials, pick up a few on the side and experiment. Dyes are not always obvious to the eye. For example, a bright red rose will become a drab greenish/brown dyebath, while the dark skin of the eggplant becomes a lovely silver blue.

In general, to make a natural dye from any of these materials, take the gathered material and boil it in water for one hour, or until you can see the dye seep into the water. In order to have maximum strength, most natural dyes act like hot–water dyes: that is, the material to be dyed must be boiled in the hot dye for approximately one hour. However, a less strong dye can be made by boiling the dyestuff in water, then cooling it and using it with or without a thickener directly on the fabric. Mordants also strengthen the durability of the dye. In regular natural dyeing, the material to be dyed is often treated with a chemical which helps keep the dye fast. Alum, chrome, and tannic acid are common mordants, or chemicals, used. For natural dyes to be used in fabric painting, it is possible to add the mordant to the dye bath near the end of its hour boiling period. Or the cloth that is to be painted can be boiled for one hour with a mordant to insure color fastness. In order to learn the specific amounts of the mordant needed, as well as what types of dye materials need which type mordant and which type of cloth, it is best to look at books on natural dyeing. *Gentle Dyeing*–Cheryl Brooks and Carol Higgins, and *Mother Nature's Dyes and Fibers*–Will Bearfoot, are good sources.

To paint with natural dyes, you simply use a brush and paint to create designs with blendings of color and soft–edged, as opposed to hard–edged forms. An ink pen can be used for detail. Natural dyes vary in their strength. Some are very strong and remain so even when thinned with water. Others may need a thicker solution, with less water and more dyestuff. After painting, let the dye dry, then heat set it by ironing with a dry iron. Handle delicately, and do not over expose natural dyed items to direct sunlight for long periods of time.

NATURAL PAINTS

Natural dyes can be thickened to make a "natural" paint. To do so, merely add a thickening agent to the cooled dyestuff. Gum arabic or tragacanth gum can be used for thickeners, and can be found at some art or drug stores. Try corn starch or carrogeen moss. Carrogeen moss is used in the marbling process, explained in chapter VI. Sodium alginate is another thickener which is used with cold–water dyes. Dylon's Paintex, Procion dye thickener or Fibrec's dye thickener can be used. (Fig. 100)

Natural paint is thicker than natural dye: therefore there is more control with the brush. The paint can be applied directly, with medium large brushes, for a large amorphous design. Or they can be painted around a blocking out medium, such as starch–paste resists. Painting with natural dyes and paints is somewhat experimental, and should be approached in this manner.

There are several household items which can be used in connection with natural dyes and paints to change their color. Some of the mordants mentioned above can be used to darken or change the color of a dye. Copperas, for example, turns any dye a darker color. Household items such as baking soda, vinegar, cream of tartar, and ammonia can be used in combination to effect color change. Vinegar and cream of tartar work together, as do baking soda and ammonia. Just add a small amount of these to the natural dye and see if you like the new color !

I have enjoyed experimenting with natural dyes and paints in connection with fabric painting. One afternoon in the fall, I remember making "sycamore soup", a mixture of sycamore leaves, wood, mud, twigs, and bark gathered from a field behind our house. I had never seen sycamore leaves mentioned in any book on natural dyeing, and so was curious to see whether or not it would react with the other substances, including alum, to form a dye. It did not, and the beautiful deep goldbrown sycamore leaves, to this day, remain on the ground and a mystery to me.

MORDANT PAINTING

A step away from experimenting with homemade paint is the process of mordant painting. Mordant painting is probably the oldest form of fabric painting known. It has been mentioned in the writings of Pliny and was used by the ancient Egyptians in their clothing. Records state that fabric or clothing was smeared with chemicals and then thrown into vats of various colored boiling dye. The cloth was multicolored because of the reactions of the different chemicals to the different colored dyes.

Essentially, mordant painting is using chemicals to both block out areas of the cloth and change the colors of the dyes used. A cloth dyed with only one color of dye could have four or five different contrasting colors due to the type of chemicals used. The most popular ones today which are used for mordants are alum, copperas, chrome, tannic acid, and blue stone. (Some of these chemicals are extremely dangerous; use them with adequate protection, and **never** let children use them or be around them)

In ancient days, muds and clays were smeared on clothing and used as a dye. Both tannic acid and metal salts are in muds

FIG.100: THICKENING AGENTS AND OTHER CHEMICALS USED IN NATURAL PAINTS. CARROGEEN MOSS, GUM ARABIC, IODIZED SALT, CORN STARCH.

and clays, so that the resulting dark brown colors were fast. Even today, the Japanese press leaves inbetween a piece of cloth to force the tannin in the leaves into the fibers of the cloth.

Designs which do not detract from the blending of colors are good to begin with when experimenting with mordant painting.

As well, you can paint more representational forms although they may be rather indistinct, and will probably not have hard edges. If these shapes are planned out in terms of color, a nice design can emerge from the different chemical reactions in a way similar to the process of batik, with one color bath influencing another.

The basic instructions for mordant painting are as follows: mix the mordant or chemical with some water and then dip the brush into the chemical and onto the fabric where you wish to have a color different from your dye or paint. When you have used all the different chemicals you wish, paint over the fabric with dyes, inks, or textile paints.

DYES

Dyes are the next group of paint materials to be discussed for fabric painting. Although there are many types of dyes which can be used, only dyes which can be applied directly, with or without a thickener, will be considered. In other words, dyes which must be used with immersion techniques will not be considered. Since fabric **painting,** not dyeing, is the subject of this book, direct application of dyes with a brush or other tool can be considered painting.

There are, nevertheless, many, many different types of dyes which can be used in this way. **Fiber–reactive dyes** are a pop–ular and versatile type of dye. Other classifications of dyes which can be used include **disperse, direct, acid, naphthol, household, Pre–metalized, and basic.** There are also liquid dyes, such as fiber–reactive **liquid dyes** and liquid dyes for silk.

The use of dyes is so extensive and its history so vast, I will only focus on one aspect of using dyes—and that is in a thickened "paste" form for handpainting, and in a more liquid form for use with spraying, watercolor techniques, or as a drawing ink. These applications have also been described as either "thin" or "thick" applications.

The dyes are used primarily with cold water, and are not ever boiled or used in a hot dyebath.

ADVANTAGES

What are some of the advantages of using dyes? Dyes are readily available, with many choices. There is a wide range of colors from which to choose, and you can intermix colors to create your own. Dyes are a versatile product, with many effects possible. They are inexpensive to purchase, and will last a long time if properly stored. Their washfastness and lightfastness varies, depending on the type and brand. They can be used on a variety of fabrics, and most importantly, they do not disturb the hand of the fabric. Unlike some paint materials, dyes will never stiffen the fabric. Some beginners may find working with dyes overwhelming. Because of the variety of types of dyes, plus the various chemicals which are used, working with dyes is certainly more complex than just opening up a bottle of textile paint and beginning to paint! I have always had a certain block towards using dyes, due to a certain amount of impa–tience; I just want to jump in and start painting. Once a person has learned about a certain type of dye, how it works, what chemicals are needed, much of the complexity of working with

dyes is removed. Still, there are certain disadvantages of the material.

DISADVANTAGES

The greatest hazard in working with dyes is that they **are** a hazard. I would not recommend that children be allowed to use them, except for Inkodye, which is a premixed vat dye, and can be used safely from the bottle. A mask should be worn while mixing them, as small particles can be inhaled and cause health problems. Rubber gloves should also be worn while handling dyes. Most companies that stock dyes now list the precautions on their instructions.

The other disadvantage in working with dyes, is, as I have stated earlier, that they are complex to use. One must assemble a number of small containers in which to mix the various colors. I use plastic egg cartons for small amounts of dye. An eye dropper can be invaluable for adding small amounts of thick–ener or color to a certain color. For larger amounts of dye, it is best to use a separate container for each color. Certain distribu–tors carry plastic bottles for this purpose; I use whatever is convenient from the amassed bottles in our pantry. If you plan to do a lot of painting with dyes over a period or time, try to store the mixtures in dark–colored bottles away from the light. They will last longer this way. I find empty vitamin bottles good for this.

Other problems with using dyes concerns staining and water usage. Some dyes, no matter how careful you are, will inevita–bly stain your surroundings. Or, you are constantly washing up, finding more dye particles, then washing up! Fiber–reactive dyes especially need a lot of water, since they must be rinsed out until the water runs clear. Most experts recommend that you don't work in your kitchen—the dye particles can too easily get in food and on cooking utensils.

Since each type of dye has particular effects, other advan–tages, disadvantages, and ways of usage will be discussed under each classification of dye.

FIBER–REACTIVE DYES

Fiber–reactive dyes are one of the most popular types of dyes used in all surface design techniques today. One reason for this is that the dye molecules bond chemically with the fiber molecules, creating a very washfast and lightfast dye. The colors are also quite brilliant for a cold–water dye. Although there are many brand names, **Procion dye** is most commonly identified as a fiber–reactive dye. There is **Procion–M, Procion H, and Procion–MX.** Other brands include **Fibrec, Fabdec, Dylon, Cibacron F(Ciba), DyeHouse, Putnam Color Fast, Hi–Dye, Pylam, Calcobond, Remazol, Cavalite, Levafix, and Reactone–Geigy.** These dyes are in powder form. Createx fiber–reactive liquid dye is produced by Color Craft Ltd. They also carry an "R" series for silk and wool. **PROChem Liquid Reactive Dye** is also a fiber–reactive dye, as is **Liquid Procion H dye.**

PROCION DYE

Procion dye, the original fiber–reactive dye, was produced in England in the mid–1950's. Many brands, such as **Dylon, Fibrec, Fabdec, Putnam Color Fast, and Hi–Dye** are actually packaged Procion, sometimes with additives. While the pack–aging makes for an easier time mixing the ingredients, experi–enced painters will find the bulk Procion dye much more economical. All these dyes are readily available, either in an art or fiber/needlework store, or through a distributor.

Colors vary on the type of Procion dye used. **Procion MX dyes** have a wide color range, with 52 colors. They have 6 yellows, 4 oranges, 7 reds, 8 purples, 8 blues, 7 greens, an interesting shade called havacado (between the olive drab and the rust brown), 7 browns, and white, grey, and black. Pro Chemical and Dye Inc. carries 32 colors starting with 2 oz. packages. Actually, they are packed in screwtop jars, which minimizes health and storage problems. Procion–M has around 15 standard colors, while Procion–H has 16 different colors.

Generally speaking, the two different types of Procion dyes are the **Procion–M and MX and the Procion–H.** The latter is used only for painting or printing, and is used with a "thin" or "thick" application of chemical water. It cannot be mixed with the Procion M's. With Procion–M and Procion–MX dye, the descriptive name and the product name are not always the same Keep this in mind when ordering dyes from various distributors.

Procion dyes can only be used on natural fibers, such as cotton, linen, rayon, silk, and wool. They cannot be used on synthetics, polyesters, nylons, etc. They are a reasonably priced paint material, especially when purchased in bulk. They are extremely versatile in their use, and very popular with fiber artists and fabric painters. Since there are so many different brand names of Procion dye, with different accessory chemicals, I will discuss each one separately under its brand name .

Procion–M dye is a cold–water dye, and can be used for immersion techniques as well as for direct application. Certain chemicals must be added to the dye for direct painting (Some distributors stock pre–packaged chemicals; others offer the bulk chemicals for you to mix. All Procion dyes follow the same procedure that I will now describe.)

The standard "chemical water" that is the base for both "thin" and "thick" applications is made from Calgon (also called sodium hexametaphosphate), urea, and Ludigol (Also sold under the names Resist Salt L, Sitol, and Nacan). To thicken this mixture, sodium alginate is added.

To make a quart of chemical water add 1 tsp. of Calgon and 10 tbsp. of urea to 2 cups of hot water. Mix and then add cold water up to 2 cups. This mixture can be used when one wishes a thin application of dye, either by using a brush, or a spray bottle or other tool. Take a small amount of dye (several teaspoons are adequate) and add a small amount of the water. (I do this by putting small amounts dye in various containers that will hold the finished dye product—jars, yogurt containers, etc. Then continue adding the chemical water until you have used all of it. One quart can be used for up to 8 teaspoons of dye, so you can divide up your colors and the chemical water.)

Baking soda and washing soda (also called sal soda, soda ash, or sodium carbonate) are added last to activate the dye. After they have been added, the dye will be useful for only a few hours; at the most, four hours. This is because the dye will be reacting with the sodas. 4 teaspoons of baking soda plus 1 teaspoon of washing soda are used per 1 quart chemical water. (This translates down to 1 teaspoon baking soda and 1/4 teaspoon washing soda per cup of water. Mix the washing soda in a little hot water before adding it to the mixture.

Working with dyes is not an exact science. There are various opinions upon measurements for dyes and how long they will last. The Procion–M series is said to last for up to 2 days if refrigerated (after having added the soda). The chemical water can last indefinitely if refrigerated, and the dyes (without the soda) are said to last up to 4 days if refrigerated. I have tended to use these dyes within a week's period with good effects.

How much dye should be used is another area with wide opinion. I have always judged the amount visually rather than measuring it. However, for those of you who are more comfortable with precise measures, use 1/4 teaspoon per 1 cup of water for pale shades, 1 teaspoon for medium shades, 2 teaspoons for deep shades, and 4 or more teaspoons for very deep shades. This is only for the Procion–M series; there are different measurements for the Procion–H dyes.

There are an infinite amount of colors possible by mixing the standard shades. Ann Marie Patterson and Ron Granich of Cerulean Blue have created a very interesting system of color mixing. For those of you who are interested, it is clearly explained in **Surface Design for Fabric**– Jennifer Lew and Richard Proctor (1984), a wonderful book on many surface design techniques. Colors such as salmon, coral orange, apple green, and copper brown are possible to mix, using three colors : Magenta, Cyan, and Yellow.

As well as the "thin" application of dye, a "thick" one can be made by adding sodium alginate, also called **Keltex, Lamitex, or Manutex.** Sodium alginate is extracted from seaweed in the form of a gum. Either of two types can be used: a high viscosity mixture (Type "H") and a lower viscosity one (Type "L"). The higher viscosity mixture makes a very thick paint mixture, using very little of the alginate. With the lower viscosity type, one still gets a thick mixture, but it is not as stiff or bulky to stir, and it washes out more easily from fragile fabrics. Other names for the high viscosity product are **Keltex S, Lamitex H, Manutex RS, plus Pro Chemical and Dye's PRO Thick SH. PRO Thick F, Kelgin LV, Lamitex L–10, and Manutex F** are other types of the lower viscosity alginate.

The "thick" application is useful for direct painting, for the sodium alginate controls the dye, and it works very much like a fabric paint in terms of application. From the finest brush to a big housepainting brush, the thickened dye works equally well. Hard–edged shapes, wavy lines, rubber stamp prints— many techniques are possible. And you can vary the thickness of the solution by adding more chemical water.

Sodium alginate is added to the chemical water in the ratio of 4 teaspoons to one quart of water. Agitate this mixture, either by hand or with an electric mixer, until it is well blended and smooth. This mixture is now called the "stock paste". It can be refrigerated indefinitely, available to be mixed with dye whenever you are ready to paint! Store it in a closed glass container for maximum shelf life.

When you are ready to add the dye, simply pour off an amount of the stock paste. Add dye (in the same proportions as for the "thin application") to the paste, first blending it with a little hot water. Then add your sodas, again, 1 teaspoon baking soda and 1/4 teaspoon washing soda per cup stock paste. Mix these also with a little hot water before adding to the mixture. Now your thickened dyepaste is ready for use!

With the color added, the Procion–M dye mixture will last 3–4 days if refrigerated between use. With the sodas added, the longevity drops to between 1–2 days.

After using the dyes, let your fabric dry for 24 hours. It must then be steam set by one of several various methods: atmospheric steaming, using a canner or steam cabinet, pressure steaming in a pressure cooker, steam baking in an oven, or steam ironing. The first two methods are discussed under "Notes on Steaming". I have found the next two methods adequate for most projects.

Steam ironing is the easiest way to set your fabric. Simply iron the fabric at its appropriate temperature for five minutes. It is preferable to iron on the wrong side. For delicate fabrics, do not bear down on the iron too hard. Steam baking in an oven requires rolling the fabric in butcher paper, muslin, or paper towels so that no painted surface touches any other. Place this wrapped fabric on the rack of the oven, with a container of boiling water beneath. Bake for 30 minutes at approximately 285 degrees for fabric up to one square yard. Larger pieces should be rerolled and baked an added 30 minutes. Be sure to keep adding water in the container, so that there is an adequate amount of steam.

After steaming, unwrap the fabric, and rinse it in cold water until the water runs clear. Then increase the water temperature until the water runs clear with hot water. If desired, the fabric can then be boiled in a mild synthetic detergent (Synthrapol is being distributed by many dye suppliers especially for this purpose). Boiling the fabric in the detergent helps to wash away any migrating dye molecules that may have bled into white areas of the fabric. Rinse your fabric in cool water, then dry it.

Rinsing out fiber–reactive dyes in a home work area requires lots of water and space. I find using a shower area for a large piece of fabric and a large wash basin for smaller pieces adequate. When working outdoors, using a garden hose is an easy way to rinse fabric. Use an apron to protect your clothing when rinsing fabric.

The following chart may help you with the basic principles of dye–pastes, chemical water, "thin" and "thick" applications.

DYE–PASTES : a dye–paste is a mixture of dye, in this case Procion–M and a number of chemicals which is used as a painting medium.

CHEMICAL WATER: Chemical water is made by mixing 1 tsp. Calgon, 10 tbsp. Urea, 2 tsp. Ludigol and adding this to 2 cups hot water. Stir well. Then add 2 cups cold water. This will make 1 quart of chemical water.

CALGON is a water softener. It is also called sodium hexametaphosphate. It chemically reacts with any minerals in tap water that might interfere with the dyeing process.

UREA is synthesized from ammonia and carbon dioxide. It is a fertilizer and retains moisture in the dyeing process.

LUDIGOL is a sodium salt which helps to achieve maximum color yield. It is especially crucial to use with dark colors, such as navy blue and black.

DYE AMOUNTS: For thin application, add the following amounts per quart:
pale shades–1 teas.
medium shades–4 teas.
dark shades–8 teas.
very dark shades–16 or more teas.

The same applies for "thick" application.

THIN APPLICATION: Pour out appropriate amount of chemical water into small bowl. Add appropriate amount of dye which has been blended with a small amount of water. Then per quart, add 4 teas. baking soda and 1 teas. washing soda, having first blended the sodas with a little water.

LONGEVITY: Chemical water can last indefinitely (try and use within a month) if refrigerated. **Thin applications** of Procion–M dyes last 4 days when refrigerated. This is without sodas added.

Thin applications of Procion–M dye **with** sodas will last 1–2 days if refrigerated.

THICK APPLICATION: Add 4 teas. of **sodium alginate** to 1 quart of chemical water. Agitate. Then add appropriate amount of dye which has been blended with a little water. 4 teas. of baking soda and 1 teas. of washing soda are then added, again being blended with a little water.

LONGEVITY: Longevity of thick applications are the same as for the thin.

DRYING: Let all painted fabrics dry for 24 hours.

SETTING: In most cases, set by steaming. Iron with a steam iron for 5 minutes at a temperature appropriate to the fabric. Oven steaming, pressure steaming, and atmospheric steaming also possible.

RINSING: Rinse with cold water, then increasing temperature to hot, until water runs clear. Boil with a synthetic detergent (Synthrapol is good) 5 minutes, using 1/8 cup to 3 gallons of water. Rinse again in cold water. Let dry.

SODA SOAK APPLICATION

There is a "short–cut" method which can be used for both thin and thick applications. Prewash your fabric, then soak it for 15 minutes in a solution of 1 gallon of water and 1/2 cup of washing soda. Let the fabric dry if desired, or use it damp. Apply the thin or thick dye–paste, but omit the baking soda. After painting, let the fabric air dry for 24 hours. No steam setting is needed, simply rinse out the fabric as with the other methods and let dry.

PROCION TIPS

As can be seen, there is quite a bit to learn about using Procion, or fiber–reactive dyes. Here are a number of other ideas which may be useful.

1. Use synthetic, such as nylon, brushes when working with dye–pastes. Natural–fiber bristles absorb too much water and soon become unmanageable.

2. Always prewash your fabric. If you suspect the fabric has a permanent finish on any other type of finish, it can be removed by doing the following :

REMOVING PERMANENT PRESS FINISH

Prepare a solution of muriatic acid (a 30% solution of 30% hydrochloric acid available from Pro Chemical and Dye company) by adding .5 liquid ounces of muriatic acid to 2 gallons of cool water. Add the fabric, putting it in an enamel or stainless steel pan. Heat over a stove to 185 degrees F and stir the fabric occasionally up to 20 minutes. Remove from heat, rinsing thoroughly.

3. The color black has some special considerations. Often it is difficult to get a true black with dyes. Procion–H does have a good black—use it up to three times stronger for desired results. Or, mix 3 parts scarlet, 3 parts yellow to 6 parts navy for a good strong black.

4. The washing soda in the grocery stores has been cut with additives which interfere with the dyeing process. It is best to order your washing soda from a supplier.

5. Painting on silk with dye–pastes requires special awareness. Procion–M dyes will only dye the silk in light to medium shades. Also don't steam–bake or use a pressure cooker to steam silk. It can be ironed or used with the atmospheric steam technique (canning kettle or steam cabinet). Another consideration with silk is that only the low–viscosity sodium alginate should be used with it. It is much easier to wash out of the fabric. Pro Chemical and Dye uses the PRO Thick F rather than the PRO Thick SH. Print Base Kit "L" is another product used for silk and wool.

PROCION–M AND PROCION–MX DYES

Procion–MX dyes are included in the Procion–M series. The Procion–MX dyes are exceptionally brilliant. They come in about 52 different shades, and these are intermixable. They can be used on cotton, rayon, wool, and silk. They do not have to be steam set; instead of this process, replace the adding of sodas with the "soda–soak" method, described earlier in this chapter. After following this process, let the fabric set overnight, covered in plastic to prevent evaporation.

PROCION–H DYES

This is another type of Procion dye which is becoming very popular today with fabric painters. It is especially designed for painting and printing, and cannot be used for immersion techniques. Neither can it be mixed with the Procion–M series dyes. Another difference with the **Procion–H dyes** is that they will react on silk with very bright and brilliant colors, rather than just tints or light shades. They are, therefore, highly recommended for painting on silk.

The other advantage of using Procion–H dyes over the M–series is that the dye–paste can be kept for 4 weeks or longer. This greatly facilitates planning and executing a painted work, for one does not have to either continually mix up the dye–paste, or count the available working days.

The third difference in Procion H dyes is that there is little migration of dye molecules during the wash–off process. This means it is less likely that white areas of the fabric will be stained with dye.

In general, the same procedures are followed when using either type of Procion dye. The same proportions are used when making the chemical water, and the same amount of sodium alginate is used for a thick application. The only difference is that baking soda is used solely; washing soda is not added to the dye. There are approximately 16 stock colors—and they can be intermixed to make many more. If refrigerated, and without the addition of baking soda, some sources say that the stock colors can keep up to 8 months. With baking soda added, these Procion–H dyes will still keep for 1 month. Be sure to label all refrigerated items.

Procion–H dyes have the same characteristics of brightness of color, good light and washfastness, as do the Procion–H dyes. When measuring dye quantities to mix with the chemical water, I find it useful to add approximately 2x the amounts given for the H–series. For example:

pale shades: 2–4 teas.
medium shades: 4–8 teas.
dark shades: 12–16 teas.
very dark shades: 24 or more teaspoons. These amounts are

for 1 quart of chemical water.

Add 1 teaspoon of baking soda to each *cup* of chemical water used, along with the proper dye amounts. Then you will be ready for painting! In general, Procion–H dyes must be steam–set. The only exception to this is using **Pro Chemical and Dye's PROFix LHF**–a liquid alkali which will fix the dyes without steaming. It can only be used on cottons. Fabrics should be steamed by the *atmospheric steaming method,* which uses either a steam cabinet or a canning kettle.

ATMOSPHERIC STEAMING

Atmospheric steaming is accomplished by wrapping the fabric loosely in either butcher paper, muslin, or paper towel. Be sure that none of the painted surfaces touch. Place this wrapped fabric onto the rack of the canning kettle or steam cabinet. Cover the fabric with an aluminum foil "tent" so that no water or condensation gets onto the fabric. Steam the Procion–H dyes for 30 minutes. (Refer to **Contemporary Batik and Tie–Dye** –Dona Meilach for a complete explanation of steaming with a canner)

OTHER STEAMING METHODS

There are alternative choices to atmospheric steaming. If you pressure steam (just like with the Procion–M dyes), steam for 5 minutes instead of 3. With oven steaming, set the oven at 300 degrees and steam for 45 minutes. And with a steam iron, iron for 10 minutes instead of 5.

Other steaming ideas are to wrap your cloth as you would for atmospheric steaming, and place it in a sauna for 15 minutes, at a temperature of 250 degrees. Or, use a shower and run hot water to create steam, but hang the fabric well away from the water source. If you live in a humid environment, you can air dry the fabric for one to two days!

PROCION–H TIPS

1. With the black dye, substitute washing soda (3 teas. per cup of chemical water) for the baking soda. This is only true for the color black in the Procion–H series. Also, it is helpful to use less urea in the chemical solution—3 1/2 tablespoons instead of the usual 10 per quart of chemical water.

2. When steaming silk, only 15 –20 minutes is needed when using Procion–H dyes. After steaming and rinsing, add 1 cup of vinegar in the final rinse to restore the lustre to the silk.

OTHER BRANDS

There are a number of other brands of Procion dye which are packaged for use with fabric painting. Some of them are marked as either Procion–M or Procion–H; others are not. They include **Fabdec, Fibrec, Dylon, and Jacquard Fiber–Reactive Dyes.** There are a number of other fiber–reactive dyes as well, including **Fibracron Fiber–reactive Dyes, Dyehouse, Aljo, Cibacron F dyes, and Cibacron F dyes.**

Fibrec carries a dye thickener which is prepackaged, to be used for silkscreen, printing, and painting. Dylon carries **"Paintex"** also a thickener for painting. Dyehouse is supplied by Dharma Trading company—they have 27 different colors and a prepackaged thickener or the bulk chemicals for use. There are a number of other fiber–reactive dyes that I have not used: **Putnam Color Fast, Hi–Dye, Pylam, Calcobond, Remazol, Cavalite, Levafix, and Reactone–Geigy. Aljo Cold Process Dye** has 20 different colors, and uses a gum tragacanth thickener rather than sodium alginate. They also carry the other needed chemicals in bulk.

These prepackaged dyes are especially good for beginners, since they can easily mix the dyes and focus on design and color. When working with these various dyes, keep organized and everything will go more smoothly! For example, label and date every bottle of dye before putting it in the refrigerator. Make a chart with samples when mixing your own colors—this way you can easily repeat your favorite color mixtures. If you work with one type of dye until you are comfortable with it, it makes it easier to "learn" a different one.

QUALITIES OF PROCION DYES

In order to sum up the vast amount of information about Procion dyes, the following chart may be helpful :

Use: Extremely popular and very versatile

Quality: Excellent quality art material for fabric painting

Price: very economical

Ease of Use: fairly complex to learn how to use

Hand: Excellent hand

Washability: Good to excellent

Usage: used for many items: T–shirts, tops, pants, dresses, pillow cases, lampshades, curtains, wall hangings, soft sculpture, etc.

Fabrics used: cotton, linen, rayon (viscose),silk, and wool. Only natural fibers that do not have a finish of any sort can be used

Productivity: Good results, once dyes are mixed

Availability: art stores, fiber/needlework stores, many suppliers

Lightfastness: Good to excellent

How set?: steam iron, oven steaming, pressure steaming, or atmospheric steaming

CIBACRON–F DYES

Cibacron–F is another type of fiber–reactive dye. (It is sometimes called Cibacron Reactive dye or Ciba dye) It is a lower reactive dye than the Procion–M or MX dye, meaning that it takes a longer time for the dye to completely react. 24 hours is needed for it to cure.

There are 20 different colors available from Pro Chemical and Dye These colors can be intermixed with each other, but it is best not to mix them with other fiber–reactive dyes.

Since these are fiber–reactive dyes, they follow the same process as do the Procion dyes. One advantage is that they may be stored for up to two weeks (refrigerated and without the added soda) with no color loss. They do not need to be steam set; rather they can be "cold batched" (the name for the process

of letting the fabric cure for 24 to 48 hours under a protective plastic wrap)

LIQUID FIBER–REACTIVE DYES

There is one more type of fiber–reactive dye available to the fabric painter: the liquid variety. There are several brands on the market at this time: **Createx Liquid Fiber Reactive Dyes, Liquid Fiber–reactive "R Series" Dyes, Liquid Procion H Fiber–reactive Dyes, and Liquid Reactive Dyes.** In general, these dyes are used in a manner similar to the powdered reactive dyes. They are mixed with a chemical water solution, and can be thickened with sodium alginate. One reason for using these dyes in a liquid form is that there is less danger from inhaling the airborne powder of the dry dye.

The dyes can be fixed by a number of methods. They can be air cured if you live in a warm, humid environment. Let hang for 2–3 days. Or put in a clothes dryer for 30 minutes on the highest setting. They can be steamed. They can be treated using the "soda–soak" method .They can be baked in an oven for 15 minutes at 225 degrees. They can be ironed for 5 minutes at a steam setting appropriate to the fabric used. Other fixatives include PRO FIX LHF and Createx Fast Fix. PRO FIX LHF cannot be used on wool, and it should be handled with caution as it contains a strong alkali. Createx "Fast Fix" is a product which eliminates any type of heat setting. It works on cotton, linen, rayon, and silk.

Createx Liquid dyes are unique also in that they can be used on some synthetic fibers—nylon and Lycra, specifically. Their "R Series" dyes do not need heat for fixation on certain fabrics: silk, wool, nylon, and Lycra. Citric Acid is used as the fixative.

SUMMARY OF FIBER–REACTIVES

As can be seen, there are a great many different fiber–reactive dyes available to the fabric painter. They are a very popular kind of dye, since their colors and bright and their fastness is good.

Procion–MX dyes are the most highly reactive dye on the market. They are followed by the Procion–M dyes, then Cibacron–F (half as reactive as the MX's), then come the liquid fiber–reactive dyes at 10 times less reactivity than the MX dyes, and at the last, the Procion–H dyes. Depending up on your method of work and what you are doing, each one of these types of dye can be your best choice. Just remember that, the more reactive the dye, the faster it loses its full color, and the less likely that you will be able to store it. On the other hand, the dyes that are highly reactive need less complicated forms of fixing or steaming (the MX dyes need no steaming at all)

DISPERSE DYES

Disperse dyes are the next category of dyes to be discussed.(Fig. 101) They can be used in two ways: as a transfer paint or for direct application using chemical water and thickeners. In chapter VI, under "Transfer Painting", directions are given for using disperse dyes as a transfer paint. I will discuss here the methods of direct application.

Disperse dyes are used for synthetic materials. They can be used on acetate, triacetate (Arnel) nylon, Lycra, dacron, kodel, fortrel, and mylar, as well as polyesters and synthetic blends. Disperse dye is very concentrated; a little goes a long way.

FIG. 101: SUSAN SPRINGER MODELS A QUIANA BLOUSE SHE PAINTED WITH DISPERSE DYES. PHOTO BY PERRY SMALL.

Colors range from 9–22 colors, including yellow, navy blue, emerald green, and magenta. Brands include Polydye, PROsperse disperse dye, and Aljo acetate nylon dyes.

Disperse dyes are mixed with the same chemical water and sodium alginate thickener that is used for the fiber–reactive dyes. To refresh your memory, use 1 teas. Calgon or other water softener, 10 Tbsp. Urea, 2 tsp. Ludigol, and add 2 cups of cold water to this mixture. Then add 2 cups of hot water, mixing well. For a thick mixture, sprinkle up to 4 tsp. of sodium alginate into the chemical water. Then add 1/4 to 4 teas. of dye per cup of chemical water. One important change with the disperse dyes is that, for each teas. of dye used, add 1 Tbsp. of white vinegar. Another change is that monogum thickener is often used with disperse dyes rather than sodium alginate. Add 2 teas. of monogum to 1 quart of water, sprinkling the thickener over the chemical water until it is thoroughly mixed.

After direct application of the dyes, fix in the following ways: steam iron for several minutes at a setting appropriate to the fabric used; bake at 375 degrees for 45–90 seconds (watch carefully—synthetic fabrics can burn easily); or pressure steam at 260 degrees for 30 minutes. Replace the urea with water (10 tbsp) when using this method of fixation.

The fabric should now be rinsed just like for fiber–reactive dyes. Start with cold water, increasing the temperature to hot. Use Synthrapol or Ivory Liquid to wash the fabric. Follow with a hot water rinse, and you will minimize the problem of "bleeding"

Disperse dyes that are applied directly have a different effect than those applied by heat–transfer. With direct application, the dyes appear very soft, with slight blending into the fibers due to capillary action. Watercolor effects, with blending of colors on top of each other, is possible. By using a greater amount of thickener, hard edged looks are possible. However, with heat–transfer, textures are possible since the painted paper can be crumpled or torn before being transferred by ironing to the fabric.

QUALITIES OF DISPERSE DYES

To sum up disperse dyes, refer to the chart below:

Use: moderate use by craftspeople. Especially useful and versatile where synthetic materials are used

Quality: Good quality art material

Price: very economical, as it is highly concentrated

Ease of Use: Fairly easy to learn how to use

Hand: Excellent hand

Washability: very good

Usage: used especially for dancewear, costumes for the theatre, hosiery and lingerie, accessories such as scarves. Also used for outerwear, dresses and blouses, curtains, etc.

Fabrics used: Polyesters and synthetics such as acetate, nylon, acrylics, plastics, mylar, dacron, etc.

Productivity: Good results

Availability: primarily ordered through dye houses and fiber arts supplies

FIG. 102: LISA HENSLEY MODELING SILK DRESS PAINTED WITH FLORAL DESIGN.

Lightfastness: very good

How set?: steam iron, pressure steaming, oven baking.

ACID DYES

Acid dyes are used on silk, wool, and nylon. There are quite a variety of them, including **Miyako, Ciba Kiton, PRO Washfast acid dyes, Aljo Silk and Wool Acid dyes, Fezan Batik dyes, Calcocid, Ciba Acid, and Lanaset.** (Fig.103)

Some of these dyes are for use on silk and wool, others for wool and nylon. There are different processes for the different fabric types, and various brands have a variety of recipes that are used. Therefore, it can be seen that working with acid dyes is a complex procedure.

There are a number of different chemicals used with acid dyes. These include glycerin (available at most all drugstores), tartaric acid (available at a medical pharmacy), glacial acetic acid (available at photographic supply stores) acetic acid (photographic or dye suppliers will carry this), ammonium sulfate (available from dye supply houses), and ammonium oxalate (also available from dye houses). White vinegar is also used in some recipes. Sodium alginate and locust bean thickener (indalca gum) are also used to thicken acid dyes.

These chemicals should be handled with extreme care, as some of them are poisonous. Wear a mask, rubber gloves, and a plastic apron, and do not work around a kitchen area.

One of the difficulties in using acid dyes is that each color acts individually— there are no hard and fast rules that are true for all colors. Also, the dyes act differently depending on the fiber or fabric used. The primaries red, yellow, and blue do not dye well on silk (of the Ciba Kiton series), as they will only yield tints or pastel shades. Tests must be made in order to be assured of certain colors.

Acid dyes give brilliant colors, and this is one of their best features. Although they are lightfast, some sources suggest keeping them away from direct sunlight. Their washfastness is not good, and it is best to have articles dry–cleaned. The one exception to this is the series PRO Washfast Acid Dyes, which gives very good washfastness and fair lightfastness.

Most suppliers stock between 11–14 colors except Aljo, which carries 30 different colors, including rubine, lily rose, violamine, milling blue, topas yellow, and pearl grey. All the acid dye colors can be intermixed to expand your palette.

ACID DYE RECIPES

There are a number of recipes for acid dyes. Several will be given here: look for others in books on fabric dyeing as well as instructions given with the acid dyes them selves.

Thickened dye for silk, using glycerin and tartaric acid:

Sprinkle 1 teas. dye over 1/4 C. water. Add l Tbsp. glycerin. Heat this mixture briefly until the dye is warmed and dissolves. Cool. Then add 1/2 cup of thickener. (See below) Then dissolve 1 and 1/2 teas. of tartaric acid in 1 and 1/2 teas. of hot water. Stir this into the mixture to make 1/2 cup of dye paste.

Thickener for acid dyes on silk

To make 2 cups:
1/2 teas. Calgon

2 C. hot water
2 teas. sodium alginate
Add together and mix well.

After painting, steam set the fabric. Different weight fabrics use different methods. For example, light weight silk such as China silk can be steam set with an iron. Heavier silks and light–weight wools can be oven steamed or put in a steam cabinet. Heavyweight wools and heavy silks must be steamed in a pressure cooker or auto clave. Steam for 1 hour at 185 degrees. Rinse in cold water, gradually increasing the temperature of the water. Wash with a light detergent to minimize "bleeding".

Fezan "Batik" Dye for Silk with thickener

Take 1 Teas (heaping) dye and mix a little hot water with it. Then add 1/4 C. white vinegar. Add 3/4 teas. of plain salt, then add 2 cups of hot water. Stir this mixture, then add 2 cups of cold water. Finally, sprinkle from 1/4 to 1/2 teas. of sodium alginate over this mixture and agitate it. After painting, steam fabric, then rinse it until water runs clear. For best results, dry clean fabric to remove thickener.

Here is a recipe for making liquid silk dyes from acid dye. Take 1 teas. glacial acetic acid and mix with 1 teas. acid dye. Mix this with a mortar and pestle until it is blended. Then slowly add two cups of hot water. This mixture can be stored indefinitely.

This liquid dye can be used directly on the fabric with the serti method—that is, painting on silk using gutta as a resist. Or, one can use a thickener, such as the ones listed below:

Gum Arabic thickener for acid dyes (for silk, wool, or nylon)

To make 1 cup:
1/4 teas. Calgon
1 C. hot water
3 Tablespoons gum arabic (or more if needed)

Gum Tragacanth thickener

To make 2 cups :
1/2 teas. Calgon
2 cups hot water
2 teas. gum tragacanth

Locust bean(indalca gum) thickener

To make 2 cups:
1/2 teas. Calgon
2 cups hot water
1 teas. locust or carob bean flakes

With all these recipes, the thickening agent is sprinkled on top of the water, and then mixed thoroughly. Let the solution sit for at least 10 minutes before using.

Thickened dye for silk, wool, or nylon, using Ciba Kiton dyes

Make a thickener by adding 1 teas. Calgon to 2 cups water; then sprinkle up to 4 teas. sodium alginate on top. Mix 1/2 teas. dye with 2 teas. glycerin. Add 1/8 C. boiling water. Let cool.

FIG. 103: PAINTED SILK GOWN:"IRISES" BY CAROL RACKLIN. CHINA SILK, ACID DYES & WAX LINES.

Dissolve 1 teas. ammonium oxalate in 1 tablespoon hot water. Then add 1/4 C. of the thickener. Add the dye mixture to this, plus 1/2 C. water.

After painting, steam fix for 1 hour, under moist steam conditions. Then rinse under cold running water and wash with Synthrapol to minimize bleeding. Rinse again in cold water.

TIPS FOR ACID DYEING

1. If using acetic acid, white vinegar can be substituted. 2 tbsp. of acetic acid equals 1/2 C. vinegar.

2. Although acid dyes do tend to migrate on the fabric, causing bleeding, and because they are not generally washfast, it is possible to handwash silk in cool water with a mild soap. This will help washability.

SUMMARY OF ACID DYES

Use: Moderate among fabric painters. More popular among weavers and those who dye their own wool. Used a lot by silk painters, however.

Quality: quality of acid dyes varies with the type dye; in general, a good quality paint material

Price: very reasonable

Ease of Use: quite complex to use, with many chemicals, some of them dangerous

Hand: Excellent

Washability: fair to poor, except for PROWashfast Acid Dyes.

Usage: silk scarves, blouses, dresses, wool clothing, nylon clothing and accessories

Fabrics used: silk, wool, nylon, other animal or protein fibers, some other synthetics

Productivity: fair, since mixing dyes takes time; also complex procedures in applying and steaming

Availability: ordered primarily through dye houses and fiber arts supplies

Lightfastness: good

How set?: steaming by oven or pressure or steam cabinet or autoclave

The colors of acid dyes are what makes their use worthwhile for the fabric painter. By testing a variety of colors, one can create a vocabulary of beautiful brilliant colors.

DIRECT DYES

Direct dyes are in less use to day because they have been surpassed by dyes with greater washability. Still, they are inexpensive, easily available, and easy to use. (Fig.104) Some of the brands available are **Miyako, Calcomine, Aljo Cotton and Rayon Dye, Deka–L, and Fezan.**

Direct dyes are used on natural fibers and fabrics such as cotton, linen, silk, wool, and viscose rayon. They are available in a range of 33 colors, including antique rose, wine red, cornflower blue, russian green, salmon, copper, old gold, fawn, mode brown, and deep black. Direct dyes are one kind of dye where it is possible to get a true black on cotton. Direct dyes are attracted to cellulose fibers, and the colors are good. For direct painting, it is suggested that double the amount of dye be used. Washability varies with direct dyes. One solution to this is to handwash each item separately in cool water with a mild detergent. Another solution is to dry clean all items. And a third is to use a product called **Fixanol**. The fabric is soaked in this solution after dyeing and it improves washability.

There are several ways to thicken the dye. One is to follow the procedure for fiber–reactive dyes, and omit the sodas. Or, use the following recipe:

1–2 teas. dye
5 teas. urea
3/4 cup hot water

Mix dye and urea with hot water. Add 1 cup plus 3 Tbsp. thickener (gum tragacanth) which is made in the following way:

Sprinkle 2 teas. gum tragacanth over 2 C. hot water. This will make 2 cups of thickener. Add 1.5 teas. disodium hydrogen phosphate (available at a pharmacy) and mix well. Then apply to fabric. Direct dyes must be steamed thoroughly in order to approach fastness. Steam for 1 hour using either a steam cabinet or an autoclave. Although the washfastness and lightfastness of direct dyes vary, they have very nice colors and are an inexpensive way for the beginner to experiment with dye–pastes.

FIG. 104 :"PLAITED PIECE"– ANNE MARIE NICKOLSON. DIRECT DYE APPLICATION, PLAITING WITH RAYON BRAID.

Use: Declining but still available

Quality: only a fair paint material due to dubious washfastness

Price: Inexpensive

Ease of Use: very easy to use

Hand: Excellent

Washability: varies, but generally poor to fair

Usage: clothing and other fabric items

Fabrics used: natural fabrics such as cotton, linen, silk, wool and viscose rayon

Productivity: In terms of time, good, but not recommended for salable items

Availability: readily available in fiber/needlework stores and dye suppliers

Lightfastness: fair to good

How set?: by steaming

HOUSEHOLD DYES

Household dyes are a blend of a variety of dyes, most commonly acid and direct. They are very good to use with blends of fabric, such as poly–cotton or synthetic blends, for more of the dye will "take". A cotton fabric will only use the direct part of the dye, while the other dye molecules will wash off in the rinse. The same is true if you are painting on silk or wool: the acid dyes will react, while the direct dyes will wash off. One way to get deeper colors is to double the amount of dye used for hot dyeing when painting with dye pastes.

Household dyes can be used on cotton, linen, silk, viscose rayon, wool, acetate, nylon, and synthetic and polyester blends. They are readily available in grocery stores, drugstores, or dimestores. They are sometimes called "union dyes". Some of the brand names are: **Rit, Tintex, Putnam All Purpose, Cushing's, Dylon Multipurpose, and Union.**

Household dyes are not particularly lightfast or washfast. They can, however, be dry-cleaned. Or, wash each item separately in lukewarm water. This will prolong their washfastness.

Here are some recipes for dye pastes using household dyes:

1 teas. dye
1 teas. Glauber's salt
5 tbsp. glycerin
3/4 cup water

1 C. thickener (sodium alginate or gum tragacanth) This recipe is for cotton and cotton blends, linen, other cellulose fibers. This recipe will dye synthetics to a pastel shade. I also found the washfastness of this recipe very good; there was no migration of dye during the washoff as there was with the direct dyes thickened with sodium alginate.

This is a recipe for silk and wool, using household dyes:

1 teas. dye
5 Tbsp. glycerin
1 Tbsp. acetic acid
1/2 C. water
l C. gum tragacanth thickener

In both these recipes, mix the dye, Glauber's salt or acetic acid, and glycerin together and heat briefly until the dye is dissolved. Cool, then add thickener. After painting, steam fabric by atmospheric steaming, pressure steaming, or oven steaming. Small test pieces can be steam–ironed. Rinse and wash with a mild detergent.

Household dyes can be useful for beginners as they are easy to find and their washfastness is fair. However, fiber–reactive dyes are far superior for long–term use. Another use of household dyes is for overdyeing of fabrics. Certain painted works using white fabric can be overdyed with no change in color. Household dyes are good for this.

SUMMARY OF HOUSEHOLD DYES

Use: used primarily by beginning fabric painters

Quality: fair to good

Price: moderately expensive except for use in small amounts (due to high packaging costs)

Ease of Use: Fairly easy to use

Hand: excellent

Washability: moderate but varies

Usage: good for beginner's products, small samples, casual clothing such as T–shirts

Fabrics used: natural fibers and synthetic blends–cotton, linen, viscose rayon, silk, wool, and synthetic and polyester blends

Productivity: good

Availability: readily available

Lightfastness: fair to good

How set?: by steaming—atmospheric, pressure, or oven–steaming 45 minutes.

BASIC DYES

Basic dyes are known for their brilliant colors. They can be used with a thickener on cotton, linen, wool, silk, and synthetics, but the cotton and linen fabrics must be mordanted, either before or after applying the dye–paste. There are several brands available, including **Aljo Alcohol/Water Dye, Batik Tintout Dyes, Astrazon, and Calcozine.** These last two dyes are available only in bulk amounts (100 pounds and up). Up to 22 different colors are available, including gold, dark brown, red, pink, black, fuchsia, sky blue, and turquoise. The colors are intermixable for a greater variety of combinations.

The washfastness and lightfastness of basic dyes is not good; therefore it is best to make items that will not receive direct sunlight. Basic dyes can, however, tolerate artificial light. They should be dry-cleaned, if possible since their washfastness is poor.

There are several different procedures for using the thickened dyes. For cotton or linen, the fabric must be mordanted either before or after the painting process. In the following recipe, the mordanting occurs afterwards.

BASIC DYE–PASTE ON COTTON

1–4 teas. dye
5 teas. glycerin
4 teas. glacial acetic acid
Mix these ingredients together. Add:
1/3 C. hot water. Mix together with this:
2 teas. tartaric acid
Let this mixture cool and then add:
1 and 1/4 C. of thickener, either gum arabic or gum tragacanth)
Then mix 5 teas. of tannic acetic acid by mixing 2/3 teas. tannic acid and 2/3 teas. glacial acetic acid with 4 teas. of water; add this to previous mixture.

After painting, steam fabric for 1 hour. Then immerse the fabric in a bath of 1 teas. of tartar emetic mixed in 2 cups of hot water. Immerse only for 30 seconds, then rinse fabric in cold water.

Tannic acid, tartar emetic, glacial acetic acid, and glycerin can be purchased through a pharmacy.

BASIC DYE–PASTE ON SILK AND WOOL

1–2 teas. dye
2 and 1/2 teas. glycerin
2 and 1/2 teas. glacial acetic acid
2 and 1/2 teas. cold water
Mix these substances together. Then add:
3/4 C. hot water. Mix well.
Then add a gum arabic or gum tragacanth thickener. Add 1 C plus 1 and 1/2 tablespoons thickener.
Dissolve 5 teas. tartaric acid in 5 teas. of water. Mix this into the dye mixture. Apply to silk or wool fabric. After the fabric is dry, steam for 1 hour. Rinse in lukewarm water.

BASIC DYE–PASTE FOR SYNTHETICS

1–2 teas. dye 2 and 1/2 teas. glycerin 2 and 1/2 teas. glacial acetic acid 3/4 C. plus 4 teas. warm water. Mix these ingredients together. Add: 1 C. thickener (gum arabic or gum tragacanth) After painting, steam fabric for 1 hour. Rinse in warm water.

Basic dyes are not widely used by fabric painters. This is due primarily to their poor washability and lightfastness. However, they are effective for painting on silk and they are considerably less in price than the liquid silk dyes. Their bright, brilliant colors are their "selling point".

SUMMARY OF BASIC DYES

Use: limited usage

Quality: fair to good

Price: reasonable

Ease of Use: easy to use on silk, wool, and synthetics;

slightly more complicated on cotton and linen

Hand: excellent

Washability: generally poor; dry cleaning recommended

Usage: good for silk clothing and accessories: other synthetics such as scarves, acrylic knits

Fabrics used: natural fibers are possible but best results on silk, wool and synthetics

Productivity: good

Availability: not easily available

Lightfastness: good on synthetics

How set?: Steam set

PRE–METALIZED DYES

There are several pre–metalized dyes in use for fabric painting. They are Cibalan, Irgalan, Lanaset, and Telana. Pre–metalized dyes are very lightfast and good in their washfastness. While their colors are not brilliant, I find that they produce deep shades on most types of fabrics.

There are only 10 different colors, but they can be intermixed. Certain shades are deeper than others, and are called super milling dyes. Pre–metalized dyes can be used for silk, wool, nylon, and certain synthetic blends. When used as a dye-paste, the dye does not spread or migrate. This gives hard-edged, clear images, a desirable feature of the dye.

RECIPES FOR DYE–PASTES

The following recipe can also be used with acid dyes. However, with pre–metalized dyes, the recipe will work on synthetic blends as well as the standard silk, wool, and nylon.
1–4 teas. dye
5 teas. glycerin
2/3 C. water
Mix these substances together and heat briefly, until dye dissolves. Cool. Then add 1 and 1/4 C. of thickener, either gum arabic or gum tragacanth. Mix 2 and 1/2 teas. tartaric acid with 2 and 1/2 teas. water. Add this to the thickened dye paste.

Note: When painting on silk, add only 2 and 1/2, rather than 5, teas. of glycerin.

After painting fabric, let it dry and then steam for 1 hour. Rinse, wash in a mild detergent, and rinse again in cool water. When rinsing nylon fabric first rinse in a mixture of 3/8 teas. washing soda per quart of water. Then wash in a mild detergent. Rinse again with 2 teas. of white vinegar mixed in 1 quart water. This will minimize "bleeding".

Pre–metalized dyes are especially good for use with direct painting. They can be used on a wide variety of fabrics, and they do not bleed. Their washfastness and lightfastness are also good. Here is a summary of their qualities:

SUMMARY OF PRE–METALIZED DYES

Use: a somewhat popular paint material

Quality: a high quality dye

Price: reasonable

Ease of Use: fairly straightforward. Some mixing of hazardous chemicals

Hand: Excellent

Washability: very good

Usage: particularly recommended for synthetic blends, silk, and wool; scarves, dresses, other clothing and accessories; also wall hangings, curtains, quilts, etc.

Fabrics used: silk, wool, nylon, and some synthetic blends

Productivity: Good

Availability: not readily available

Lightfastness: very good

How set?: steam–set

LANASET DYES

I want to mention briefly that Lanaset dyes are available in 15 intermixable colors. These colors produce more stable results on different fibers, such as silk and wool. They are a wool reactive and 1 : 2 metal complex dye. These dyes have good washfastness and lightfastness.

VAT DYES

Although there are a variety of vat dyes, only **Inkodye** will be discussed here as it is a soluble vat dye with the quite hazardous chemicals already mixed in. There are 14 intermixable colors and an extender, called Inko Clear. Inkodye, like other vat dyes, appears clear or pale until sunlight develops the colors. Therefore, color mixing cannot be done by dye, and making test swatches is extremely important. Colors are mixed like pigment: red and yellow make orange; yellow and blue make green; and red and blue make purple. The simplest way to make tests of colors is to use a hot iron to develop them quickly.

Inkodye is sometimes called a "sun dye" as it is most common to develop the colors outdoors on a sunny day. (Fig. 105) This type of paint material is also popular with children as it is premixed, easy to use, and fun to apply! The colors are exceptionally light and washfast. Inkodye can be used on natural fibers such as cotton, linen, and viscose rayon (Inko Silk Dye, which is used on silk, will be discussed under "Liquid Dyes"). It can also be used on certain synthetics and fabrics with a finish.(Fig.106, Fig.107)

To use Inkodye, simply use from the bottle, with or without a thickener. Sodium alginate can be sprinkled on top of the dye and left to sit for 10 minutes or so. Sunlight will develop the colors in 30 minutes. Some artists like working under a sunlamp, for they can see the colors as they develop. While still damp, the fabric can be ironed, and the colors will develop this way as well. If you prefer to let the fabric dry, steam iron the fabric. Another method of processing the color is to oven bake at 280 degrees for 15 minutes up to 1 hour. Check the fabric periodically to make sure it is not scorching.

No further setting is needed. Just wash and rinse the fabric. Keep the Inkodye away from the light. Store it in a cool, dry place away from the light and it will last for up to 2 years.

Inkodye is an easy–to–use paint material for all ages. Its results are pleasing, as well. To summarize :

SUMMARY OF VAT DYES (INKODYE)

Use: popular use with versatility

Quality: a good quality paint material

Price: reasonable

Ease of Use: very easy to use

Hand: excellent

Washability: excellent

Usage: children's products such as T–shirts, toys, dolls; also quilts, clothing, accessories

Fabrics used: cotton, linen, viscose rayon, some synthetics

Productivity: very good

Availability: available from dyehouses

Lightfastness: very good

How set?: by ironing, oven baking or exposing to sunlight

NAPHTHOL DYES

Although naphthol dyes can be thickened and used for direct painting, I am not including them in this book. They require the use of strong chemicals, such as lye, and they are no longer easy to find.

FIG. 105: JUDY HANKIN IN EUGENE, OR. USING INKODYE TO PAINT A SILK PARACHUTE

LIQUID DYES

There are quite a number of liquid dyes on the market today. They are used primarily for silk and wool, but there are a few manufactured for other fabrics, such as for polyester and cotton. The liquid dyes include **Inko Silk Batik Dye, Tinfix, Super Tinfix, Tinsilk, SeriTint Liquid Dyes, Seidicolor, Princefix color, and Du Pont Silk Dyes.** Liquid dyes for other fabrics include **Tincoton and Tincoton II and Du Pont Dyes for Cotton.** I shall discuss these dyes depending on the type fabric they are used with. The most extensive dyes are the silk liquid dyes.

SILK DYES

Silk dyes are often an acid dye or a mixture of acid and direct dyestuffs. (Fig. 97–A) Since they are premixed, they are ready to use without any added chemicals or procedures. They come in a wide variety of colors, depending on the brand, and can be intermixed. Often they are used with gutta, a resist which is used with the French gutta serti method of painting on silk. Silk dyes can also be used on wool, even thought they are usually just called "silk" dyes. Most silk dyes require steaming, but there are some brands which bypass this step.

Inko Silk Batik Dye has 8 colors and 1 clear shade. This dye is thicker than many of the others, and therefore is much easier to control without using a resist. It is a mixture of acid and direct dyes. Tinfix is an acid dye. It is manufactured in France by the Sennelier company; if you come across "Sennelier Silk Dyes", reference is being made to one of the Tinfix dyes. These dyes come in 58 different, brilliant colors. Tinfix dyes can also be used with a **Silkscreening Thickener** to achieve hard–edged results. Some of the colors include: Chinese vermillion, Peony Red, Pollen Yellow, Tyrien Pink, Persian Blue, Almond Green, Prussian Blue, Nut Brown, Indigo, Slate Blue, and Rosewood. Both of the above dyes need to be steamed.

Super Tinfix is also an acid dye. It is a concentrated form of dye, and must be mixed with a solution of water and alcohol. There are 22 colors which must also be steamed. Tinsilk varies from these other dyes in that they do not need to be steamed. They are an acid dye, available in 21 different colors. After applying directly, let dry for 48 hours. Some of these intermixable colors include : Anthracite, Tropical Blue, Persian Red, Moss Green, California Poppy, and Cinnamon. Tinsilk, like Tinfix, is fairly liquid: a resist is helpful unless watercolor effects are desired (one of all liquid dyes' assets!)

SeriTint Liquid Dye is another liquid dye used for silk. There are 49 colors—Buttercup, Watermelon, French Rose, Blueberry, Holly Green, Blue Spruce, Jade, Curry, Cappuccino, Butternut Brown, Terra cotta, Champagne, and Eggplant. Fabric painted with SeriTint is machine washable—a unique feature. Seri–Tint can be used with or without a thickener. **Seidicolor Colors** are another silk dye that can be used without steaming. After painting the dye on silk, let dry and then brush on a **Fixer.** Let the fixer sit for 1 hour and wash off. Seidicolor Colors are often used with the **Seidicolor Resists** especially the colored resists! These are unusually nice resists available in 10 colors. This allows you to paint and apply a resist simultaneously. These resist colors will not be removed with either washing or dry-cleaning. Seidicolor Colors offer a unique silk painting experience with both resist, fixer, and no steaming. As well, the dye can be thickened with sodium alginate. Simply sprinkle a little sodium alginate over a small amount of dye.

FIG. 106: A CAFTAN BY SUZANNE LARSEN. POLYCOTTON–WRINKLE GAUZE DYED WITH CUSHING DYES. LINES DRAWN WITH INKO–DYE.

Agitate, then let sit for up to 10 minutes or until dye appears to have thickened.

Another product used in silk painting is **Presist.** It is a nontoxic alternative to wax or gutta resists. When **SilkPaint!Water– Soluble Resist** is used, one can paint while the resist is still wet. Dharma carries this, as well as **Dharma Stop–Flow Primer.** This is painted onto the silk *before* painting. Let it dry. The dyes will now hold their shape, and it is like painting with regular fabric paint. This primer washes out easily.

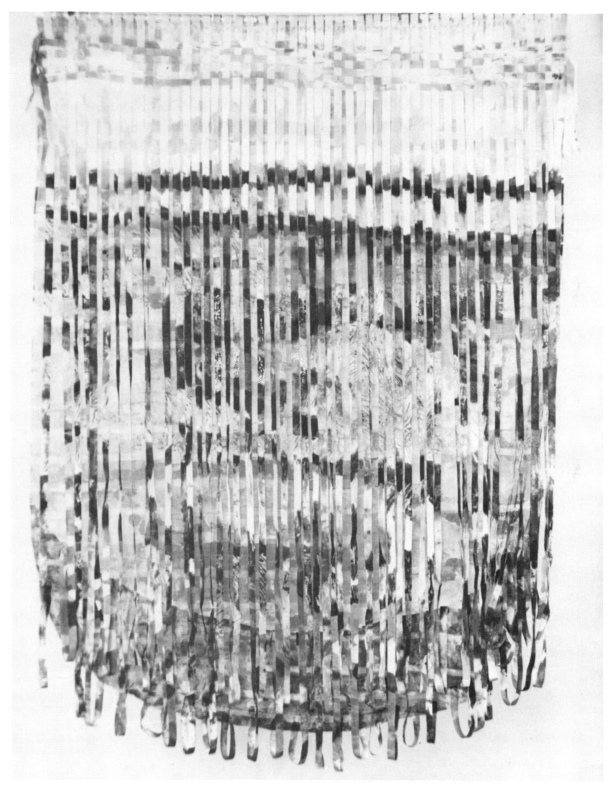

FIG. 107: *"SEASONS AT KENTFIELD MARSH"* –BY LOUAINE COLLIER ELKE. PAINTED WITH INKODYE, WITH PASTE RESIST. RAYON RIBBON OVER COTTON ORGANDY.

FIG. 107: SHAWLS BY SHERRY DE LEON. THE
ONE ON THE RIGHT IS HANDPAINTED SILK.

I have used all these silk dyes and find them all to be a very satisfactory paint material. The following silk dyes I have not tested, but they are a popular paint material, used by others. **Princefix Color Concentrate** comes in 29 colors, including Corn Poppy, Geranium, Red Cherry, Pansy Hearts, Petrole Blue, Night Blue, Hazel Nut, and Bordeaux Wine. These brilliant colors require no steaming, only hand washing after painting. The Princefix dye is mixed before painting with a Dilutant–Fixative to make the colors permanent. **Du Pont Dyes Par Excellence** for silk come in 170 colors : They also carry a thickener for silkscreening and handpainting. **Pebeo Nebotatik** is another silk dye with 20 colors. **Orient Express Silk Paints, SilkPaint! resists, Jacquard Silk Colors and Pebeo guttas** are other silk paint products available on the market today.

NEW SILK PAINTS AND PRODUCTS

The trend in the newer silk paints are similar to that of the fabric paints, that of ease of use. Several of these products do not need steaming to be set. Silk painting was traditionally more complicated due to the need to steam set. One can argue the merits of the brightness of color via steaming, as well as, when once learned, it is not that difficult. Still, it is very nice to have the choice. If you are in a hurry, you can paint a quick silk scarf for a gift overnight. When working in the studio on a regular basis, one can steam.

Peintex Sennelier Silk Paints are a high quality silk paint which can be used on all fabrics. The colors are clear and with good tone. Some of the 29 colors include carmine, prunella, pine tree, and violet. They can be easily mixed. Peintex has both a thickener and a medium. The **Peintex Thickener** is of a smooth consistency, and it helps control the paint flow. When you are painting with it, it has a kind of "cornstarchy" look, but as the paint dries, this disappears. Most all silk paints are like water in consistency. The **Peintex Medium** allows you to lighten the shade of the color of the silk paint. Both the thickener and the medium can be used simultaneously. Peintex is one of the newer silk paints which does not have to be steam set. It is set by ironing on the wrong side with an iron at the silk setting. Iron long enough for the fabric to get "hot", and your paint is set!

Deka Silk, while not new, has added some new lines to its silk painting products. Deka Silk paint flows fast and spreads. It mixes easily with other colors. There are now 18 colors, including skyline blue, poppy red, and shamrock. Deka Silk can be used on all fabrics, not just silk and wool. **Deka Silk Resist** comes in clear, colors, black, and metallics. It is very nice in my opinion. Some of the colored resists look like dimensional paints, with pearlescent or metallic looks. Deka Silk Salt is used with the salt technique. You drop the individual table grade crystals on the freshly painted silk. I found it interesting to continue painting **between** the salt crystals, adding small amounts of paint, and increasing the moisture content. The results were very unique and pleasing. **Deka Silk StopFlow Primer** is used directly on the fabric areas where you want to have more control. It is applied with a foam or other large soft brush in a very thin application. After it has dried, directly apply Deka or other paints. This will be much like painting directly on paper.

Deka is a popular silk paint line in that, among other reasons, it does not have to be steam–set. After letting air dry for 48 hours, one simply irons on the wrong side of the silk for 2–3 minutes at silk (or a low) setting. Also the resists can be dry-cleaned and they will not lose their color. This is not true of all resists.

SilkTint Silk Paint is another popular and high quality silk paint. It is a very concentrated paint, and needs to be diluted with **SilkTint Dilutant,** or a mixture of 50/50 water and alcohol solution. Dilute the paint in a ratio of 1 part paint to 2–3 parts solution. Therefore, if you had 1/4 teaspoon of paint, you would dilute it with 1/2 to 3/4 teaspoons of solution.

SilkTint, like other of the more traditional silk paints, needs to be steam set, and can only be used on silk and wool, as it is an acid–based dye/ink. SilkTint can be intermixed with both Tinfix and Super Tinfix colors and their dilutants. Its colors can be intermixed easily. There are 20 colors, including Chinese red, Sea blue, and Tyrien purple. Included in this are also 5 pre–mixed tints. There is also a **SilkTint Gutta,** in black, and clear. The gutta flows well, and can be used with small tipped resist applicators.

Three newer silk paints which I have not yet tested are **Orient Express by Pebeo, Setacolor by Pebeo, and Jacquard Silk Colors.**

LIQUID DYES FOR COTTON AND POLYESTER

Other liquid dyes include dyes for polyesters and cotton. Polydyes have 9 intermixable colors and do not require the addition of chemicals or steaming. **Tincoton and Tincoton II** can be used on cotton, linen, and other vegetable fibers. The

Tincoton II does not need steaming, while the Tincoton does. They come in 15 intermixable colors. A fixative is used with the Tincoton II dyes in place of steaming. I found that the Tincoton dyes were not especially bright; the colors are subtle. **Mli Dyes by Du Pont** are another liquid dye for cotton. And lastly, there are **Fabric Colors by Rosco Haussmann** used for silk, wool, and certain synthetic stretch fabrics. They come in 15 colors, with a thickener and fabric resist. They must be steam–set.

SILK PAINTING RESISTS

Specific resists are made for painting on silk. **Gutta serti** is one of the most familiar silk resists. It is a liquid rubber resist, and can be used straight from the can, or or it can be thinned with a gutta solvent. 75% gutta to 25% solvent is the standard ratio. Fine lines can be made with gutta with a squeeze bottle or a cone similar to a tsutsu cone. It gently dissolves in water, and will definitely be removed by dry–cleaning. Gutta serti is the resist used for the famous French serti technique of silk painting.

Seidicolor makes a nice water soluble resist called **Seidicolor resist.** It makes very nice sharp lines and comes in a plastic applicator bottle with a convenient cone–shaped top. It is used primarily for silk painting, but it can also be used on other natural fibers, such as cotton, linen, and wool. It can be thinned with water if necessary. Be sure when applying it that it soaks through both sides of the fabric, otherwise your dye will seep through.

Another nice silk resist is called **Rezist Bien.** It can be used with squeeze bottles and brushes. It needs several hours to dry. It works best on silks,and washes out with cold water.

Silk painters will find another product advertised along with the regular silk resists. These are the **colored resists.** You can add a dab of oil paint to the plain gutta for color. Dharma Trading company carries a fancy line of metallic gold and silver colored gutta. The Seidicolor resist comes in ten colors, and it is unique in that it won't wash out either with regular washing or with dry-cleaning (most gutta resists will come out if dry–cleaned, and this includes the colored ones!) Createx line resist can also be made into a colored resist by adding liquid fiber–reactive dye. After adding the dye, add 2/3 teaspoon of sodium bicarbonate and 2 tablespoons of urea (for every four ounces of resist.)

IVY Crafts Import's Silkscreen Thickener can be used with the French Sennelier Colors for silk and wool. This thickener comes in a powdered form, and can also be used as a resist. It is also of medium weight, and works well with squeeze bottles. **Resist applicators** are now available from many fiber arts suppliers.These are small plastic bottles with 3mm and 5mm metal tips. These provide more control than plastic squeeze bottles without tips.

I find the **Deka resist** and the **Silk–tint Gutta** especially easy to use. The resist just flows and you can draw just as if you were drawing on paper. The hand and wrist can relax and make flowing motions on the silk, with no resistance. For people who love to draw, silk painting is wonderful!

DISCHARGE DYES

Discharge dyeing is really a process of bleaching or lightening colors. A thickened paste can be made, or a premixed paste, called **Inko Discharge Paste,** can be used. In both cases, the

FIG. 108: CAFTAN BY GLORIA RIGLING. CHIFFON WITH DIRECT APPLICATION, THEN TIED, DISCHARGED, AND REDYED.

areas that are applied with the discharge will, in some cases, totally remove the color and in others will lighten it. Interesting effects can be created by painting, then discharging, then overpainting.(Fig.108) The discharge process can be used on colored fabrics to lighten certain areas; then these areas can be painted.

To make a thickener, mix 1/2 C. hot water, 1/4 teas. Calgon, and about 1 teas. sodium alginate. The amount of the alginate can vary, depending on how thick you wish the paste to be. Add 1/4 C. liquid bleach and mix well. I have found this mixture to be very effective on cotton and cotton blends, both colored fabrics and painted white fabrics. Do not use the discharge process on silk or other delicate fabrics, as the bleach may weaken the fibers and ruin the fabric. Formasol is another discharging agent, sold under the name **Dygon** or **PreDye.**

The Procion dyes will discharge, as well as direct dyes. Vat dyes, disperse dyes, and fabric paints do not discharge. Sometimes the fabrics will discharge to colors such as tan, grey, cream, rust, and other pastel colors. There are certain discharge fabrics which can be bought which are particularly dyed for discharging. Using bleach on black T–shirts is also very popular today.

DYEING ON COLORED FABRICS

No mention was made in the summaries of the various dyes as to how the dyes would react on colored fabrics. This is due to the fact that, unlike paints, which can be made more opaque with an "opaque white", dyes react with the fiber molecules. Most dyes will, therefore, change color when painted on already colored fabrics. The same principle works when under and overpainting with thickened dyes.

OVERDYEING PAINTED FABRICS

There are some instances where overdyeing of the fabric is desirable. Sometimes it is not desirable to always paint on a white background yet painting on already dyed or colored fabric does not yield the desired results. One solution is to overdye the white fabric after painting. Acrylics paints work best with this process, as there will be no color change. Oil paints also work well with overdyeing. Certain markers or dye pastels may change color, especially the lighter colors. Many times the colors will be more subdued after overdyeing.

Textile paints vary in their response to overdyeing. On a test run using Eurotex fabric colors, Texticolor Iridescent, and Createx Hi–Lite colors, I found that the last two did not change color with an overdye of household dye–paste. The Eurotex blended with the dye when both were wet, creating a lovely purple color. The textile paint that was not covered with the dye remained blue.

Another instance where overdyeing is desirable is when working with fragile art materials for fabric painting. For example, there are a number of art materials that are not washable, and really are not suited for fabrics which are going to be washed. Yet, when overdyed, they can be used for certain types of articles. One example of this is using chalk pastels to draw on muslin. By overdyeing, the fragile pastel is stabilized.

There are two ways of overdyeing pieces of fabric. Small pieces can be painted with a dye–paste, preferably with a large brush. Large pieces of fabric, as for clothing, should be immersed in a dye–bath. Fiber–reactive dyes are especially suited for this.

NOTES ON STEAMING

1) Steaming may look harder than it really is! Reading about it is really more complicated than the actual process.

2) First, wrap your fabric in paper towels. Then wrap with newsprint or in muslin. Be sure no part of the fabric touches itself. This is your fabric bundle.

3) Be sure that the bundle does not touch the edges of the pot used for steaming. Wrap the fabric loosely enough so that the steam can get to the fabric.

4) With a canning kettle, which is atmospheric steaming, wrap the bundle in a "tent" of aluminum foil and steam 15 minutes. Some fabrics will take up to 1 hour to steam.

5) Protect the fabric bundle by wrapping other protective material around the bundle. Do not let this protective material touch the sides of the pan, either.

6) For both oven steaming and steaming with a canner, have the water steaming before putting the fabric bundle into the oven or pot.

7) Look for steamers at a restaurant or hospital supply house. You may be able to purchase them used.

8) Most dyes need 1 hour of steaming— between 180 and 210 degrees F. Fiber–reactive dyes need only 30 minutes.

9) Unwrap the fabric immediately after steaming so that the condensation does not cause the colors to run.

• •

CONCLUSIONS ABOUT DYES

As can be seen, dyes are a very extensive paint material. The amount of material about dyes could be seen as overwhelming. It's best to choose one type of dye and learn about it well before going on to another type. Your knowledge from one type will build a foundation and learning about the next type will seem easier. Sometimes ordering the primary colors (in most cases, red, yellow, and blue) and learning to mix them is a good way to "break in" a dye.

The greatest problem with dyes, other than the vast amount of information about them, is that many of them require steaming when they are applied as dye–pastes. Steaming takes time and is a skill which must be learned. Other aspects of dyes can be seen in the following chart :

Use: the most popular and versatile paint material for fabric painting

Quality: a very high quality paint material

Price: very reasonable, especially when ordered in bulk

Ease of Use: somewhat complex to learn how to use, but once techniques are learned, fairly straightforward

Hand: excellent

Washability: varies, depending upon the type of dye. Some are excellent, others poor

Usage: Usage is vast. Clothing, both casual and formal, accessories quilts, wall hangings, curtains, lamp shades, toys, soft sculpture,etc.

Fabrics used: Most dyes take either all natural fibers or synthetics and polyesters. Some are for silk and wool; others for cotton and linen.

Productivity: fair to good, depending upon procedures used

Availability: very available, from drugstores to art and fiber stores to dye suppliers

Lightfastness: good to very good

How set?: generally, steam–set either by steam iron, oven steaming, pressure steaming, or atmospheric steaming with a steam cabinet or canner.

INKS

Inks are the next category of paint materials which can be used in fabric painting. There are two different kinds of inks: oil–base textile printing inks such as silkscreen inks, block printing inks, etc; and permanent waterproof drawing inks. We shall first discuss the textile printing inks.

These printing inks are sometimes known as "pigment pastes". They are more viscous than regular textile paint, but in many ways they are similar to textile paint. They are usually a combination of ground pigments, a binder, an extender, a thinner, and a transparent base. Many of them can be found in art stores, under silkscreen supplies or block printing supplies. They can also be ordered from a number of distributors.

Brand names include: **Inko–Tex,** which is a water–base fabric ink coming in 17 colors (water–base inks which are *textile inks* are suitable for fabric painting); **InkoFab,** (a solvent based fabric ink); and **PROfab Textile Inks.** These last inks are a waterbase textile ink that comes in 16 different colors. They can be used on both natural and synthetic fibers, and are especially good with poly–cottons. They can be used on white or light fabrics as is; and they can be made more opaque by adding a **White Color Concentrate.** They only need to be heat set for 3–4 minutes with a dry iron. The 16 colors are intermixable, and a **PROfab Color Concentrate** is also available to make colors deeper, or for you to mix your own colors. The **Print Base Extender** will make the colors lighter and allow you to mix pastel shades. Add a little water when doing direct painting.

PROFab Textile Inks are especially nice and easy to use. They are contained in a plastic screw–top jar, so they can be easily stored and used. The hand of the fabric remains smooth with these inks, although they, as most other inks, give a "flat finish" look (meaning the dried ink has a matte, rather than a glossy, look).

Naz–dar Fabric Ink, Hunt/Speedball Textile Screen Printing Ink, Hunt/Speedball No Heat Textile Screen Printing Ink, Advance Textile Silkscreen Printing Ink, Hunt/ Speedball Oil–base Block Printing Ink, and Shiva Oil–base Block Printing Ink are some of the more popular textile inks that are available in art stores. **Naz–dar Fabric Ink** is used on cotton and other natural fibers; while **Hunt/Speedball Textile Screen Printing Ink** can be used on most natural and synthetic fibers. Both of these are also very nice inks: they are only slightly rough to the touch.

Colonial's silkscreen inks are stocked in bulk amounts, the smallest being 1 quart. **Perma–Print Ink** comes in 15 colors and can be used on T–shirts and sweat shirts. **Poly–Print Ink** can be used on waterproof nylon garments. **Denim Ink** is used, obviously, for denim material; **Aqua–Bright** has 24 colors including fluorescents. **Texdye Pigment** is used for clothing, hand and beach towels; **Hydro–Tex D.G.** is used for dark fabrics. **Stretch Ink** has 40 colors and can be used for T–shirts, sweat shirts, as well as to make heat transfers. **Dyno–Print Plastisol Ink** is especially good on poly–cottons, and **Pro Print Wet–on–Wet** can also be used as a heat transfer paint. **Mul–T–Print Plastisol** is used on woven or knitted cottons.

I find that these textile inks are most satisfactory on cotton, muslin, and medium–weight fabrics. On lightweight fabrics and synthetics they are apt to stiffen in an undesirable way. They are also very good in combination with overdyeing, especially when making fabric yardage. Textile inks are easy to apply and quite inexpensive to use. To summarize:

Use: fairly popular

Quality: a good quality paint material

Price: one of the most inexpensive paint materials

Ease of Use: easy to learn how to use

Hand: fair to good, depending on type of fabric used

Washability: very good

Usage: Clothing, wall hangings. Especially good for fabric yardage

Fabrics used: natural fibers such as cotton and muslin are good; some synthetics

Productivity: very good, as inks are quick drying

Availability: readily available at art stores and silkscreen supply houses

Lightfastness: very good

How set?: generally set with a dry iron

DRAWING INKS

Drawing inks are the other type of ink that can be used for fabric painting. In general, drawing inks are not wash–fast, even if the ink is described as a waterproof ink. Sometimes, the fabric can be dipped in cool water without soap and the ink will not run, but these inks should not be used for clothing that needs washing. A fine–tipped brush or pens with a variety of pen tips can be used with these drawing inks. There are a number of different types of ink that can be used for fabric painting. I have tried **Pelican Drawing Ink, Luma watercolors, FW Drawing Inks, Koh–i–noor, and Higgins Permanent Ink, and found Pelican** to be the most washfast. Lettering pens and drawing markers can also be used directly on fabric.

When working with pen tips, use a light touch, and work on smooth, evenly woven fabric rather than a stretchy knit or textured fabric. Drawing and lettering such as is done on paper can also be done on fabric. (Fig. 109) Drawing inks are best used for small, delicate pieces; fabric cards, small pictures that can be framed, dolls and soft sculpture. Their colors are luminous and give a soft look to fabric. To sum up their characteristics :

Use: limited in use

Quality: not a high quality paint material for fabric painting due to poor washability

Price: Moderately priced

Ease of Use: Moderately easy to learn how to use. Always stretch fabric before drawing

Hand: Very good

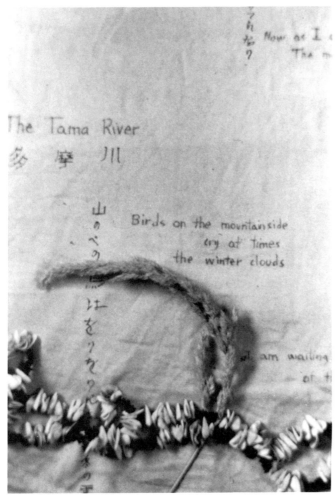

FIG. 109: CLOSE–UP OF HAIKU WRITTEN ON NYLON PANTS–SUIT WITH MARKING PENS.

Washability: Poor

Usage: Small wall hangings or pictures, dolls, soft sculpture, fabric

Fabrics used: all types of fabrics such as cotton, poly–cotton, polyesters, synthetics, silk

Productivity: very good

Availability: Readily available in art stores

Lightfastness: fair to good

How Set?: No setting needed

FABRIC MARKING PENS

Fabric marking pens and marking pens are other paint materials that are used with fabric painting. The most permanent markers are those which are made specifically for fabric, but some "permanent" design markers can also be used. In the latter category, I have found **Design Marker** to be fairly permanent in most colors. Some of the brands of fabric markers include **Loving Touch Permanent Fabric Marker, Setaskrib,**

Deco–color pens, Superfine pen, Nepo pens, Niji pens, and Glad Rags Marker. Sharpie laundry marking pen, though labeled permanent, did not test out for permanency.

Setascrib has 12 colors, and is especially good for cottons and T–shirts. Deco–color pens also have 15 colors, while Glad Rags has 10. The other markers mentioned can be found in most fabric or needlework stores.

Newer fabric markers which I have tested include **Niji FabricColor Superfine Markers, Niji Fabricolor Calligraphy Permanent Fabric Pen, (now called Niji FabricMate Jumbo Chisel–Tip Fabric Markers,) Pentel Color Pen Fine Point, Marvy Fabric Marker (Fine–Point, Chisel–Tip Fluorescent, Broad Point), Uchida's Deco–Color Fine Line Opaque Paint Marker, Pigma Micron Extra Fine Point Fabric Marker, Faber–Castel's Uni Paint Marker, Dylon's Color Fun Marker, and Duncan Scribble's Outline Pen.**

Niji FabricColor Pens are very nice to use. They are smooth and are easy to control on fabric. The **Calligraphy Pen** is nice as well, though more difficult to use on ribbed or textured fabric, such as a T–shirt. Stretch your fabric when using these pens. **Pentel Color Pens** are one of my favorites, as they are very smooth on the fabric, and detail work is easy to do with much control. **Marvy Fabric Marker** is another popular fabric pen, and is widely available. From the fine point for detail work to the very large broad point, there is plenty of variety in tip size. I found the **Uchida DecoColor Paint Marker** to have slightly fuzzy lines on cotton, meaning that the ink was thinner than in some other paints. **Faber–Castel's Uni Paint Marker** was similar. **Pigma Micron Fabric Marker** is very crisp and clear. **Dylon's Color Fun Marker** works especially nice on knit fabrics, as well as on fine textured cottons or silk, as it moves very smoothly over the fabric. The **Scribbles Outline Pen** is very nice! It is black, moves easily over fabrics without catching on the weave or knit. It works well in tight spots, making it a well–designed outline pen. It works well on stretchy fabrics such as T–shirts and sweatshirts.

Other permanent markers that are generally found in art stores that can be used include **Sanford Hi–Impact Intensive Color Markers and Sanford Permanent Calligraphic Pens.** These are permanent markers that are waterproof. All "art markers" should be tested, as some will withstand water but not soap, and others are not really permanent at all.

Markers are the best paint material to begin with for drawing on fabric. They require practically the same techniques as would be used on paper. There is a very good book, called *Painting with Markers*–Troise and Port, which gives many ideas for using marking pens in a painterly way. As well, markers are good for intricate designs as they come in fine enough tips to execute precise lines. Lattice work, lace, iron wrought fences, sculpture, calligraphy, and embroidery are intricate designs which could be drawn on fabric. Markers are also good for gesture drawing, quick sketches, and cartoons. I also use them for the preliminary drawings for some paintings.

On smooth–weave cloth, such as cotton or muslin, markers make fairly contained lines. Any close–weave cloth will produce a consistent line; however the rougher the fiber, the less consistent the mark or line. Fabric markers and marking pens are easily available, easy to learn how to use on fabric and come in a wide variety of colors. Their disadvantages are that they really should be tested to see how washfast each individual brand is. They are best used on nonwashable items, such as wall hangings, toys, soft sculpture, etc, rather than clothing. They can be used on most any type of fabric.

MARKING PENS AND PENCILS

There is also a washable marking or transfer pencil used in sewing for marking designs on fabric which is also useful in fabric painting. **Bona Venture** carries this type of pencil, in blue, red, and green. **Scribbles Disappearing Ink Pen** is a good brand. Disappearing ink pens are good when you are doing spontaneous scribbling or drawing which you might or might not want to keep; and for tracing patterns which are going to be painted in light colors. (Usually if you are painting with dark colors, I find that colored pencils work quite well, when you need a guide or outline. This also works with light colors if you match the colored pencil to the paint color.) **Mark–B–Gone** is another disappearing ink pen. Look in fabric stores for these types of marking pencils and pens.

TRANSFER PAINT MATERIALS

Transfer paint materials include **transfer paints, pencils, pens, crayons,** (See under "Fabric Crayons") as well as **iron–on transfer designs.** These items are part of **Heat–Transfer Processes** (see Chapter VI for a discussion of this technique).

TRANSFER PAINTS

Deka iron–on transfer paint is a popular transfer paint. With it, one can paint on paper, let it dry, and then transfer the image to the fabric via a hot iron. The colors range from lemon, orange, and pink through the reds to light blue and green, and finally brown and black. The colors are darker in the bottle than they are on the fabric, but much brighter on the fabric than on the paper !

The paint has a very nice consistency like fingerpaint! It is conducive to trying out textile designs, since one is painting on paper rather than on fabric. (Similar to making "croquis" textile designs painted on paper before being adapted to textiles.) Another technique is to paint on leaves, ferns, or other natural items.

Transfer paint can only be used on synthetic fabrics, preferably 100% synthetic. If your fabric is at least 60%, you will still be able to transfer the design, but it won't be quite as bright. (Read about "Transfer Painting" in Chapter VI for more details on this process).

Another transfer paint which are available but I have not yet tested is **Palmer's Shaded Transfer Paints.**

TRANSFER PENCILS

Scribbles Iron–On Transfer Pencil is is a wonderful invention for making your own iron–on transfers as well as drawing directly onto fabric. **Deka Transfer pencil** is another brand available. (See Heat–Transfer Processes in Chapter VI for technical information)

There is a lot of freedom inherent in this slender simple looking tool. It opens up to you worlds and worlds of designs, including many wonderful designs in craft books and is a real help for people who do not have a natural ability to draw!

TRANSFER PENS

There are also transfer pens available. The **Sulky Iron–on Transfer Pen** is available in a number of colors, including black, green, blue, yellow, purple, and red. I find it very useful, for two reasons. One, you can copy any design from anywhere! Two, you can use it to reuse ready–made iron–on transfers. I find this pen, with its thicker nib, easier to use when recopying most designs.

IRON–ON TRANSFER ART

Iron–on transfers are one of today's very popular transfer paint materials. (See Chapter VI on Iron–On Transfers about this technique). Gick, Scribbles, Dizzle, Tulip, and Aunt Martha's, are some of many companies who offer these transfers. ***Scribbles Fashion Decorating Books: Iron–On Patterns and Projects*** includes several different lines. They include such topics as: Victorian Florals, Night Moods (designs for evening wear), Southwest Scribbles, Lingerie, and Hit the Beach (motifs for beachwear). ***Hot Off the Press*** is a small publisher who includes iron–on transfers in their fabric painting booklets. The booklets have color photos of either full–length projects or details from. They suggest specific paints and colors, so they are good for the beginner as a guideline towards a successful project. Gick also carries a line of iron–on transfer patterns. They are easy to use, and are already designed for a particular garment (such as **Gick's mini–transfers "Shirts".**) This makes it easier to have a successful looking garment, as the transfer is already designed for a particular style of clothing. Dimensional paints work well with these small designs, as do small brushes. Fabric paints are much easier to work with than dyes, since the designs are small and intricate.

Dizzle's Glitterlooks is an iron–on glitter design which does not need to be painted. Simply cut out the individual design and, placing the design face down onto the fabric, iron for 20–30 seconds. Then peel the backing off of the design.

Iron–on transfers which are available but I have not tested yet include: **Tulip Big and Easy Iron–On Transfers; The Beadery's Chic Boutique Iron–on Pattern Guides** (to be used with rhinestones, cabochons, and mirrors) and **Dimensions Iron–On Fashion Transfers** which can be used "as is" or embellished with fabric paints.

EMBROIDERY PAINTS

Embroidery paints are another type of marking tool that is used in fabric painting. It has been on the market for a long time, and is usually found in needlework stores, in the embroidery section. Embroidery paints can also be mail–ordered, and are often advertised in women's magazines and needlework magazines. Another name for embroidery paints is decorator paints. Some of the brand names of embroidery paints are **Cameo Silhouette Designs, Vogart Ball Point Paint Tubes, Minuet, Craft–tint, Deco–write, Artex Decorator Paints, Aunt Martha's and Tri–Chem.** Tri-Chem is a dealership of embroidery paints which sells their product through dealership parties. Other brands also use this method. Embroidery paints are applied to fabric by pressing hard on the tip of the tube of paint, and allowing the paint to flow. (This is why they are called paints rather than markers) The tube should be held firmly from the bottom, but never squeezed. Since the paints need pressure in order for the color to show, they do not work very well on stretchy material or on thick textured fabric.

They are best used on cotton, muslin, and other smooth–weave fabrics. There are many embroidery stitches which can be used effectively with embroidery paint. (Fig.110) In general, stitches which are composed of long running lines, and those which do not use twisted or overlaid threads to create their pattern, can be drawn so as to look like authentic embroidery. Besides, painted embroidery is not supposed to copy thread embroidery; it is an emphasis on line,whereas in embroidery, there is more of an emphasis on texture within line. Embroidery paints can also be used for plain line drawing, and for filling in small areas. They work especially well with small delicate types of designs. Certain types of paint give unusual results; the Glo–lite, metallic, and pearlite paints are especially popular. Embroidery paints can be used on a variety of fabric. They do not need to be heat–set.

FABRIC CRAYONS, DYE PASTELS, AND OTHER ART MARKERS

The last major group of paint materials to be discussed is fabric crayons, dye pastels, and other art markers such as regular color crayons, Stabilotone markers, etc. Crayola Craft markets a **fabric crayon** which is used on synthetics. It is actually a disperse dye in a wax base, and works like other transfer paint materials. First the design is drawn on paper, and then transferred to fabric by ironing with a hot iron. Only 8 colors are available, but it is a popular item with children.

When drawing the design, it is important to remember that it will transfer in *reverse.* If this is not desired, lightly trace the design in pencil in reverse on the paper by recopying the lines of the original design. These lines can then be marked over with the fabric crayons, with the entire design transferring correctly. Fabric crayons are an excellent way for children to wear some of their favorite coloring book characters. For adults, Dover carries a marvelous series of coloring books with many interesting topics: books on the ancient near east, the middle ages, and a medieval alphabet are some of their many titles. Paint crayons are also marketed for use in stenciling. **Stencil Crayon** from Stencil Decor is an oil base wax crayon which can be applied directly to fabric. It can be rubbed on, then a brush is used to blend it into the fabric. **Artist Paint Crayon** also from Stencil Decor, is another oil based crayon for stencilers. It is packaged in several coordinating colors, including Southwest Floral. This crayon can be applied directly, as well as rubbed onto a palette first, and then the colors can be applied using a paint brush, palette knife, or rubbed with ones' finger. Turpentine can also be added for extra brushability. This particular crayon is not washable, so it can only be used with fabrics where this is not an issue. It has a smooth creamy texture and is easy to use, with or without stencils.

Shiva/Markal Artist's Paintstiks are another interesting marker. They are actually a solid oil paint, in marker form. They can be dipped in turpentine before using, or used straight. Delta/Shiva also manufactures an **Iridescent Paintstik marker.** This is a fine crayon to use in fabric rubbings, and over dark fabrics. It can be used in conjunction with **Delta/Shiva's Glit–terstik** markers. These are shimmery metallic crayons, and are excellent for use for evening wearable art creations! Although fabric crayons are easy to use, they do require strength in ones' arm muscles. And, just like color crayons, they require a certain amount of patient diligence to use!

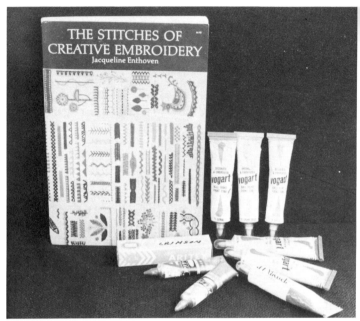

FIG. 110: LAYOUT OF EMBROIDERY PAINTS AND EM–BROIDERY BOOK

DYE PASTELS

Another type of "crayon marker" which can be used is called a **Dye Pastel.** Dye pastels are marketed by Pentel. 15 colors are available, including red, yellow, buttercup, pink, green, turquoise, white, and black. These pastels are similar in consistency to an oil pastel. They are best used on natural fibers, such as cotton and muslin, but will work on some synthetic blends. Unlike the fabric crayons, these pastels are used directly on the fabric. It is best to stretch your fabric, using either an embroidery frame or other stretching frame. Use short, swift marks. Be careful not to let little flecks of the crayon land on white parts of the fabric. After drawing, set the pastels by ironing with a medium hot iron. Use a soft cloth to cover the drawing and protect your iron. Overdyeing works well with both these pastels and the fabric crayons. Or, use an acrylic wash after drawing with these crayon markers.

REGULAR COLOR CRAYONS

Color crayons can be used with limited effects. They can be used directly on certain fabrics, such as cotton or polyester blends, with very nice effects. Wall hangings, soft pictures, or other nonwashable items should be made with the colored fabric. Color crayons can be heated, using a crayon, and drawn in a soft or semi–melted state, onto fabric. This approaches a crude method of batik, and the fabric must be pressed with a hot iron to remove the wax. This method is best used when subsequent overdyeing occurs. Another possibility is to draw with crayon over fabric which has been painted with an acrylic wash. Heat–set all these methods by ironing.

■ ■

OTHER ART MARKERS

There are a number of other art markers which I have used on fabric for decorative purposes. One is called the **Stabilotone marker.** Its texture is similar to an oil pastel, and it works very nicely using a combination of direct drawing and washes. It is a waterbase marker.

Oil pastels and **regular chalk pastels** can also be used. For the oil pastels, stretch your fabric as the marker will work better that way. Oil pastels are good to use when making rubbings, or any other textured or relief effect. (Fig.111) **Caran D'Ache Neocolor I,** a wax oil, is also used with turpentine. To summarize:

Use: Limited

Quality: a fair to good quality paint material

Price: reasonable

Ease of Use: very easy to use

Hand: Very good

Usage: wall hangings, fabric pictures, soft sculpture, dolls, curtains, some washable items

Washability: Poor for all items except dye pastels and fabric crayons

Fabrics used: Synthetics for fabric crayons; all types of fabrics for others

Productivity: very good

Availability: very available

Lightfastness: good to very good

How set?: no setting or by ironing

A PAINTING VOCABULARY

■ ■ ■ ■ ■ ■ ■ ■ ■ ■ ■ ■ ■ ■ ■ ■ ■ ■ ■ ■

As you gain experience with all these various fabric paints and dyes, you may find that certain particular paints become your favorites. As you get to learn and know certain paints, it is as if you are adding to your paint vocabulary. Then, before starting a particular project, you can with certainty pick out particular paints and dyes, already knowing their effects!

For example, I decided to paint a T–shirt. I chose a color scheme, then went to my samples of fabric paints and dyes, and picked out particular metallic and puff paints of which I liked the effects. I already knew what I was working with, so I had more control over the outcome. Some of these particular paints will become like good friends, in that you will grow fond of certain colors and certain types more than others, and find that you have good success when you use them.

FIG. 111: "REFLECTIONS IV"– BY VICTORIA RIVERS. PROCION ON VELVETEEN, OIL PASTELS, STUFFED.

ACCESSORY PRODUCTS FOR FABRIC PAINTING AND DYEING

● ●

GLITTER

Glitter is *fun!* It's hard not to get good results immediately. Glitter is marketed just as glitter, in other words, not mixed into a paint base as are the glitter fabric and dimensional paints. It usually comes in smaller and large shaker jars, and also can be ordered in bulk. The larger the holes in the shaker, the less control you have as you shake the glitter out over the paint or glue. You can use it with fabric, dimensional, and acrylic paints. Glitter can also be used in conjunction with adhesive glues by simply being sprinkled over it. When the glue dries, it will be transparent, and you will have a nice glittery surface. Glitter can be sprinkled over any type of fabric paint as long as it is wet. It is nice to use in a contrasting color from the paint below it.

Designs can be made with glitter. Simply draw a design with fabric paint or glue and carefully sprinkle the glitter thickly onto the underlying paint or glue. When dry, all you will see is the glitter design.

Another way to use glitter is with **Glitter Fashion Transfers by Aleene.** The transfer is like a stencil, and **Aleene's OK–To–Wash–It Glue** is applied to the open spaces of the design. Then glitter is sprinkled on. After the glue has dried, the glitter will adhere and the stenciled transfer can be lifted up, leaving a very nice glitter design.

Some of the available glitters which I have tested include: **Gick's Original Prisma Glitter, Metallic Glitter, and Sparkles.** The **Prisma** is iridescent and transparent. It allows the paint to show through the glitter. Let dry for 2 days. The **Metallic Glitter** is very nice, and covers very thick. Its colors include purple, fuchsia, and copper. It is best to use a paint color similar to the glitter. Sparkles is a nice glitter with small stars in it. Another product I have tested is **R and R Ltd Multifine Glitter.** This particular glitter comes as jewelescent or crystalescent. It is a very fine grade glitter, and comes in 15 colors, including turquoise, royal, emerald, black, copper and gold. The gold glitter look white in the jar, which can be confusing, but it shows up gold on a dark fabric or any color of paint. The crystalescent glitter comes in ultrafine, fine and medium grades. Its 5 colors include gold, violet, and multicolor.

Other available glitters include: **Gick's Prisma Stardust, (tiny metallic stars) Hologram and Glow–in–the–Dark, (speciality glitters) Prisma Pastels, Metallic Mixes, Prisma–Tallics (a mixture of metallic and Prisma colors); and Mark Enterprises Halo Glitter.**

TEXTURAL MEDIUMS

These are similar to glitters, but simulate snow. **DecoArt's Snowtex:** (a textural medium which simulates snow), is one I have read about, but have not been able yet to locate for testing.

GLACE

Glace is a handmade plastic like material with varying textures, metallic sparkles, and hologram effects. It comes in four distinctive styles from Stanislaus Imports (filigree, gemstone, reptile, and confetti.) It can be cut, shaped, and glued for use in wearable art as well as jewelry. It is used with fabric painting primarily in the context of sweatshirt art, and other wearable art, such as T–shirts, hats, shoes, and other accessory items.

FOIL

● ●

Iron–on foil is used in conjunction with sweatshirt art and other wearable art projects. (See Chapter VI under Sweatshirt Art for specifics). It comes in plain sheets in a variety of colors as well as in finished designs. It can be found in craft and art stores.

TRANSFERS

Iron–on transfer designs are a common items sold along with fabric paints. They are sold individually and in books. Transfer pens and pencils allow one to transfer original designs and individually collected artwork from books, magazines, etc. Transfer glues, gels, and paints are also part of the transfer art process. This is all discussed in Chapter VI under Heat Transfer Processes.

GLUES

Glues have numerous uses in craft art in today's world. For example, in fabric painting and especially in sweatshirt art, glues are used to adhere jewels, (rhinestones, pearls, mirrors, cabochons, etc). They are used as a base to adhere glitter, galafetti, sparkles, sequins, etc. They are used in the process of foiling, or foil art. And then they are used in transfer art, to transfer black and white or color pictures to fabric. It's really quite interesting how many uses there are today for glue in crafts work and especially in surface design.

I've used **Aleene's Jewel Glue,** to put on acrylic rhinestones, that worked very nicely. It was very easy. I used **Aleene's OK—to—Wash–It Glue,** and spread it with a brush onto fabric. Over this I spread some "galafetti", some sequins, and some glitters. I also used some dimensional paints along with this, to see how it would work in comparison to the glue. Really they are similar, except that the glue is clear. The glue can be applied in little squiggly lines. Then spread some glitter, sequins, and confetti over it. It gives a "light" effect, kind of glitzy, and this is easy and fun to do! You can actually use the glue in a similar way to how you use the dimensional paint, except the glue is going to be a little different. You are not going to have a color. You are going to have your sparkles come forth to the surface. However, the glue becomes some what of a dimensional texture in the fabric painted surface.

There are numerous brands of glues. I have had success with all of them. Aleene has a product line which includes **Aleene's Jewel Glue,** to be used for rhinestones, beads, pearls, and mirrors, and **Aleene's OK–to–Wash–It Fabric Glue,** which can be used with painted applique. They also carry a transfer glue, simply called **Aleene's Transfer Glue.** Delta/Slomons carries **Stitchless Fabric Glue,** which is also used as a transfer medium when transferring photographs and magazine pictures to fabric. There are numerous other brands, including ones from Adhesive Technologies, and Fibre–Craft Materials Corp. **Acrylic Gel Mediums,** such as Liquitex, can be used both as a glue, and also as a transfer glue. **Duncan Foil 'n Accent Adhesive** though used in conjunction with foil art, is a good adhesive for a number of fabric painted decorative projects. Foil designs, bonding of rhinestones, buttons, studs, ribbons, sequins, and other embellishments are all possible using this adhesive. Acrylic

RHINESTONES, CABOCHONS, PEARLS, STUDS, BELLS, BUTTONS, BEADS, ETC

Acrylic rhinestones, pearls, studs, and other various items are now commonly used on sweatshirts, denim jackets, T–shirts and other clothing articles. When used in combination with fabric painting, it has often been suggested to simply drop the rhinestone into a dab of fabric paint (usually dimensional paint). Although this can be done, I find that rhinestones and other acrylic stones are more successfully secured to fabric with the use of fabric glues, specifically those made for jewels, rhinestones and other items. Although the dimensional paint will indeed secure the stone, often the paint messily seeps around the stone and the stone does not look as "clear" as it does when it is glued down. The reason for this is, in order for the rhinestone to really adhere to the fabric, the paint is pushed up through the holes, thus affecting the clearness of the stone. It is best not to dry–clean rhinestones, but they are washable. Some types of rhinestones include **Shafaii Snap–on Stones, Elvee/ Rosenberg acrylic gemstones, and Mangelsen's.**

STUDS AND NAILHEADS

Studs and nail heads are attached by pressing the prongs into the fabric and then pressing them down, usually using a small screwdriver, so that the metal hooks are secured. Some nailheads and rhinestones, as well, are attached with a special tool which places them into the fabric.

BRUSHES

We fabric painters are lucky today in having available to us brushes manufactured specifically for fabric painting. Rather than having to hunt amidst art brushes for appropriate brushes, we can now buy brushes specifically oriented for fabric painting. Some of the large manufacturers of brushes include Marx Brushes, Loew–Cornell, Robert Simmons, Silver Brush, and Grumbacher. Special brushes for stenciling include **Stencil Ease, Adele Bishop, Stencil Decor, and Quilting Creations** (see Stenciling Paints and Accessories in Chapter IV for a detailed

description of these brushes.)

Scribbles carries **Soft and Stiff Fabric Brushes by Grumbacher.** They include: liners, shaders, soft flat, soft round, round scrubber, angular, flat scrubber, fan, and filbert.

Marx carries a number of brushes and spreaders. The regular bristle brushes come in soft round medium, soft flat medium, stiff round, stiff flat liner, fan shape, as well as a brush cleaner, conditioner, and brush sizing accessories. **Marx Spreaders** are plastic shaped spreaders which allows one to spread the fabric paint in interesting textural ways. Four differently shaped spreaders can make waves, swirls, blending of colors, and streaks and stripes.

Loew–Cornell carries fabric brushes, including fabric painting soft brushes in round, flat and liner for silk painting and fine fabrics; fabric dye brushes in rounds, flats, detailers, and liner; a fabric spotter, and several white nylon brushes, in liners, rounds, flats, and detailers; stencil brushes, and bamboo and Oriental brushes. Some Oriental brushes are made from horsehair, others from boar's hair. These brushes can run very big, and are good for painting on yardage. (See Fig. 111A, 111B)

Foam brushes are another recent invention for painting in general. Foam brushes cover large areas quickly. They work well with soda–soak on clothes and fiber–reactive dyes. When used with dyes, you can blend colors easily. They are good for large areas or lots of garments, for example, tops or sweatshirts. It's nice to start with large brush, lay down a light color, (for example, yellow). use a medium brush to put in more color and design, and then add accent colors with a small brush.

Foam brushes come in small, medium, and large sizes and are available at regular art and craft stores as well through surface design suppliers.

Robert Simmons carries a number of interesting brushes including oval and pat sponge blenders, (available through Dharma Trading Co.) and deerfoot stippler art brushes and dagger stripers. They also carry Tolemaster brushes in round, blenders, shaders, oval mop, liner, script, and fan.

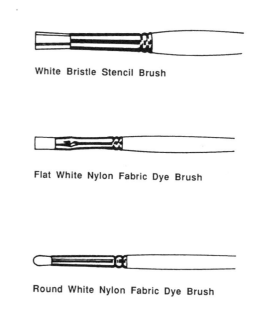

White Bristle Stencil Brush

Flat White Nylon Fabric Dye Brush

Round White Nylon Fabric Dye Brush

FIG.111A:ILLUSTRATIONS OF LOEW–CORNELL BRUSHES

PALETTES

• •

Palettes sold at art stores are helpful, I find, in the fabric painting process. They help one to organize one's colors, and to plan color themes. Right now, no one is really marketing or selling palettes for fabric painting. As well as the plastic and metal manufactured palettes, I have found it useful to make a homemade palette of cardboard (in a regular palette shape, even with a hole in the middle so you can hold it!) which is sealed with Varithane. This makes mixing colors easy, as well as the clean–up, especially with acrylic paints. Acrylic paints as well as some fabric paints mixed on plastic palettes will dry and harden

I recommend having many forms for various projects. It is a lot easier than the old "newspaper–and–pin–everything down" technique! Frames and forms are where it's at!

CARDBOARD FORMS

■ ■

There are a number of cardboard forms which are very helpful in fabric painting. Shirt forms, (see below), stretch the fabric and keep it taunt, making it much easier to control one's work. Homemade card board forms can be helpful when painting three dimensional items such as socks, tights, and other stretchy clothing.

Cardboard T–Shirt Forms: It's really helpful to use these manufactured cardboard shirt forms for painting. I recommend the ones that Gick manufactures, which are coated with a waxed sealer. Buy several if you are working on several projects, so while one shirt is drying you can go right ahead and work on another one.

Homemade Forms: For smaller items and certain techniques, it's easy to make your own forms. A cardboard form is needed for marbling almost any clothing item, so you don't marble the back side by mistake. When you are painting socks, it helps to have a cardboard form. In order to keep your cardboard from getting paint all over it, you will want to protect it with a sealer.

Cut out the form a little bit bigger than the item, so that it can stretch a little bit and be taunt. Brush on a varithane clear liquid finish which will seal the form. Any paint or marks can then be simply wiped off!

FIG. 111B:LOEW–CORNELL FABRIC BRUSHES

STRETCHERS

There are several kinds of stretchers used in fabric painting and surface design. Stretcher bars are used primarily in silk painting, and can be found through mail order suppliers of surface design materials. (See Chapter VI for discussion of stretchers, as well as *my companion volume 1001 PRODUCTS AND RESOURCES FOR THE FABRIC PAINTER AND SURFACE DESIGNER*, for an extensive listing) With so many good paint materials at hand, it is possible to learn a whole vocabulary of "painterly" techniques for fabric. We'll look, in the next two chapters, for inspiration and ideas for painting.

5   *PERCEPTION, INSPIRATION, CREATION*

Inspiration for design ideas can be found everywhere! The wider ones' perception, the more possibilities for fabric painting. In fact, sources of inspiration for fabric painting cover a very wide area: ideas can be found in biology books, tree identification books, in a geography or history book, in an auto parts store, in the anthropologists library, or on a trip by bus into a downtown area; as well as in the area generally called the humanities—art history, music, literature, drama, dance. I want to describe some unusual and unapparent design sources as well as presenting familiar ideas—flowers, colors, lines, etc.

The main question when forming a design for fabric painted cloth and clothing is: 1) is the design functional to painting, and 2) is the design functional to clothing? As was explained in Chapter III, there is no use in designing something which would be easier fabric printed. There is, however, such a wealth of design ideas that are unique to fabric painting that it is soon easy to discern what type of design to bypass.

With direct painting, for example, there is no need to use repetition of image or placement, unless it is desired. At the same time, a design with scattered images without any unity is not the aim of fabric painting design. Cohesive variety is the aim. This means that a variety of ideas, images, colors, and compositional devices such as line, texture, shape, etc. are used within a larger unifying structure. A larger unifying structure could be composed of different **types** of musical instruments drawn on the fabric, with or without, a background. This basic idea could be used with any number of images types of metal clasps, old lace patterns, or words and poems in different languages—any number of **types** of images can be used in combination to achieve a pictorial unity for fabric painted cloth.

As well as various types of images within a certain category, a theme could be any short subject from which variations are developed. I have been working on a series of designs which evolve from "organic design" where the main theme is nature, both the materials in nature and the idea of natural growing processes. A theme could include a certain type of design motif, a certain garment design from the area or time of the motif, and a way of putting the two together that would not be a traditional pattern.

Another example of this is correlating an archaic design or material with a garment design from the same period. Songs from the ancient troubadours (such as the ones compiled by Raynaud, entitled "Chanson de Richart Coeur" or "Chanson du roi de Navarre") could be combined on a dress with other motifs from that historical period, and, as well, the design of the dress could be similar to those worn by the ancient troubadours. There is an immeasurable amount of unfamiliar design material stored away in library books in the forms of designs, diagrams, photographs, drawings, pictures, music, and words. Research could be combined with fabric painted textile design to create numerous images that would be visually interesting, intellectually stimulating, and rarely seen. At the same time, a beautifully drawn flower is a new design, since arts' capacity—or magic, if you will—can present a new vision of an old idea. Research does not pretend to be original, but it can expose ideas and designs long forgotten.

Research used in connection with textile design is very functional as concerns fabric painting, and in general this approach also works for the design being functional to clothing. For now, we shall focus on design ideas in two–dimensional space, independent of their relationship with the clothing form. Let us then turn our perceptual eye to the world and see what visions we can create for fabric painting.

Since fabric painting focuses mainly on painting, I would like to describe some of the origins of painting, and how the process of painting formed into design. There are three forms of painting: painting as writing, painting as drawing, and painting as sculpture. Early prehistoric painting was a rough form of writing, as the painting recorded events of the hunt, wild animals, battles with other humans, and the general comings and goings of various peoples. From a realistic recording of events, prehistoric painting evolved into symbolism, with medicine shirts which contained powers for healing, due to the symbols and images painted on the shirt. When this primitive "painted writing", or pictographs, began to become more symbolic, painting and writing began to separate. Painting began to be more representational, and writing began to be more abstract, with symbols that were subject to certain rules of usage and capable of being deciphered by other people. This separation has not been quick, nor even complete. For example, just in the past fifty years have the Mayan hieroglyphs been deciphered.

One type of pictograph began evolving towards alphabets: starting with hieroglyphs, such as Mayan and Egyptian, then the cuneiform (a simplified version of the hieroglyph) which was used in the writing of the Babylonian–Assyrian periods), then Chinese characters, and hence to our present day standardized alphabets. Some older languages retain more of the pictorial in their alphabets, such as the aforementioned Chinese, as well as Arabic, Russian, Eskimo, and Tamil. As well, our regular alphabet is modified and illustrated by calligraphy. The divorce of painting and writing is seen to be slow. Illuminated manuscripts are an example of the combination of painting and writing, being as equally pictorial as written. Even today, alphabets and words are used both as symbols for information and as design forms.

The other type of pictograph began to evolve into drawing, as it became more representational and less symbolic. Painting as drawing usually concerns the first stage of painting—the making of a form. When a painting is of form, rather than formless (or abstract), drawing is an integral part of the painting. In many paintings, the drawing portion remains visible in the finished painting. For example 14th and 15th century paintings began with an outline of the subject matter, then marked out areas of light and shade. Only later was color added.

If a painting is solely the application of paint upon a surface, with no consideration of form, then painting is not involved with drawing. "Painterly painters" of the 1970's, such as Larry Poons and William Pettet concern themselves with the mechanical application of paint upon the surface, yet even they are as concerned with form (and therefore drawing) as they are with color and texture.

It is hard to differentiate painting from drawing. A line could be a streak of color. A color could be a line.

Painting as sculpture concerns the interchangeability of the two art forms. Painting can render three–dimensional sculpture in two–dimensional space. So, is it an illusion? It can be done. In ancient Egyptian and pre–Columbian art, painting and sculpture were combined. Much sculpture was colored; the Parthenon was painted brightly. Certain periods of painting are considered "painterly", others "sculptural". Renaissance painting is sculptural, while Baroque and Hellenistic sculpture is painterly.

These, then, are the roots of painting. All three forms are still evident in todays' modern art, and form the basis for the history of design. We shall now explore design images, which can be used in fabric painting, in a somewhat chronological order, beginning with design images from prehistoric art.

DESIGN IDEAS FROM PRIMITIVE ART

Prehistoric art found in caves consists of hand silhouettes, animals such as bison, wild horses, and some deer. Examples of painting and sculpture are found in caves in France, Eastern

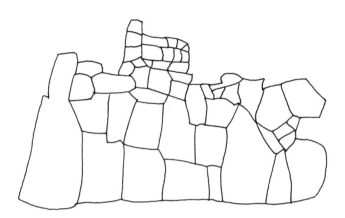

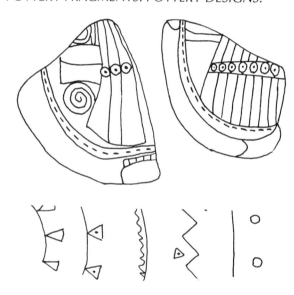

FIG. 112: DRAWINGS OF PREHISTORIC ITEMS: ROCK FORMATIONS AT SACSAHUAMAN, PERU. POTTERY FRAGMENTS. POTTERY DESIGNS.

Spain, North Africa, and Norway. Carved menhirs, which are stone monuments found in Brittany and Italy, Neolithic pottery with great amounts of geometric ornamentation, and Bronze age weapons and utensils from Scandinavia are other art objects from prehistoric times that can be used in fabric painting design. As well, there are numerous examples of pictographs found in cave paintings. In general, inspiration from the fruits of archaeological digs and anthropological studies gives the fabric painter a wide range of subject matter. (Fig.112)

As well as using images from prehistoric art, one can use the ideas behind the images which are the basis for this art. In other words, one can understand the reasons for ancient peoples making what they made, and then simulate the reasons in a modern context. Probable reasons for painted animals were to appease a dead animal, attract live ones, or record the events of a hunt. Other motivations for prehistoric painting include recording of seasons and time, painting for healing (Fig.113), painting as magic and power, painting visions and dreams, and painting to record social history. You could paint your dreams (night or day), your visions, or symbols which give you a sense of strength and power. Or you could paint a series of events which mark time.

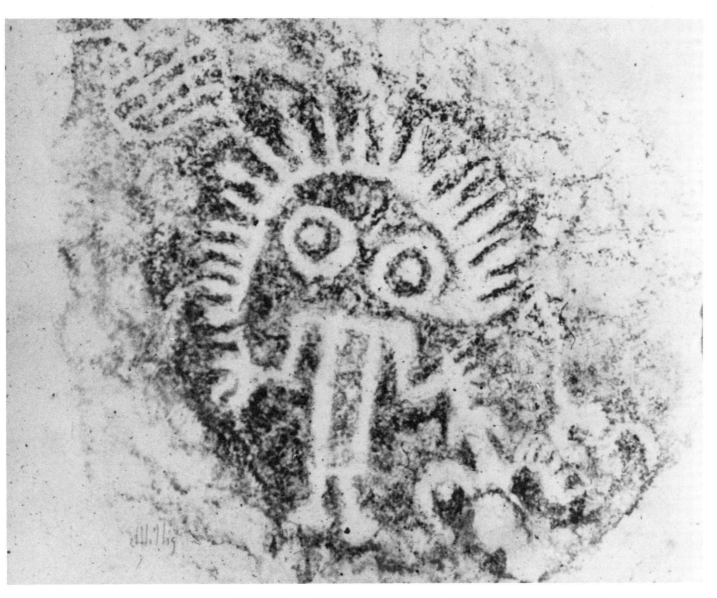

FIG. 113: "MEDICINE MAN"–BY JEANNE HILLIS. A RUBBING TAKEN FROM AN ANCIENT PETROGLYPH (1500-2000 YEARS OLD) FOUND ON THE OREGON SHORE OF THE COLUMBIA RIVER.

Sandra Longmore, a fiber artist, eloquently states the impact of working with ancient symbols.She states, "There has been recent thought that the ancient symbols are an alphabet in connection with our Source. As the symbols are drawn each day, over and over, some kind of connection is being recognized. The connection feels like a global connection of peace, where all of us are—this place is of all things very humorous, spontaneous, alive and free to see each image as the unique, wonderful creation it is. This work and its symbols often occur in the form of dreams, where I consciously interpret but the interpretation that feels true comes only after, and during the drawing of the image,and this interpretation is not a verbal (one). It's before spoken language, or thought, and it rings very true, very wise, and very deep."

Very close to design ideas from prehistoric art are design ideas and images from alphabets and other symbolic forms. Pictographs, Egyptian hieroglyphs, Mayan hieroglyphs, and cunieforms are the most primitive alphabet forms. (Figs.114–118) Occult signs and symbols, such as can be found in *The*

Book of Signs–Koch (Dover), zodiac signs and musical notations are other symbolic forms used with fabric painting. Foreign languages can be used as a design form rather than a symbol, thus taking a symbolic form and making it more abstract. Chinese characters are another alphabet form which is easy to use as a design form.(Fig.119) There are a number of good calligraphy books, such as *Calligraphy*–Baker (Dover), *Written Letters*–Suaren, *Calligraphic Lettering*–Douglass (Watson-Guptill), and *Letter Forms*–Lambert, which show different calligraphic forms of the letters in a large format so that it is relatively easy to learn to paint calligraphic letters. As well, calligraphy and lettering can be done regularly with pen and ink on smooth cloth. (Fig. 117) Illuminated manuscripts, which use a combination of calligraphy and decorative painting, make intricately beautiful painted clothing.

Alphabets in the forms of words can be a very beautiful design form to use in connection with clothing. I find that using an alphabet and a language which is not one in common usage gives me a new perspective on the form and shape of the words,

FIG. 114: TED COTROTSOS MODELING T-SHIRT WITH MAYAN HIEROGLYPHS DRAWN WITH MARKING PENS.

FIG.115: DRAWING OF SIOUX AND ARAPAHO PICTOGRAPHS, BY PHYLLIS THOMSPON. AFTER **PRIMITIVE ART**– *FRANZ BOAS, 1955*

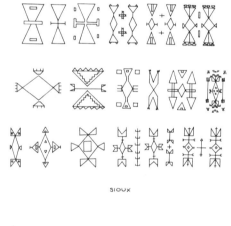

SIOUX

ARAPAHO

FIG. 116: DRAWING OF CUNIEFORMS

FIG. 117: TED COTROTSOS MODELING A LONG–SLEEVED COTTON PULLOVER WITH EGYPTIAN HIEROGLYPHS AND MOTIFS.

as they are not connected to images and ideas. I once made a shirt using phrases written in the Eskimo language. They can be pure design to those who do not know the language, or they can be a word–symbol if translation is added to the design. I have seen tops printed with French words that are fairly familiar, which becomes a design that combines pure design with some symbolic meaning. Many languages can be used in this way.

When the word becomes less of a pure design form, and more of a symbol, then the painted word and words begin to evolve into literature. Taking the idea of books and connecting it with the idea of clothing can be very exciting. Children's literature is an especially good inspiration as there is a maximum of pictures and a minimum of words. It would be easy to make an Alice in Wonderland shirt or a dress with illustrations from **The Little Prince** (St.Exupery). The composition of the painting in a garment is similar to the layout of the pictures and copy in a book, with the juxtapositioning of pictures, colors, words. There is also a connection with this type of design to movies, which are a series of pictures which move after each other in rapid succession. The composition for fabric painting can be made in a linear way to show a "picture-movie". As well,

these designs go beyond the one–dimensional idea of pictorial decoration; there is meaning in the visual images which accompany stories and myths.

There is a wide range of literature which can become painted literature; it is not limited to certain genres or centuries. In fact, painted literature (although not on clothing) is a historical fact, with epics such as the Ramayana being painted into tapestry wallhangings in Persia. Poetry ranging from the long epic to the very short haiku can be used in fabric painting design.

Stories and fiction become design ideas, with or without pictorial elements. (Fig.121) Stories from books are nice; making up your own stories and putting them on your clothing can also be a lot of fun. If you add drawings and pictures, it is like a comic strip, or a walking book!

Real comic strips can be used in a limited way with clothing, by lifting the ink colors from the paper with acrylic gel(See Chapt. VI on Glues and Gels for a discussion of this) onto some clothing. The comic strip "Peanuts" is fun to wear on clothing.

Titles from books can be a design inspiration. Quotations which form around a general theme are good design material

*FIG. 118: (LEFT) DRAWING OF EGYPTIAN HIERO–
GLYPHS (RIGHT) FIG. 119: DRAWING BY PHYLLIS
THOMPSON OF CHINESE CALLIGRAPHY. FROM
CHINESE CALLIGRAPHY– BY CHIANG YEE.*

*FIG. 120: NAME SKIRT: (ABOVE RIGHT)BY EVELYN
BYATT.COTTON AND INKODYE. AN EXAMPLE OF
LETTERING ON CLOTHING.*

*FIG. 121:(RIGHT) AVA LAKE MODELING A COTTON
DRESS WITH AFRICAN TALE WRITTEN IN
ORIGINAL ALPHABET, ORIGINAL LANGUAGE
WITH ROMAN ALPHABET, AND ENGLISH
TRANSLATION. MARKING PEN AND ACRYLIC
GEL TRANSFER.*

for fabric painting, as the theme unites loosely linked material. It can be seen that painted literature can take many forms, from the very intellectual and sophisticated forms to the comic book and humorous tales.

I find the idea of using book ideas and clothing ideas together as very exciting. Many ideas for books can be created in clothing, with similar wide exposure. This would refer primarily to short works, although a larger body of work could be painted on a larger piece of material. Fabric can be a walking book as the pages or the book can be spread out on the fabric. Think of the form of the body as a natural landscape and the character (of your book) adventuring in different parts of the landscape—the points and planes formed by the body in motion and at rest.

Wearing words in public via painted clothing makes them a stronger message and an identity linked to you. Therefore, do not paint what you really do not believe, or are not willing to defend. It is much more personal to wear a sign than to carry one, since clothing is today an extension of personality. As well, words so close to the body change their meaning somewhat, for they relate to the body. Close–fitting garments emphasize the relationship between body and word much more than words on looser parts of a garment. Material which drapes from the body rather than forming to it, creates a detachment between the meaning of the words, and the body.

Sizes and shapes of words have varying relationships to the shape and form of the garment. Words can be written small or big, but very small print may cause people to come up close to you to read what is written, unless they only see the visual (rather than visual and verbal) effect. Large print allows others to read the clothing without stopping you or coming close. (See Fig.120) What size letters you use depends partly on what type of relationship you wish to have with other people when wearing painted clothing.

Another variation on this is to write small words small and big words big. This illustrates not only the meaning, but the shape and sound and dimension of the words. The shape of a poem can be integrated with the shape of a garment, as different words go better with different shaped garments. Flowing words need flowing clothes. Poetry which must show every word in order to be coherent should be lettered on a flat sturdy garment which is rather close–fitting. The progression of a poem can be graphically shown: action such as running can be lettered on the cloth, running around and through it. Directions such as behind, above, and below can be graphically spaced. The form of a poem and the form of a garment and a body can interact in a more meaningful way without being gimmicky.

Some of the most successful words to use on clothing for the beginner are images which relate to clothing: images dealing with texture, color, action and motion, either abstractly or specifically. Specific images would be words connected with sports and dance, as they describe movement. In deciding on the composition for painted literature, think of the body as a landscape. This will draw it out of its purely physical and sexual meanings, allowing for a larger range of thought in design. The landscape could be timeless or surreal, or it could be a setting with a specific time and place; such as the woods in winter, or the city in the spring. This gives the garment a setting much like our summer and winter clothes, with certain colors, material, and styles which are actors within the setting of the real weather. To bring time and place into the garment only adds another dimension.

Another source of design ideas comes from motifs from various cultures, such as pre–Columbian, American Indian, African, Chinese, Japanese, the Far East, Persian and Indian,

Asian, South American, Russian, Scandanavian, Eastern Europe, and European. Some of these cultures or areas are richer in motifs than others, but all should be explored for their possibilities.

Motifs from pre-Columbia include stylized birds and animals, woven and embroidered designs, and geometrics in earth tones from pottery. Sculpture, fabrics, architecture, and pottery can be explored to find many interesting design ideas.(Figs. 122–123).There are a number of Dover books, including **Mayan Hieroglyphs**–Morley, **Design Motifs of Ancient Mexico**–Enciso, and **Pre-Hispanic Mexican Stamp Designs**–Field, which include many motifs from pre-Columbian America. American Indian motifs are extensive and can be found in their fabrics and weaving, painted tipis and hides, and pottery.(Figs.124, Fig.125).African design holds interest with its mixture of primitivism and modern awareness. There are a number of printed fabrics with design motifs and layout inspired from African design (Figs.126,127, & 128), and Oceanic art.

Designs from the Far East (China, Japan, and Korea) and the Near East (India, Persia) are quite different from the above, but are equally applicable. For example, the motifs can be used on American clothing, (Fig.129) within a traditionally Eastern garment form such as a kimona, (Fig. 22) or as pillows (Fig.130–131) Rugs, bedspreads treasures, music, and literature are other sources for Persian and Indian designs. The bright stripes of Mexican, Spanish, or Russian clothing (Fig.132), and the unique layered looks from Asian clothing and Eastern Europe are other design sources. As well, there is the whole of Europe

FIG. 122: LESLIE ALLEN OF LEXINGTON,
KENTUCY, MODELING A PRE–COLUMBIAN
PAINTED SKIRT. ACRYLIC ON COTTON.

FIG. 124: NORTHWEST COAST INDIAN MOTIF PAINTED ON MAN'S COTTON SHIRT. TIM RENN MODELS SHIRT MADE BY CINDY TURNBALL, BOTH OF EUGENE, OREGON. THE DESIGN REPRESENTS A THUNDERBIRD FROM THE KWAKIUTL INDIANS OF SOUTHWEST BRITISH COLUMBIA. VERSATEX PAINT.

FIG. 123: DRAWING BY PHYLLIS THOMPSON OF A MOTIF FROM THE CODEX ZOUCHE–NUTTALL (MIXTEC) FROM **THE CONQUISTA-DORS** BY HAMMOND INNES.

*FIG. 125: DRAWING BY PHYLLIS THOMPSON OF A MAN'S SHIRT FROM TLINGIT, ALASKA, AFTER **INDIAN ART IN AMERICA**– F. J. DOCKSTADER*

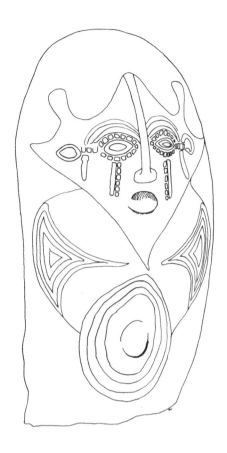

FIG. 126: DRAWING OF E. NIGERIAN STONE CARVING, AFTER **AFRICAN STONE SCULPTURE–** BY PHILIP ALISON. DRAWING BY P. THOMPSON.

FIG. 127: DRAWING OF BAKONGO STONE CARVING. AFTER **AFRICAN STONE SCULPTURE–** P. ALISON. DRAWING BY PHYLLIS THOMPSON.

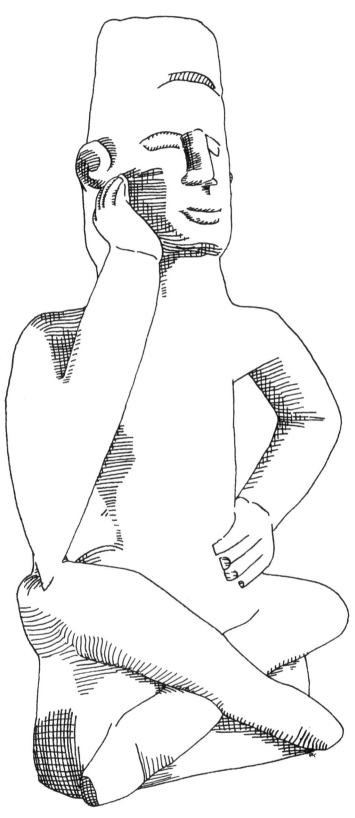

FIG. 129: HANDPAINTED T–SHIRT BY KIM AND LEIGH LACAVA WITH CHINESE MOTIF.

FIG. 128: DRAWING BY PHYLLIS THOMPSON OF A CONGOLESE STONE FROM NTADI, BAMBONA. AFTER **AFRICAN STONE SCULPTURE**– PHILIP ALISON

FIG. 130–131: MONSTER PILLOWS BY VALERIE GUIGNON. THEY DEPICT THE FIERCE AND FRIGHTENING VISAGE OF AN EASTERN MYSTIC SYMBOL IN A COLORFUL AND CUDDLY FORM. PROCION DYE ON COTTON.

*(ABOVE) FIG 132: DRAWING BY PHYLLIS THOMPSON OF A SPANISH STRIPED SKIRT FROM AVILA, SPAIN. AFTER **PEASANT COSTUME IN EUROPE**--KATHLEEN MANN*

process of crochet into other mediums. Drawing and painting can be approached as well, as a journey. (see the books, **The Dot and the Line**–Juster, and **Taking a Walk With a Line,** for inspiration).

There are many new design ideas concerning crochet. Old patterns are still used, but new ideas in construction have come about. **Crochet:Discovery and Design**–Del Pitt Feldman, and Creative Crochet–Edson and Stimmel (Watson–Guptill) describe many new ways of crocheting. One simple idea with a lot of potential is to crochet simple shapes such as squares, circles, triangles, and loops and then attach them in various ways and crochet around that area; perhaps adding on another separate piece somewhere and crocheting around more. This type of composition could also be painted on fabric.

Lace and macrame are two more fiber structures which can be reproduced by drawing. With pen and ink, an expert draftster can reproduce intricate lace designs. (Fig. 133)Needle made lace with the many buttonhole bars as anchors are especially graceful designs for clothing. There are many types of lace made in different ways. unfortunately, hand-made lace is becoming a rariety. Yet, for the purposes of fabric painting, books on lace can bring lace designs alive again. The designs can be copied and worked with pen and ink, markers, and stencils and paint. As well, real lace can be used as a stamp. (see Chapter VI under "stamps") Macrame, which is formed in a manner similar to lace, can also be used as a design form. Different kinds of needlework, point to different kinds of ideas for fabric painting. For example, needlepoint, with its limited number of stitches, yet its wide variety of designs, is a wonderful place to draw inspiration for "painterly" scenes. (Latch-hookrug designs are another good source). Scenes such as baskets of

and Scandinavia to be considered, and it will be given more extensive treatment later in this chapter, in "Design Ideas from Historical Costume and Dress". By working in these geographic areas, as seen above, it is possible to experience the atmosphere of that area without necessarily wearing what might be felt to be a costume. Modern day designers and manufacturers have been using this technique for a number of years. In an ad for Dan River fabrics, the following types of fabrics are described: Persian peasant looks, spicy Mexican serape stripes and prints, North African mosaics, light refreshing Indian batiks and gauzes, and potluck patchwork plaids. All of these fabrics have the vivid interest of costume without the ensuing nationalism, nor the inappropriateness that a costume sometimes has.

When talking about design ideas from needlework, one does not intend to capture the textural interest via painting to the extent that it can be created by thread and needle. However, certain needlework stitches can be copied into the language of painting. It is impossible to recreate the textures and body of yarn with paint in knitting, for example, but knitting stitches can be approximated in fabric painting by their design. Texture resembling needlework has been shown in paintings by Van Gogh ("Starry Night"and "Wheatfields") with the straight, sharp brushstrokes.

Design ideas evolving from knitting include painting brushstroke textures similar to the textures created by the knitted stitch, or copying the whole design in a garment, such as the textured patterns in the Ayran or fisherman knit sweaters. As well, knitted pieces can be used in fabric painting, for a collage-type effect.

Design ideas from crochet deal more with the process of crochet than from the end result. For example, by thinking of the yarn as a long unending line (which it is) and the crochet hook as the guide, director, or seeker, it is easy to transfer the

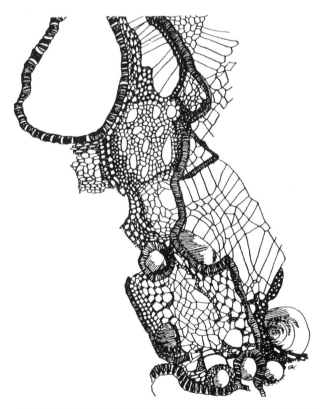

*FIG. 133: DRAWING BY PHYLLIS THOMPSON AFTER UNTITLED LACE ON PLEXIGLAS BY OTTO THIEME, IN **LACE**– BY V.C.BATH*

flowers and farm scenes, all stitched in one or two basic stitches, could be painted with small brushstrokes similar to the techniques of the French Impressionists and Pointillists. Bargello needlepoint reminds me of some types of weaving, and could be translated into fabric painting by working with marking pens, oil paint and textine with small brushes, or pen and ink.

The term "stitchery" is sometimes described as painting with a needle, because of its freer design. Many paintings have been copied into stitchery, and stitchery ideas can be used for fabric painting. Stitchery is a more modern term for embroidery, and focuses more on the composition of the design and less on specific intricate stitches.

Traditional embroidery, on the other hand, has many types of stitch with numerous effects possible. It is easy to copy embroidered designs with embroidery paints, marking pens, and with regular textile and acrylic paint using small brushes. "Stitchery"–type effects, rather than "painterly", are likely. Also, **painted** embroidery designs are much quicker to complete than sewn embroidery. What is lost in texture is gained in line. (Fig.134)

Historical examples of embroidery give good ideas for the placement of embroidery on garments. As well, it is possible to copy the designs without having to have the technical needlework skills. **Erica Wilson's Embroidery Book** has excellent color pictures of historical embroidery.

Weaving, tapestry, applique, and patchwork are four other types of needlework which can be used as inspiration in fabric painting. The design, rather than the technique, of both weaving and tapestry should be considered. (Fig. 137) On the other hand, designs evolving from applique and patchwork rely on process as much as design.

Applique, collage, and the Cubist movement in art are all very closely combined. I am using the term "applique" to apply to abstract design which is first cut and then pasted or sewn onto the material. Collage usually has more of a message, either psychological or sociological, and often uses newspaper clippings and lettering in its composition.

Henri Matisse used paper cutouts for some of his art. These paper cutouts were previously painted with gouache and then experimentally composed into a variety of layouts. Some of Ferdinand Leger's earlier work, such as "The Smokers" and

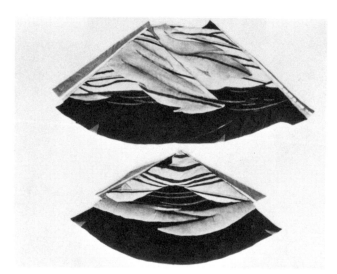

FIG. 135: **"TIME ENLARGING II"**– BY VICTORIA Z. RIVERS. PROCIION DYE ON VELVETEEN, BEADS, AIRBRUSH, APPLIQUE, HANDPAINTING, QUILTED AND STUFFED.

FIG.136 : **"UNTITLED: GREENS"**–VICTORIA Z. RIVERS. PROCION DYE ON VELVETEEN, AIRBRUSH, BEADS, QUILTED, STUFFED, SCREENED, AND HAND PAINTED.

FIG. 134: DRAWING OF EMBROIDERY STITCHES WHICH CAN BE USED IN FABRIC PAINTING. BY PHYLLIS THOMPSON.

FIG. 137: (FOLLOWING PAGE) DETAIL OF **"ICARUS"**– BY JUDY FELGAR. PAINTED WEAVING, DOUBLE WEAVE PICK-UP IN WOOL, SAX'S COLORTEX.

"The Woman in Blue", though painted rather than pasted, are very good guides for painted applique. The shapes are geometric with straight edges and look like cut–paper shapes, yet the colorings within the shapes have a variety of shadings and texture. This effect can be created in applique with cut shapes of fabric which are painted and composed into a design. (Fig.135, Fig.136) Design evolving from applique and applique processes can be found in the work of other painters and needleworkers.(Fig.139)

Patchwork can be used as design and technique in fabric painting. Chapter VII goes into detail about painted patchwork as it is such a unique combination. However, for design ideas from patchwork, two approaches can be followed. Various patchwork patterns can be drawn and painted onto fabric, eliminating the tedium of sewing together small pieces of material. Or, painted material can be cut and pieced in the tradition of patchwork. (Figs.138 and 140)

As well as needlework, there are other crafts, both fabric and nonfabric, which can be a source of design ideas for fabric painting. Batik, pottery, ceramic sculpture, jewelry, wood, glass, enameling, and soft sculpture are some of the many crafts at which to look. Batik, with its emphasis on bright colors, color overlays and swirling lines caused by the motion of the tjanting, is a good design source for fabric painting. Other methods of fabric decoration, explained in detail in Chapter 1 should also be looked at for design ideas. Ideas from pottery and ceramic sculpture include drawing the three–dimensional forms onto the fabric, thereby translating the medium of clay and fire into color and form. Ancient and modern pottery and ceramics

should be explored. Another possibility for design ideas comes from analyzing the methods used in making pottery, and adapting these techniques of construction to painting and the forming of garments. For example, the coiling method could be transferred to cloth, creating coiled skirts, either with sewn or painted coils. The technique of handbuilding with clay, along with the process of adding various sections of clay to a main form, could be used in an approach both to sewing and painting.

Jewelry and metalwork form another category for design inspiration. (Figs. 141) Expressions in wood, ranging from a wooden house to a wooden carving, form design ideas. Glass, enameling, fiber wrapping and twining, in fact, **any** other form of art or craft can be a design inspiration for fabric painting.

DESIGN IDEAS FROM SEWING

The history of sewing, generally known as historical costume and dress, yields up much useful information about how ancient peoples dressed, what types of materials they used, and what type decoration they used in their clothing. There are so many ways to approach design ideas from the category of historical costume and dress. The outline of the clothing can be drawn to fit the wearer, and then if there are variations within the garment, they can be painted in. Or, pattern pieces can be cut, painted, and then sewn together to form the dress. Or, just the form of the clothing can be used as inspiration, with a modern design painted in or left plain. Or the design could be decorated in another way, such as embroidery. In general,

FIG. 138: "COLLOGRAPH QUILT" –BY JUDITH STEIN. COLLOGRAPH ON UNBLEACHED MUSLIN, PIECED AND QUILTED. OIL–BASE ETCHING INK USED (GRAPHIC CHEMICAL'S PERFECTION PALLETE INKS). 70 X 70"

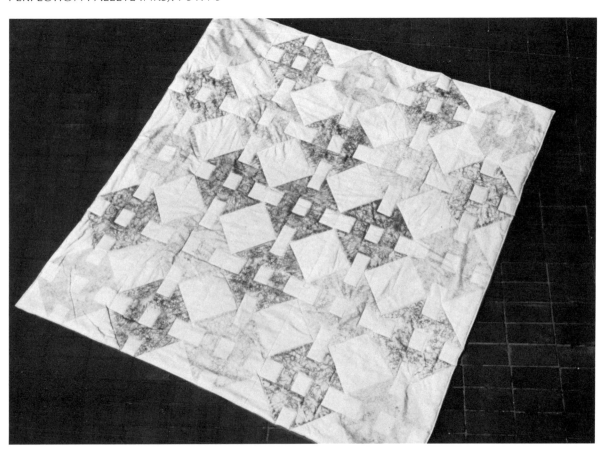

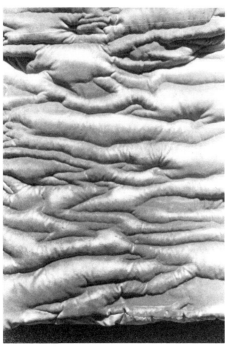

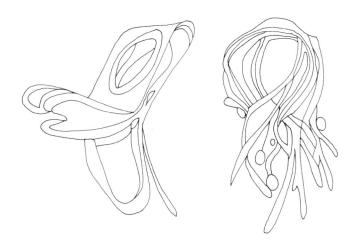

FIG. 141: DRAWINGS OF JEWELRY RINGS. DESIGNS FROM SCANDINAVIAN ARTISTS. FROM **NEW DESIGN IN JEWELRY**- DONALD WILLCOX

(ABOVE LEFT) FIG. 139: **"HOMAGE TO FURR AUDITORIUM"** BY JAMES H. SANDERS III. AIRBRUSH AND TRAPUNTO (A TYPE OF QUILTING). (BELOW) FIG. 140: LAYOUT OF PATCHWORK DESIGNS: BOOK AND UNFINISHED SHIRT

designers and the clothing industry use historical costume as a base for new designs, but what they can do is regulated by consumer interest, production costs, and available mechanical techniques. The fabric painter has the advantage of considering only the designs themselves, basic painting techniques, and the way in which they themselves would best like to use the design.

Certain historical periods may yield more of interest, but all have possibilities. Greek, Egyptian, Roman, Byzantium, Medevial peasantry, Early Renaissance, 17th, 18th, and 19th centuries in Europe, Russian, Slavic, and the Far East offer a wide range of costume and dress. (Figs.142,143,144,145) Most of these designs are just the outline and decoration. Learning how to take such an outline and form a pattern is called flat pattern drafting. Available books can guide you in such a pursuit. Historical dress can also be found in paintings, with accurate portrayal of the colors and fabrics of the fashion season.

It is exciting to make a dress from a very old pattern. It has a flavor of tradition, yet its design is aimed towards modern use.

Fabric painting is especially helpful here, as frilly dresses, ruffles, pleats, and intricate and perhaps cumbersome patterning can simply be painted on a dress. Painting can create visual illusion.

So many sources for design ideas, still there are more! Nature, the fine arts, and the history of textile design are three more areas in which to look for design ideas. Design ideas evolving from the physical and natural sciences include material from biology, botany, zoology, human physiology, chemistry, geology, and astronomy. Such material might include skeletal structures of animals, different kinds of wood, bark, leave, plant, and flowers, different parts and organs of animals, drawings from microscope samples of various parts of plants and animals , drawings of the arrangements of atoms, photographs of chemicals, fossils, minerals, rocks, clay and earth, and the stars, planets, and galaxies. This material can be abstracted, analyzed, or altered to fit specific design needs.

DESIGN IDEAS FROM NATURE

Nature is familiar to us in everyday forms. Art transforms in order for us to see again, in new but somehow familiar ways. The eye sees that which is close and that which is far, but it cannot see closely enough to see atoms, nor far enough away to see the shape of stars. Microscope eyes and telescope eyes show us other ways that nature is: the pen and brush record it and show it to our eyes. (Fig.149, Fig.150)

Design in nature is abundant. Grasses and twigs suggest line. Something as small as bark, as well as a large overview of rolling hills interspersed with streams and twigs, suggests texture. Rocks and leaves provide one with simple shapes and forms. Many different species of flora and fauna can be drawn, both realistically and in an abstract way. (Figs.147,148) As well as rocks, minerals are very good as inspiration. They are crystalline, and offer a variety of composition with their many planes. Some look like paintings themselves, with deep blues and golds and with marbled greens and blacks. Stibnite, microline, and azurite are particularly colorful.

Not only can designs be drawn from nature, as in the previous examples, they can be used directly on the fabric. (This is discussed in detail in Chapter IV) Bark, pieces of wood, twigs, leaves, seeds and pods can be coated with polymer gel and then glued onto the fabric. Natural or commercial clays can be shaped and fired, and either glazed with a ceramic glaze or painted with acrylic as a sealer. Beads are especially nice when made from clay and then pasted or even strung and sewn down on the fabric, creating a type of organic clothing.

Materials in nature can also be used as stamps and the image can be imprinted onto the fabric. Twigs, grasses, and delicate dried weeds are particularly good, for it is difficult to duplicate their intricacies by brush. The paint is brushed onto the object and then it is pressed onto the fabric. Leaves also produce an interesting, though sometimes imperfect, replica.

It can be seen, therefore, that there are many design ideas to be found through study of both the natural and physical sciences. Nature is always looked to as a design form, but I feel that the category of nature should be expanded to include other sciences, as mentioned above–sciences which are not so commonly thought of in terms of design or form. Other large categories to explore for design ideas come through an examination of art history and through modern textile design.

Although the history of painting and the works of various

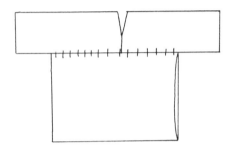

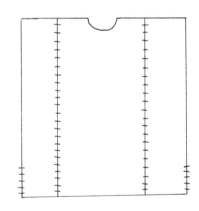

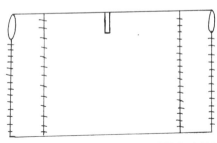

FIG. 142: DRAWINGS OF HIUPTLS, A BASIC MEXICAN CLOTHING SHAPE.

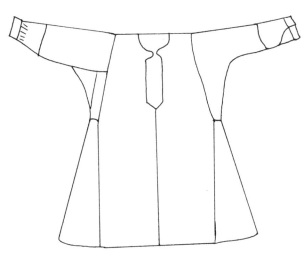

FIG. 144: DRAWING OF RUSSIAN CLOTHING
FROM THE TRIBES OF THE CASPIAN STEPPE.
FROM **COSTUME PATTERNS AND DESIGNS**–M. TILKE

FIG. 143: DRAWING OF MEDIEVAL CLOTHING

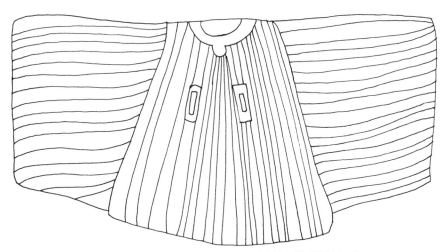

FIG. 145: DRAWING OF AFRICAN CLOTHING,
EAST AFRICAN, WESTERN SUDAN, FROM
COSTUME PATTERNS AND DESIGNS–M. TILKE

FIG. 147: **"PERSIAN PONIES 1"**– BY MAGGIE KENDIS. DIRECT DYE APPLICATION WITH WAX RESIST. COTTON POPLIN WITH PROCION DYE. 36" X 52"

painters are good as a source of inspiration, not everything is possible on fabric that is possible on canvas or paper. All through the ages, the concept of "design" has been relegated to cloth, while canvas and paper have expanded many painting techniques. Cloth is as equally creative.

However, there are differences in the two materials. Cloth has various textures, and therefore can create more resistance to paint, especially when doing subtle and delicate techniques of shading, or small lines. You cannot slide paint onto all fabrics like you can with oils on canvas. Certain types of paint will simply soak into the fabric, while others will stiffen the surface of the fabric. When looking to art history for design ideas for fabric painting, the technical differences between fabric painting and canvas painting should be kept in mind, but you can also keep an open mind to the possibilities of **any** art form for fabric painting.

FIG. 148: *"YOUNG BUCK IN THE BIRCHES"*--*BY MAGGIE KENDIS. PAINTERLY BATIK DONE WITH DIRECT APPLICATION OF PROCION DYE ON COTTON POPLIN. 22" X 28"*

DESIGNS FROM THE FINE ARTS

Within art history, there is drawing, painting, sculpture, printmaking, and architecture. The differences and similarities between drawing and painting have previously been discussed. Very simply, drawing is the first part of painting, but it also stands on its own as an art form. Drawing can be simple or complex. You can simply draw lines, one after another on a piece of fabric. Doodle drawings and cartoons are another category. The most popular category of drawing may be figure drawing, and the graceful drawings of Renaissance artists are particularly effective when drawn on long, flowing robes. When a human figure is drawn on cloth, it usually expresses the body in some form of motion–standing, sitting, resting, or moving. It is best that the style of the garment harmonize with the type of movement expressed in the drawing. For example, Degas' full–skirted ballerinas would be consistent when drawn on a loose flowing garment; they would be inconsistent if drawn on a tailored suit, with its emphasis on constraining movement and maximized efficiency. The category of figure–drawing has within it a great many ideas which can be used in fabric painting. One last interesting thought is that drawing figures on clothing is an overlay, for the figures are on clothing which contain *within them* figures; and if the painted or drawn figures wear clothing, there are four different realities: painted clothing on a painted figure on clothing which is painted, being worn by a real person!

When considering painting, one can look at various artists and historical time periods, or one can look at categories such as still–life, landscape painting, portraiture, religious painting, or abstract. Look at the following historical periods for design ideas. **Prehistoric and early historic art,** covered earlier in Chapter V under prehistoric art and cultural motifs, includes Greek, Egyptian, and Roman art. In Greek art, for example, vase painting limited itself to a few motifs which were perfected, and painted either as black or red figures. Many different garments could be created from this basic theme from Greek art.

The next large period of art was greatly influenced by the church. **Early Christian, Byzantine, Early Medieval, and Romanesque art history** includes mural paintings, tapestries and beautiful illuminated books.(see Figs.151-153) **Gothic art** was also influenced by religion, but less so by the church. Much of Gothic art was expressed through architecture. Stained glass and painted manuscripts were also popular during these times, and could be easily translated into designs for fabric painting.

From 1400-1600, the influence of **Renaissance art** was felt. Some painters include the Van Eyck brothers, who began to use oil paint with good effects, as well as Leonardo Da Vinci, Michelangelo, Raphael, and Titian. The last artistic period before Modern art was the age of the **Baroque and the Rococo.** These periods, which extended from 1600-1800, aimed for dramatic effects and the portrayal of emotional intensity. Paintings stressed space and dissolved form in color and light, unlike the preceding Renaissance, which emphasized form. The light touch, light but sensuous, exhibited in the works of these painters, are effective for fabric painting, as fabric painted clothing should suggest a certain effect or emotion rather than be permeated and weighted down by it.

Look to Watteau, Boucher, and Poussin for figures with rich lustrous clothes set in atmospheric landscapes of spacious light. Chardin, Rembrandt, and Vermeer portrayed still life, while

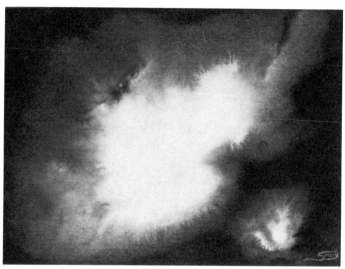

FIG. 149: *"THETA ORIONIS"–BY FERNE SIROIS.AN EXCELLENT DEPICTION OF THE MULTIPLE STAR IN THE ORION NEBULA. ACRYLIC STAINING ON HEAVY CANVAS.*

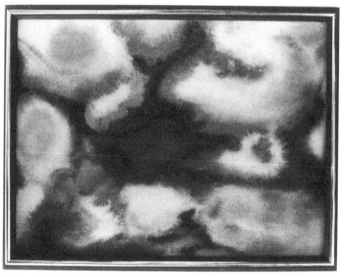

FIG. 150: *BY FERNE SIROIS. ANOTHER EXAMPLE OF STAINING ON CANVAS.*

robust and country life was portrayed by Rubens and Hals. Reynolds and Velasquez painted portraits, Gainsborough and Lorrain concentrated on the countryside, a countryside full of light, space, water and air. Caravaggio and Turner are well remembered for their paintings of light The Baroque and Rococo periods are full of interesting ideas for the fabric painter.

Modern art began around 1800 and continues into the present day. After Napoleon's rise to power, **Neo-Classicism** was the dominant style, with David, Ingres, and Angelica Kauffmann as some prominent painters of the time, as well as the now well–known Maxfield Parrish. Following Neo–Classicism came the **Romantic movement,** which rebelled against the restraints of the NeoClassicists. There was a lyrical manner in the Romantic treatment of color and form. Corot, Millet, and Rousseau were Romantic painters, as were Rosalba Carriera and Elisabeth Vignee–Lebrun. Emotions and colors were emphasized, subjects were glamorized and made heroic. **Realism**

FIG. 151: DRAWING BY PHYLLIS THOMPSON AFTER BYZANTINE GOSPEL COVER, MID 900'S. SILVER GILT WITH ENAMEL. AFTER **ART OF THE BYZANTINE EMPIRE**–A. GRAVAR

FIG. 152: **"VENUS"**–BY JUDY FELGAR. EXAMPLE OF RELIGIOUS ORIENTED FABRIC PAINTING. DOUBLE–WEAVE PICK–UP:WOOL.TEXTILE PAINT.

FIG. 153: **"NINE"**–BY JUDY FELGAR. DOUBLE–WEAVE PICK–UP: WOOL WITH ATLANTIC TEXTILE PAINT

and **Naturalism** occurred midway through the 19th century. The artist, rather than presenting her own thought or feeling, was merely a neutral recorder of the objects observed. This was most true of Naturalism, which tried to reach the perfectionism of photography. Realism, however, allowed for some distortion for emotional emphasis, a kind of poetic license. Millet, Courbet, and both early Degas and Renoir were included in this period. Women artists include Rosa Bonheur, Lilly Martin Spencer, and Sarah Miriam Peale.

In the late 19th century, a small group of artists in France became intrigued with the effects of sunlight on various objects, particularly outdoors. Monet, Manet, Pissarro, Renoir, Degas, and Sisley watched water, haystacks, and cathedrals at various times of the day, painting "impressions". They sought only momentary occurrences; yet the spots of paint fused into a shimmering color field, the effect of which was far from momentary. **Impressionism** has been an important development in the history of painting. Berthe Morisot and Mary Cassatt are two important women Impressionist painters. Morisot emphasized painting directly from nature in low–keyed color harmonies. She caught the evanescent effects of light in shimmering color just as her male colleagues did in their paintings. Cassatt's goal was to paint the concerns of "the feminine" motherhood, the charm of womanhood, in a strong manner. Her success is evident in her now famous pastels and oils.

Seurat took the technique of the spots of paint one step further in **Neo–Impressionism.** It was a short lived experiment based on the science of optics, and dealt with certain complementary colors being placed next to each other in small dots. The colors would fuse on the retina at a certain distance, creating greater luminosity. This idea would appear in the next century, in Op art.

Among others, Paul Cezanne, Van Gogh, Gauguin, and Suzanne Valadon comprise what is today called **Post–Impressionism**. Cezanne began a new trend which aimed at form, which evolved into the artist being personally inventive in handling **both** color and form. Cezanne stressed a solid yet sensitive composition, and the basis of his painting can be found to continue further into modern painting. With their bright colors, textured brushstrokes, and lyrical subject matter, the styles of the Impressionists and Post–Impressionists are particularly adaptable to fabric painting.

Cezanne, Van Gogh, Gauguin, and Valadon planted the seeds of abstract art: Cezanne, with his emphasis on form, Van Gogh, Valadon, and Gauguin with their bright colors and emotional style leading to Expressionism. Abstract art concentrated on a conscious elimination of natural forms, or an abstraction from objects in the environment.

Picasso, Mondrian, and Miro were the beginners of **abstract art. Cubism** evolved from abstract art, with the emphasis on pure form, with a resemblance to objects coming second. It destroyed the ordinary forms of things, recreating them into colorful and highly textured decorative compositions. Picasso and Braque were the founders of Cubism. There are a number of famous women artists of the Avant–Garde of this time. They include Romaine Brooks, Gwen John, (Dora) Carrington, Vanessa Bell, Marie Laurencin, Gabriele Munter, Marianne Werefkin, Paula Modersohn–Becker, and Sonia Delauney.

Abstract art became the dominant style of modern art. In the 1920's, Cubism was followed by Futurism, Nonobjective art, Expressionism, Fauvism, and Surrealism. Futurism came out of Italy in the early 1900's, with an emphasis on the machine age. Artists painted speed, excitement, movement. Paint was swirled on the canvas, and the form of the object was not seen, only the object in motion. **Non–objective art,** very similar to abstract art, can be seen in the works of the Russian artist, Kandinsky. By the 1930's, artists were completely free to devise and improvise from their imagination rather than using man or nature as a frame of reference. Kandinsky formed a group called "the Blue Horsemen", which included Paul Klee and Franz Marc. The space relationships in their paintings seemed, to the onlooker, to be very free, yet they are formed from calculated relationships. The paintings of these three men have associative properties, but they are not connected to any outer reality. The paintings move us to recognize our inner reality.

Expressionism, which began in Germany in the late 1800's, emphasized the emotional experiences of the artist, their inner feelings. The colors in Expressionism were bold, vivid, executed with rapid brushstrokes, often symbolic. Van Gogh, Gauguin, Valadon, Matisse, Picasso, Rouault, Kirchner, Nolde, Vlaminck, Munch, Kokoschka, Kollwitz, Dufy, Munter, S. Delaunay, and Kandinsky are all Expressionists. **Fauvism** grew out of Expressionism, with Henri Matisse as the leader. Fauvism emphasized color, swirling bright thick color, unrestrained combinations of color. Faces might be blue or pink, bridges red, rivers yellow. Realism was not a concern of the Fauves; expression was.

Another group, the **Dadaists,** felt that the intellectual mind could only produce sterile ideas, when it concerned art. They deliberately pursued chaos. Close to Dadaism was **Surrealism.** Pursuing a psychological point of view, Surrealism depicted the visual symbols of the unconscious. Space was often seen as endless, with moody dreamlike landscapes and strange figures frozen in space. The Surrealists were very intent upon communicating this new "language" of the unconscious to the general public, so they used traditional painting techniques in order to present their imagery in as clarified a manner as possible. Leonor Fini, Remedios Varo, Leonora Carrington, and Frieda Kahlo were all exciting Surrealists.

Americans were watching and following from overseas these various forms of abstract art flourishing in Europe. They broke with the European tradition in 1910 and created what is called **American Modernist painting.** A number of painting groups and techniques abounded. The Ashcan School in New York was unique in that this group of painters focused on painting the city. Edward Hopper depicted the city as a lonely place, while George Bellows' landscapes were peopled with forceful, energetic types.

Regionalism and Social Realism were the two major art movements of the 1920's. **Regionalism** was a reaction of Americans from foreign influence. Artists painted romanticized landscapes of the Mid–West, the farms, the people, the simple everyday lifestyles. Grant Wood, Thomas Hart Benton, and John Curry were foremost Regionalists. (Look at their work for good examples for landscape fabric painting.)

Contrasting with this was **Social Realism,** which focused on the pain and suffering caused by the economic Depression. Ben Shahn is a well-known artist of this period. Other famous painters from 1920-1935 include: John Marin, who did watercolors of the sea, Joseph Stella, and Georgia O'Keeffe. Other movements include the **Color Painters** or **Synchromists** (who followed the influence of Sonia and Robert Delaunay in Europe), and the Cubist Realists. These artists would foreshadow approaches and techniques appearing again in the great movement of the 1940's–Abstract Expressionism.

Abstract Expressionism began in New York in the 1940's. Abstract Expressionism, or **Action Painting,** as it is sometimes called, is an intuitive activity demanding automatic, and nonplanned responses. The painter empties herself of conscious direction, then allows for intuitive direction. One application of paint demands further applications, the placement of which depends upon what happened initially. In a sense the painter is building upon impulse, not preplanned thought. The Abstract Expressionists were not looking for conventional visions or traditional techniques when they painted, and so the paintings cannot be judged or perceived from that perspective. The paintings exist as ends in themselves. Jackson Pollack was well known for his spatter, or drip, paintings. Hans Hofmann, a German Modernist who resided in the U.S. was also instrumental in the beginnings of Action painting. Other famous members of this group were Mark Rothko, William de Kooning, Adolf Gottlieb, Robert Motherwell, Mark Tobey, Grace Hartigan, Franz Kline, Joan Mitchell, Lee Krasner, Arshile Gorky, Sam Francis, and Helen Frankenthaler.

Abstract Expressionism is an exciting inspiration for the fabric painter due to its bright colors, its abstract shapes, and its emphasis on *color* being the expressive force in the painting. Modular unit painting and repeat motifs would work well with these techniques. Not limited by form or specific subject matter, this allows the painter the free flowing of color onto the fabric.

Several painters have emphasized painting, or staining, on raw canvas. In 1953, Morris Louis began staining his canvases with acrylics, inspired by the staining of Helen Frankenthaler, who used acrylic or polymer resins on canvas. By the 60's, this form of art was being labeled **Color–Field Painting,** or **Abstract Imagery,** and was a reaction to Abstract Expressionism. Other painters of this time doing this type of work were Jules Olitski, spraying colors on canvas, Sam Francis, and Sam Gillian, who stained and then draped his canvases so they look similar to painted fabric. These artists are, I believe, especially exciting inspirations for fabric painting.

Artists branched out from Abstract Expressionism into a variety of techniques and movements. Post–Painterly Abstractionists brought form back into their paintings, while still using the techniques of the Abstract Expressionists. **Hard–edge painting** was one form of this movement. Hard–edge painting is related to the language and structure of form. It is intellectual painting, with flat color application and abstract subject matter detached from the direct problems of life. The **soft–edge** form of this movement was similar, except that their paintings were soft–edged!

Pop art bloomed in the early 60's as a reaction to the intuitive processes of the Abstract Expressionists. It relied upon mass–media images such as were used in advertising. Andy Warhol, Jaspar Johns, and Robert Rauschenberg, are some famous names in Pop art. **Op art** was also popular in the mid–60's. It sought expression thru a sharp stimulus of the retina. It is based on scientific calculations of the theories of vision. There is a kinetic quality to most Op art; the lines seem to "swim" or vibrate before our eyes.

Two more art movements became well-known in the mid–to late sixties. They are Photo Realism, and Minimalism. **Photo Realism** was cool and noncommittal, like Pop. The artist would often project a photograph onto canvas, then paint it so it looked just like a photograph. Common themes were suburban neighborhoods, cars, city buildings. **Minimalism** emphasized clarity and understatement, and was a reaction against what the Minimalists saw as the excesses of Abstract Expressionism.

Other art movements continuing into the 1970's include **Constructivism** (an interest in geometric shapes), **Conceptualism** (focus on the process rather than making an art object), **new**

image painting, and **pattern and decoration.** Joyce Kosloff's work in pattern and decoration is an excellent source for using peasant design, embroidery motifs, and decoration in painting. Other important painting history to look to for inspiration includes: **Modern Native American Painting, African–American Art, American Folk Painting, and Feminist Art.**

With each day, there are more painters, developing ever new ways of seeing, which, over time, develop into major art movements. One of the distinctions of modern art lies in its versatility; scientific and intellectual schools blossom simultaneously with the very intuitive and the emotional. All of these painting schools and movements, focused on the two–dimensional surface of the canvas and the picture hung upon the wall, can be changed into the painting of fabric, and fashioned into clothes of ones' creative choice and fantasy in fabric and color.

While not all paintings are suitable in textile design, there is much to be pulled from these paintings and formed into a three–dimensional statement of color, texture, and balance. What's important is to *look* at lots of paintings and get ideas for your own. I personally feel that certain painters and times are more of an inspiration for fabric painting than others, but I wanted to walk you through all of art history, so you can make your choices. I feel that the Impressionists, the Expressionists, the Abstract Expressionists, the ColorField Painters and the Synchromists, and the school of pattern and decoration are especially useful. Look at Paul Klee's whimsical paintings, Sonia Delaunay's brightly colored paintings and sketches for fabrics, Hans Hofmann's brightly colored squares, among thousands of other equally important painters.

It is rarely recognized that the world of painting and the world of fashion can be merged. Because of this, we have an untapped wealth of creativity waiting in all those paintings on the wall, waiting for those of us to consider that fabric is yet another canvas.

DESIGN IDEAS FROM SCULPTURE

There are several basic ways to use sculpture in design for fabric painting. The outline of the sculpture can be drawn on the fabric (Fig. 154), as repeats, in groups or in various compositions. The *textures* from sculptures can be sketched used in design. Instead of the outside form of the sculpture, perhaps the textures would form in your mind as a design.

Look to geographic works of art, such as African art, or Russian art, to find sculpture typical of the area. As well, books on the history of sculpture trace their various schools, many of which parallel the trends in painting, and well known artists. Henry Moore, Picasso, Brancusi, and Giacometti are some familiar modern sculptors.

It is also possible to make very small sculptures which can then be glued onto the fabric. For example, primitive figurines, abstract shapes from wood, clay, or acrylic modeling paste can be shaped and then glued with acrylic gel onto the fabric. It is important that these shapes are not a hindrance to the wearing of the garment. They should be placed where they will not be scratched, or broken.

One way of experiencing the sculptural effect with fabric painted clothing is to put the clothing on a dressmaker's bust, (first covering the bust with plastic so the paint will not damage it) and then paint the clothing. This will give the painter a different experience than when painting on a flat surface.

DESIGN IDEAS FROM PRINTMAKING

Printmaking is another category of the fine arts which should be considered for design ideas. Included in printmaking is woodblock printing, etching, engraving, intaglio, and drypoint. Books on printmaking yield interesting ideas which can be painted or drawn onto fabric. An especially diverse book is **101 Prints-the History and Techniques of Printmaking-**Norman R.E. Eppink.

DESIGN IDEAS FROM ARCHITECTURE

Architecture should also be considered as a source for design ideas for fabric painting. Buildings are beautiful in three dimensions with real stone or wood, but drawings, diagrams, and paintings of buildings are equally interesting, and especially if the drawing is on such a grand scale that it would rarely be seen in the real. Simple tents, yurts, barns, and huts (see **Shelter**-Shelter Publications, Random House) or grandiose palaces and churches are both equal as design material. (Fig. 155)

DESIGN IDEAS FROM PRINTED TEXTILES

Design ideas from printed textiles is the last category that should be looked to for design ideas simply because they are designed for clothing. General rules for design for clothing can be followed, but the limitations on design imposed by technology can be overlooked or gone beyond with fabric painting. In some cases, design created by complex technological processes **cannot** be simulated by fabric painting, and it is best to accept the limitations of fabric painting, as well. However, fabric painting can go beyond the repeat motif, scenes, stripes, and abstract textures of printed textiles to include all of those effects, if desired, in one length of fabric.

I find it helpful to analyze a piece of fabric by verbally describing its components. An overview of several printed textiles shows: delicate pink flowers with green leaves in small clusters; a black background with shapes in hot pink, turquoise, rose red, bright orange, and bright purple; grey, cream and lilac zigzags running parallel; and a geometric knit with blue, sienna, rust, and midnight blue. Each of these designs is repeated at some point in a printed textile. A painted textile can combine these designs.

The magazine, **"American Fabrics and Fashions"**(Doric Pub–lishing Co.) is an excellent source for modern designs used in textile printing today, as well as clothing designs using these materials. An advertisement for a **Color Source** book, listed in the above publication, shows the wide range of sources that modern technology uses in designs for printed textiles. The Color Source book lists the following as historic or modern color palettes: Persian miniatures, Egyptian colors, Ancient Peruvian textiles, Japanese woodcut, Illuminated manuscripts, African mask colors, Williamsburg, batik colors, Scottish tartans, Victorian colors, Greek pottery, Indian textiles, Persian carpets, Coptic textiles, Mozarabic colors, American Indian, Gobelin tapestry, Aubusson tapestry, Empire colors, Wedgwood colors, Giotto's palette, Titian's Venetian Palette, El Greco's palette, Ruben's Baroque palette, Velasquez Colors, Gauguin colors, Monet's palette, Vermeer's palette, Italian Mannerists, Turner's palette, Delacroix colors, Renoir and Impressionism,

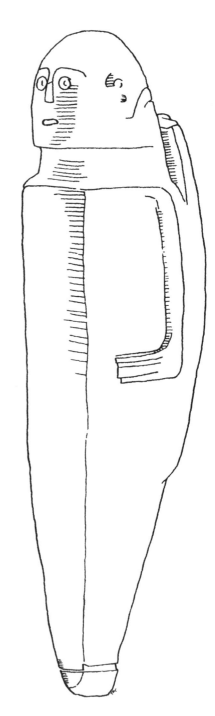

FIG. 154: DRAWING BY PHYLLIS THOMPSON AFTER RHODESIAN MALE FIGURE, ZIMBABWE IN **AFRICAN STONE SCULPTURE–**BY PHILIP ALISON.

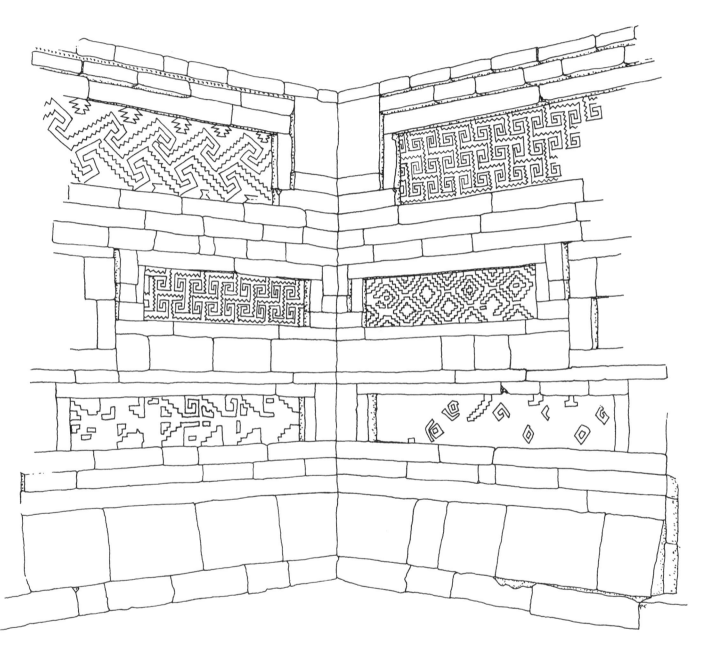

*FIG. 155: DRAWING BY PHYLLIS THOMPSON AFTER LATE ZAPOTEC WALLS, OAXACA, MEXICO, IN **MEXICAN ART**–BY JUSTINO FERNANDEZ*

Tiffany colors, Fauve colors, Kandinsky colors, Matisse colors, Art Deco colors, the Braque palette, Chagall's colors, Miro's colors, and Pop art colors. It can be seen from the above list that there is much to draw from for inspiration for fabric painting and textile design!

There are many other areas in which one could go to find design ideas for fabric painting. The list is almost overwhelming as it is. I feel it is important to present to the reader the idea of the possibilities of textile design beyond the flowers and nature designs with which we are all quite familiar. It is not to be assumed that every category mentioned in Chapter V will provide material for a successful design for fabric painted clothes. I feel it is better to widen the mind a little too much—rather than too little. Areas which I have not mentioned but which may provide interesting material are music history (actual written music, designs of instruments), psychology (mandalas, archetypal drawings,) and geography (maps, diagrams of land usage, etc.) Doubtless there are more.

6 *TECHNIQUES AND METHODS*

Over the centuries, the rules of painting have changed. Painting is not under the strict rules that it was in Leonard da Vinci's or Michaelangelo's time. Painting is no longer strictly defined. Although many painters do follow the old rules, using oils, doing under and overpainting, and doing many preliminary drawings, many more painters are breaking these rules and following their own. Some of these new found paths are becoming rules, and so there are more techniques from which to choose, more methods of expression. This development in painting goes along with the general increase in technical knowledge in scientific and humanistic fields. As we learn more about the outer world of space and the inner world of the mind, painting expands its boundaries to express in more abstract terms these events.

Techniques of painting which are very basic for beginning fabric painters are discussed in Chapter III. Techniques which are particular to a certain medium are described in Chapter IV. In Chapter VI, I will discuss a number of techniques which are used in fabric painting as well as a few other techniques used in surface design.

For our purposes, painting techniques can be divided into three categories: direct, indirect, and spontaneous. (I am indebted to Anthoney Toney for describing these categories in his book, *Creative Painting and Drawing*) **Direct painting** refers to traditional painting, where the paint is put onto the brush and then onto paper or fabric. Direct painting usually involves a general preplanned design, or at least, conscious action and direction. In fabric painting, direct painting occurs when the paint and cloth interact to form a design, usually with a direction and control through a tool, the brush. **Indirect painting** methods differ from direct painting in that there are stages of preparation needed before the paint contacts the fabric. Often there's a substance needed (besides the traditional brush) to apply paint to fabric. **Spontaneous painting** refers to painting which allows chance occurrences, often concerning nature, to effect the design.

Most of the techniques and methods which have not been described earlier are included in the category of indirect painting, and it is here that we shall begin. Indirect painting includes **monopainting, marbling, collographs, stamps and found objects, rubber stamps, airbrush painting, spray painting, stencils, resist processes including wax resist, cassava paste, flour and starch resist, clay resists, Japanese stencil dyeing with paste resist, and Japanese nori or rice paste resist, rubbings, fold–and–dye methods, bound resists (wrapping, tying, or clamping fabric before painting) and heat transfer painting.** As well, a preview to the use of photographic stencils and emulsions is included in indirect painting. Indirect painting is a way of using the advantages of fabric printing and surface design without straying from the idea and techniques of painting. In fabric printmaking, the design is formed on a material other than the finished product and then transferred. The design idea is *worked out* on other materials. In fabric painting, however, there is a direct relationship between paint, cloth, and brush; the design idea is worked out primarily as an idea, perhaps sketched first, but then put directly onto the fabric.

In the processes of **marbling** and **monopainting,** the painted design is formed by the influence of a liquid or a semi–liquid substance, something which forms and shapes the paint differently than would a brush. With **collographs, stamps, and found objects, rubber stamps, rubbings, and stencils,** something solid influences the paint and the design. In **spray painting and airbrush painting,** the gaseous substance, air, shapes and directs the pattern of paint. **Resist processes, and fold–and–dye methods** deal more directly with the action of the paint with the cloth. So it can be seen that there are many different "indirect" substances influencing the paint in indirect painting.

The historical sources of indirect painting are drawn from printmaking. Blake for example, in making a monoprint, would make several prints from one plate. Of course, each print was different, but each has a similar source. This irregular type of printmaking led to a recognition of what is now called indirect painting.

It is important to recognize and accept the differences and limitations in fabric painting when compared with printing methods for fabric. Painting is, in a sense, the primitive or root of printmaking. What ideas can you experiment with, evolve, and extend? Abstract and invent? What ideas are realistically limited to fabric printing as they cannot be repeated by painting without arduous effort?

There are a number of effects which indirect painting create more easily than either direct fabric painting or fabric printing. These advantages include working with intricate designs on certain materials, working with texture, and working with similar forms. Certain effects of texture cannot work on fabrics with a heavy nap (such as corduroy or terry cloth); neither will these fabrics allow for delicate lines with direct painting. By painting the impression or design on a surface *other* than the fabric, and then transferring it to this type fabric, certain delicate designs are possible on thicker fabric.

Textures are emphasized by many processes of indirect painting. Suppose you want a large painted textured background for a fabric design. Monopainting, marbling, spatter or airbrush painting could be very effective. Designs from monopainting and marbling often resemble oil on water, frosted windows, or the forms and colors of rocks and minerals embedded in canyon walls. Indirect painting methods differ from direct painting in that something is done to paint, brush, or cloth before the painting is done, in order for a measure of spontaneity or lack of control in the painting. Because of this spontaneity, the paint is more active in forming the design, and often the mark of the paint is texture.

Another advantage of indirect painting lies in using it for design ideas which are too tedious for direct painting. Suppose you want to use a large number of similar forms in a design. If they were the same shape, size, and color, a block print would work. If they were in a group with a rotation of shape, size, and color, a silk–screen would work. But suppose all you want is a simple repeat pattern of African motifs, say seven or eight, in three different colors. And you want sharp straight edges. And the material you plan on using is thin, with a tendency for capillary action. In this case, a stencil or paste resist would be a better choice of technique.

Stamps and found objects are another way of quickly creating a repeat shape. An allover print made with found objects could be an interesting design idea.

Indirect painting, then, can be seen to have many uses different from the painting techniques discussed in previous chapters. Let us now look more closely at the individual techniques, including new techniques and updated information on traditional techniques.

NEW TECHNIQUES AND PROCESSES

As I began to research new paint products to include in the revised edition of **THE COMPLETE BOOK OF FABRIC PAINT-ING,** I found that there were many new products and processes for me to learn about and test. Chapt. IV contains information on all the new **products** available; while Chapt. VI has information on new and updated **techniques** available. These include *new* techniques such as **needlepainting, texture painting, sweatshirt art, transfer processes, and foil art,** as well as the updated information on **silk painting, marbling, rubber stamping, and stenciling.** As there is more sophistication in fabric painting processes, there are many accessory items for these updated techniques and they are included as well.

MONOPAINTING

Monotype, monoprints, and monopainting are terms which all refer to a technique of printing one impression (as opposed to printing duplicate impressions). A discussion of the wide range of interpretations of monotype is found in the book, Printmaking with Monotype–Henry Rasmusen (Watson–Guptill). Monotype is a unique impression produced by painting a design on a surface and then transferring it to another surface. Monopainting was used more extensively than real-

ized throughout the history of art. Blake used the technique for some of his illustrations of "Songs of Innocence and Experience", as well as in other singular works of art. Gauguin was another artist who used monopainting.

When monopainting for fabric, paint your design on a flat sheet of glass, plastic, or metal. (Use the back of a flat cookie sheet, or the glass from a picture frame, for example). When the design is as you wish it, press the cloth onto the flat surface and pat evenly over the entire surface. Then lift up the fabric. Some paint may still remain on the glass or metal surface, and this serves as the origin for another monopainting. More paint can be added, or another piece of fabric can be pressed upon the remaining paint.

The size of your fabric will be determined by the size of the glass, metal, or plastic surface upon which you use to paint your design. It is possible to use a small surface and a larger piece of fabric, and this will create a type of repeat design. It is not necessary to limit the plain surface to a flat piece of metal, glass, or plastic. With imagination, monopainting with fabric can be extended to painting on large, curved, or cylindrical surfaces, and wrapping or pressing pliable fabric around these surfaces to create unusual designs.

There are other possibilities for monopainting. After mixing your paint material, swirl it on a piece of glass, then press the material into the design. Or put paint onto a piece of glass, then press this with another piece of glass and the paint inside. This will form a design. Also, take water or a paint thinner, put this first on the glass or metal surface. Then apply the paint onto the surface and press the cloth into it to obtain a delicate running together of color.

MARBLING

Another method of indirect painting is **marbling**. It is sometimes called waterpainting, as when the paint is dropped onto the surface of water rather than another type surface.

Marbling is the process of putting paint on a liquid or semiliquid surface and letting the surface tension affect the design of the paint. Water, buttermilk, starch paste, and carrogeen moss are four such substances used with marbling. The action of the water or semi–liquid base is similar to the action of wind and water in nature, and many times the designs created by marbling resemble the random patterns of oil on water, as well as the mottled variegated look of marble itself.

It's important to find an appropriate container when marbling. It should be large and flat, rather than deep, so that you do not need to use excessive amounts of starch paste, moss, or buttermilk. Since only the top layer is used, one or two inches is deep enough for the container. Lightweight aluminum baking tins are one good source, and are easily found. Ideally, the container for marbling should be wide enough and long enough to easily place the fabric flat onto the surface. It is possible to use a large table spread with plastic wrap for the container, using wooden supports at each edge. This method will only work with carrogeen moss or starch paste.

Once an appropriate container is found, the base mixture should be put into the container. Water and buttermilk prove no problem; starch paste can be made by boiling a few tablespoons of cornstarch with several cups of water, adding water if the mixture is thicker than whipped cream. Pour the mixture after it has boiled and thickened into the container. Carrogeen moss is also mixed with water and boiled until thick. Instructions come with the moss..

Paint is then poured onto the surface. Acrylic, oil, textile, ink, and dye paint materials have all been used with success. You can use nails, a comb, a stick, or other objects to cut across and break the tension on the surface, thus changing and influencing the design pattern. Also, different types of paints react differently. Oil on water is particularly interesting, with the beads of paint rapidly spreading across the surface of the water. When the pattern is as you desire, put the fabric upon the surface and gently press it onto the surface. Then carefully lift up the fabric, holding it by its edge. The pattern of the paint should have transferred itself onto the fabric. With a buttermilk surface sometimes a layer of buttermilk is also transferred, so not until you wash it off (after the fabric is entirely dry) will you see clearly the paint design. Let the fabric dry and then fix by pressing or steaming if the paint material used needs fixing. Be sure and also rinse off the base mixture for marbling after you've fixed the paint.

NEW MARBLING METHODS

There are two origins of marbling: marbling which is used on hard surfaces, and marbling which is originated with hand bookbinding and marbled papers for bookbinding. Fabric marbling is indeed patterned upon marbled papers made in the bookbinding process (See "Texture painting" for the other type of marbling).

Marbling on fabric has evolved into a very sophisticated technique. One reason is because there are better products for its use. It also used to be an inexact process with limited results. There are now a number of techniques that allow for controlled effects, rather than just getting spontaneous variations of design and color. Variables include: the kind and weight of paint used; the *order* in which the paint is placed on the size; atmospheric conditions; the age of the paint; the kind and age of the size, as well as the type pattern used.

Marbling is not something that most people learn overnight. It takes some time and testing, with trial runs, and records kept, to learn to control the many variables. Today the fiber artist has more control over these variables, due in part to powdered sizes and specific paints made for marbling. The main size used in the past was carrogeen moss (also called Irish moss). It was even more frustrating and difficult to work with than is today's carrogeen moss powder. Today's powdered sizes make it much easier to do marbling.

Marbling can be either two or three-dimensional. Two-dimensional marbling occurs where the fabric is laid on a flat surface of size. In three-dimensional marbling, the object is immersed into a bucket of size. Shoes and caps are commonly marbled this way.

Marbling on fabric is a process of spreading *paint* in a pattern over a *surface,* (called a size) such as water or other semiliquid or gelatinous substances. The pattern is produced by the *movement* of various objects (such as picks, combs, nails, needles) through the paint and its size.

There are three variables: the paint, the size, and the tools. With more materials at hand to use with which to control the process, marbling has become a more technical skill producing ever more varied results.

Within each of these categories, there are many variables. With the *paint:* one must consider the kind, its age, used in combination with what other kind. With the size: one considers what kind of substance it is made from, its age, its condition, and the temperature. With the *tools,* what type, what specific patterns are created with which specific tool? Additional variables include the *fabric:* what types, how the fabric interacts with the paint used. From all of this, one can see how marbling has *not* been an exact or simple technique.

Marbling originates from the Japanese, in a process called **suminagashi.** It was also done in China and Persia, mainly on paper. Europeans learned the craft, and used marbled paper as end–papers of books. In the 1960's and 1970's, there was a renewed interest in paper marbling, as craftspeople began to revive the art of bookbinding. By the late 1980's and early 1990's, marbled fabric, clothing, and accessories began showing up at craft fairs and in boutiques.

There are lots of things that one can marble. For two–dimensional projects, consider: T–shirts, socks, ties, silk scarves, throw pillows, quilt squares, fabric inserts for jackets, skirts, and shirts, yokes for skirts and shirts, pillowcases, leggings, a canvas book bag, and fabric yardage to be made into clothing. For three–dimensional projects, consider canvas shoes and tennis shoes, and caps and hats. Marbled cloth can be made into skirts, shirts, shorts, pants, kimono's, etc. Ready–made clothing can also be marbled, although this is a more challenging project.

MARBLING BASICS

Fabrics: Smooth weave fabrics give better results than textured weaves. Wash fabric to get rid of any sizing, or use ready–to–print "printables" without sizing. Fabrics such as woven cotton, muslin, China silk, cotton lawn, and rayon are good choices for beginning projects. Ready made items, such as socks, caps, and ties, should also be washed first.

Paints: Many types of paint and ink can be used in marbling. Printer's ink, oil base printing ink, oil colors, and acrylics can all be used in fabric marbling. Experiment with other paints and even dyes. Printer's ink, and block printing inks will give results of translucent veining. **Deka Print Silk–screening Ink, Sennelier Texticolor fabric paints, Createx marbling colors, and Liquitex acrylic paints** are some paint materials that have been used with success by various fiber artists. Try **Badger Air–Tex airbrush paint** (and other brands of airbrush textile paints) for marbling, as it is the right viscosity.

Paint Additives or Surfactants: Wetting agents which break down surface tension are also called **surfactants.** These substances can be added to the paint which will then make the paints float and spread better. They include: **Ox–gall** (used by watercolorists), **Photo–flo** (used by photographers), **Acrylic flow releaser or Acrylic water tension breaker, olive oil, and dish soap** (such as Dawn or Joy). These additives are added, one drop at a time, to the paint. They are recommended for acrylic paint, but can also be used with other paint materials.

Size: The solution that the paint is laid upon is called the "size". An older product which has to be mixed is carrogeen moss (or Irish moss). Today, this product can be found premixed in powdered form, and is much easier to use! Other sizes found in premixed form are Delta Marblethix and Deka Marbling Medium. Corn starch with water creates a thin size. It is a good place to start with experimentation. One method of marbling on paper is a technique called *starch papers.* This method can also be used on fabric.

Delta Marblethix: This is the easiest to mix up. Place 1 tsp. Marblethix into 1 quart of warm water. Let stand 6–12 hours. Then pour into a marbling pan. Marblethix tends to be a fairly liquid size, so some of the combing results are different from a thicker size. However, I find the results very pleasing. To get a thicker size, simply add a larger amount of the powder. Also, with Marblethix, you do not immediately rinse your fabric in water, as you do with the carrogeen size. Instead, pull out your fabric and place on a line or drying rack to dry.

Deka Marbling Medium (a methylcellulose sizing*)*: Take a gallon of distilled water. It's supposed to be hot, so if you are using distilled water put it in a canner on the stove and heat it up! Then agitate in 5 Tbsp or one small bottle of the marbling medium. I used a chopstick to agitate it in. It will get soapy. Then put in 2 teas. of ammonia. This can be bought from the grocery store. It is supposed to be clear or pure ammonia. When the solution cools down add some white vinegar and let set overnight. This is fairly easy to mix up, and is comparable in ease of use with Delta Marblethix.

Carrogeen (also spelled **caragheenan or caragheen**): Even the powdered carrogeen, a true improvement over the carrogeen moss, still has a strong fishy smell. Heat distilled water and add the moss powder (2 quarts water to 5 Tbsp. of carrogeen powder). Bring slowly to a boil. Stir for 5–10 minutes while mixture simmers. Add 2 quarts of cold water, stir, and allow to stand for 24 hours. Then add another 2 gallons of water. This mixture then needs to be strained through a nylon stocking. After straining, pour into marbling tray. Let sit for one hour. Skim off bubbles with a newsprint "skimmer". This is a rolled up newspaper which is used also to clean the size inbetween inkings.

Marbling Tools: Tools such as nails, needles, combs, etc are used to "distress" the paint over the surface. African picks, such as used for hair combs, regular combs, decorative combs used by women for their hair, and homemade marbling combs made with plastic hair rolling picks stapled or glued onto wood or cardboard are very useful to make the patterns. Various size nails are useful, as are other metal objects: pins, tacks, push-pins, and paper clips. What you want to look for is variance in size and width of these objects. A homemade pin comb can be made by cutting off a row of sewing pins from its paper. Secure it by glueing it onto a sturdier cardboard holder. You can vary the position by pulling out every other pin and leaving just the alternate ones in. This will provide different lines of color when it is pulled through the paint. A cardboard comb can be made by cutting out a comb–shape from heavy cardboard. Make sure the spatulates of the comb are wide enough to cause paint displacement. Actually, anything with ***prongs*** can be used. This includes objects such as forks.

Containers: A good sized marbling pan is very important. It can be plastic, wood or metal. The following are some ideas for marbling containers:

1) A cookie tray, (the kind with the 1" sides)
2) Any plastic container or pan such as a plastic dish pan, a plastic dish drainer, a new plastic cat box
3) A metal pan lined with plastic wrap
4) A wooden planting box
5) A cardboard box lined with plastic
6) Homemade wooden frames lined with plastic
7) Your bathtub (for large projects)
8) A child's outdoor plastic swimming pool (for large projects)

When you get into larger projects, more creativity is needed to find the right size boxes and containers. Sometimes a cardboard box lined with a heavy plastic will work. Remember that the box does not have to be very deep. The emphasis is more on length and width.

For very large projects, you can make your own marbling trays. Use 1" by 4" framing wood; join with glue or metal angles that are screwed in, and line with a 1 ml plastic (like a plastic drop cloth, found in the paint section of your home improvement store). Also, the bathtub can be used to marble fabric lengths.

I have found the easiest frame to use is a plastic open bottomed frame (4 wooden sides and open bottom) plus the plastic 1 ml liner. The plastic *easily* washes off, whereas with other metal or plastic pans, the colors from previous marbling ventures often remain, no matter how hard one scrubs! As well, the plastic is easily storable, is flexible, and comes in many sizes.

Other Needed Items: Squeeze bottles for acrylic paints (thinned with water in a 1/3 ratio); laminated cardboard forms (can be homemade) to put inside clothing, such as T–shirts and socks, so that the marbling pattern does not soak through.

MARBLING TECHNIQUES

First, soak your fabric in **alum.** Alum is a chemical which, when the fibers absorb it, allows the color to adhere to the fibers. Without alum, the color will not absorb. The general ratio is 8 Tbsp. per gallon of water. At first, use distilled water for more control of results. This solution of alum water will keep for several days, and will be enough for several yards of fabric yardage, many silk scarves, or several T–shirts.

There are several kinds of alum that can be used. One is **plain alum** (aluminum sulfate) found in art supply stores and distributors which stock marbling supplies. Two other kinds that can be used are **ammonium alum** (found in pharmacies) and **potassium alum** (also found in pharmacies). Alum, which is an astringent, is also a pickling agent and can be found along with canning supplies in grocery stores.

Soak the fabric, then hang up on a clothesline to dry, so that the piece will dry stiff. There should not be any spots on the fabric. If there are, it means that the alum did not "take" in that spot. Resoak the piece in the alum. After the fabric is dry and stiff, iron it on a low temperature. There should be no wrinkles in the fabric.

Starch Papers Method: This technique was originally created for paper, but can be adapted to fabric. Measure 2 Tbsp. cornstarch and 2 Tbsp cold water. Mix this together. Add 1 C of boiling water. Boil, then cool, then add batik or fiber–reactive dyes. Put several tablespoons of the cornstarch mixture into small dishes and create your colors by adding some dye to each mixture. Generally speaking, 1 teas of dye will be adequate. Brush this wet mixture on fabric. Then take a cardboard comb (see above) and press it across the thickened dye. This will displace the ink and cause veining to occur.

MARBLING PATTERNS

Marbled patterns are created by laying down the paint and then "distressing" the surface of the size. There are a number of specific patterns that create attractive designs. They are:

Peacock Feather Pattern (or Eye of the Feather): First, drop with an eye dropper or a small spoon the paint material in large dots 3 across and 3 down. Then take a nail and pull from left to right then looping down right to left and swirl again back left to right through the circles. This will create a feathered pattern of paint.

Arcs: Drop the circles of color exactly like you did in the peacock feather pattern. Then use a comb, or a pin comb, to vertically draw down through the color. This will produce attractive arcs of color.

Feather Pattern: In this feather pattern, use the same color pattern as previously described. Use a comb or a pin comb and, starting at the *front* of the sizing, move the comb away from you, up towards the top. This is the opposite motion that you used for the arc pattern.

Heart–Shaped Pattern: Drop the paint into circles as described above. Then, using a large nail, point at the center of the drop and make an s–shaped swirling motion (a loop) ending up *above* the circle. You can also do this by positioning the loop as a regular s–shape ending to the *left* of the circle.

After a print has been pulled, another piece of fabric can be laid down on the remaining impression. It will usually be lighter. This is called **shadow marbling.** You can also put a darker image *over* the pale one—ie after lifting a second image, reapply a darker paint and put another piece of fabric on the sizing. If desired, a nail can be drawn through the sizing for yet a different type of pattern. When marbling, you can *intentionally* produce irregularly shaped patterns. This is done by simply jarring or tipping the pan of sizing and paint. This usually produces an angularity to the initial pattern.

Further Techniques: Use a small stiff brush or bundle of straws tied together (such as from a broom). Dip in the paint material and then shake over the sizing. Droplets of color will fall in a random fashion. Shake the brush again, and smaller droplets of color will fall. You can then repeat the process with a second color.

BEGINNING PROJECTS

The easiest beginner's project is to marble small squares and lengths of fabric. These can be then made into throw pillows, small coin purses or sachets, or be kept for a quilt. They can also be used as inserts in clothing, whether ready–made or made from scratch. Square silk, rayon, or cotton scarves are another easy project; as are rectangular belts. (However, remember when you are marbling on a silk scarf, you have only one chance to make it come out beautiful!.) One thing that is popular now is marbled silk, using small strips of marbled fabrics in clothing inserts. That's a nice way to start out!

There's a big difference between marbling large pieces and marbling small pieces of fabric or clothing. You have a lot more control over a small piece of fabric than a large piece. With large pieces, often at least two people are needed to lift the fabric off and onto the size. And large projects require large amounts of size! Marbled clothing is more challenging anyway, and is best left until you have had some experience just marbling smaller things. (Professional craftspeople who do marbled clothing often build huge frames specifically for certain sizes of fabric)

INTERMEDIATE PROJECTS

In my opinion, marbling on T–shirts is an intermediate project. It is harder to handle the front and back sides of the shirt, plus getting the sleeves to print "cleanly". In one design, only a center circle of the T–shirt is marbled. This is done by using an embroidery hoop, and laying the stretched fabric onto the size. The rest of the shirt can be dyed or fabric painted, or left plain. Reverse marbling is done by blocking out the center with a design, such as a heart shaped template, and then marbling the rest of the shirt. Cut a design from contact paper and stick it to the shirt. This should suffice as a "resist".

To marble an entire T–shirt, take a shirt and put a laminated piece of cardboard the size and shape of the shirt inside, so that when you marble one side of the fabric, the paint will not soak through to the other side. You can buy forms like this in sewing and art supply stores, in the fabric painting section. Then lay one side of the shirt on the size. When the color shows through, lift it up. After adding more paints and preparing your design, lay the other side down onto the size. (When doing this process, I found it hard to tell when the size had permeated the shirt.)

Items such as socks, shorts, leggings, pillow–cases and other clothing items should follow the same procedure as described above. I think this is a fairly technically difficult process and you should expect to "lose" a few items of clothing while learning this process!

MARBLING FABRIC LENGTHS

It is easier to get a "clean" look with clothing by marbling fabric lengths or by marbling the already cut out pieces of unsewn clothing, and then sewing it together. I actually think marbling fabric lengths is easier, in that the fabric remains intact. If you cut your pattern pieces first, then it is important to pay attention to the grain and the direction of the marbled pattern, so that there is consistency in the finished piece. However, it is a challenge to be able to marble a *number* of fabric lengths with a similar pattern and color structure. This would occur when making a more complex item such as a kimono or a longsleeved shirt. In this case, it's best to cut the pattern pieces out and then marble them separately.

However, marbling fabric lengths is also a lot of fun, in that there are several ways to approach the concept of the design of the yardage. One idea is to be as consistent as possible and make all the yardage look alike. A second concept is to do shadow marbling, where the first imprints are then followed by other imprints that have second designs over them. Some consistency is retained, but with added design. A third concept calls for using a consistent color scheme and varying the patterns, such as using stone and combed, or wave and feather.

Use a bathtub to marble fabric for several items such as a pair of shorts and a cotton V–neck top. The fabric can be pulled from several prints, all of the same colors, but with some variations in pattern. Another design idea would be to marble several yards of cotton and then sew a loose African style top.

One of the specifications in doing marbling with fabric yardage is to have a garage or a basement, somewhere where you can really spread out. It's not possible to do it in a small space.

COMMON PROBLEMS/ SOME SOLUTIONS

When you are marbling, the colors you mix are the colors that are going to be on your garment. They are not going to blend after you lay them down on the size. It is real important that you have the colors that you want already mixed. I did a project using red and blue, thinking they would blend into reds, blues and purples. I didn't mix my colors before I dripped them on the size. After combing the pattern, I ended up with a red, white and blue scarf. No purple!

Some writers on marbling will say that you can't mix **brands** of colors or different **types** of dyes and paint materials, because the weight of the paint will vary. I've actually found that marbling is very temperamental and, within the same brand of paint, there are variations in terms of the weight of different colors. As a beginner, I would say it is really easier just to go ahead and merrily mix whatever paints you have.

As you marble, your size will get dirtier, depending on the weight of your paints. Sometimes it's harder to see what's actually on the top, so depending on what you are doing, you can experiment and find out or you can mix up another batch of size.

If you are doing a lot of marbling, it is always good to have an extra already–mixed–up–and–ready–to–go batch of size, so that you don't have to stop and wait overnight.

Marbling gets easier with practice. I would suggest to you to not give up on it if the first few times don't work. Also, the prep work with marbling is time consuming as well as extremely important. Prepare to learn marbling in several segments.

COLLOGRAPHS

Collographs are another form of indirect painting. Although it is by strict definition a form of printmaking, I include it in fabric painting because it is a unique form of printmaking. The word collograph explains its definition. "Collo" comes from "collier" (French, to glue or paste), and "graph" meaning to write (from the Greek, "graphein"). A collograph is a process of design where various materials are pasted together on a surface, and paint or pigment is spread over them, and then imprinted on paper or fabric. In many cases, a collograph is a collection of textures and so it is well suited for fabric painting. (Fig.156).

The collograph is fairly recent. Its roots grew from collage, as the idea of taking the textures created by collage and printing them onto another surface became apparent. The collograph allows for a wide range of expression as much of the design is defined by the objects used in the collograph. Since fabric painting can involve using large amounts of space, the collograph can expand and use this space easily. A collograph can be as large as the artist wishes. The main creative problem for the artist is the spacing and choosing of the objects for the collograph, and these can be laid out and seen before they come into contact with the fabric.

To make a collograph, assemble a number of objects, usually objects with texture and ones about the same weight, and paste or glue them onto a sturdy surface,(a piece of plywood, for example). When they are all assembled, brush the surface with an acrylic medium, such as acrylic gel. This will protect the surface of the materials without obscuring them. Then brush your paint materials over the collograph and either press the print onto the fabric, or press the fabric over the print. If your collograph is made with objects of different sizes, it might be easier to press the fabric over and into the shapes created by the various objects. Certain types of materials and objects which might be interesting to try are: crumpled paper, towels, leaves, string, grasses, metal objects with textures, fabric, and pins and nails. The collograph can be painted with one or more colors at the same time, and reprints can be made over the same area of fabric for a different effect.

There are certain other processes which I include in fabric

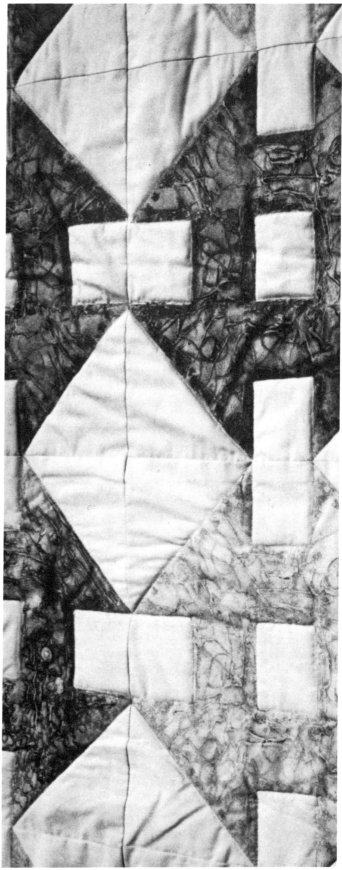

FIG. 156: "COLLOGRAPH QUILT"–BY JUDITH STEIN. DETAIL. OIL–BASE ETCHING INK ON MUSLIN.

painting which are between the printing/painting process. By using natural materials such as leaves and grasses as the brush, you can make interesting textures, and if used in a well–thought out way, they can be an interesting composition. For example, rather than having just a border of leaves, look at the many variations of patterns of leaves in a summer tree. Look at the way nature grows: a field of wheat, with dense textures, the foliage of shrubs, the differences of every tree in winter, a field of flowers with overlapping shapes and petals on many linear planes. Using these materials as brush–prints allows you to focus on the composition and let the brush become the drawing.

FOUND OBJECTS

Found objects become a brush–stamp or brush–print. They are the marks of our present civilization just as the American Indian art emphasizes wind and rain by symbols, showing their involvement with natural forces. Stamps found in the ancient pre–Columbian societies are believed to have been in the possession of the shamans or sorcerers, and these were used to appease the spirit world. Future generations of scholars may study the pop top bottle tops imbedded in the pavement with the same precision that archaeologists use in their diggings today. Although we look at the stamp designs of ancient cultures as something of interest, their perception of these marks may be as mundane as our perceptions of Coke bottle tops, due to the blindness that each generation has of its own time while still living in it. Future generations will notice the marks of these stamps and found objects as interesting, since they are an important, if not vital, part of our life today. Using found objects as art in the present day is a challenge and most people have found that by making the practical use of the object non–apparent, it becomes artistic. Automobile parts, machinery, kitchen utensils, and tools can be used as stamps without the marks made by them being identifiable.

STAMPS

Found objects and stamps are objects which can be used to imprint onto another surface a mark or design. By coating the surface of the object with paint, and then pressing it onto paper or cloth, a mark, or stamp, is made. There are many objects which can be "found" and used in fabric painting. For the fabric painter, the found object is a brush, a contact from paint to cloth. And the brush is squeezed, crumpled, broken, and made subservient to the processes and demands of good design.

In other countries, people have used mud to make stamps and stamp dies (molds) as well as using thick leather from certain animal hides for stamps. They then use dye–pastes made from natural materials for the colorant and stamp geometric patterns onto fabric. Stamps are commonly made from the calabash (a gourd from West Africa) and other hardskinned gourds.

One modern adaption of this in this country would be to carve primitive stamps from gourds, such as the rind of pumpkins and certain squashes. The inner meat is first scooped out, then using linoleum cutting tools the stamps are carved in geometric patterns. Use a dye paste such as Procion dye, for the colorant.

Potatoes, long used for simple stamps in children's art, are currently also being used by adults to make sophisticated patterned stamps.

Modeling clay or plasticine can also be used to make stamps. Plasticine can be rolled and then pressed onto a texture. Ink is then put onto it, and pressed as a stamp. This is an easy way to make some nice textile designs to augment fabric painting. I made one with plasticine where I pressed a small circle into the clay with a bottle cap. It made a very nice graphic design.

Foam also can be used as a stamp. It can be glued onto a wooden handle and used as a stamp. Clearsnap, Inc. has created a new product called **Pen Score Foam Stamp Set,** where you can create your own stamp set by engraving the design with a pen or pencil and then molding the design by holding it over a heat source (300 degrees heat). Felt can also be used in the making of stamps. It can simply be glued onto a wooden block, and then the design, cut out in felt, can be glued onto the base square of felt. Homemade rubber stamps can even be made from blocks of paraffin, which are generally known for candlemaking.

Glue itself can be used to make a stamp block. Trace a design in glue onto a wooden block. Use a casein–base white glue, such as Elmers, etc. Other homemade type stamps can be made successfully from our common friend, the potato. It is best to use basic shapes which can then be combined, such as a variety of geometric shapes. Much ethnic art patterns are derived from the successful combining of geometric shapes. Another "homemade stamp" idea is to use cardboard as a base, with shapes being cut out from heavy paper and glued to this base. Also glue fabric, leaves or grasses to the cardboard base in the same way. Stamps like these can be easily inked with an "ink pad" which is a cheesecloth filled with foam and tied at the top. Like a blotter, it can easily be dabbed lightly over these homemade stamps. These stamps can also be made more permanent by glueing them onto a wooden block, then varithaning lightly over the fabric or natural materials. They can then be reused.

RUBBER STAMP ART

Rubber stamp art has progressed from the mid 70's when there were books about how to make your own rubber stamps from gum erasers. In general, like with other processes of fabric painting and surface design, people have specialized to create products which the rest of us can use to make the design process more efficient and with higher quality. Stamp pads, including multicolor ones, embossing powders, rubber stamp fabric inks, and carving tools are available along with a myriad of manufactured rubber stamps. Therefore, there are many products for rubber stamping besides rubber stamps!

Rubber stamps can be used in conjunction with other fabric painting techniques, most commonly dimensional paints, sponging, and painting with dyes using foam brushes. Of course, there are many other mixed media techniques that can be used.

There is a very wide market interest with rubber stamps for kids. In this market are stamps of bugs, toys, Halloween and Christmas themes, and animals. For adults, stamps images can be used on pillows, clothing, for doll clothes, and other craft items. Rubber stamp artists go beyond the repeat motif and use their stamps in wild, wonderful ways. Carol Zastoupil makes postcard–shaped canvas pieces with rubber stamped images of travel scenes, while Sam Evans stamps her art on wearables. Cats, dinosaurs, scary faces, insects, fish, bunnies, stars, stamps and postage markings, hands, alphabets, musical instruments, and cameras are some of the many hundreds of images on manufactured stamps!

Rubber stamping, in the realm or category of fabric painting, is an **accessory,** in the way that scarves and jewelry are acce–ssories to the main focus of clothing. They **can** be used by themselves, for fabric lengths, or for making **printed** fabrics (such as stamping bears in a pattern all over a piece of fabric for a tablecloth or for a child's pajamas). However, the rubber stamps that can be bought along with the accompanying stamp pads, are, in themselves, too uniform to be seen as a central part of fabric painting. For painting is not uniform. The technique of rubber stamping is more closely allied to fabric **printing** than it is to painting, yet it is a surface design technique, and one that is very popular. Just be aware not to fall into the trap of consumerism and standardized (and uninspired) designs.

Therefore, when used within this framework, rubber stamping can be a welcome addition to other forms of fabric painting. Rubber stamps are, after all, images which are generally used repeatedly within the context of a larger design. I have seen some very nice T–shirts, using applique and rubber stamped images, or rubber stamped images augmented with handpainting, dimensional paints, glitters and rhinestones.

BASICS OF RUBBER STAMPING

Finding Rubber Stamps: There are essentially three ways to find stamps. The first saves time but not money. Simply buy the manufactured "art" stamps from catalogues and craft and fabric stores. These will run from $3.00–$7.00 each, and the bigger ones are even more! (In the trade, people who buy large numbers of stamps with a large outlay of money at one time are called "stamp junkies"!) Some of the companies which have catalogues include All Night Media, RubberStampMadness, and Bizarro Providence, RI). They also have pads and ink, so you can get to stamping in a hurry! (For a complete listing of stamp sources, see my companion volume **1001 Products and Resources for the Fabric Painter and Surface Designer)**

Stamp sizes vary include regular, mini, and jumbo. Jumbo stamps are sometimes as big as 14" by 11", and are often made of foam. Jumbo stamps are especially appropriate for use on fabric yardage. A unique stamp is **Rollagraph,** from Clear–snap, Inc. This is a roller stamp, so that rows of designs can be made.

The second way is less expensive with some expenditure in time. Scrounge around in dime stores and toy stores, and you will find some rubber stamp kits marketed for kids. Alphabet stamp kits are especially prevalent. If you are just curious about rubber stamping, this is an easy way to get started. Stationary stores, stores which carry old printing paraphernalia, school and office supply stores (especially those with close–out sales), garage sales, antique stores that sell old desks, and mail–order catalogues such as Lillian Vernon are good places to find second hand stamps. Also today you can buy uniquely shaped erasers which can be used, as is, for stamps.

The third, and most time intensive way, is to make your own stamps. Pencil erasers are a common material which can be carved into a wide variety of creative designs, as well as textures. (see section on "Making your Own Stamps")

Stamp Pads: There are two kinds of stamp pads: plain ones and multicolored ones. Since many stamp pads are marketed for stamping on paper, be sure that you are getting a pad with **permanent ink** for textiles. Some brand names to look for include All Night Media. Several companies, including Bizarro, Inkadinkado and Co–Motion provide a dry ink pad which can be inked with permanent textile ink. Another solution is to make your own stamp pads (see under "Making your Own Stamp Pads")

USING MULTICOLORED STAMPPADS

Some stamp pads, such as the Colorbox ones from Clearsnap, Inc. are multicolored, or "rainbow" colored. They will have at least two different colors, sometimes three, and sometimes a multitude of colors. Stamping with these pads presents particu-lar challenges. It is important to press the same way each time on the pad; otherwise the colors will muddy. (For example, if your pad has red, yellow, and blue, you might stamp first on the red and yellow sections, and later stamp yellow and blue.) It is also very important to clean the stamp between inkings by stamping it onto a wet paper towel. After usage, the stamp can be cleaned by rubbing it with a rag and denatured alcohol.

INKS FOR FABRICS

A variety of textile inks are now being marketed specifically for rubber stamping. These inks, which include **Co–Motion fabric inks, Stamp Dabber's Fabric Ink, and All Night Media's Stamp Dabbers,** are permanent upon stamping. Fabric paints, fabric dyes, silk paints and other textile inks are also permanent when following the specific instructions for each material. Metallic fabric paints make a good impression, but they can build up a residue on the stamp. Specific brands which have been used successfully include : Deka textile paints, Deka dyes, Createx pigments, Hot Air Textile pigments, and indelible, or laundry inks. Another unique product is an invisible ink, in which the stamp will be invisible until exposed with a black light. Use with an uninked felt pad.

Fabric markers are another important part of the rubber stamping process. Use the ones with the "feathery like" tip (such as Niji Markers); they make it easy to apply color. The color can be applied directly to the stamp to make a multicol-ored stamp. The design can also be colored in after stamping with black ink. This method works especially well with a complex stamp.

It has been predicted by craft stores and retailers that, in the future, more slow–drying inks will be developed specifically for rubber stamping. Inks and paint products for rubber stamping on fabric are still in the beginning stages.

CLEANING YOUR STAMPS

The care and maintenance of rubber stamps is very impor-tant. They can be cleaned with water and a mild soap (such as Ivory Liquid) if you are using a waterbase fabric or acrylic paint. Use window cleaner or denatured alcohol when using solvent based paints. Solvent based stamp cleaners, such as Rubber Stampede's Stamp Cleaner, are also available. Nail polish remover is another solvent, but be sure to keep the remover away from the other portions of the stamp, such as the glue, the felt, or the wood.

Clean the stamp by pressing it on a wet paper towel which has been soaked with solvent or water. If further cleaning is needed, use a toothbrush to scrub off the ink. The bristles can really get into the grooves of the stamp design !

All these procedures worked well on manufactured stamps. I had some trouble, however, cleaning the hard shaped erasers (hearts, words, animals, etc) which I had bought. With the hard rubber surface, I found that only a good scrubbing right away with soap and water kept the surface relatively clean of ink. It's a good idea to always keep a wet paper towel nearby when stamping, so one can clean off a stamp between inkings.

EMBOSSING POWDERS

Embossing powders are sold along with rubber stamps and ink. On paper they cause a raised image, on fabric, they fuse the ink to the fabric. They are primarily used to bond a slow–drying *waterbase* paint or ink, such as are sold with many rubber stamps, to the fabric in order to make it permanent. They are not needed with any textile inks, silk dye, thickened dye, or fabric paints. Nevertheless, this process is fragile, and is suggested more for items that will not be worn. As well, the process works best on smooth finished fabrics where the paint lays on the surface of the fabric rather than soaking into it. Satin, silk, acetates, and satin ribbon are examples of fabrics which work well. Embossing powders come in a variety of colors and types, such as clear, sparkles, silver, gold, sparking white, confetti opaque, pastel confetti, stardust, and pearlized. Use the clear powder if you wish to keep the colors of your design the same; use other powders to enhance or change the colors that you stamped.

To emboss a stamped design on fabric, simply stamp the image onto the fabric. Then sprinkle with embossing powder. Shake off the extra powder and save it for another application. Hold the fabric over a heat source, such as an iron set on the cotton setting, a hair dryer, or over an electric burner for 8–10 seconds. You can also put it on a piece of aluminum foil, lay it in an oven set at 300 degrees, and let it melt for 2 minutes. This works very nicely. However, do not iron over this image, and do not dry in a dryer. These items can only be handwashed.

MAKING YOUR OWN STAMP PADS

There are times when making your own stamp pad is more practical than buying a number of different colored ones. This is especially true when one is experimenting with rubber stamping. Uninked stamp pads can be made quickly from common items.

Felt Pads: Buy some felt squares from a fabric store. I would recommend white. Cut them into various square shapes, large enough for your stamps. Also make some squares large enough for multicolor stamps. Then stack several layers of the felt together, and place them onto waxed paper or plastic. If possible, place them in small plastic boxes (such as can be found at office supply stores), so they do not dry out. Another easy way to keep your felt pads moist is to cover them in plastic, such as wrapping them in a small ziplock plastic baggie. To ink the pads, simply immerse the pad with the textile ink, fabric paint, or fabric dye. I feel that textile inks and fabric paints are the best choices for stamp pads. And there you have your own stamp pads in various colors!

Foam Stamp Pads: Stamp pads can also be made from foam, such as is found in craft stores and that is also used in packing materials. Foam stamp pads are best used with stamps which are carved from erasers, because they need to *sink* into a surface for an even distribution of ink. Foam stamp pads do not work well with regular stamps, as it can be difficult to get an even distribution of ink on the surface of the stamp.

Sponge Stamp pads can be made from sponges.

Multicolor stamp pads: These are made from longer squares of felt or foam. Apply the colors from light to dark, and in general, from left to right, in stripes, or in other patterns. Multicolor stamp pads can be very inventive in how you apply your colors.

An easy way to make your own stamps is to use erasers.

MAKING YOUR OWN STAMPS

Types of erasers used are **artgum, vinyl, typewriter erasers,** and the **rubber erasers** on pencils. Brands include: Eberhard Faber (the green ones and the pink ones), Artgum, Niji soft plastic eraser, Staedtler Mars Grand, and RubKleen. The textures on these are especially suited to carving. Generally speaking, handmade stamps are created by carefully transferring a design onto the face of an eraser and then cutting out the design to produce an indentation on the surface. Use X–acto knives to cut your stamps, also use linoleum block cutting tools (sometimes called gouges). Gouges are especially helpful to cut curved lines and circular images. Gouges are also best to used when the material you are cutting is hard, (like a gourd). A sharp knife or scalpel will also work for many materials.

Pencil erasers are the best place to start, as they are easily carved and make nice small designs, like circles, half–circles, triangles, and triangles with notches. Begin with 10 new pencils, carve them into designs, and then add them to your brushes. They really are another brush that can be used in the fabric painting process. These can be worked closely together to make nice geometric patterns. The old–fashioned typewriter erasers are a little hard to find these days, but also make a good stamp.

Artgum erasers are soft and crumbly, so a knife really slices through them! You can carve a design on one or both sides, making geometric designs which then can be combined into nice fabric stamp art. A wonderful book full of techniques and ideas is *Stamp It!* and I recommend it to you for more details. Another good book is *Rubber Stamps and How to Make Them.*

Be patient when carving the design, and try to keep the surface edges flat. If nicks or bumps are encountered during the work, you can carefully sand the eraser down to smooth out its surface.

A design can be first traced onto paper. It may even come from a stamp catalogue. Trace it with a transfer ink pen and then place the design onto the rubber stamp. Using a brayer or a burnisher, press the design down and it will transfer onto the eraser. Then it will be much easier to carve. In general, the best designs to handcarve are ones that are fairly simple. Also try making stamps with textures on them. It is much easier to buy the complex designs, as they really cannot be approximated by hand. It's fun to make stamps, as well as to buy them. Stamps run around $4.00–$5.00 each these days, even the little ones, so it's not a bad idea to carve some of the simple designs on your own.

I've had some real good luck making rubber stamps from erasers. I used as a base some wooden handles (from a bag of wooden accessories used for toymakers and hobbyists). I cut out a piece of felt and glued it down onto the wooden handle. Then, I glued the eraser to the felt. Sometimes, more than one piece of felt needs to be used for thickness. If the design calls for the rubber eraser to be cut into several parts before glueing, use tweezers to place the parts onto the felt. Rubber stamps can also be made from cutting out shapes from an old bicycle inner tube.

STAMPING TECHNIQUES

Contrast stamping (light and dark). Stamp once, then several times without reinking. This will give a feeling of motion.

Overlap stamping: First stamp onto paper, then cut out the image. Continue stamping onto fabric in a straight row. Then, cover part of one of the stamped images with paper, and stamp over it (and behind) with a ***different*** stamp. The result will show an image behind the other row of images. This is a very useful technique, which, when mastered, can be used to create depth in stamped images.

Silhouette image: A silhouette image is made by using a fabric marker to fill in a silhouette of the stamp. Then use Pentech Erasables, a liquid eraser. The stamp image and color will disappear, leaving only a silhouette.

Painting and stamping: If you want to stamp images ***before*** or ***after*** having painted or dyed a garment, the underneath colors will show through. This can be especially effective when using black ink for the stamped image. However, if you want the color of the fabric to remain the same after stamping, (for example if you are stamping a black inked image on a white piece of fabric, and you want the whiteness to remain), and you are planning to paint more of the T–shirt, be sure and paint ***around*** the stamped images. Another way to keep the rubber stamped image "clear" is to paint with transparent fabric paints over black inked items.

BEGINNING PROJECTS

Buy several rubber stamps, several fabric ink stamp pads, and a length of fabric. Practice stamping the stamp onto the fabric, varying the colors. Practice with a one–color stamp pad and a multicolor one. Notice the difference in stamping techniques.

Using Fabric Markers: Use felt tip textile markers, such as Niji FabriColor Pens, to color the stamp ***before*** stamping. Lovely affects can also be achieved by coloring in a design with permanent fabric design markers. Make the design by stamping with indelible black ink onto cotton or linen. Then color the design with the fabric markers.

Decorating T–shirts With Rubber Stamp Art: To insure that you like your composition, first stamp your stamps onto paper, cut out the designs, and place them until they look the way you want them to look on the fabric. Then, stamp away! One idea would be to do a painting with a lot of wash and colors and abstract designs and then put in your stamps as little figures here and there in the landscape, then maybe adding some glitter.

Fabric Yardage: Using one or two stamps, make borders and allover fabric yardage, such as a spot technique, to make your own printed fabric. Add painted touches such as a watercolor wash or dimensional paint lines. When you feel comfortable with this, proceed to decorate a T–shirt or other piece of casual clothing.

Other design ideas: Stamps can be used for the background as well as the main image. Textured stamps, many of them easily homemade, are useful for this.

RUBBER STAMP DESIGN

Historically, rubber stamp art has had several styles. One is a political, curious, and even odd style using scrounged stamps in an avant–garde fashion, which was used on wall hangings, quilts, or small hangings. Calligraphy was popular, using alphabet stamps to write poetry or sayings. More recently in the late 1980's rubber stamp art has infiltrated the craft market, and the themes are more likely to be are flowers, bears, or hearts. Some companies are making stamps for transfer embroidery designs, and stamping them on fabric.

A SHORT HISTORY OF RUBBER STAMPS

Rubber was created by Charles Goodyear, when he mixed up a rubber and sulphur mixture that accidentally hit the stove by mistake, and "set". It was then called vulcanized rubber. In the 1800's rubber stamps were used in dentistry, and vulcanizers were created to make the stamps.

AIRBRUSH PAINTING

Airbrush painting is another form of indirect painting. Airbrush painting has been fairly popular on clothing since the late 1960's, when the counterculture began decorating their clothes and themselves with buttons, bells, and beads. It has also been used extensively by commercial illustrators for poster art, signs, touch–ups on photographs, as well as for photographic type illustrations for advertising of new products. It is also used for painting toys, ceramics, and automobiles and motorcycles. The airbrush is, indeed, a very versatile tool!

There are two types of airbrushes on the market today: the double action brush and the single action brush. The **double action** is used for finer work and thinner dyes, and both the flow of the air and the flow of color can be changed simultaneously by depressing two levers with ones' fingers. The **single action** brush is used with heavier paint materials and the amount of color cannot be adjusted while using the brush. A double–action brush is preferable for most airbrush painting on fabric.

The other important feature in airbrush work is the air supply. You can use a compressed carbonic (CO_2) airtank, an electronic air compressor, or an air compressor with a tank. The first is most common for regular use. A small air–compressed aerosol can is available, but it will not last very long for anything other than small amounts of work.

Although the airbrush is successful when used alone, it is common to use it in conjunction with a variety of masking devices. With these devices, specific effects unique to the airbrush can be produced. **Acetate** is used as a masking device and can be cut into various shapes for both **stencils** and **templates. Friskets** are made from thick paper covered with rubber cement (or can be store–bought) and are used to mask out areas while airbrushing ***within*** the masked area. Friskets block the overspray that would occur without them. In the following discussion on "Stencils", more ideas will be given for making stencils which can be applied towards air brushwork.

For fabric painting, it is imperative that you purchase an airbrush with color ***jars,*** rather than color ***cones.*** The jars screw onto the brush and will hold your paint material. To begin painting, attach the airbrush to the air supply hose. Pour your paint material into the jar, up to 2/3 full. (Thinned acrylic paint, airbrush textile colors, and fiber–reactive dyes have all been used successfully). Regulate your air pressure to 25–30 pounds. Holding the airbrush like a pen, keep it perpendicular to your work. Push down onto the lever to release the air, then pull back to release color. Practice will help you to control your "brush" strokes.

Be sure to clean your airbrush correctly after using it. Improper care with the airbrush is the most common reason for problems. (When you purchase a brush, the accompanying instructions should tell you how best to clean your specific model).

Special effects are possible with an airbrush. These include fine gradations of tone, color overlays (without disturbing the hand of the fabric), and subtle shadings using masking devices. You can draw fine lines, or thick lines, or dots! The following are techniques which are useful in airbrush painting: flat wash, graded wash, spotlighting, and softhandling and hardhandling of common shapes the cube, spheres, cone, and cylinder. To do a **flat wash,** go back and forth with the airbrush lightly, from top to bottom. A **graded wash** is created by working up from bottom to top, left to right, leveling out towards the top. Repeat from the bottom, leveling out sooner as the overspray will build up.For **spotlighting,** mask the area to be spotlighted and airbrush toward the corners with most of the paint landing on the mask. Start with lighter tones, then add the darker ones. **Softhandling** of various shapes involves drawing the shape, frisketing around various parts while airbrushing others. The tone gradation with this method is similar to achieving tonal areas portraying volume in oil painting. In **hardhandling,** each side of the shape has a more similar tonal value than in softhandling, thus having the object appear hard, or solid.

Fabric artists use the airbrush a number of ways. In the 1970's, airbrush painting on T–shirts using stencils of "cosmic" scenes, rainbows, and ecological themes were popular and seen at craft fairs and in boutiques. This has been expanded to using various stencil methods to create designs for clothing and art pieces. Frances Butler silkscreens yardage using the airbrush to create the silkscreen positive. (Figs.157 ,158 ,159) Cate Fitt handpaints and air brushes silk wearables using fiber reactive dyes. Melody Weiler makes intricate designs with the airbrush and up to 100 stencils on a shirt. She uses thinned acrylic paint and builds up her image with lighter values, then darker.

Other artists use the airbrush for surface design, wall hangings, or art pieces and show the surface treatment and color effects possible. (Fig.160)

SPRAY PAINTING

Fabric painters also use spray bottles for another form of airbrush painting. Any bottle with a spray attachment can be used. A Pre–Val spray unit, plant sprayers, and old Windex bottles are good for this type work.

Spray painting is very popular with fabric painters since it is quick and easy to use. Diluted acrylics, textile paints, and dyes work well with spray painting. Stencils and templates can be used just like with airbrush work. Sprayed backgrounds for wall hangings and spray–dyed garments are popular. (Fig.161)

TEXTURE PAINTING

Texture painting is developed from decorative painting techniques used in home decoration, such as painting on walls, floors, furniture, and other hard surfaces. Many of these techniques can also be adapted for use on fabric, canvas, and clothing. Decorative paint surfaces are a popular technique today and a number of books are now available on the topic. Many of the following ideas come from the book: *Recipes For Surfaces:Decorative Paint Finishes Made Simple*–Mindy Druc–ker and Pierre Finkelstein.

Texture painting includes: sponge painting (or sponging), cloth distressing (which includes ragging,rag rolling, and cheeseclothing), spatter painting, stippling, color washing, marbling (which includes tortoiseshell painting, vinegar painting, crackling, and wood graining), combing, and dragging.

In **sponging,** a sponge is pressed over the paint to create the design, leaving spongelike impressions. **Cloth distressing** is a

FIG. 157: *"JAPANESE ACROBATS"*– BY FRANCES BUTLER. AIRBRUSHED SILKSCREEN POSITIVE.

*FIG. 158: **"INSECTS DETAIL"**– BY FRANCES BUTLER. THE AIRBRUSH IS USED TO CREATE THE DESIGN ON THE SILK–SCREEN AS A POSITIVE. YARDAGE IS EASILY MADE THIS WAY.*

general term where rags are manipulated with paint, creating textures. **Ragging** is a process where a rag is rolled and either used to put the paint on or to take it off. **Rag rolling/on** is a process where you roll up a rag to make an oblong bundle, dip the rag roll in paint, and roll back and forth. This makes a shaded, impressionistic background. **Rag rolling/off** occurs when you first apply paint to the fabric, then take some off by rolling the rag roll back and forth. This also makes a subtle, textured pattern. **Colorwashing** is a process of applying thin glazes of

paint to fabric, using a brush or a sponge. **Marbling** is one pro–cess where a transparent color, a glaze, is applied to a surface and then, while still wet, the paint is moved or "distressed". The "distressing agents " include sponges, combs, and cloths or rags. In **combing,** after the paint is applied, a comb is run through the paint, creating a bold design of lines. **Dragging** is similar except a stiff brush is used, making finer, closer lines. **Spattering** occurs when the paint is brushed off from a stiff brush, such as a stencil brush, onto the surface. **Stippling** is a technique where first the paint is applied to the surface, then a stiff brush is bounced and struck on the surface. This produces a mottled effect. Stippling is a common technique used in canvas painting.

BASIC PROCEDURES

These techniques are being adapted from painting on hard surfaces, usually with latex paints. As such, different types of paints are used, and different surfaces. I have used these techniques successfully on a variety of fabrics, including heavy canvas, cotton duck, muslin and cotton sheeting. I have used some of the latex and enamel paints, and also acrylics, oils, fabric paints, silkscreen inks, and alkyd paints. All of these have worked well.

Be sure to use rubber gloves or latex medical gloves when applying these techniques, as most of them get fairly messy. Also use a drop cloth on the floor and some plastic underneath your canvas or fabric. It's important to have good ventilation, especially when working with the latex and oil paints. Also be sure and wear a protective apron to keep your clothes from getting spattered. (It's also a good idea to wear old clothes as well when working with these techniques).

Most all of the techniques can be adapted for fabric as is. One technique, however, needs some explanation. When

FIG.159: "BEACH ROCKS"–BY FRANCES BUTLER. RUNNING YARDAGE. AIRBRUSHED SILKSCREEN POSITIVE.

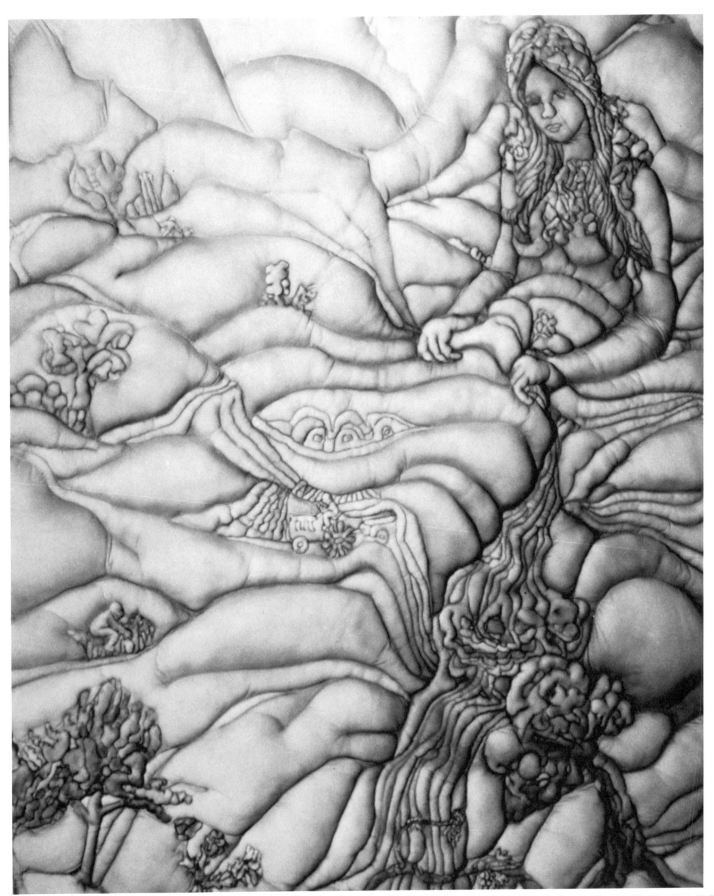

FIG. 160: **"PASTORAL BEDSCAPE"**–LINDA NELSON BRYAN. PAINTED AND STUFFED RELIEF (AIRBRUSH AND TRAPUNTO ON ANTRON NYLON BLEND MATERIAL WITH ACRYLIC PAINT.

using textured techniques on hard surfaces, a base coat of paint is often put down first. It is usually a glaze. How does this translate to fabric? There are two choices: consider the fabric to be the "base coat", and continue with the technique. The other method is to lay down a base coat of paint and then proceed with the technique. This second method will make for a more stiff fabric, so it is generally restricted to fabrics such as heavy canvas and duck. However, you can use thickened dye as the base coat and stiffening will not be a problem. Plus, there is a nice intermingling of the subsequent coats of paint with the base dye coat.

SPONGING

Sponging is relatively new in the field of fabric painting, yet it is a very simple concept. It is basically using a sponge to press paint onto fabric. The most important technical detail about sponging, however, is to dampen the sponge with water, and then *squeeze almost dry.* If you do not do this, your colors will run and you will lose the effect of the sponge's mottling. Another important technique is how you press the sponge onto the fabric. The sponge prints should not be able to be counted. They should overlap. It's important to let the background show through as well. Vary your hand slightly from side to side.

Use a regular painter's tray when sponging. This will give you enough room to load the sponge with paint. The sponge needs to be loaded with paint, but not so much that it is going to drip onto your work or leave a muddy imprint. Don't squeeze the sponge, but rather hold it lightly and bounce it on the fabric!

Sponges: There are three types of sponges available for use: one is already shaped, such as in the form of alphabets, hearts, stars, crescent moons, or toys. The second type are sea sponges.

A sea sponge has an irregular shape and its surface will help create a mottled texture as well as overall blending of colors.. Different *species* of the sea sponge are made into different *types* of sponges. They also have different sized holes, just like Swiss cheese! Regular household sponges, bath sponges, and sponges used with ceramics were originally sea sponges, and will leave diversely textured imprints.They are available in paint stores, cosmetic sections of drug stores, in health food stores, as well as in the ceramics/clay section of art supply stores. It's important to get at least one good natural sea sponge, as you will get a better effect with it. They are expensive but you can get a very small one for around $6.00. The larger ones run $15.00 and up. A third type of sponge is made from a die–pressed material (Miracle Sponge Co. is one source). This sponge can then be cut and shaped by the craftsperson. When dampened, it swells up to regular dimensions.

BEGINNING IDEAS

Sponging is really a lot of fun! Experiment with different types of sponges, on different types of fabric, and with a variety of paints. Use large pieces of fabric to record your results. Both paints and dyes, such as acrylics, fabric paints, drawing inks, and fiber reactive dyes can be used with sponging.

Also remember to use specifically shaped sponges with fabric paint. Press the lightly dampened sponge into a small amount of fabric paint. (The pearlescents, metallics, glitters, opalescents, and fluorescents make especially nice effects). Then press the sponge gently on the fabric. When successful, you should have a specific image with the mottled effect from the sponge.

FIG. 161: "SANCTUARY"– BY MICHAEL FORAN. SPRAY PAINTING, DIRECT APPLICATION. CANVAS WITH ACRYLICS, CUSHING DYE, BLEACH, TEXTILE PAINT. 19' X 9'.

SPONGING TECHNIQUES

Background color blending: a technique where a small sponge imprints colors onto fabric, leaving the mottled image of the sponge shape. Various paints and dyes can be used, however I find that acrylic paints and fiber–reactive dyes work well. Thin the acrylic paint to the consistency of thin cream. Dampen your sponge, then *squeeze it almost dry.* Press your sponge on the fabric in an allover fashion. More than one sponge can be used, or the same sponge can be used with different colors. (With fiber–reactive dyes, it is necessary to have a separate sponge for each color, since the dye will color the sponge).

Combination effects including two–tone sponging, then spattering in a third tone.

Sponging Off: Apply the paint almost like a runny glaze with a brush. Then criss–cross the paint and follow this with the sponge, sponging off by patting lightly with the sponge dampened in mineral spirits or turpentine. (Be *sure* to use a household sponge for this, rather than a natural one.)This works on canvas, floor cloths, and wall cloths. (This technique will also work using water rather than turpentine.)

Sponging off and on: In this case first use a thin glaze with a brush or roller. Sponge off with a damp sponge, then put on a thick glaze with another sponge. You will get multitone colors and an interesting textural difference.

Dark and Light: If you use dark fabric, use a contrasting color, for example black fabric and a purple paint (light over dark). Or start with a dark base coat such as a dark fabric or fabric dyed or painted with a dark color—then add oil color or latex in light shades.

Three–Color Sponging: Apply a vertical strip with the medium color, go back and sponge a horizontal strip with the darkest color and then apply another vertical strip with the lightest color.

Four–Color Sponging:
1) Use a medium color over the entire surface, occasionally dragging the sponge.
2) Put a dark color in in random patches.
3) put a light color and fill in areas but leave some untouched and cover over others,
4) put on another light color of a different hue to soften the finish. This can have an interesting painterly effect.

CLOTH DISTRESSING

Cloth distressing is an overall category of techniques in which rags are manipulated with paint to create subtle textured patterns. Some of the various techniques are: **cloth distressing (sometimes called ragging on), subtractive cloth distressing (sometimes called ragging off), cheeseclothing, rag rolling/on, rag rolling/off, and combinations of these. (two–tone cloth distressing, cloth distressing and cheeseclothing, subtractive cloth distressing and cheeseclothing in two colors, subtractive cloth distressing and cheeseclothing: light over dark).**

Cloth Choices: With all of these techniques, there is a wide variety in the type of fabric used for the rags. Try cotton and linen fabrics, such as old T–shirts and sheets. Cheesecloth can be bought in packages at hardware stores or home centers. Other textured materials which can be used for the same technique include: crumpled plastic wrap, paper, plastic netting (such as some vegetables come in), burlap (from burlap bags), and other textured items which can be crumpled in your hand, hold paint, and do not have loose ends which would cause the paint to "straggle". It is important to use good quality rather stiff fabrics, such as cotton, linen or burlap, so that the imprint of the fabric will not be lost in the heaviness of the paint.

Paint Choices: Oil paints, acrylics, alkyds, tempera, some fabric paints (the heavy bodied ones) and latex paint can all be used. Turpentine or mineral spirits, rather than water, is used as the liquid agent on the rag.

Ragging On: Take a rag and crumple it in your hand. Immerse it in paint, using a painter's tray or shallow plate to hold the paint. Press the rag lightly into the fabric, moving around to imprint various areas. Then recrumple the rag in order for the impression to vary. Repeat the imprints. "Twist your wrist" as you work, also, so the imprints will vary! Reapply paint when needed. This works very well on canvas and fabric, and is easy, besides! Use latex, acrylic, oil, alkyd, or textile paints as well as silkscreen inks.

Ragging On/Two Tone: After using the previous technique, repeat in a darker tone of the same color. This can be extended to three tones if desired, for three–tone ragging on. Be sure and let the first application dry before starting the second. In both cases, allow the surface color to show through, be it a dye, the original color of the fabric, or the first base coat. As well, the end result should be a random yet controlled or definite pattern, subtle, but asymmetrical. In other words, it is not a symmetrical design where each "rag print" can be defined.

Ragging Off: In this subtractive technique, apply paint with a brush or a roller. Break up the surface of the paint with short flicking motions of a smaller brush. Then apply the crumpled rag (which has been dipped in turpentine or mineral spirits) and press lightly to take off the color. Change hand positions often. When the rag is filled with paint, rinse it out with turpentine and continue. The finished product should resemble suede.

This technique provides very subtle effects on canvas. It is more challenging because the turpentine can drip and stain the cloth. It's best used on heavier fabrics such as canvas, duck, etc. rather than fine woven fabrics, but it can be used successfully on cotton or muslin when used with acrylic paints.

Cheeseclothing: In this subtractive technique, glaze is applied with a brush or roller. Then take a piece of cheesecloth, fold it in a square, and using it as a "stamp", apply paint liberally to it. The purpose of this is to keep the cheesecloth from absorbing too much paint. *Lightly* dab the cloth onto the surface of the canvas. This will remove paint and also leave an attractive netlike pattern.

Cheeseclothing can also be used as an additive technique. Ink your cheesecloth square in a contrasting color to the laid down color, and lightly press over the fabric, varying your wrist motions to allow for a fine textured surface. This technique looks very nice on fabric. I have tried it on both canvas and cotton muslin. It is very soft with lots of texture. It can also be used without a base coat.

Ragrolling/On: The additive technique of rag rolling is extremely attractive for fabric lengths. It is an easy technique as well. The shape of the rag provides the distinctive pattern, while the motion of rolling the rag provides a rhythmic linear pattern. Large areas of fabric can be covered in a short amount of time. Take a large, solid rag. Immerse it in paint, then squeeze it so it will not drip. Fold it in half, then roll it into a long, loose cylinder. Roll it over the fabric like a rolling pin, keeping a continuous motion. The final impression is controlled yet varied.

Ragrolling/Off: This subtractive technique is also subtle

when used on canvas. Again, apply glaze with a brush or roller. Dip your rag in turpentine or mineral spirits and squeeze until dry. Twist the rag and roll it into a cylinder. Then roll this rag over your painted canvas or fabric, allowing it to pick up paint and leave a "ragged" impression. Like ragging/off, this technique is best used on heavier fabrics due to the use of the turpentine.

As well as being applied individually, some of these techniques can be combined.

Ragging/Off & Cheeseclothing: Ragging/off can be combined with cheeseclothing for a soft textured effect. Paint on a glaze with a brush in a crisscross manner. Rag off vigorously using a dry rag, rather than a rag dipped in turpentine. Then lightly pat with a cheesecloth square. This will soften the textured effect.

Two–Color Ragging/Off; Cheeseclothing: Paint on two colors, one light and one dark, with random shapes using a medium size brush. Rag off, blending colors as you go. Then use the cheesecloth pad to soften the effect. Another variation on this is to have the dark color be the base, or the fabric color, and a lighter color of paint over it. In this case, paint a random array of strokes in a wavy pattern with the light glaze. Rag off. Finish with cheesecloth. More subtle effects are possible in this way.

COLOR WASHING

Similar to work done by the artist Helen Frankenthaler with her stained unprimed canvasses, color washing is done by applying thin glazes to canvas or fabric. Color washing can be done using sponges or brushes.

Sponge Washing: A watery glaze of acrylic paint is applied with a brush, in a crisscross fashion. The, using a sea sponge, sponge off the paint, changing the position of the sponge (by dabbing, rolling, and dragging it). It can be further smoothed out with a soft brush. There are many techniques that can be used with sponge washing. You can use a light color over a dark base coat or fabric color. Three, even four colors, can be used to have an interesting blended background.

Brush Washing (Two Tones): Use a large enough brush so you can splay out the bristles. Apply a light glaze, using an uneven number of brushstrokes but having them in a balanced pattern. Then, with a small brush, apply a darker glaze. Now, with a wide flat stiff brush, smooth and blend these two colors together. Continue blending with a stainer's brush. The end result is a soft cloudlike design.

Three–tone Brush Washing: Another technique with brush washing allows for a light tone to gradiate into a dark tone. Start with a light glaze and brush it across the top of your fabric. Then start a medium shade, working up towards the light but not quite touching. Do the same with the dark glaze. Now, using a dry brush, do a crosshatch or basketweave pattern, working down from light to dark. Don't work back up. This will create a nicely gradiated color band of blended colors. This technique works well with latex, alkyd, oil, or fabric paints.

MARBLING AS TEXTURE PAINTING

We usually think of the word marbling in conjunction with the popular fabric decorating technique. Marbling as texture painting means *painting* on fabric or canvas to approximate the look of marble. While both techniques are meant to replicate the look of marbled stone, learning to paint a marbled look requires certain techniques. Some of these are: broken color techniques, veining, cissing, and softening and blending. Marbling can be done using either water or oil–based paints.

Historically, marbling has been used as a painted finish. Some early examples are on plastered Roman temple columns, Mycenean pottery, French Renaissance ceilings, doors and walls. It was used to decorate all types of woodwork.

Marbling on surfaces is a process of adding more and more shapes and veining in many subtly mixed tones of colors, in order to approximate the look of marble. Keep tones of similar value, hue, or intensity. Using a sketch or photograph of marble as a guide, one can paint white, red, green, or black marble. This is the technique for white marble: 1) using a sea sponge, first apply a neutral hue, then add small dabs of other colors (black, ochre). 2) Use a small brush and blend in a light pattern of these darker colors. 3) With a small brush and the chamois cloth, blend the pattern more. 4) Paint in veining by using a very small brush and painting "veins" (fine cracks which squiggle slightly). Pick up different colors for variation, such as black, raw umber, dark blue. Don't outline the shapes exactly; rather, have some veins cross over. 5) Create depth by using a well–worn sponge, and sponge with a white acrylic glaze over the entire piece.

For other colors, see the text *Recipes For Surfaces,* from which this was also adapted.

Wood Graining: One can, with practice, approximate the textures of wood with a paint brush. Although this is used more commonly in canvas painting or painting on walls, there may be a use for this technique as well for painting on fabrics. One use that comes to mind is in the theatre, such as clothing for elves or munchkins in dramatic pieces!

Here is the technique for painting a "pine–looking" texture.

1) With a small brush, copy the grain of wood, using a drawing or photograph, onto the fabric.

2) Using a toothed spalter brush, paint some straight grain lines

3) Add knots.

4) Shade, using a regular spalter brush.

5) Shade more, using a cotton cloth to soften glaze.

6) Begin with a latex paint, then use acrylic for the detail work, and an oil glaze at the end.

For an "oak" texture: Follow as above in #1 and 6, except use metal combs in #2) to pull down straight through the glaze. Soften with a cloth.

DRAGGING

Dragging is a technique where a tool is dragged through the glaze, creating a pattern. Tools which are used include: steel wool pads, or a hard bristle brush or wire brush. Latex house paint, alkyd, oil, and silkscreen inks work well for this technique, because they are viscous. First, apply a base paint to the fabric. Then put down a glaze in a contrasting color. Immediately after painting, pull a steel wool pad or a brush through the paint. The steel wool will create a grain effect; while the brush will cause contrasting lines to form.

COMBING

Combing is similar to dragging. With combing, a comb is used to pattern the surface. Many different types of combs can be used: plastic, cardboard, or metal. They can be homemade. Plastic hair combs can be used. If making one from cardboard, make the teeth of different widths, and with angled and squared edges.

First, apply a base coat to the canvas or fabric. Then apply a glaze. Stipple the surface. Begin combing through the paint. You can do various patterns, such as crisscross, crosshatching, basketweave, moire (wavy lines) and a folk technique called colonial graining, by using a cardboard strip and weaving it through the paint.

SPATTER PAINTING

Spatter painting looks easy to do, but predictable results takes practice. Though it is technically easy, it is hard to control the results. Spatter painting requires using a brush and hitting the paint off the brush into "spatters" which land onto the fabric in a random fashion. You can hit the loaded paintbrush with the handle of another brush, or a thick wood stick. This will produce random spatters. Another method is to use a regular butter knife and run it across the bristles of the brush. More control is possible this way. A very find dot pattern is possible by running a toothbrush loaded with paint over a metal screen.

There are several rules in spatter painting. The closer you are to your surface, the more control you will have and the finer the spattering will be. Conversely, the father away you are from the surface, the less control you will have and there will be bigger blobs of paint along with the finer ones. It is also important that your paint medium be a certain consistency. If it is too thin, it will drip and run. If it is too thick, it will be difficult to spatter it onto the fabric.

Spattering off is a technique where, over a basecoat of oil, latex, or Japan paint, one spatters turpentine or mineral spirits. This is best done in a shop or basement. Be sure to wear goggles.

Spattering/Sponging: Spatter painting combines well with sponging, making a nicely textured surface. First, sponge in the background. Then spatter with a small brush. When used with complementary colors, a speckled stone–like surface is produced. Up to 4 or 5 colors can be spattered successfully.

All these techniques are similar to the effects produced with an airbrush. Another tool which can be used in large work is an airgun which is used for painting cars. These can be rented through auto body shops.

STIPPLING

Stippling is commonly used in regular painting. Stippling creates lots of tiny dots in a blended pattern. A regular stippling brush can be used, as can a clothes brush, a shoe brush, a scrub brush, a vegetable brush, or a stainer's paint brush.

Apply a base coat with latex, alkyd, acrylics, oil paint, or keep the fabric unpainted. Then, dip your brush into paint and gently bounce the brush down onto the fabric. You can do this pretty hard. The paint will be displaced into many tiny dots onto the fabric. This technique can make an even pattern of dots across the fabric. If you do apply a base coat, it can also be stippled. This will make the color of the glaze even richer. Stippling is another technique which is easy to do and very attractive on fabric.

ROLLER TEXTURE PAINTING

This technique is simply using a paint roller (a narrow one or one of regular width) across fabric. It's good when you have a lot of surface to cover, such as for fabric lengths. You can mix your colors and in the case of latex paints, marble them on the surface. I tested a latex enamel white base coat with other enamel paints and the result showed a variegated yet regular pattern as the roller made the same marbled imprint every few inches. Many other techniques can be developed from roller painting.

IDEAS FOR FABRIC YARDAGE

Texture painting is idea for making fabric yardage, as ideas can be implemented quickly and easily. One idea I had for fabric yardage is to take some brown cotton fabric with the following paints: white latex, white oil paint, white acrylic, cream colored acrylic, and a dark brown acrylic. Apply various texture painting techniques while shading the fabric from light to dark. Then make into a pair of casual cotton pants and a casual slip–over top. Another idea is to use sponging and rag rolling with acrylics, oils, latex, and some fabric paints. Stippling fabric lengths is another quick project where the finished product is unique and interesting. By using various colors over other colors, many variations are possible.

WALLCLOTHS

Wallcloths are similar to floorcloths (see after "Stenciling" section) in that one paints a piece of canvas or other heavy thickly woven fabric, but instead of putting it on the floor, it is tacked onto a wall. This can be used in a situation where a wall is plain and you wish to use decorative techniques, but you do not desire to paint the wall directly. This technique allows for flexibility, as these wallcloths can be moved and changed depending upon the decor of the room, or one's mood.

These cloths, being cut first, can fit into crevices and oddly shaped areas of an apartment or house, such as the foyer or stairwell. They are similar to paintings *on* a wall, but since their main purpose is a decorative one *of* the wall, they serve the same function as when stenciling or using other painted surface techniques (sponging, rag rolling, marbling, etc.)

Many techniques can be used with wall cloths. One idea is to use latex and tempera paint with sponging techniques. It is fun to use lacquer paints and lay the paint on quite thickly! Latex paints, alkyd, acrylics, oils and lacquers can all be used in texture painting for wallcloths. Wallcloths can also be stenciled with stencil paints.

STENCILING

Stencils are a very old and common way of creating a design, both on fabric and on paper. A stencil is a stiff piece of paper or cardboard, or it could be a thin sheet of metal, acetate, or plastic upon which a design is drawn and then cut out. (Mylar plastic in 3 mils is a good thickness for beginners). Then the stencil is placed upon the material upon which you wish a design, and paint is brushed in the open spaces, and around the edges of the stencil. Stenciling produces a clear, sharp, design.

Because stenciling is such a common way of creating a design, it is easy to overlook the creative use of stencils. But there are many sources of inspiration for creative stencil art. Dover publishers carries a nice selection of stencil designs, including designs from ancient Egypt, Japan, China, Art Deco, Early American, Pennsylvania Dutch, and Victorian. As well, folk art designs such as Scandinavian rosemaling, Islamic designs, African, and Native American are well–suited for stencil work. The design ideas of stenciled folk art symbols which were so popularly used in houses, on doors and doorways, on wooden objects, and on tinware can easily be transferred for use on fabric and clothing.

An easy way to make a stencil is by using lightweight paper, which is then folded several times and cut similar to when one makes paper snowflakes. Scissors can be used when making this "practice stencil". If you use waxed paper, you won't have to worry about the edges of your stencil getting fuzzy, as they may with regular paper. Once you have made a practice stencil, it's time to make one out of stencil paper. You can find the materials you need at an art store: waxed stencil paper, stencil board, a stencil knife or an X–acto knife (#11 or #16 blades for the X–acto knife are recommended).

You can use the designs you made with the folded–paper stencil and simply transfer them onto your stencil paper. Just trace the cutout parts with a pencil onto your stencil and then cut them out with a knife. A regular design on tracing paper can be transferred with carbon paper.

You can use more than one color in an individual stencil if the shapes are far enough apart. When working with a design where the colors lay side by side, or are superimposed on each other you'll need to cut more than one stencil. Cut out the center part of your design, and then lay the cut–out stencil over another piece of stencil paper. Trace this center shape onto the paper along with the other parts of the design, so that they can "line up" with each other correctly. Then cut out the remaining parts of the design.

Megan Parry, in her book, *Stenciling,* has explained these methods and more, in great detail. As well, she has expanded the concept of stenciling to an exciting art form. Hers is an inspiring source for designs and projects!

Acrylics, textile paint, blockprint inks, oil paint with turpentine and thickened dyes have all been used successfully with stencils. When painting a stencil, be sure to move your brush **from** the stencil down into the empty area rather than the opposite way. If you work from the center outwards, the edges of your design will not be sharp and crisp, and paint may seep beyond the area delineated for the design.

Stencils can be used for many types of designs. Many stencils are quite small, from two to four inches. The imposed design is then repeated over and over on fabric or paper. Remember, however, that it is possible to make a very large design, twelve inches square, twenty–four inches, etc. Border repeats with folk art motifs can fit in very nicely on the hems of clothing; they could either be petite and delicate or very wide designs.

Another type of stencil device is masking tape. It can be used where a long straight line is needed. Tape can be used as a design tool by simply putting tape wherever you do not wish paint. Another popular masking device is **contact paper.** It can also be cut into shapes and used like a stencil. Both of these materials block out areas, just as stencils do.

NEW IDEAS IN STENCILING

Stenciling, a traditional craft with a long history, has been made immeasurably easier with the manufacture of a number of new products. These include stencil–plates, brushes specifically designed for stenciling, and fast–drying paints manufactured for the stenciling process.

Stenciling was originally used to decorate wallpaper and rugs since these items were mostly unaffordable to our rural ancestors. At first, freehand painting was used, but people found that by using a stencil, a more even design could be made. The early stencils were made of whatever was handy,

including paper. Their design ideas came from their rural lifestyle: shapes of farm animals, trees, flowers, fruits and vegetables from the garden.

Today, as more rural acreage is eaten up by development, interest in the "country" look grows. Stenciling has reemerged as a popular craft, and country themes are popular. Thus, craftspeople look to the past, to traditional themes in stenciling. With the wealth of materials available today, stencilers can duplicate the old–fashioned, rustic hand–wrought look of the rural stenciler's efforts, or, on the other hand, create a pristine, perfectly neatly painted modern design. One can replicate the rustic look of old–fashioned stencil work, or create a modern design. With today's pre–cut stencils, either look can be easily achieved.

Old–fashioned motifs and modern designs work equally well with stencilling. Old applique and Amish quilt patterns provide excellent designs for stenciling. Like Amish quilts, stenciled images are simple, even quaint. Appliqued designs are so similar to stenciled images that they are can be the same design rendered in a different technique. You can stencil fabric yardage, and make sheets, tablecloths, and scarves. Stenciled bedcoverings were a popular folk art in America in the 1820's, as they replicated the costly embroidered bedcoverings of the period. For stenciled sheets, I would recommend bright colors, since they will undergo frequent laundering. Wash them in a coldwater wash, so they will not fade. You could pick up a design from a quilt and having a matching bedroom set, with a quilt, and then a border design stencilled on your sheets and pillowcases! Other coordinated projects similar to this could be matching colors and designs in your kitchen, such as dishtowels, pot holders, placemats, and stenciled wall designs.

In the past, even as recent as 10 years ago, stenciling required a long involved amount of prep work. First, you would trace or photocopy a suitable design, transfer the design to the stencil material (plastic such as Mylar, waxed stencil paper, vellum, or heavy cardboard), and cut out the design using a stencil knife. If the design had small intricate parts or curved lines, it was hard to cut it neatly with this knife. As well, making your own stencil required understanding the concept of "the bridge"—that part of the design which had to remain intact in order for the stencil to also remain intact after cutting! Learning how to put bridges in a designs is very challenging, so it was easier to use a design from a stenciling book which had already figured out this technical problem. Only after all this work was done could the stenciling begin.

Today we are lucky to have the best of the designs of this traditional craft without having to master the more difficult aspects of it. Today, much of the tedious work of designing and making stencils has been eliminated. This is due to the creation of pre–cut stencils. As well, specifically designed stencil brushes along with premixed acrylic paints with the correct consistency for stenciling make it possible for the craftsperson to start in on the *art* work, rather than having to take a lot of time doing the *prep* work!

BASICS OF STENCILING

Pre–cut stencils, also called stencil plates, are commercially produced plastic stencils. There are two types: one–part stencils and multi–part stencils. With **one–part stencils** the entire design is on one sheet. The **multi–part stencils** are made on several sheets, and you place each sheet subsequently over the ensuing design. Each sheet is numbered so that the design can be correctly aligned. The stencils also have "register marks" or dashes which show exactly where one plate lines up with another.

There are several types of stencil designs that are manufactured into pre–cut stencils. One is called a **spot stencil.** The spot stencil is usually one subject, such as a flower design or a motif and is usually used alone, often in a center of a space. They can also be used in sequence, such as a splay of flowers placed around the hem of a dress. They are usually shaped within the parameters of a square, and tend to be large. By contrast, the **border stencil** is shaped within a long and narrow rectangle. The design is used continuously or repeatedly along vertical and horizontal edges. Borders tend to be a series of geometric shapes, or flower tendrils. You can use these two types of stencils interchangeably, however. Stencils **can** be put wherever you want them!

Today's stencil paints are fast drying, with pre–mixed colors.They can be either a fabric paint or an acrylic paint. The acrylic paints are often called water–soluble textile paint, but they are not a true fabric paint. Rather they are an acrylic paint which is used on fabrics. Products labeled as "craft paint" also can be used for stenciling. What distinguished stencil paint from other fabric paints is that it needs to be of a thick consistency. (See Chapter IV under "Stencil Paints and Accessories" for a discussion of specific brands of stencil paint and how they work.)

Another type of stencil paint used particularly for walls, floors, and floorcloths is Japan paint. Japan paint is an oil–based paint with a hard, glossy surface. It must be thinned with turpentine. It is good for intricate designs as it is easy to achieve a sharp outline. It is best used for floorcloths, painted folding curtains, painted tents or tipis, and other projects where you would use a heavy canvas fabric. Whereas textile paint produces a "thin" stencil through which the underneath surface shows, Japan paint produces a thick, shiny surface that is not translucent.

Another kind of paint which can be used is a spray paint, such as an enamel or acrylic spray paint. Simply spray through the stencil. Though similar to airbrush painting, this is easier and does not require the set–up or equipment of airbrush painting.

Brushes for stenciling are specifically made for this technique. They tend to be rather stiff and squat, so that you can "bounce" them gently onto the fabric. They come in various sizes. I find the smaller stencil brushes easier to handle. Sometimes the fabric creates friction with the brush, so the closer the brush is to the fabric, the more I can control the brush.There is also something called a **stencil shield,** which is a piece of plastic with a straight edge and a curved edge. It is used in shading techniques.

The best type of fabrics to use for stenciling are smooth, flat–weave natural fibers and blends. Don't stencil on wool or other "nubby" fabrics. Knitted fabrics will not work well alone, although if you put a piece of sandpaper underneath a knit to "grip" it and keep it from stretching, you can stencil T–shirts and other knits. Silk can be stencilled. Be sure and wash out any sizing before stenciling.

STENCILING TECHNIQUES

Brush Techniques: I have found it best to hold the brush straight up and down. It is a good idea to practice on paper first. Tip the brush into paint, then wipe it off on a paper towel as if you were trying to wipe it **all** off. Try this for the translucent look.

After you feel comfortable stenciling on some paper, switch to muslin and continue with practice strips. It is important to keep the edges neat and clean, and this requires a good brush technique. The key is to have just the right amount of paint on the brush. With too much paint, your paint will smoosh underneath the stencil and ruin your design. So, it's always better to have too little paint on the brush, and keep adding!

Flat and Shading Painting Techniques: There are two possible "looks" in stenciling. With one, you use a small amount of paint on the stencil brush, and, painting towards the center of the design, fill up the space until the finished design has a flat, even tone. The end result is a **printed** look, with clear, crisp edges and an even color throughout. Pre–mixed paints make this easy, since you will produce the same tone and shading over and over again. A more traditional look is possible by using almost no paint on the brush. Take the brush, put a very small amount of paint on it, and then roll it into some paper towel. Beginning from the outside work in towards the center of the stencil and delicately "shade" the paint into the design. The finished design will be shaded, delicate, and **painterly.**

Shading is what gives stenciling its old–fashioned or traditional look. The key to shading is to use the appropriate amount of paint on your brush, which is almost none. By doing this the shading can occur naturally. As you bring the brush towards the center of the design, the heaviest reside of paint will lodge against the edge of the stencil, while, as you bring your brush towards the center, it will have very little paint on it. The results of this are that the edge of the stencil will be a crisp, clear image, while the middle will be more lightly shaded, producing an image of three dimensions.

With either of these techniques, it is best to lightly bounce the brush onto the fabric. Hold the brush in an upright position. To make a darker color, simply keep bouncing with some paint on your brush. With either technique, it is very important to barely touch the brush to the paint. Paints marketed specifically for stenciling work best for shading, as the paint is the appropriate consistency for stenciling and the jars are wide enough to just lightly "dip" your brush. Be gentle.

IDEAS FOR STENCILING

There are many many things you can do with stenciling. With a little bottle of stencil paint and that stubby brush, plus lots of patience, much can be made more beautiful. All fabric items can be stenciling: from outdoor furniture down to socks. Outdoor furniture and coverings made of heavy canvas, such as deck chairs, cushions, canvas hammocks have added interest when stenciled. Plus, your lawn furniture can be unique and coordinated! Moving inside the house, one can stencil the entire array of bedroom fabrics, from bed linens (sheets, pillowcases, quilts, comforters, pillows) to the curtains and rugs. All types of clothing and accessories can be stenciled, from coats down to stenciled socks. Other items to be stenciled include small accessory household items such as pincushions, handkerchief's, doll cloths, and hair ribbons.

Predyeing fabric: You can dye your fabric a background color before stenciling and this can make up into a nice garment, for example a T–shirt or other casual knit dyed a purple or deep blue and then stenciled with a flower design. Do remember that the textile stencil paints will interact with the dye on the background, however.

MAKING YOUR OWN STENCILS

If you desire to make you own stencils, here is some helpful information about the process. This information is also helpful for *designing* with stencils.

Repetition and Movement: One important principle deals with how to avoid static repetition in stenciling. Stenciling can appear static looking since it entails the repetitive application of an outline or pattern. In order to avoid this, it's important to introduce movement (as opposed to statis) so that the eye is led in a variety of directions. There are two possibilities you can consider: symmetrical and asymmetrical. With symmetrical design, there is uniform space and the design is self–contained. With asymmetrical design, the space extends outward in a variety of directions. Usually, in a stencil design, you will want to have both of these elements. By mixing them, they can balance each other and they establish a pace. The symmetrical element is the "object" and the asymmetrical elements are the path or "movement". Working together, these can produce very pleasing stencil designs.

Layout: One of the advantages in terms of designing stencils is that you can learn how a pattern fits together by taking a simple combination of shapes and playing with them in different ways. For example, take a simple flower motif. Make a number of prints on plain white paper. Flop it over. Make more prints. Add a few other motifs (leaves and a stem). Cut these out and begin to arrange them on a grid layout. (3" squares, for example). Use these same elements for a border layout. Next, try a "staggered" layout. Still using a symmetrical motif, place the motifs in alternate squares of space with squares of the motif. And, lastly, find a fabric that you like a lot and try to "copy" it using a stencil and noticing especially the layout of the motifs on the fabric.

Bridges: The next important principle to note about stenciling is how to form "bridges". A successful stencil design drawn from a *line* drawing is dependent upon connecting strips which are called "bridges" or "ties". These bridges keep the middle of the stencil connected to the outside, so your design doesn't fall out completely when you cut it. The most important feature of designing a stencil is to break down the *outline* of the design into 1) the stencil openings and 2) the interlinking bridges. The bridges serve 2 purposes: they prevent the stencil from collapsing and they separate different colors within one element of a pattern. Bridges strengthen stencils—for example, a long, narrow stencil can buckle and warp—bridges will keep it nice and flat. After you've painted your design, if you wish, you can paint in the area where the ties were, creating an unbroken line.

The basic rule is to have *space* between the elements of the stencil. Also, in order to have a multi–color stencil, you will need a different stencil for each *color.* The number of stencils needs for a given outline depends upon the number of colors you want and the number of bridges required to hold the stencil. If you have only one color in the stencil, you will generally only need one stencil, but it does depend upon the design. A very intricate design may need more than one stencil. Since designing stencils is, in itself, an art form, we are lucky now to have so many pre–cut stencils available, so that we can get to painting and making art.

Many of the stenciling books listed in *1001 Products and Resources for the Fabric Painter and Surface Designer* give more detailed instructions as to how to make your own stencils. Look especially for the older books, as they have detailed instructions for the reader for this particular process.

FLOORCLOTHS

Floorcloths were used in place of rugs during Colonial times. They played an important role as they simulated the tiled floors that the settlers had had in their European homes. The rude wooden floors of the cabins in the new land were made colorful with brightly painted cloths with geometric designs. Also, at that time, there were no manufactured carpets available!

At first the designs of the floorcloths were primarily geometric designs covering the entire floor, but later they became more ornate, with many flowers and trellises. In both cases, rug designs were the origin of these floor cloth designs. Popular motifs include: checkerboard, stripes, squares, diamonds, quilt designs, boarder designs, Oriental, Islamic, Persian, Arabic, Mexican, Turkish, and other popular rug designs.

With the recent emergence of interest in both country and American folk art, there is a renewed interest in the floor cloth. But you may ask "What exactly is a floor cloth?"

It is a stiff, smooth, shiny, and colorful piece of canvas which is laid on a wood or hard surface floor. It is not a rug, therefore, it is not to be laid over a carpet as one would a throw rug. However, it can also be used on hard supportive surfaces, such as on a back patio, a wooden deck, or a cement basement floor. Floorcloths can be mopped and vacuumed, just like a linoleum floor.

In general, they are made from heavy canvas and cut square. However, it is not necessary to limit oneself to squares and rectangles; floor cloths, because they are cut out from canvas, can be made in any possible shape. They could be circular, oval, hexagon, octagonal, shaped like a whimsical animal, such as a big fish or a lizard, (especially good for a children's room). You could have a matching sun and moon, with the sun floorcloth near the child's door, for waking up and getting up, and the moon cloth near the child's bed,

To get started, first obtain some heavy canvas, such as is used for tents, tipis, awnings, and sails. Both an awning store or a sailcloth supplier are possibilities. Check with your local art store or fabric store to see where they get their canvas if other possibilities don't check out. Also, remember to check your yellow pages under "canvas goods".

The best canvas is a #8 or 10 duck canvas. These come in widths of 3, 4, 5, 6, and 10 feet. Be sure you purchase something that is chemically *untreated,* so that your paint and lacquer can penetrate the fibers. It's best not to fold the canvas on your way home—better to roll it up.

Floorcloths can be made from treated or untreated canvas. First I will discuss making the treated canvas.

Treated Canvas: Cut the canvas in the desired shape. For a beginning floorcloth, you might want to cut a 3' by 5' one, just to keep it simple. Soak the canvas in water, the staple it to a stretcher just as if you were stretching a canvas for painting. (For this you will need stretcher bars which can be obtained in an art supply store. Or, find some plywood, nail it in a square or rectangle the size of the canvas, and attach the canvas to the wood). When it dries, it will be nice and taunt

Next, apply Liquitex (or another brand) gesso in thin coats. Use a regular wide paintbrush, or a polybrush. After applying, sand with sandpaper. Repeat this step three times. As you are nearing the end, take out the staples and replace them with pushpins. Gesso over the holes where the staples were. Move the push–pins around and gesso in the needed areas.

Another way to treat the canvas is to paint it with a flat latex or oil–based paint, rather than using gesso. This will also make the canvas stiff. Paint in broad strokes or a wide brush or use a regular paint roller. The paint will cause the canvas to shrink, so it is important to allow for an additional 2–3" in either direction.

First put down newspapers or butcher paper on the floor or table. Use masking tape or push pins to secure the canvas. Use a semi–gloss latex paint for the background, applying two to three coats, one at a time, with a 24 hour drying time in between. Do not sand the coats between layers. Paint with smooth, even strokes. Polyurethane can be used to seal the paint.

Another option is to use a latex spray paint. This is quicker and easier, but will not leave as thick a background coat.

Untreated Canvas: For untreated canvas, you simply omit the step of gessoing or lacquering before painting. The first decision then to make is whether or not to paint the canvas a back ground color or to leave it natural. If you decide to paint a background color, you can either use a glaze, by painting a thin coat of paint with a brush, or you can use a sponge, and have a mottled background or a fully covered background. Either way, gloss or semi–gloss paint is generally used.

There are several advantages to putting down a background glaze first. By painting the background, if you make any mistakes when stenciling, it is easy just to wipe off the design and start over. Certain designs, however, will look better with the unprimed canvas as a background. Be sure the paint is thoroughly dry before starting to stencil. If it feels at all damp or sticky to the touch, let it dry more thoroughly.

If you choose to stencil directly on the canvas, be aware that the canvas will soak up the paint quickly, so you will need to continue to apply it and rub it in. Eventually it will reach its saturation point and you will have a successful design. Remember, if you put the paint on too heavily and it comes through the stencil, your project cannot be saved. Therefore, the way to successful stenciling, especially on unpainted canvas, is "be sure your brush is dry".

PAINTING TECHNIQUES

In both cases, you are now ready to paint your design onto the floorcloth. A latex or acrylic paint works well. Japan paint also is a good paint for floorcloths. It does need to be mixed with turpentine, but it has a shiny and hard finish, which withstands wear. Bright colors and brightly patterned designs such as Mexican or pre–Columbian weavings, abstract modern art, and other folk art motifs are popular designs for floorcloths. Place your stencil over the canvas fabric and, using a stencil brush, carefully paint the design, bobbing your brush up and down onto the canvas. The treated canvas is going to have a shinier, harder surface than the untreated and may be slightly harder to paint on at first. After painting all the open areas from the stencil, carefully remove the stencil and let the floorcloth dry.

FINISHING TASKS

Hemming: The next task is to hem your floorcloth. One way is to turn up a narrow hem and use a hot glue gun or some craft glue to secure it. Another easy way is to use a self–stick tape on the back. Hemming or sewing canvas is not really very success-ful. The canvas fabric is so thick that on a regular sewing machine, you are going to find it tough going. If you do decide to hem by sewing, it must be done before priming and painting your cloth.

Sealing: Now it is time to put the final seal on your floorcloth. Use a polyurethane varnish, either flat or gloss. I prefer the flat, as the gloss will sometimes deter from the design. Of course, a brightly colored gay design would be compatible with a glossy finish! Use 3–4 coats for a good strong seal. After this has dried, you can wipe your floor cloth with a sponge or even mop it. Over time, you may need to revarnish it, depending upon how much wear it gets. Another popular idea is to have the "antique effect". Do this by tinting the final varnish with raw umber oil paint. This can look very nice as a complement to wood floors.

Now, for the final grand moment, which is putting your floorcloth down! Simply lay the floor cloth on the hard surface that it was designed for. It should lay flat (or nearly so). Walk over it and see if it shifts. If it does, use double–sided carpet tape and tape the corners to the ground.

As you can see, making a floorcloth is not entirely a simple matter, but it can be very satisfying. There are many interesting designs that can be used for floorcloths. Floorcloths do not necessarily have to be stenciled, but they look very nice with the technique.

RESIST PROCESSES

There are a number of processes which come under the category of resist processes. These include using wax, com-monly known as batik, using flour and starch, rice, and clay pastes, as well as more exotic substances such as cassava paste, which is used in Africa as a resist. As well, many companies now make special resists to be used with fabric design. The **resist process** allows sections of the fabric to be blocked out while other parts are painted or dyed. Usually the "resisted" design remains white, with other areas of the fabric being colored. Many nice effects can be created in this way. **Colored resists** are used to add color to areas at the same time that they work as a resist. They are popular with painting on silk. (Fig.162)

Most resists are used in a liquid or semi–liquid state. They can be brushed on, used with a tjanting or cone tips (either the Japanese tsutsu cones or cake decorating tips), or squeeze bottles. After the resist is applied to the fabric, it is left to dry. When dry, textile paint, dye–paste, or cold–water dyes are directly applied to the surrounding areas. The fabric is fixed in a manner appropriate to the paint material used, and then the resist is removed, usually by washing in hot water.

Wax is used as a resist in either hot or cold form. **Hot wax** as a resist is called batik. Paraffin, beeswax, and sticky wax can be used. Hot wax penetrates both sides of the fabric, and is commonly applied with the tjanting. (Please refer to books on batik for greater details of using hot wax.) I find **cold wax resist** preferable for fabric painting as it approximates certain features of batik, yet one does not have to deal with the vagaries of hot wax. The cold wax resist is applied to the fabric with various tools and is left to dry. Then the fabric can be squeezed to break and "crackle" the wax. The crackling makes a very nice visual effect.

Since the cold wax resist solution can be very pourable it is best used with a brush or squeeze bottle. After it dries, color can be applied and set. The cold wax is washed off in hot water and can be used on all types of fabrics. (Figs.163,164)

Flour and starch paste–resists are easy to mix up and use. Recipes for flour and starch paste–resists don't have to be exact. Basically, if you want a thick paste, use more flour or starch and less water. If you prefer a thinner paste, use more liquid. Here are a few recipes for flour and starch paste–resists.

Take 1 Tbsp. of flour, 1 Tbsp. of rice flour, 1/2 Tbsp. of laundry starch, and 1 and 1/2 C. of hot water. Boil this for fifteen minutes. Let the mixture cool until it thickens, then brush it, spoon it, or otherwise apply it to the fabric. After it dries, apply your color and fix it, then wash off the paste. Another recipe calls for 3 Tbsp. of flour, 1 C. of water. Let this boil briefly, then apply it, while hot, to the fabric. This technique allows for interesting yet nebulous shapes, and a somewhat primitive effect.

Very nice effects can be created by using various kinds of flour, cornstarch, and laundry starch. A simple idea for yardage would be to brush on your resist showing evenly spaced brushmarks, then with a wider brush, apply lines of dye–paste going in the opposite direction. Flour and starch paste–resist is an excellent beginning material for the resist process.

Rice flour has been used by Japanese textile artists to create a special resist technique called **norizome,** or nori. (Japanese paste–resist) This process is derivative of an ancient Chinese recipe for an insoluble resist made from ground soybeans and slaked lime. When the Japanese used sweet rice as a resist material, they found that it was extremely glutinous and had strong adhesive properties. It then became the most desired type of resist process.

The rice flour is mixed with rice bran water, salt, and slaked lime to create the paste. In the technique of **tsutsugaki,** the paste is squeezed through cones made from mulberry paper with brass tips, much like a cake decorating tube. Japanese nori paste is also used for **katazome,** the art of stencil dyeing with paste resist. This technique will be discussed later in this section.

Nori paste–resist is a more complex resist method than the previously mentioned flour and starch resists. General instructions will be given here, but I would like to recommend that you read Japanese *Stencil Dyeing: Paste–Resist Techniques*–by Eisha Nakano and Barbara Stephan (Weatherhill Publications) for a thorough explanation of norizome and katazome.

Take 1/4 cup sweet rice flour, and 3/8 cup rice bran. Mix these together, then add approximately 1/6 cup of water. Mix this well to make a batter and knead it, just like you would bread dough. Then shape your batter into a few donuts. Wrap these donuts with a damp piece of cotton fabric. Put them in a steamer (just like a vegetable steamer) and steam them for 45–50 minutes. Remove them and mash them with a pestle or potato masher. Gradually add 1 to 1 1/2 tablespoons of uniodized salt, dissolved in 1/8 cup of water. If the weather is humid, you'll need less salt, if it's dry, more. Mix together 1/8 cup of water and 1/2 tablespoon slaked lime (also called calcium hydroxide). Let it settle for a few minutes and then pour off the top liquid into the paste mixture. Continue beating the paste. Its color will change from light brown to light yellow. Continue adding

FIG. 162: *"PERSONAL SPACE"–BY EVE ZWEBEN–CHUNG. PROCION DYE PAINTED ON COTTON WITH INKODYE RESIST, CRAYOLA FRABRIC CRAYONS, AND VERSATEX PAINT.*

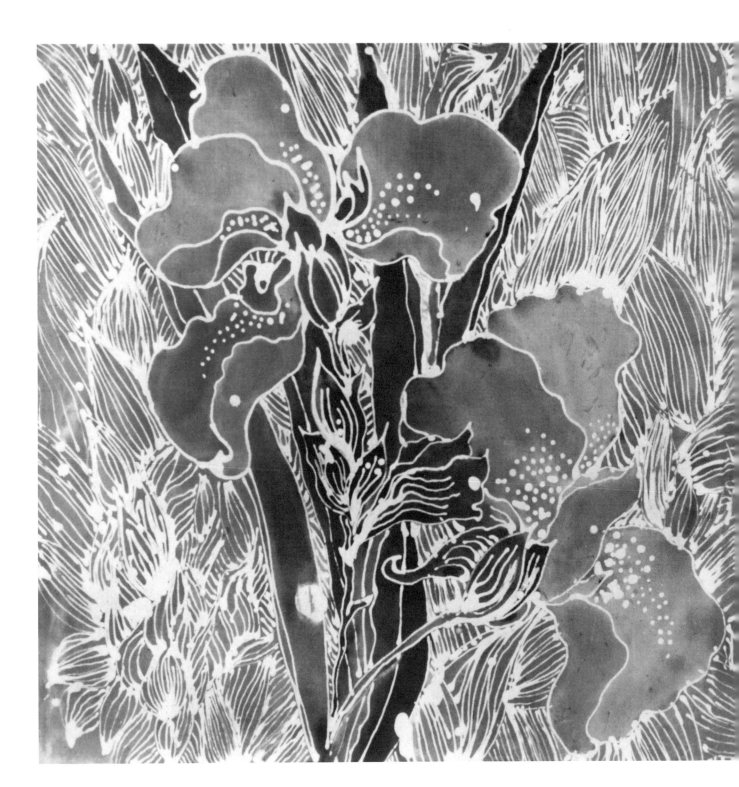

FIG. 163: *"IRISES"–BY CAROL RACKLIN. WAX LINE RESIST. COMMERCIAL BATIKDYE APPLIED DIRECTLY WITH BRUSH*

warm water until you can stir the paste easily. It is then ready to use.

If you are using the Japanese **tsutsu cones,** first soak them in water to make them more flexible. Attach the metal tips securely and fill the cone half–way with nori paste. If using cake–decorating tubes, attach the proper tips and again half–fill the tube. Squeeze with an even pressure to draw lines and other designs. Let your paste dry (this will probably take at least overnight,) then apply dyepastes or textile paints. Fix your paint material before washing out the paste.

Japanese nori paste is ***extremely*** tenacious. For this reason, it is not the easiest method to use successfully for the beginner. Be sure your paste is thick enough to flow through the tube— otherwise little globs will come out of the tube and you will have no control over your design. Once you've made up a few recipes and learned how to do it properly, it is a wonderful resist technique!

Switching cultures, nori paste is also used as a resist in Africa by being applied to the fabric with a spatula, combed through with a plastic comb, and left to dry. Sweet rice flour can be purchased at an Oriental food store. Rice bran is available at health food stores. Uniodized salt is available at a regular grocery store. Slaked lime can be found locally at a garden center.

Clay resists have primitive origins. In Africa, mud and clay were smeared onto cloth, and the metallic salts in the mud sometimes themselves would color the fabric; other times it was necessary to pour a hot dye onto the fabric. To use clay today as a resist, take a small amount of potter's clay and put it in a container—a small dish, for example. Add water to soften the clay, then use it as a resist in a manner similar to the flour or starch paste resists. Sometimes the clay will react to the paint material, leaving a nice blending of colors. Clay is an easy resist to try.

Cassava paste–resist also originates from Africa. The cassava root was pounded down and ground into a paste and used much like the starch–resist pastes mentioned earlier. **Inkodye Resist,** which is used along with Inkodye, is much like cassava paste. It can be applied with a brush, squeeze bottle, stamps,or through a stencil. After drying, it can be cracked just like wax to produce the batik–like "crackle" effect. It is washed off with hot water.

Other ready–made resists today include a line resist called **Createx Line Resist.** It is a medium–weight water based resist, and is best used with a brush or squeeze bottle. It has to be washed out with Createx detergent and tri–sodium phosphate. Other resists, such as gutta, are used specifically in silk painting (see below).

A colored resist using paraffin wax and regular **color crayons** is described in ***Batik and Tie–Dye***–by Dona Meilach. A particular color of crayon is melted with some paraffin and then applied to the fabric with a brush, squeeze bottle or tjanting. After other paint materials are applied and fixed, the wax is removed by a hot iron, and the colors from the crayons will remain intact.

As can be seen, the resist process is quite varied and extensive. Its roots are in ancient cultures. Resist processes have been found throughout most of the worlds' cultures for many centuries. (***The Dyer's Art:Ikat, Batik,Plangi***–by Jack Lenor Larsen is an excellent sourcebook which tells of this fascinating history.) Resist process contain an element of surprise, as they do not adhere to hard and fast rules. Part of their appeal comes from the difficulty in pinning down the effect through certain procedures or an exact recipe. As they are part of the process

*FIG. 164: **"LADY WITH HAT"** – BY CAROL RACKLIN. WAX RESIST WITH FIBER–REACTIVE DYES.*

of something handmade, they also have the variety and sometimes the irregularity which is part of the appeal of the handmade item. Their look is the opposite of the hard–edged look of most stenciling, which is interesting in that they both operate under the same basic principle, that is of the block–out technique.

PAINTING ON SILK

Silk painting is one of the most popular and well–known of fabric painting techniques today. Many fiber artists have perfected this type of painting to its highest form. (Fig.164–A) Techniques of silk painting need to be practiced in order to be perfected. Classes and workshops are helpful towards this end. However, with today's new silk paints which do not require steaming, the painting process is easier than in the past.

There are numerous preparations necessary for silk painting. One needs to locate frames or stretchers. Besides silk paints, dyes, and resists (see Chapt IV), and silk fabric, one needs to know about the various accessories used in silk painting.

Stretchers: Stretchers are a very important tool in the silk painting process. In silk painting, the fabric needs to be stretched taunt enough so the paints can be applied evenly and the resists can be applied thoroughly. Stretchers can be bought, made, or found. Types of stretchers include: canvas stretcher strips, quilting frames, stitcher and needlework frames, embroidery hoops, small oval quilting frames, and Japanese bamboo stretchers called sushi (a bent bamboo stick). You can also buy specific silk stretchers through different distributors.

There are two kinds of stretcher or frames: the **nonadjustable** (or fixed frame) and the **adjustable.** Nonadjustable frames are glued or nailed together and will only fit one size. Old picture frames, wooden window screens, artist stretcher bars, or specifically made stretcher bars used for silk painting which snap together are all fixed frames. They can be used for beginning "practice pieces" or for a particular item, such as a certain sized silk scarf which you might intend to paint numerous times. It is problematic, however, to have endless numbers of frames of varying sizes unless you are a professional silk painter.

The advantages of the fixed frame are that they are strong and sturdy but the disadvantage is that you can't move the silk on the frame. The frame, in other words, is the size of the silk product. Also, if you live in a small place, you need a lot of room for all these different sized stretchers.

The other type of frame used is an adjustable frame, with wing–nuts, that slides to adjust to the size of the piece on which you are working. Therefore, it can be used over and over again, regardless of the size project. Sometimes it is necessary to restretch the silk while in the middle of a project, and this is far easier to do on an adjustable frame. One problem with an adjustable stretcher is that, with the movement of the adjustable sides, the other two sides are left open, with no support. The fabric can be clipped to the sides with something called "crocodile clips". Someone skilled in carpentry could also easily make a homemade adjustable frame with 2 by 4's. This is the ideal situation, because several basic sizes could be made for a very reasonable cost, and you can tailor the sizes to your needs.

Another easy way to make a similar type stretcher is to use canvas stretcher strips. These wooden strips are available in art supply stores as they are frames for regular painting canvases.

It is possible to experiment with other objects just to stretch the silk fabric taunt, which is after all the stated goal. Embroidery, stitchery, and quilt frames have all been used as stretchers. Try what is available to you and remember that silk painting works best when the silk is taunt and not touching any other surface.

Another type of stretcher used in Japan and very popular with silk painters is a bamboo stretcher. It has needle points on the end, so that the stretcher is positioned from selvedge to selvedge on the fabric. For a square silk scarf, the stretchers are crossed, as in an X, and each needle point is placed in the corner of the scarf.

From all these choices, I find the most appealing stretcher is the adjustable one that is manufactured. So I highly recommend using the products that are now available. I think it's best for a beginner to take advantage of the products that are available for you and not try to do too much of making your own stuff.

Silk Tacks and Pins: Fiber art distributors carry special tacks and pins used in silk painting. These have very fine points which do not cause the silk to snag, and which do not leave holes.

Brushes: Brushes that are commonly used for silk painting include: watercolor brushes, foam brushes, wash brushes, Oriental brushes, cotton swabs, and pieces of cotton secured with a clothespin. Watercolor and wash brushes are especially suited to working on the fragile surface of silk.

Fabrics: A source of silk, such as already hemmed silk scarves, make a good first project. Or you can simply purchase some China silk to work on your "practice pieces".

Paints: There are numerous silk painting products available, especially dyes, paints, and resists. (Most silk paints are actually an acid dye.) Some popular paints are: **DekaSilk flowable paints, Sennelier Paris Peintex Ink, Sennelier Tinfix Fabric Colors, IVY Crafts Silk Tint Silk Colors.** Resists include: **Deka–Silk resist (in clear, gold, silver and colors), IVY Crafts Silktint Gutta (clear, black).** Other popular products include: **Deka–silk salt, Peintex thickeners, and Peintex medium.** (See Chapter IV under Silk Paints for detailed information) If you are doing a whole lot of

silk painting and want to be economical you can use an acid dye and then dilute it with one part of water to one part of alcohol. I wouldn't recommend this for beginners, however because most silk paintings are small projects such as scarves and you really can go a long way with a few products or a silk painting starter set.

BASICS OF SILK PAINTING

Certain basics are consistent in all types of silk painting. Products such as stretchers, brushes, and paints remain the same regardless of technique. Tracing a pattern is the same. The basic process is also the same. Let's go through the basic procedure for silk painting and then I will describe the different techniques.

First, wash your silk to remove any sizing. Put it on your chosen stretcher. Be sure and pin it so that it is taunt and firm. When pinning or tacking, first secure the four sides, then work out from the center to tack the rest of the silk onto the frame. If you have a design that you want to transfer to the silk, you will need to trace the pattern.

Tracing the pattern: To do this, put the pattern or design beneath the silk and trace with either gutta (if you are using the resist technique) or with a disappearing fabric marking pen. Be ***sure*** to test the marking pen first. Some really do disappear, and some don't, especially on a fragile fabric such as silk. If the silk you are using is opaque, such as a heavy silk noil, use a non-oil transfer medium such as Saral paper to transfer the pattern.

After you have transferred the pattern, you are ready to paint! When painting on silk, use the paint ***sparingly.*** This cannot be emphasized enough. You want to have a gentle touch on the silk. It doesn't take much color to permeate the fabric. This is because the fibers in the silk are so slender that capillary action happens immediately: the paint spreads whether or not you have a resist on the fabric.

The best approach is to apply the paint to the middle of the design, not right next to the resist line. For watercolor painting, allow room for the expansiveness of the paint so that you can control your color blending. Using small soft brushes, such as watercolor brushes, makes it easier to control the paint. Also, use this spreading action to advantage in your design.

In general, the older silk paints which must be steam–set have more brilliant colors which emerge after steaming. Therefore, when using these paints, do not overpaint, because you may either get too much paint runoff during the steaming process, or your colors may turn out darker than you wish.

Set the silk paint or dye by ironing on the back side of the fabric for 2–3 minutes. Another method is to steamset. (See below) Also you can use an oven and wrap the silk in butcher paper or aluminum foil at 300 degrees in the oven, with a pan of boiling water beneath the fabric packet. Launder to remove any resists. Boiling with Synthranpol will remove excess or fugitive dye.

SILK PAINTING TECHNIQUES

Silk painting includes techniques such as **resists or gutta serti, salt techniques, watercolor or blending, stenciling, and batik.** The most widely used ones are the resist method and the watercolor techniques.

Gutta Serti Resist Method: Resist methods derive from the French method of gutta serti. Gutta is a thick and somewhat rubbery substance used as a resist. Guttas are clear, colored, and metallic. They either come in small plastic squeeze bottles or are used with a plastic applicator.In the gutta serti method, first the gutta is applied to the silk, then the paint is applied. The gutta acts as a resist, allowing the artist to paint within the resist lines. Gutta is also used to trace the lines of a design or pattern, by simply laying the silk on top of the pattern or design.

Applying gutta: When applying gutta, make sure that all of the lines are completely enclosed as the dye can easily seep out. Use a firm stroke. When tracing the pattern using the gutta, be very firm with the applicator so that the gutta penetrates to the other side. This is important because the gutta is what is keeping the design intact. If the resist is not put on well, the paint will often bleed out. This is a common problem with beginners. However, the guttas that are available today are very easy and pleasant to use. Using them is like drawing quickly on a very nice smooth paper with a fine charcoal or smooth pencil.

After the resist is all applied, let it dry. Then apply the paints or dyes. Use the paint very sparingly. Since the silk is such a fine fabric, the paint will just rush out towards that resist. Apply the paint in the middle of the design, not next to the resist line. The paint is going to go speeding towards that resist line and you just hope you have enough of a barricade up to keep it in!

Gutta Serti with Blending Techniques: Silk painters often incorporate both resist painting and watercolor or blended color techniques in the same piece. They can make beautiful items using blended colors with specific designs. I recommend this technique as a first project. Take your colors and just paint within the lines. There are so many beautiful colors available it's easy to make something real pretty right off. Another variation on this method is to first draw your gutta lines. Then, without even attempting to keep within the lines with the color, paint in a watercolor or blended way. The gutta lines will show through the blended colors very delicately.

Salt Techniques: Salt is an easy and fun way to make interesting patterns. The principle behind salt techniques is that the salt will draw up the water in the dye, leaving behind "starburst" type patterns. The larger the salt crystal, the bigger the starburst. Many kinds of salt can be used: table salt, Deka–silk salt, Kosher or course salt, sea salt and rock salt. Also, variations on the water/salt ratio will produce differences. More water will produce a softer design, while less water will create more jagged edges.

Apply color to the silk. One minute after the dye has been applied, place or sprinkle some grains of salt onto the wet area. Lots of granules will produce a lighter colored design with more pattern. Placing only a few granules will produce less drawing up of water, so the dye color will remain the same except for the patterns created by the separate granules. This is a easy technique with which to experiment!

Salt Soak Technique: This technique leaves a spiky or lacy edge to the design. Soak the fabric in a solution of 1 C boiling water to 2 Tbsp. salt. Soak the fabric. Let it drip dry. Then paint the silk. Fabric will glitter with tiny salt crystals and the paint spreads very little, leaving many crystal–like designs. A variation on this is to brush the salt solution onto the already stretched silk.

Watercolor or blended technique: Another technique is the watercolor or blended technique. It's a good idea to use your cotton ball "brushes" (the cotton balls with the clothespin holder) so that you can blend your colors. To blend colors, put down water first. Then start blending in your colors, just like as if you were working in a regular watercolor wash method. Blend from one edge to the other. The more you wet the fabric with water, the less intense the color. Let areas dry first when you want hard–edged shapes. Remove color with cotton swab to highlight area. You can use resist, or gutta serti, techniques, together with the blended colors. If you are not familiar with these and other watercolor techniques, refer to the section "watercolor techniques" in Chapter VI. Use paper towels to blot up water.

Stenciling on Silk: Stenciling on silk is the same as on other fabrics except that the silk is more porous. Dry off your brush very well, and rub it in a circular motion. I would recommend pre–cut stencils, rather than cutting your own. Stretch your fabric and tape or pin it to a board or cardboard. Putting sandpaper beneath the silk will keep the fabric from slipping. Use very little paint on your brush. Use a circular motion. If you get very much paint on the brush, it will bleed underneath the stencil design and cause "blobs" of paint to form.

Stenciling, as a technique, is very meticulous. This is especially so on silk. It requires a steady hand.

Silk Batik techniques: The batik look is easy in silk painting. Paint your design directly on the fabric, then brush on a hot beeswax/paraffin blend. When the wax cools, take the silk off the frame, put it in the refrigerator for a little, then "crinkle" the fabric together. Now spread the silk out again and put it back onto the frame. Apply a dark color with a brush. Remove the wax by ironing between several layers of butcher paper, or let the wax melt out during the steaming process.

BEGINNING PROJECTS

Take some scraps of silk and try out different techniques (resist, blended colors, watercolor, stenciling, batik, etc.) Mix colors. Most importantly, watch how the paints "bleed". Do they always bleed in a certain direction (ie along the horizontal or vertical lines of the fabric, or in all directions?) Paint color squares using different colors and brands of paint. If you are at all serious, you will want to keep a record book, putting swatches of silk and the various techniques tried. Silk painting is something you can learn to do in stages, and since it is an imperfect science, it is best to keep records of your techniques.

SILK PAINTING IDEAS

Silk painting can be a very meditative, quiet, and soothing experience. However, expect to "practice" on your first pieces. In spite of what the books and pamphlets say, what is supposed to work doesn't always. For example, the gutta or various resists which are used in resist work are not resistant enough to stop the flow of the thin silkpaint or dye. The trick is to work slowly, use a small brush, use very little paint. Lightly touch the paint to the silk in the middle of the design. The tendency is to want to paint at the speed that one would paint with regular fabric paint. I find that this does not work. It's important to let the paint spread out into the edges of the resists, rather than using the brush to add more paint. This requires patience

I have also found using these new silk paints is easy and pleasant now that I've gotten the hang of silk painting. It is nice to mix colors together, both before painting and also in a watercolor method. I find using silk paints in conjunction with both metallic or pearlescent fabric and dimensional paints enhances the already luxurious look of the silk. Also, using silk paints next to areas painted with fabric paints gives more textural contrast. In fact, I find that I can use dimensional paints successful to "mop up" mistakes that occur with fast–spreading silk paints. If the paint goes into an area that I do not wish it to, I can control it with a quickly drawn line of dimensional paint.

STEAMING SILK DYES

In order for the colors to be fast, many silk dyes must be steamed. They need dry steam rather than wet steam in order that the dyes do not run. The best techniques to use are pressure steaming or atmospheric steaming To pressure steam, roll the silk in an absorbent paper (steaming paper is available from various suppliers). Seal the ends of the paper with adhesive tape. Carefully fold in sections and put into the wire basket of a pressure cooker. Be sure and place the basket on a trivet so that its bottom will not touch the bottom of the pan. Add 1/2" of water. Cover the rolled fabric bundle with a hood of aluminum foil. This will keep condensation from touching the paper, thus wetting the fabric. In one recipe, the next step is to steam for 45 minutes. Another recipe suggests bringing the pressure cooker up to 3 pounds of pressure before putting in the fabric bundle. Then steam for 20 minutes. With a regular steamer or steam cabinet, follow instructions for its use.

JAPANESE STENCIL DYEING WITH PASTE RESIST

The nori rice paste–resist mentioned earlier is also used in another process: **katazome,** or Japanese stencil dyeing with paste resist. In this resist process, the nori paste is pushed through a cutpaper stencil with a wooden spatula, called a hera, to produce the design. The paste is left to dry, then a dye paste is painted directly onto the fabric.

The process of katazome has many steps, and again I refer you to *Japanese Stencil Design:Paste–Resist Technique*–by Eisha Nakano and Barbara Stephan, for a description of the complete process. There are also many different types of Japanese stencil dyeing. For example, **komon** is a technique where a small repetitious design is cut on the stencil and only one color dye is used for the background. This produces a small overall pattern in monochrome. In **chugata,** the patterns are medium sized and are perfectly aligned on both sides of the fabric. **Bingata** is a brightly–colored method which combines cone and stencil dyeing. It is an especially interesting design technique, since the stencil can easily reproduce fine textures while the tsutstu cone drawing produces fine line drawing.

Colored paste, or **ironori,** is used in katazome in the same manner as the colored resists mentioned previously. **Yuzen** means fine–lined cone drawing of colored paste with delicate handpainting inside. **Stencil yuzen** occurs when the colored paste is stenciled onto the fabric.

The design and cutting of the stencil is an art in itself. The two most common stencil design techniques are colored ground, and white ground. In colored ground,or **jizomari,** the design remains white while the background is dyed. With **jishiro,** the design is colored and the background remains white. The cutting of the stencil for jishiro would be completely opposite than for jizomari. Other techniques are senbori, or cut outline, and kukuri, or "string", where extensive use of bridges is needed.

There are various types of cutting styles, as well. **Awl cutting** and **thrust cutting** create arabesque and floral shapes. Tool punching uses a **dot punch,** which punches out the design. **Pull cutting** is a technique which creates very fine stripes.

In order to do katazome, you'll need some kind of stencil paper, a stencil knife or X–acto knife, silk gauze, a wooden spatula or hera, possibly some dot punches, nori paste, soybean liquid for sizing the cloth, and the dye–paste or thickened dyes for coloring the fabric.

In Japan, the type paper used for stenciling is a handmade paper of mulberry bark which is laminated with the sticky tannin–rich juice of persimmons. This paper is very strong and resilient, and much of the success of katazome is due to this paper. This stencil paper is called **shibugami.** Other alternatives for this paper are the regular stencil paper sold in art stores, contact paper or vinyl sheeting (sold to cover kitchen shelves), or firm paper which has been brushed with wax and then ironed between sheets of waxed paper.

To start your design, you can use white tissue paper or special Japanese tracing paper (minogami) over a design and then transfer the tracing paper to the stencil paper with a spray adhesive. Then you're ready to cut your design. This is really the most important part of the process, since the stencils can be used repeated numbers of times. It pays to try and do a careful job of both planning and cutting your stencil. After you've cut your stencil, you can make it solid and secure by attaching a piece of silk mesh, called **sha,** over the stencil. (I've found that this step is not always necessary). If your stencil design does not have enough connecting bridges or ties (refer to the section on stenciling for more detail on this), you will need to lacquer the sha to your stencil.

The next step is to brush your fabric with a sizing of soybean liquid. Secure your fabric and put the stencil on top of the fabric. Then lay the nori paste down onto the stencil, putting the paste in the middle and spreading it outward to the edges. I find a kitchen spatula is sufficient if you do not have the wooden hera. If your paste is of the right consistency, without lumps, this part of the procedure will be very easy. I found that using a blender to mix the nori paste makes it smooth and manageable. Smooth the paste with a firm stroke, so that you will force the paste through the stencil. After laying several layers of paste,carefully lift up your stencil off of the fabric.

The stencil can be washed off and reused many times, if carefully handled. Let your paste dry, then brush the thickened dye over the fabric. Fix the paint material after it has dried, and wash off the nori paste with warm water. You may need to soak the paste before it comes off.

Over the centuries, the Japanese have refined katazome to a fine art. These instructions are but the rudiments of the art of stencil dyeing with paste–resist.

RUBBINGS

The next type of indirect painting is very different from either stenciling or resist processes. **Rubbings** have recently been noticed as an art form. A rubbing is an impression taken by rubbing a crayon over a piece of paper which is put upon a certain textured surface, which is the desired impression. Subject matter for rubbings include gravestones, stamps and seals of buildings telling of the date of their erection, grates and markers in streets, and other large markers to be found around cities. In order for a successful rubbing to be taken, the object used must be thick enough to create a raised surface in contrast with the paper, but it must not be so thick or bumpy that the paper cannot be laid fairly flat upon its surface. For example, a large sculpture in a graveyard or museum which has great contrasts in its surface, with some parts out quite far and other parts barely raised at all, would not be suitable for taking a rubbing. A more even texture is helpful. (Fig.165)

FIG. 165: "ELK"–BY JEANNE HILLIS. RUBBING DONE ON POLY–COTTON WITH OIL PAINT.

▬ ▬ ▬ ▬ ▬ ▬ ▬ ▬ ▬ ▬ ▬ ▬ ▬ ▬ ▬ ▬ ▬ ▬

Taking rubbings with cloth varies a little from using paper. One advantage is that cloth is more flexible and can be wrapped on a more uneven surface, like that described above. However, it is still necessary to move your crayon evenly across the surface of the fabric, in order to pick up the impression rather than eradicating it into a crayon scrawl! A square–shaped crayon such as a pastel,works more easily than a round crayon,and the bigger the crayon, the better. When first taking rubbings, hold the crayon and move it *lightly* across the surface of the fabric with smooth even strokes. Move the crayon in *one* direction rather than in short back and forth strokes. If you have never taken a rubbing before, it might be better to first try it on paper in order to learn how to use the crayon correctly.

Some most interesting rubbings have been made of the ancient Maya sculptures. The book, *Maya Sculpture of an Ancient Civilization Rubbings* by Merle Greene (Leder, Street, and Zeus) is full of beautiful rubbings which were done on rice paper. These rubbings were made from the various stelae, sculptures, and the stucco relief and ornamentation found on the temples.

Two paint materials are especially suited for taking rubbings. One is a soft oil–like pastel called Pentel pastel dye sticks. The other is oil paint mixed with turpentine or textine. The oil paint can be used with a brush, and with a very light touch one can pick up impressions from various textured objects—lace, leaves, in fact, *any* kind of textured object. Smooth, fairly thin cloth works best, as it allows the impression to be clearly recorded.

FOLD AND DYE

Fold and dye is another technique which can be used in fabric painting. Fold and dye is simply folding the cloth in a number of sections one way, and then folding it some in the reverse direction, and then dipping the cloth into dye, or brushing dye or paint into corners and on edges of the fabric. This technique was originated for use with decorative papers, which are used in connection with bookbinding or card making. Fold and dye was seen as applicable for surface design as well.

Flat lengths of material can be folded and dipped, or a whole garment can be used. The garment does not have to be evenly folded, and part of the appeal of the method is the surprise in finding what kind of design is created from the random brushmarks or dippings that have been done. If on the other hand, you wish a more even design, simply fold the length of cloth more evenly, and dip the fabric in an even manner.

For the actual process, you will need wide shallow cups for the dye, ink, or other paint material. Fold your fabric, and press the folds with an iron. Then moisten your fabric with water, and gently pat it damp. This is an important step so that the dye will be drawn up into the folds. Clothespins are handy to use as a handle and to keep the folds together. Dip your fabric into the various containers. Let the colors blend and spread. Or, if you wish, use a brush to paint on designs. Gently press the fabric together, so that the designs will penetrate to the innermost folds.

Fold and dye looks simple and easy, but it takes practice to achieve predictable results. The most common error is to not get the dye into the innermost folded areas. If you are sure to moisten your fabric enough, and if you don't have too many folds, this problem should recede.

After you have dipped the material, set it on some butcher paper to dry. Try and keep it in the same shape as when it was dipped. When it is partly dry, it can be spread out for further drying. Set your dyes if necessary.

Fold and dye works especially well with cold water fiber–reactive dyes. Most all types of fabrics can be used, and other types of paint materials, such as acrylics, oil paint, and textile paint, can also be used with good results. The key to good results with fold and dye is practice, since its effects happen somewhat by chance.

BOUND RESISTS

Very close to the process of fold and dye is the **bound resist technique.** With a bound resist, also called plangi, the fabric is rolled into a rope–like shape, firmly bound with various types of cords, rope, or pieces of fabric, and usually immersed in a dye–bath. For the process of fabric painting, this is modified to applying the dye directly with a brush, or dipping the bound fabric in a manner similar to fold and dye. (In both fold and dye and bound resists, the dye is mixed with chemical water and soda and washing soda in order to be effective. Refer to Chapter IV, under "Thinned Applications" for instructions)

Only a few tools are needed for bound resists. String, cord, twine, rope, and strips of fabric are used to bind up the fabric. Sometimes artists will wrap round objects in the fabric as a resist. Seeds, pebbles, stones, beads, rubber balls, marbles, and other round objects are used.

To proceed with bound resist, take your fabric and roll it up into a long "rope". It's best to not have your fabric real wide, but you can have it as long as you wish. If you wish to wrap objects in the fabric place them along the length of the fabric and secure them by tying them with string or thread. Then continue rolling your rope! The fabric is then bound with various ties, ropes, and strings. It is then dipped in various dyes, just like in fold and dye. The ties will act as a resist. Paint can also be directly painted onto certain sections of your fabric "rope".

For a more complex design, let the fabric dry, then unwrap your ties and strings, and retie them in different ways. Repeat the process and dip areas that are undyed. This process can be repeated several times. After the final drying, unfold your fabric, set your dyes and paints, and untie any objects that were tied in.

For beginners, bound resist processes depend largely on chance. However, in Africa and Asia, where these techniques have been used for centuries, they are highly developed. One such method is the clamp resist technique, where a wooden or metal clamp is used to secure the fabric together. For more ideas, refer to **The Dyer's Art,** a wonderful sourcebook for bound resists.

Fiber–reactive dyes, textile paints, thinned acrylics, and Inkodye all work well with bound resist techniques. Bound resist is really no more than a "wrap and dip" method. There are many possible effects from changes in wrapping and how the paint material is used. One last point, if you fold or roll your fabric lengthwise, you'll get a linear design. If you wish a circular design, pull your fabric up from the **center** and begin wrapping it like a rope. This will produce a circular design, commonly seen in tie–dyed T–shirts of the 1970's, as well as today.

HEAT TRANSFER PROCESSES

The **heat transfer process technique** uses a type of dye (disperse) which is activated by heat and then adheres to synthetic fibers (such as polyester and nylon). This disperse dye is used in three forms for the heat transfer process: **in powder form,** to be used with a thickening agent, on pre–manufactured **heat transfer paper,** and in a solid wax form—**fabric crayons.** These three forms have different effects, are applied in different ways, yet can be effectively used together in a complementary fashion.

In the heat transfer process, the design is painted or drawn directly onto **paper,** left to dry, then the paper is placed, face down on the synthetic fabric. Butcher paper is placed, beneath and on top of the fabric, and the whole area is ironed until color shows through the top paper. The heat "transfers" the dye molecules from the paper to the fabric.

Heat transfer requires few materials. Have a ready supply of butcher paper—you'll need a lot when ironing your fabric and it's also good for painting designs! Other suitable paper: heat–transfer Thermal Master paper (available from silkscreen supply houses), or any other smooth nonporous paper. Various types of brushes can be used for the thickened dyes, and scissors will be needed for the transfer paper. Since this technique utilizes textures, you may wish to collect string, lace, or other items which will create textures when pressed with the fabric.

One of the nicest aspects of this process is that you can reuse your patterns. You can recolor them, in which case they will approximate the original, or you can make a second, weaker image from the original. Areas of a painted design can also be cut out in various shapes for use as an independent image. Any technique that you are used to doing on paper can be done and transferred to fabric. You can tear your paper, or cut it in geometric squares like patchwork, or leave it in big open sheets. Watercolor effects, line drawings, collage, all can be done with the heat transfer process!

The powdered disperse dyes are used with a thickener for direct painting. The recommended thickener is monogum thickener. Take one part monogum to 10 parts water, and sprinkle the monogum over the water. Agitate your container so the particles blend into the water—this should happen fairly quickly. Mix about 1/4 teaspoon of dye with a bit of boiling water (approximately 1 and 2/3 teaspoon). Then mix the thickener with the dye mixture (I find plastic egg cartons convenient to mix up small quantities of a number of different colors of dye) and you are ready to paint!

I've encountered only a few minor problems in using this technique. The drying time for the paints interferes with a continuous production of craft items. You have to be patient ! Also, with the transfer process, the colors are only transferred to one side of your fabric. If you want to make a neck scarf, for example, you might want to repeat a weaker image on the wrong side of the fabric. Sometimes, while ironing, the image will "slip" a bit, but a double–image effect can be used to work with the design rather than against it.

Many nice effects are possible with disperse dyes. The colors blend well, with a softness to them. As mentioned before, watercolor techniques are very effective. The already painted paper can be cut up in various shapes for overlays of pattern and color. And the colors themselves are especially bright, particularly on 100% synthetic fabrics. If you don't wish to mix up your own thickened dye, **transfer paints** are now available from Deka. They are applied just like the thickened dyes, and come in eleven different colors: lemon, orange, pink, light red, crimson, violet, light blue, dark blue, green, brown, and black.

Heat–transfer paper is also used with the heat–transfer process. This paper has been manufactured with the disperse dyes already on it. It's very easy to use and produces a clean sharp image. The same method is used for transferring the color from paper to fabric. Simply place the paper, cut or torn in various shapes, face down on your fabric. Cover with white paper, and iron with a dry iron for up to one minute. Your colors will be bright, and very smooth. It's easiest if you cut your shapes from the **back** of the transfer paper, since the image will be reversed onto the fabric. This way, what you are cutting, and what you see on the fabric will be the same. Heat–transfer paper designs have been sold as transfer prints for T–shirts commercially. Try making your own T–shirts using this paper; it works well!

Fabric crayons are the last category of paint material used in the heat transfer process. A similar procedure is followed, with the design being first drawn on the paper. The wax in these crayons has a tendency to "flick" off from the design, causing miniscule smudges, so be especially precise when coloring, and try and blow off any crayon specks before the ironing process. One solution to this problem is to use the crayons in conjunction with the dyes—they compliment each other wonderfully and your smudging problem is solved. (Refer to chapter IV under "Crayons and Fabric Markers" for more details about these crayons.)

All forms of the disperse dye reach out and "grab" the synthetic material, so you do have to be careful when transferring these dyes to not have your pattern accidentally brush up on some fabric. These dyes can be used on white or lightly colored fabrics, and the colors will undergo interesting transformations on colored fabric. Any fabric that is at least 50% synthetic can be used successfully with the transfer processes. Acetate, nylon, polyester, poly–cotton, triacetate, and dacron are some good synthetics to try. Be sure and put a pad of newspaper on the ironing board before laying down the butcher paper; this will give you a cushion when you iron.

The most challenging aspect of heat transfer is the reversibility of the image when it is transferred. One solution to this is to plan abstract designs. Another is to sketch your design in pencil, then turn the paper over and go over the design in fabric crayon or thickened dye. This way the desired image will appear "right–side up" on the fabric. Color blending is also different from other dyes. Rather than the red, blue, and yellow primary colors of color **pigments,** disperse dyes work on the theory of colored *light.* Yellow, turquoise, and magenta are, therefore, the best colors for mixing.

IRON–ON TRANSFER PATTERNS

Iron–on transfers are another heat transfer process now very popular for fabric painting. They are simply designs drawn on paper with heat transfer inks. Iron–on transfer patterns are very familiar to needleworkers and cross–stitchers, as they have been produced over the years to that market. More recently they have been introduced to the fabric painting market, for use with fabric crayons and now the entire gamut of painting products, including dimensional paints, fabric paints, plus the various embellishment products (glues, glitters, fusible appliques, etc). Many of today's designs still originate from needlework, embroidery and cross–stitch.

Iron–on transfers are sold individually or in thick books with many hundreds of patterns. In general, transfer books only have line art, or regular iron–on transfers. However, individual patterns come in at least five different types of transfers. There are large selections in both categories, and Plaid, Gick, Dizzle, Tulip, and Aunt Martha's are some of the companies who carry iron–on transfers.

Regular transfers are composed of line art for use on light fabrics. Some of them come in big books of 1000–2000 designs which can be used more than once. This allows for a lot of creativity! **"Brite" transfers** are for use on dark fabrics. They actually are a type of an acrylic silkscreened image. The design transfers onto the fabric as a raised image, and you merely paint between the lines! **Iron–on pre–shaded transfers,** while seem-ingly easy to use, are fairly standardized. Your decisions as a craftsperson include deciding if the design will "work" on the clothing or fabric item you have chosen, and what types and colors of paints to use in painting **over** the shaded design. In some ways I find them harder to paint on than starting from scratch. **Colored iron–on transfers** do not need to be painted. They are used in combination with embellishments, usually on wearable art. **Iron–on transfers which do not require painting** are the last category. These include **reflective foil iron–ons** (see Foiling in Chapter VI), and **iron–on "fashion accessories"**, which have glittery or hologram surfaces which can be used in wearable art. (See Iron–On Transfers in Chapt IV for various brands of iron–on transfers).

The transfer patterns that are found in books that are prima-rily line drawings are easy for the beginner. They are also good for people who are not particularly talented in line drawing. Many times the designs are larger, more simple, and therefore easier to paint. Also there can be a lot more choice on what paints to use, what colors, and how the design will turn out.

IRON–ON TRANSFER TECHNIQUES

The design is easy to apply, as you simply use a dry iron on a cotton setting (or the highest setting appropriate for the fabric you are using) and hold the iron over each part of the transfer for 15 seconds. Be sure to keep the iron still, so that the transfer does not smear.

Painting the transfers is where the creativity really comes in. It takes some experimentation to find paints which work on transfers. For pre–shaded transfers, one must find paints which don't obfuscate the details of the shading. Dizzle Tints are recommended for the **Dizzle Pre–shaded Iron–on Transfers,** as they allow the shading to show through. Tulip has a paint called Tulip Lite, also used for their pre–shaded transfers.

Both of these iron–on transfer designs (regular and pre–shaded) have a short "life", in other words they can only be used once with a full transfer, and then can be used once or twice with a "light" transfer of the image. (If your design starts to get faint, put aluminum foil beneath the fabric.) However, transfer pens and pencils are wonderful items which can be used to retrace or retouch your favorite iron–on patterns! With this pen or pencil, you can trace any pattern to make iron–on transfers. (See Transfer Paint Materials in Chapt IV for available products).

They can also be used to design your own iron–on transfers. It is possible to avoid the "mirror image" problem that occurs with regular tracing. First, trace the pattern with pencil, then turn over and retrace with the transfer pencil. You will then get the original pattern, right side up, when it is transferred to the fabric. If the pattern or design is on paper which is see–through, printed on only one side, this double tracing can be avoided. Simply turn the paper over and trace the "wrong side" image with your transfer pencil. This will correctly transfer the image for you onto the fabric.

IRON–ON TRANSFER DESIGN IDEAS

Iron–on transfers are a good way to learn how to paint, especially three–dimensional shapes such as flowers, animals, buildings, and people. Using fabric paint, you can learn how to shade simple shapes such as flowers, and produce an effective and attractive design at the same time. Fabric paints, acrylic paints, and dimensional paints are best to use for this technique.

Iron–on transfers of embroidery are very effective when used with both embroidery paints, fabric markers, and the new dimensional paints. They look especially attractive when a combination of these paint products are used, for the textural differences can be highlighted. Also, seeing painted embroi-dery on T–shirts with added lace or crochet edgings is a feminine yet modern look in casual wear.

You don't have to follow all the "rules" with iron–on transfers. I made a very nice T–shirt actually using a "brite" iron–on transfer dark fabric and I put it onto light fabric! My challenge in this project was mainly the choice of colors and placement of the design. I ended up retracing part of the design with an iron–on transfer pen, flipped it so it was a reverse flower, and put it on the pocket. Because of the raised image caused by the "brite" silkscreen transfer, I needed to match this in the flower on the pocket. I ended up using dimensional paints to duplicate the raised outlines. It made a nice windowing effect.

Traditional embroidery iron–on transfers can be used with fabric painting, on fabrics such as silks and cottons. Dimensional paints, fabric markers, and embroidery paints can all be used in the design. This close work can turn out very nice, but the real small patterns can be hard on one's eyes. I used an Aunt Martha's traditional cross–stitch pattern.

In general, iron–on transfers are a slower way to paint on fabric, as the designs must be filled in carefully. There is not the spontaneity that one gets with other techniques, however one is almost guaranteed an attractive finished product. It's fun to learn all the different fabric painting techniques and then use them as you wish!

NEEDLEPAINTING, LIQUID BEADING AND PAINTSTITCHING

Several new products have enhanced the designs which come from needlework, most especially needlepoint. When dimensional paints were first introduced, manufacturers of these paints also introduced the idea of using needlepoint designs in conjunction with dimensional paints. The technique was first called "needlepainting", where a needlepoint design can be transferred with a transfer medium to fabric or clothing. Then, dimensional paint was applied to the patterns and colors of the design.

More recently, Tulip has introduced a product called Tulip Colorpoint, which has even more control over the size and shape of the dots. As well, Fashion Show is advertising its dimensional paints with a new technique called "Liquid Beads", with kits with iron–on patterns and paint, books with iron–on patterns, and a "View and Do" Video.

Needlepainting Technique: This technique, which was suggested by Delta, combined two of their products, Delta Glitter, Shiny, and Swell Stuff dimensional paints with Delta/Slomon's Stitchless glue. First choose a needlepoint or cross–stitch pattern from a book and transfer it using the glue. (An alternative would be to use an iron–on needlework pattern). Fill in the pattern using dimensional paints rather than using needlepoint. When finished, these small designs can be cut out and fused onto other items, such as shirts.

Use a "light" touch with the dimensional paints. Lightly touch the fabric with the tip of the dimensional paint, and then "pull up" your hand. You can actually cover more ground and make many small "stitches". Be patient. Let small areas dry with space inbetween. If you are copying a cross–stitch pattern, do some X's, then let them dry before adding in more.

Enlarge some of the smaller needlepoint patterns 25% for easier coverage. You will want to match the dimensions of the needlepoint pattern to the width of the dimensional paint tube. Think of the paint as your yarn! New dimensional paints work best since older paints don't flow as easily. Some of the brands which worked for me included: **Duncan Scribbles Dimensional Fabric Writer, Tulip Polymark, Delta Shiny, and Fashion Show Dimensional Paints.**

Needlepainting can also be done directly on needlepoint canvas. Different "stitches" can be learned on various mesh sizes. Plastic canvas, regular needlepoint canvas, and counted cross–stitch cloth can all be used, to make small items such as belts, bracelets, pins, and barrettes. I have used Wally R dimensional paints and Fashion Show Dimensional paints very successfully with this procedure. The needlepainting can be used in conjunction with regular needlepoint for an interesting textural look. French knots, cross stitch, and tent stitch can all be needlepainted!

Liquid Beading is a similar technique, however its concept is to use dimensional paints to create beads. Plaid Enterprises originated the idea using their **Fashion Show Dimensional Paints (Shiny, Pearl, Metallic, and Jewel)** and iron–on patterns. The focus is on replicating the beaded look in clothing with paint. The paint relaxes into a smooth, realistic bead. Sweatshirts, sweaters, tennis shoes, dresses, tops—all have potential for the "beaded look". Rows of similarly shaped beads in the same color can make an elegant statement on a sweater or dress.

Liquid beads can be used in conjunction with rhinestones and cabochons on a garment. I found that the Fashion Show Shiny paint dries very hard and can approximate beads, as well as "painted jewels" such as pearls or cabochons. Fashion Show Pearl is a little less solid, but still satisfactory. With **Duncan Scribbles Dimensional Fabric Writer, Dizzle Iridescent dimensional paints, Tulip Polymark Dimensional and Tulip Slick, Tulip's Colorpoint Dimensional paints, Delta's Swell Stuff or Cool Stuff or Wally R's Fluorescent Dimensional paint,** it is possible to paint on drops of paint which give a beaded or jeweled look.

Recently, Tulip paints began to advertise their Colorpoint Paintstitching, with their **Tulip ColorPoint Dimensional Paints** and iron–on transfer books. Like other companies, these paints are advertised to be used to simulate the look of needlework, such as paint–stitched sweatshirts, pillows, hatbands, pictures, and tablecloths. ColorPoint paints make it easy to create beads of a uniform size. They dry into a hard bead. Other brands which are similar to Tulip's include **Delta's Shiny, Cool, and Swell Stuff, Scribble's Dimensionals Fabric Writers, and Wally R's Moonbeams Dimensional paints**. All of these mentioned paints can "peak" rather than bead, so practice some before beading a garment.

TRANSFER ART

Transfer art is a technique which originated with the creation of acrylic gel. When the gel was painted onto paper, it bonded to the ink on the paper. The paper design could then be pressed onto fabric, where the gel would also bond with the fabric. After drying, the paper part of the design could be rubbed off, leaving the paper design (though in reverse). This technique has been refined to now include b/w photographs, color photographs, and xerox copies, but can still be used with newspaper and magazine cut–outs. Along with the acrylic gel process, one can now use products such as **Fashion Show's Picture This Transfer Medium for Fabric,** as well as **Delta/Slomon's Stitchless Fabric Glue and Transfer Medium.** Another transfer medium which I have not yet tried is **Delta's Photo to Fabric Transfer Medium** (used on both light and dark fabrics). **CoMotion Fabric Transfer Ink** is a unique product which allows you to make your own customized transfer designs with **Co–Motion "Stamp 'N Iron" stamp pad).**

Slomon's Stitchless Glue Transfer Medium can be used in conjunction with photographs or pictures in transfer art. First, photocopy a b/w or color photo. B/w photographs photocopy better in b/w, but there are also color copiers for color photographs.

Magazines, with their slick shiny graphic designs, are a wealth of opportunity for abstract designs, cut and recut, perhaps with quilt patterns as the design, and placed on fabric. Using newspapers as a medium, think of what could be done just with headlines. A topic of social importance could be the theme as one makes a "statement" about current life, or politics, or our society.

TRANSFER ART TECHNIQUES

The most challenging part of this process is not applying the medium to the paper and pressing it down onto the fabric, but removing the paper after the glue or medium has dried! It's real important to be liberal in your use of warm water when rinsing off the paper. I would also suggest using a household sponge. The paper/glue mixture is going to be a lot like a gummy paper mache mixture, and it's real important to get it all off of the fabric. What happens if you don't is, when the fabric dries, the design will not be clear, but sort of smoky. That is because there are little bits of glue and paper clinging to the fibers of the fabric. Sometimes it helps to run the water full force from the faucet onto the fabric, starting with hot and moving to cold water, so that the force of the water will help release the glue from the fabric. This has helped me. Don't feel like you are going to rip the paper off of the fabric, since it is the *ink,* not the paper, which provides the design!

DESIGN IDEAS USING T RANSFER MEDIUMS

Many wonderful ideas can come from this marriage of fabric art and photography, not to mention the wealth of ideas derived from using newspaper and magazines as one's design ingredients. Within the realm of photographs, think of all the family members and other significant people in one's life who could be used as the raw material in fiber art. Many creative ideas can come from this process. For example, take a number of photographs of someone (yourself included!) and organize them in a design on a T–shirt or jacket. Various comments or autobiographical details can be added. A small quilt with patchwork photos is another creative idea, which can chronicle an individual's life or a family. Or, make a quilted wall hanging of family members, with a written biography about each member underneath their picture; or extending this idea to an actual quilt.

Another idea is to use children's art on T–shirts. One way is to photocopy several favorite pictures from a children's book, enlarging or reducing the images as desired. (Use a Color Xerox machine). Use a transfer medium or transfer glue to transfer image to fabric, being aware that the images will show in reverse on the finished project.

SWEATSHIRT AND T–SHIRT ART

Sweatshirt art is a genre of fabric painting which includes using various fabric painting techniques along with a number of craft and sewing techniques on sweatshirts and T–shirts. For example, fabric painting techniques include using the **various dimensional paints, sponging techniques, stenciled shapes, "special effects" fabric paints such as metallic, neon, puff, and glitter fabric paints, spatter painting, and watercolor techniques.** Incorporated along with these various fabric painting methods are sewing items such as: **applying appliqued fabrics with fusible webbing, adding ribbons, bows, buttons, ribboned roses, edgings, trims, fringes, laces, sequined appliques, leather fringes and strips, tassels, braids, and crocheted edgings; sewn beadwork, including glass beads, bugle beads, Fimo handmade beads, and handsewn pearls; glitzy decorations such as rhinestones, studs, nailheads, acrylic gems, sequins, Austrian crystals, Austrian crystal rhinestones, and cabochons; and using various glues and adding galafetti, sparkles, glitters, and sequins.** Other techniques used include **iron–on transfer patterns, and foil art (or foiling).** Usually a number of these

techniques are used all together, rather than just one or two. It is truly a mixed media!

SWEATSHIRT PROJECT IDEAS

Here are several ideas for making these sweatshirts or T–shirts. One is to use iron–on transfers, along with foil art and dimensional paints. Another is to start with sponging a background texture and then add appliqued shapes with fusible webbing. Finish off by adding some beads, buttons, and stenciled shapes. A third is to use dimensional paints to make squiggles, then add sewing ribbons, trims, buttons, applique, lace with metallic paint. Techniques that are popular include sponging, watercolor techniques, glitter paints, swirls, dots, the simple repeating shapes, squares, circles, hearts and triangles. Focus on elements such as shapes, texture, color, and placement.

TECHNIQUES FOR SWEATSHIRT ART

Sewn–on items: Remember also that rhinestones with holes can be sewn on, as well as items such as buttons (manufactured or handmade), beads, and bells.

Studs and Nailheads: Studs and nailheads are attached by pressing the prongs into the fabric and then pressing them down, usually using a small screwdriver, so that the metal hooks are secured. Some nailheads and rhinestones, as well, are attached with a special tool which places them into the fabric.

Don't forget to use scavenged items such as seashells, feathers, small pieces of driftwood, and small rocks and pebbles for decoration.

Handmade Figures and Shapes: Fimo and Sculpty can be molded into beads, buttons, and other small sculpted shapes and then glued onto fabric and clothing. Acrylic modeling clay can be similarly sculpted, colored (with the addition of acrylic paint) and glued. **Friendly Plastic** can be used to make decorative shapes which can also be glued. Acrylic resin historically was used to make jewel shaped pieces, so these can be used as well.

Applique with fusible webbing: Fusible webbing is a convenient sewing product often used in sweatshirt art which fuses fabric to fabric. It makes applique especially easy. Pellon **Wonder–Under** is one fusible web product available which has a paper backing. The paper backing allows you to transfer iron–on transfer designs directly onto the paper, or use stencils, or draw a design directly.

For example, let's say I decide to put some handpainted applique heart shapes on a sweatshirt. I paint cotton fabric with acrylics and dimensional paints. Then, using a stencil with a heart design, I trace it onto the paper backing of the fusible web. I then place the rough side of the webbing (which is the back) onto the wrong side of the painted fabric, and iron these together so they will fuse. Another way of doing this is to go ahead and iron the wrong side of the fabric to the fusible webbing *before* painting. The advantage of this is that, if you are using dimensional paints, you don't have to iron and squash the dimensional paint design.

To applique a shape onto a T–shirt, sweatshirt, or other item, you simply peel off the backing and position the fabric with the web side down onto the project (in other words, your painted surface will be on top). Cover with a damp press cloth, iron with a wool (or low setting), apply pressure and fuse for 15–20 seconds. Your damp press cloth should dry in that time and you can use that as a guide to the timing. With a large area, the fusing process is repeated, until all of the fabric is fused. The heavier the fabric is, the longer it takes to fuse.

FOIL ART (FOILING)

Foil art, or foiling, is a technique using foil paper where the paper is ironed onto fabric in a variety of ways. The first method is similar to applique with fusible web, in that glue is first laid down onto fabric and the foil then is ironed onto the fabric. Special foil paper can be bought at art supply stores, and comes in a variety of colors. The second method uses manufactured iron–on foil transfer patterns. Dupey carries some very nice ones with intricate designs. The third method uses glue to create a design on fabric. After the glue is dry, the foil is ironed over the glue to make a reflective form.

The first method requires that you cut or tear out the foil shapes. First put some parchment paper underneath your fabric. Then, cut or tear out shapes from the foil and place them onto the fabric or clothing. All sorts of designs are possible that are not possible with fabric. For example, snowflake cut–out designs or Chinese paper cutouts are nice, as well as little squares, circles, triangles,etc.

When you have decided on the placement of the shapes, put glue down beneath the shapes. (It is actually easier to put the glue onto the back of the paper of the foil than straight onto the fabric as the instructions say.) Use **Duncan Foil 'N Adhesive glue or Delta/Slomon's Stitchless glue.** Lay the pieces of foil paper onto the glued surface and put another piece of parchment paper over the foil. The glue can be sticky or you can wait for it to dry. Iron at a low setting such as for wool, for 10–12 seconds. Use dimensional paints to outline around the foil for a finished effect.

A second technique is similar except that the glue can be built up in globs and abstract shapes. It is left to dry from 2 hours to overnight. It should be clear when dry. Then lay a piece of foil over the glue, and, with an iron set at medium heat, iron the foil to the glue. Use the tip and sides of the iron in order to get to the hard–to–reach places. Let the foil cool. Remove the foil which did not adhere to the glued areas. It is really important to use parchment paper, because if you don't the iron will cause the foil to rub off.

This is a somewhat more complex operation than the instructions give. When you lay the foil on top of the glue and then iron it, there will be foil that is not under the glue design, and it will need to be torn off. I used a stencil knife to rip slowly and take off the foil. Another way to approach this, however, is to tear foil into the approximate shapes of the glued design. This may avoid this other problem.

This is a nice technique as long as you are not looking for precision. It can be nice for an applique on a sweatshirt.

A third technique includes using iron–on foil which has already been shaped into intricate designs. They are available from MJ Designs at Dupey Management Corporation. I have not tried these, though they look very interesting.

FOILING TECHNIQUES

It's really important when you do foiling, when you are cutting out small shapes of foil, such as triangles or squares or circles, that you lay it over on your hand, on the back, and carefully glue, starting from one corner and tracing around the *edge* of the shape with the glue from corner to corner or edge to edge. Then move the glue inward. Lightly spread the glue over the shape, and the press the shape onto the fabric very *lightly.* This will give you the best effect, for the glue will adhere to the corners of the foil and not curl up.

Be sure you have plenty of parchment paper (I used transparent drawing cover paper). If any glue gets over on top, it's going to stick to the parchment and can make things a little messy. Generally, it is hard to get the edges of the foil to lay down flat, so it is good to put some dimensional paint over that afterwards. Sometimes the foil will scratch off and then it must be covered with paint.

Another important feature is deciding where to place the foil designs. When you are decorating a sweatshirt or a T-shirt, think about the placement since the foil is a paper product and will not bend when the body moves, as will fabric. It is best to put the designs where there will not be a lot of movement or stretching, such as around the shoulder and neck area, and the front of the chest. Small shapes or "cut–out" shapes (such as a shape with openwork) are best for mobility.

PHOTOGRAPHIC PROCESSES

There are a number of processes which can incorporate photographic visual images onto cloth. They include **photosilkscreen, using photographic positives or negatives, cyanotype, photograms, brown–print, blue–print, copy–transfer, Xerography, photo emulsion, and color Xerox.** I refer you to photography books and other books on surface design for most of these processes; however, I would like to describe the last two for you.

In **photo emulsion,** a photographic emulsion is brushed onto the surface of the fabric. It is then put under an enlarger. The film is put into the enlarger and the image centered onto the fabric. The fabric is then printed as you would a picture. The emulsion can be bought or special ordered at photo stores. The fabric must be dry–cleaned, rather than washed. One idea I have had for use with this process is to take a series of pictures of houses, then make a skirt with the pictures of these houses on it, and go walking down the street in the skirt.

Color Xerox is another popular process. In many ways, it is similar to the heat transfer process. A color Xerox machine (specifically color Xerox 6500) duplicates color illustrations from magazines or books as well as color slides. It prints the image, using diazo colors (similar to disperse dyes) onto paper. The paper is now treated in a manner similar to heat transfer. Iron the print onto a synthetic fabric, and peel the backing off. In order to solve the reversal problem, you can have the slide reversed in the machine. Color Xerox machines can be rented, or you can have prints done for around $2.00 each. They can only be used once, unlike the heat transfer process. Virginia Jacobs, Virginia Davis,and Jan Cochran are some of the many fiber artists using color Xerox in their work.

SPONTANEOUS PAINTING

Spontaneous painting is the next large category of painting techniques. The roots of spontaneous painting are in the Action painters of the 1940's here in America. Instead of planning out a painting, doing preliminary drawings and slowly building up a picture, painters began to throw paint onto canvas, letting it drip, letting it soak in at random, letting it form its shape with little help from the painters' hand. In general, spontaneous painting allows for chance effects due to motion and the forces of gravity. Jackson Pollack was one of the more better known "spontaneous" art painters.

For fabric painting as well, spontaneous painting means letting natural circumstances affect your painting. A design book called ***Design by Accident***–O'brien (Dover) has many different techniques to achieve spontaneous design. Chance effects due to motion include pouring the paint around onto the fabric and then tilting the fabric in different directions in order to move the paint around onto the fabric.

Another possibility is to hang a large piece of wet fabric on a clothesline, and pour and drip paint onto the fabric. Again, manipulate the fabric in different ways to affect the direction of the paint. You can press different parts of the fabric together, or squeeze it, while it is hanging. Let the fabric dry, and see if you have the desired effect. If not, repeat the process, letting colors run more thickly in areas where the color is washed out or the design undesirable.

Another possibility: hang wet or dry cloth on a clothesline outside on a windy day. Brush and drip paint onto the surface of the fabric. Let the wind affect the design. Other examples of letting nature affect a design include using the sun, shadows, and water. The paint material, Inkodye changes color and develops with the use of the sun. Paint fabric with Inkodye and then let it sit outside on a sunny day. Use shadows creatively. Sit under a tree and draw the shadows of the leaves from sunlight. Or sit under a tree in winter with a piece of fabric laid flat on a board. Then trace the patterns of the shadows of the winter tree onto the cloth.

Spatter painting is an easy way to do spontaneous painting. Spatter painting is pouring paint onto a flat surface of cloth from various heights, letting it "spatter" into a design upon the cloth. Plastic containers, such as yogurt or cottage cheese, are useful to mix and pour the paint from. There are real differences in effects due to the size of the pouring containers, the angles at which you pour, and the speed at which you pour. As well, different paint materials react differently with different kinds of cloth. Working with four or five colors is a good way to start with spatter painting, as these colors blend into other colors without getting too messy. My favorite combination of colors is maroon, bright orange, yellow, olive green, and navy blue. Experiment with different combinations of colors.

Pouring and crumpling is another way to paint spontaneously. This entails pouring paint onto the fabric, much like spatter painting. Rather than keeping the fabric smooth, however, crumple it and then pour the paint into the cracks and ridges of the fabric. Then carefully spread the fabric out. Blowing paint is an interesting way to get a design. Try using straws for direct blowing; try a vacuum cleaner hose or a hose from an electric hair dryer as well. Think about how to move the color over the fabric.

Fingerpainting can be used on fabric. Use the motions of twisting, pulling, pressing, spattering, flicking, and pushing the paint into the fabric with your fingers. Try rubbing in the color. (Be sure and use protective gloves while doing this). All these ways are spontaneous, and you will not know the results until you have tried them. Spontaneous painting should be looked upon as experimental rather than definitive. It is not restrictive. It is, however, subject to certain rules in the same way that the effects of wind and water are governed by certain rules, even if they seem intangible.

DIRECT PAINTING

The last type of painting category I will discuss is called **direct painting.** Direct painting is what is normally considered painting, in other words painting as has been recorded in art history and that which is taught in art schools. Direct painting is differentiated from indirect and spontaneous painting in that the paint is applied directly onto the surface with a tool, usually a brush. The older books on surface design and fabric decoration only give slight mention to direct painting. They define it as spray painting, canning, using eye droppers, paint rollers, and brushes, but either assume that the fabric painter is already an accomplished painter, or do not realize the diversity of techniques with direct painting. All *art techniques* will not transfer exactly to fabric, but a background in art and painting will definitely help you as a fabric painter!

DIRECT PAINTING TECHNIQUES

Techniques of direct painting derive from **oil painting, acrylic painting, drawing, pastels, and watercolor.** One can also derive techniques from studying **still life, landscape, cityscape, seascape, figure drawing, painting flowers, and painting trees.**

Much fabric painting creates what I call a "textile style" of painting: flat areas of color much like painting on paper with tempera. **Oil painters,** however, will probably want to transfer their skills to painting in an "oil style"—using oils and textine, turpentine, or a mix of oils, turpentine, and enamel paints. **Watercolorists** might enjoy using acrylic, blending it into the fabric using a variety of watercolor techniques, and experimenting with a variety of weaves of fabric (cotton, muslin, poly–cotton, linen, canvas). Artists who draw using a variety of materials such as pencils, pens, charcoal, and pastels, could use dye pastels, inks, fabric markers, and embroidery paints on well–stretched fabrics for similar effects.

Direct painting is most effective when the *technique* of canvas painting and the *function* of fabric decoration methods are blended. To do this, one moves *beyond* painting a repeat motif on yardage. One moves *beyond* painting a picture squarely on a piece of fabric. What is really happening is that you learn an "art vocabulary" and transfer the principles of perception, perspective, tonal exercises, color exercises, etc. to fabric and cloth. When this vocabulary is learned, you are much more free to express painting that is unique to the fabric surface and the clothing form.

DRAWING

There are many exercises from drawing that are useful to the fabric painter. Drawing is one of the basics to good painting. It's crucially important to learn how to observe correctly. If one can learn how to see objects in terms of their angular relationships, tones, their relationship to other objects,and the detail of texture, sketching or drawing them is fairly basic. One problem is that the brain can distort what the eye sees. Drawing books are full of ideas in "training the eye to see".

One good exercise is to practice drawing lines with various paint materials onto various kinds of fabric. Learn to see angles to draw simple rectangular shapes such as a book on a table, a table on a floor, a house with a yard and a fence. The science of perspective must be learned. For example, parallel perspective means that all parallel lines will converge at one vanishing point (on the horizon of your picture). With angular perspective, lines which are at right angles to each other converge at separate points.

Practice drawing rectangular and cylindrical shapes using the rules of perspective. A line drawn down the body of a cylinder will always be at right angles to a line drawn through the center of the ellipse. Then practice drawing objects by using a grid. Place some cardboard drawn through with grid lines behind some objects—a vase of flowers, for example. Then lightly mark grid lines on your fabric, and practice drawing the object properly, using the grid marks as guides.

Another simple exercise is to practice drawing simple, flat shapes and notice the negative space around them. Place some simple objects in front of you, sketch them with a colored pencil, then fill the shapes in with dye pastels. Then fill the areas around the shapes with color. To learn the beginnings of tone, observe the shadows that objects cast. Practice with a simple sketch, lines to suggest shapes, then shading effects.

The crucial aspect of drawing is to be able to move back and forth from larger shapes to small and then back to large. Let me explain. Draw the outlines of flowers in a round vase. Then focus on each separate object, adding more line and tonal qualities. Continue to reduce these large areas of the picture to smaller detail. Check back to the larger area, wherever it is, to see if your shapes are correctly representing what you are drawing. If you are, continue on with the detail of the smaller areas. If not, adjust whatever mistakes may have been made.

TONAL EXERCISES

Tone creates the illusion of depth. A two–dimensional flat fabric can appear three–dimensional. The easiest tonal exercise is done in only one color. Draw a simple scene, and add tonal variations. Remember that depth is created by thick strokes in the foreground and thin ones in the background. Your one color can be darkened for darker hues, and lightened with white for the highlights.

The light source helps you decide which areas of the picture will be in light, and which in shadow. In this way, each area of the fabric is broken down into three tonal values:light, medium,and d ark. With more experience, you can refine your highlights and accentuate your shadows. Your nearby objects will be strong in tone, color, and well–defined. Objects far away will be of a lessened tonality, not as colorful, and less well–defined.

Here's another tonal exercise. Lay in washes with acrylic or textile paint. Lightly sketch your objects or design. First put down the lightest wash, then the second lightest. Add details. Then add the darkest tonalities, adding more details and highlighting with white. Also try working with just white, grey, and black, and paint gradations from light to dark in squares. Then try a simple picture that has perspective, say, looking down a road. Paint this in your whites, greys, and blacks in order to create a sense of depth.

COLOR EXERCISES

After learning about tone, it is a lot easier to put in color. You can work from the lightest tones to the darkest—in color. But first, it's helpful to learn just how to mix colors. A good exercise is to mix the three primaries—blue, yellow, and red, on a color wheel. This will give you the secondaries—violet, green, and orange,and then further blends. Then try bands of hues, going from the lightest to darkest, then overlay them with other hues to see blending.

Try a color study all in one hue, with its variations in value and chroma. Choose a variety of objects that are naturally in one color range. A pink flower, a red apple, and a rose tablecloth are some examples. Try a color study, painting the same still life three times, using a different range of colors each time. You can also emphasize the differences in warm and cool colors. (Warm colors go towards red, while cool ones go towards blue.)

An organized palette is important. Try warm colors across the top, and cool down the side. It's very important to mix the colors on the palette rather than on the fabric! Put colors together on the palette in groups, in order to see how they would look for a particular painting.

Check the color balance in your painting. If one color dominates or is isolated in the picture, it may need to be balanced by being repeated in other areas of the picture. An easy way to practice with color is to work from a color photograph. Use felt–tip colored pens to sketch a drawing, and then paint it onto fabric. There are many other ideas for working with color in painting books.

WATERCOLOR

Watercolor provides the fabric painter with many useful techniques. Watercolor uses both drawing and painting techniques, with line pictures and washes. You can lightly sketch in a design with a transfer pencil, or you can use the color itself to describe shape. Dyes, acrylics, and textile paint can all be used with watercolor techniques. (Fig.166)

It's best to practice strokes first without trying to form shapes. Allow yourself a lot of space and work big at the beginning, so you can learn to really move your brush in sweeping strokes! Watercolor is well known for using white space in a positive and unique way. Think of white shapes—sailboats, white clouds, fences, etc. and let your white fabric contrast with the blending of colors around these shapes.

Washes are very important to use. With an **even wash,** starting at the top of your fabric, brush back and forth across the wet fabric, letting the color run down, and overlapping each successive stroke. In a **graduated wash,** start at the top of the wet fabric with a brushload of pure paint. As you work down, use less paint and more water. Graduated washes can also emphasize the concentration of color in the middle or on each edge of the fabric. A **color wash** is created by brushing one color onto the wet fabric in even strokes. It will create a background upon which you can then paint or draw.

There are a number of other watercolor techniques besides washes. Splattering, stippling, blowing, dry brush, wet-on–wet, wet-on–dry, and scumbling are also used in watercolor. **Splattering** is like spatter painting or spraying. With **stippling** you make tiny dots with a brush for shading. **Blowing** just means is to apply lighter paint over darker, so that the underneath layer shows through. In both of these cases, the scumbling allows some paint to be hidden, while other paint is revealed.

I'll mention a few more of the many watercolor techniques. (Refer to *1001 PRODUCTS AND RESOURCES FOR THE FABRIC PAINTER AND SURFACE DESIGNER* for more books on watercolor). **Wet–line drawing** means drawing lines with a wet brush on damp fabric. You'll get a softened effect with this technique. **Drips** occur by drawing through areas of wet and dry fabric with a wet brush. The wet areas will drip onto the dry ones, producing interesting effects. **Partial wetting** of your fabric can be a very creative technique. It will give you contrasts in tone and types of edges. Depending upon which areas you keep dry and which are wet, you can create totally different effects with the same drawing or design.

Try mixing hard–edged and soft–edged (wet–on–wet) techniques in one painting. When doing a painting in watercolor, look at the white or negative space and try drawing **around** it as the main area of interest. For example, draw a tree, but leave its shape white. Focus on the areas around the tree shape for your color blendings. And remember, when doing tonal values, a light tone in watercolor has a lot of water and not much paint, while a dark tone has a lot of pigment and not much water.

Salt is a popular watercolor technique. While it can be overdone, if used properly, its effects are nice. Throw salt onto your wet fabric. Then paint over with your paint material. (I have found that textile paint works the best, but dye and acrylics are also possible). The wetter the paint, the larger the star–shaped spots be that will occur. Likewise, the drier the paint, the smaller the spots.

OIL TECHNIQUES

Traditional oil painting uses either layering or alla prima. **Layering, or glazing,** occurs by building up tones and colors with glazes, letting each one dry first. This can be done on a minimal scale with fabric painting, as long as not too many layers are attempted. **Alla prima,** where wet oil is mixed in and onto other wet paint, is a more spontaneous and freeform technique, and can be successfully transferred with various paint materials.

As with other tonal exercises, you can first sketch your drawing onto the fabric with a transfer pencil. Then add an underpainting with oil and turpentine, and then build up your painting with more oil and turpentine mixture. This can also be done with acrylics and textile paint. Just be sure to limit the number of layers, so that your fabric does not become stiff.

Although drawing is emphasized by many people as the foundation for painting, there are a number of oil painters who feel that it is not a crucial skill. They suggest you sketch out ideas, but primarily focus on painting. Think about color, applying colors and shapes to fabrics and see what happens.

One of oil painting's best techniques is one the Impressionists used—that of putting little dabs of color next to each other which would slightly blend into each other. Try this with oil paint and turpentine as well as with other paint materials.

FIG. 166: ARDEN DALE MODELING WATERCOLOR STRIPE PAINTED GATHERED SKIRT. THE SIMPLE DESIGN COMPLIMENTS THE SKIRT DESIGN.

using a straw to blow the paint onto the wet fabric. With **dry brush,** you pick up fairly liquid paint with your brush and then flick out most of it before painting. The thicker the paint on your brush, the rougher and more ragged the drybrush effect. Drybrush is used to create textured effects, as the fabric will show through where the brush lays down separated paint strokes. **Wet–on–wet** creates an entirely opposite effect. Take wet fabric and run color through it, letting the color spread out. This process works very well with dyes and acrylics on cotton and poly–cotton. **Wet–on–dry** allows for overlapping transparent shapes due to applying wet paint onto dry. This modulates the tone of the wet paint as it will show some of the paint below. **Scumbling** has several definitions. In one process, take thick paint with your brush and apply it with a scrubbing motion. The paint will blur, and take on a broken, rough quality. Another way to scumble

ACRYLIC TECHNIQUES

Acrylic techniques do not vary much from what has already been described in the sections on tonal exercises and oil. However, when using wet–on–wet with acrylics, you may wish to use a gel retarder to slow down the drying time of the paint. You can use acrylics with the glazing technique as previously mentioned.

One of the greatest advantages of acrylics is that they will dry quickly and then can be painted over right away. ***Acrylic Water-color Painting*** by Wendon Blake is full of interesting ideas and techniques that take full advantage of the special properties of acrylic paints. To make acrylics more transparent, add gel medium. If you desire to stain your fabric, you may want to use a water–tension breaker with the paint. It will slightly dilute your color, but will help speed the flow of the paint onto the fabric.

PASTEL TECHNIQUES

Short, direct strokes are used with pastels to take full advantage of their delicate rendering. Color is not rubbed in, and textural effects are possible by lightly handling the pastel. Dye pastels are more oily, but can be used in a similar manner and can achieve some of the same effects, particularly that of texture.

STILL LIFE

There are several ways of approaching still life. For all still life techniques, however, you'll want to set up the subjects of your painting somewhere where they won't be disturbed. Also, it's important that you have a good light source. Don't try and have too complex an arrangement for a still life. Choose a few, interesting subjects and place them in an interesting background.

One technique for painting still life is to paint the background first. Then paint the foreground. Add the main subject, and then fill out with details. Another sequence is to first draw in the horizon line, usually the edge of a table. Then sketch in the outlines of the shapes, noticing the spaces between the shapes as well. Then add washes for tonal areas. Middle–toned washes can be used to give the objects form, while areas of light can be filled in with a lightertoned wash. Add shadows and areas of shade with darker washes. Then begin adding colors of the main shapes, keeping to the tonal variations. (It might be best to mix these color tonalities on a palette separately) Then add your finishing details, such as textures, highlights, and shadows.

Still life can be painted in a very realistic manner, with tight control and lots of details. At the same time, it can be rendered with emphasis on color areas and free and easy linear gestures. **Flower painting** is a popular theme in still life. There are many good books that will give you step–by–step instructions for

flower painting. There are two ways you can emphasize a flower painting as a still life. One is to use lots of textured brushstrokes to show the complexity of the blossoms, and carefully detail each stem. The other way emphasizes blocks of color to show flower shapes. For fabric painting, a light background with just a few blooms could make a simple and eloquent statement.

LANDSCAPE

Landscape is certainly a subject matter overflowing with ideas: one has only to look outside to find something of interest to paint. Landscape painting is not just a matter of recording this or that tree, a hill, etc. but recreating an entire scene with atmosphere and light. Landscape can be abstract or realistic. Regardless of which one you may prefer, be sure to learn the techniques of both; in this way your painting can be strengthened rather than limited. Think of landscape like a patchwork quilt—there are a number of elements which must be successfully put together!

A sketchbook is crucially important for landscape painting, since ideas can be jotted down and then worked up in the studio. Take notes, also, of colors and tones.

There are many techniques in landscape painting, many ways to approach a work. You can begin by painting in the background or sky, with the light tone at the horizon. Then add the middle tones and the dark at the top. Add ground color, trees, details, etc. It's important to first draw in the horizon line. Work in masses of tone and color at first rather than shapes, so that you can get your thoughts down. Then work out the lines of trees, fields, etc. Mix your colors on your palette (rather than on the fabric) and think out your color scheme. If you like, put out colors for the trees, sky, hills, etc. on your palette in order to co–ordinate your colors.

Scale and perspective are very important, especially when working with a distant view. It's best to start with a view that is not overwhelmingly panoramic. That can come later. Try painting the same scene over and over again, from different angles. For example, stand at the top of a small hill, sketch the view below. Then walk down the hill halfway, then to the ground level. Remember that, as the forms in your painting recede toward the vanishing point, they diminish in size.

Choose an interesting eye level position. If it is high, the view looks panoramic. If it is low (from a sitting position) you can build a dramatic scene. In the middle of your canvas or fabric, the eye level will create an ordinary looking scene. Choose the one that best suits your purpose.

It can be helpful to divide your "canvas" into foreground, middleground, and background. Make a tonal chart for these three areas, before you start painting. Another helpful technique is to divide the fabric into halves or quarters before sketching in a scene. A grid, with even smaller squares, can help with perspective.

As mentioned before, landscape painting can be realistic or abstract. Abstract painting is especially suited for fabric painting. Landscape color field painting is another possibility, for colors are placed one against the other. A popular technique puts in a background of one overall color, then one particular area is highlighted in a contrasting color. With either color field or abstract painting, don't get involved in details at all. Just focus on masses of color and shape!

Landscape is successful with different mediums. Wet–in–wet watercolor is especially effective, since the blending allows for overall tonal effects of sky, fields, etc. Details can then be filled in with a pen. Washes of receding color can form interesting landscapes. Simply add a few narrow brushstrokes on the horizon for details of trees and sky. Drybrush can give very opposite effects, with rough textures representing tree bark or clods of earth in an unplowed field. Be sure to remember that when beginning a landscape in watercolor, you will start with the lighter tones and move to the foreground with darker tones. However, when working with oil or fabric paint, you start with the darker tones, and work *from* the foreground to the background with the lighter colors on top.

Field, skies, clouds, hills, trees; all are important aspects of landscape painting. **Painting trees** is especially important. Study the shapes of trees, especially in winter, when you can see the branches clearly. Study the silhouette of the tree, and how it enters the ground. See how the main branches split off from the trunk. When the branches divide farther up, notice whether or not one branch is larger than its corresponding mate. (It often is.) Notice how the leaves group themselves. Paint trees on the horizon, middle ground, and in the foreground of your painting. Paint them as trunks and branches; also paint them as blobs of color. And most of all, *study* trees. Sketch them! It's better to really learn a few tree species well than to attempt a partial success with many.

To sum up landscape, have a center of interest in your picture, create a rhythm by leading the eye on a "path" from one area of the picture to another. Contrast this with areas of calm. Make studies and sketches of all the interesting subject matter in the natural landscape.

CITYSCAPE

Cityscape is, indeed, part of our modern landscape. Towns, cities, villages, buildings are all a part of cityscape. They provide an ample opportunity to study shapes and surfaces, especially rectangles and geometric shapes. Telephone poles, bridges, chimneys, brickwork, grates, doors, windows, curtains, shutters, fences, park benches, monuments, roofs, and gaslights are just some of the features that can be used in cityscapes. They can be portrayed either realistically or abstractly, and done in all mediums.

Again, doing sketches is very important, as you will have to set up work in a studio rather than on a city street. Sketches can give you quick impressions that can be worked into future compositions. Perspective and scale are important in cityscapes, so that your buildings are in correct relation to each other. Use a grid if necessary to help you attain proper scale.

To begin a cityscape, indicate the horizon. Divide your surface into background and foreground. Note the changes in scale with a foreground building versus a background one. Use a greater amount of detail in the foreground. Sketch in the main shapes and lay washes for the sky and walls, if using watercolor.

One problem in a cityscape for a painter is the overwhelming amount of detail available. Does one try and draw every brick, every fence post? The solution is to emphasize certain details, and leave the rest in color masses. Choose what you want to emphasize, with some reasoning; otherwise, your picture will look imbalanced, with certain areas in great detail, and others looking bare.

Figures can be a part of cityscapes. Parks and ornamental gardens can, as well, be a nice place to work and have the city as a backdrop to your picture. The subject of cityscape is a challenge to the dress designer, but with the rectangular shapes, it can be a successful painted clothing design.

WATERSCAPE(SEASCAPE)

Waterscape and seascape are two other interesting subjects for painting. The subject matter is vast: skies, seas, boats, ships, clouds, fishing, shoreline, rocks, sand, pebbles, tides, tide pools, jetties, cliffs, headlands, beaches, sea shells, waterfalls, ponds, rivers, lakes, canoes, and sailboats can all be included in the theme of waterscape. Perspective and scale are very important with waterscape, as water is so fluid and invisible, as well as mobile. A stable structural background is important.

Waterscape is not the easiest subject to portray. Water can vary from being a perfectly quiet reflecting surface, through restless water that mirrors broken images, to the frothy "white" water of ocean waves and wild rivers. As well, when you add the effects of the sun on the water, with the changing light, color, and reflected light that ensues, painting water can become a formidable challenge!

One way of minimizing these problems is to do a seascape

in watercolor. First, draw a horizon line. Be sure that it is exactly horizontal, or else your ocean will appear to tilt. Fill in the sky with washes. Then add the foreground. Use the drybrush technique to put the misty spray onto the ocean waves.

Water moves and also reflects a moving sky. Water can ripple and reflect the moving trees overhead. Study the shore-lines of water—they provide interesting subject matter. Paint-ing water is also painting what is **around** the water, and how water reacts with these other elements.

FIGURE DRAWING

Figure drawing doesn't have to be as complicated as it looks. First, look at the figure as triangles, cylinders, and rectangles. Sketch the torso as a triangle (inverted) with a rectangle for the pelvis, and put the cylinders on as arms and legs.

Sketching is crucially important for figure drawing. Sketch people when you are on the bus, walking in town, sketch your friends and family. You can even learn from sketching T.V. figures! It helps to learn simplified basic anatomy, but don't worry about learning the name of each muscle.

A wooden mannikin can be helpful to learn how the various parts of the body work in motion. They are available at art stores. Stick figures are very good to learn about the figure in motion. Practice with stick figures and don't worry about details of modeling. After you feel comfortable with the figure in motion, add tonal areas of light and shadow. Then model the features of the face.

Make studies of hands, feet, and heads. Don't try for too much detail in one drawing. Draw someone doing something. It will be easier for them, as a model, and a repetitious activity, (like sewing, ironing, or even drawing) will help you study the figure in motion.

CONCLUSIONS

Direct painting is indeed an exciting technique. Even with all the specific techniques, each painter will have her own particular style. You will be learning an artistic "vocabulary" which will have your own particular stamp. As well, each painter will pick out of a scene, or a subject, particular details that have meaning to them. Beginners tend to want to paint everything in one particular painting, but as you practice and grow, you will begin to naturally choose certain colors, details, elements that you want to express in a particular work. By isolating a certain element, it can be developed and explored.

Interiors is another subject matter that was not explored in this chapter. Also, practice painting by looking from the inside out. A window facing a garden is a particular favorite.

The shape of your canvas or fabric can be an effective compositional tool. A long narrow piece of fabric, with a vertical emphasis, is different from a skinny horizontal piece. Landscapes, with 2/3 sky, and 1/3 close–up, can utilize this latter form. With long verticals, paint in an oblique direction to maximize the canvas shape.

The point of emphasis is another useful concept. Draw two crossing diagonals on a square, and you will have divided the fabric into four areas. Depending on which quadrant is empha-sized, there is a different "point of emphasis".

I hope that these techniques, be they indirect, spontaneous, or direct, will keep you busy creating new and beautiful fabric paintings!

7

MIXED MEDIA

• •

Materials have different properties. Sometimes you may want to throw every possible material and technique in one garment for its rich interplay. At the same time it is necessary to isolate each materials' characteristics and know what works best in each situation. It makes sense to use a stencil or rubber stamps when doing a series of repeat designs instead of a brush or a pen—*if* you want them exactly the same. If not, the consideration is whether or not you want to do free–hand painting.

In the preceding chapters, there have been individual descriptions of the paints and their applications. Each material has advantages and disadvantages; each material is limited in its application. Even if you were to use only one kind of paint and made many beautiful things, you would be missing out on the possible effects of other materials. By using materials in combination, it is possible to use the best qualities of each individual material, therefore extending your own growth as a craftsperson.

Fabric painting encompasses such a wide area and large amount of material that I am going to just briefly go over some ideas as to its possible varied application. I am using the term mixed media to describe three areas: different mediums combined into one whole; fabric painting combined with other fabric techniques, such as needlework, weaving, patchwork, and other types of fabric decoration methods; and the use of different ideas combined into a whole in a painting.

Different mediums combined into one whole simply means that it is possible to use a variety of paint materials, brushes, cloth, and painting techniques in one garment or project. Make sure that the paint material and the type of cloth are compatible; that the various paint materials in an item can undergo the same amount of wear, and that you keep something (a color, form, type of material or painting technique) dominant in the overall design. Try using embroidery paint, textile paint, acrylics, and marking pens on the same cotton skirt. Or, make a skirt with three or four different types of fabric, making sure they hang well together and can be washed together and paint them with dyes using various size brushes. Just be sure that in your variety there is also sameness.

Fabric painting can also be mixed with other fabric tech-

niques, such as embroidery, stitchery, knitting, crocheting, regular sewing techniques, applique, lace, pleating, quilting, weaving, and patchwork. (Fig.167,168) Painted needlework combines textural interest with variations in color. Embroidery can be both painted and sewn, thus speeding the time it takes to do rows and rows on a skirt. Embroider on woven material, then add painted motifs.

Try making a knitted and crocheted rag rug with strips of dyed and painted cloth. Knit a purse with cotton string, then paint it with thickened dyes. Make a skirt with a crocheted yoke at the top, then add patchwork, painted fabric, and put heavy material at the bottom with thick stitchery. Make a shawl from a heavy soft material, add a crocheted edge, and paint. Make a skirt with applique and painted applique.

PAINTED WEAVING

Weaving lends itself well to painting. A number of fabric artists are weavers who incorporate fabric painting in their work. You can make woven paintings or painted weavings. The warp can be painted (commonly called ikat weaving) before it is put on the loom. As well, the warp threads can be painted after they are on the loom. And the weft can also be painted or dyed.

Ikat is identifiable by the stepped blocks, arrowhead–like patterns, or feathered aspects of the dyed pattern. In native cultures of Africa and the East, the complexity of the patterning of the ikat process has reached a high art form. The warp is bound, like in a bound resist, and then dyed. Dip–dyeing is another possibility in ikat work.

Warp painting creates soft shading throughout, with vertical emphasis. Tapestry weaving works especially well, allowing for a more painterly expression in the weaving. Both textile paint and direct dye application have been used with warp painting.

Woven pieces can also be painted. Dyes, textile paint, and acrylics have all been used with direct painting on weaving. Be sure to plan your design well so as to make no crucial mistakes on your handwoven, time–consuming project!

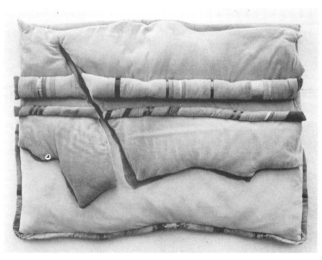

FIG. 167: **"UNTITLED–YELLOWS"**–VICTORIA RIVERS.
PROCION DYE ON VELVETEEN, AIRBRUSH, FLOCKING,
APPLIQUE, SCREENED AND HANDPAINTED,QUILTED
AND STUFFED. ANOTHER CREATIVE USE OF MIXED
MEDIA.

FIG. 168: **"RECOLLECTIONS VI"**–BY VICTORIA RIVERS.
PROCION DYE ON VELVETEEN, SCREENED AND
HANDPAINTED, APPLIQUE, QUILTED AND STUFFED.
4' X 6'. A GOOD EXAMPLE OF MIXED MEDIA.

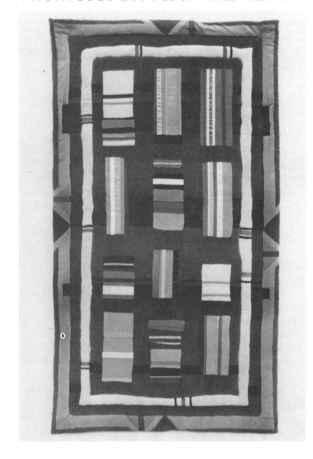

FIG. 169: DRAWING BY PHYLLIS THOMPSON. AFTER
PATTERNS IN **THE PERFECT PATCHWORK PRIMER**–
BETH GUTCHEON.

PAINTED PATCHWORK

Painted patchwork is a very nice example of mixed media. If you don't like cutting and sewing all those little patchwork pieces into intricate patchwork patterns, yet you like its effect it is possible to simplify the whole process by drawing and painting them on the fabric. And it is also possible to do the quilting afterwards, so that the sculptural quality is retained. (Fig.168, 177)

There are several different approaches to painted patchwork. One method is to paint individual squares in their respective designs; for example, the Log Cabin or the Wedding Ring. The squares are painted in solid colors, either leaving some areas white or filling in all the material with paint. One pattern can be used throughout the work, or a variety of patterns which blend well together are used. (Fig.169)

Another method of work is to paint individual pieces of material with different designs, such as is done when making fabric yardage. Cut this fabric into individual pieces of the quilt pattern, then sew them together. You will then have patchwork fabric with originally painted designs. Another variation is to paint a large piece of cloth with either all solid colors or a mixture of solid areas and patterned areas, all in a patchwork design, of course.

Patchwork is both the small square and the large quilt. There are many ways of combining the individual patterns into large pieces of fabric. Colors and fabric patterns and design patterns must be balanced out in the whole work. When the fabric is to lie flat, as in a quilt or a wall hanging, it is very important that it be well designed in all areas. However, when the fabric is used in certain garments, especially garments with gathering and pleating, the two–dimensional effect is modified by the body and movement, and becomes a three–dimensional work of art. When this happens, the design must be viewed from a new perspective.

Machine prints which are often used in patchwork (small prints, calicoes, etc.) are good guides in painting. Materials which are delicately detailed or heavily textured cannot be easily painted; it is easier to use closeweave flat smooth fabric for a patterned painting. Bright, broad splashes of color interspersed with plain colors or white are very effective. Simple rectangular shapes of various colors, sizes, and positions are very pleasing to the eye, easy to paint, as well as good exercises in working with shades and tones of color.

Another combination of painted patchwork is **woven paint–ed patchwork.** Any kind of patchwork can be used, but irregular shapes utilize the patchwork process more than squares would, because irregular individual shapes must be pieced together in order to form a cohesive unit. One large square could be woven rather than small individual pieces.

Woven painted patchwork can be formed by taking various pieces of cardboard and weaving small pieces on them. Then the individual pieces are painted with acrylic washes, textile paints, or fiber–reactive dyes. The pieces are then joined together. A small wall hanging or a sturdy purse are good ideas for this type of work.

SOFT SCULPTURE, DOLLS

Soft sculpture is a favorite technique for use with fabric painting. Many contemporary fabric painters use the techniques of soft sculpture to make dolls, containers, toys, soft jewelry, and other soft sculptural items.(Figs.170–175)

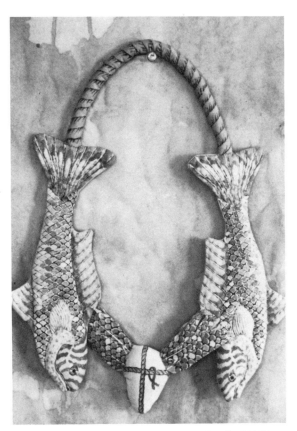

FIG. 170: **"FISH TRANSFORMATION"**– BY K. LEE MANUEL.

FIG. 171: **"PAINTED DOLL"**–BY K. LEE MANUEL.

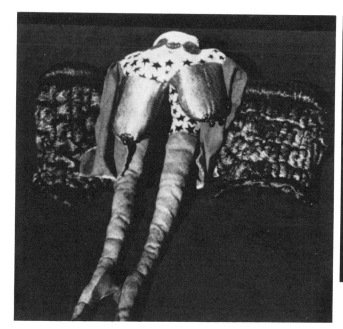

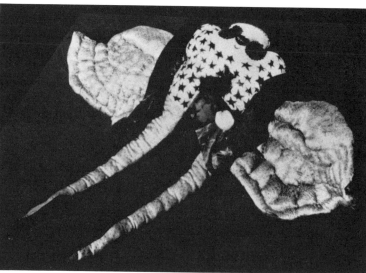

FIG.172: (TOP) *"FEMALE DOLL"*– BY NORMA ROSEN.
COLOR ETCHING ON SATIN. 36" HIGH, 54" WIDE.
(BOTTOM) FIG. 173: *"MALE DOLL"*– BY NORMA ROSEN.
COLOR ETCHING ON SATIN. 36" HIGH, 54" WING SPAN.

FIG. 174: *"WINGED BEAST"*–BY DOROTHY CALDWELL. COTTON WITH PROCION DYE. THIS TOY HAS A VARIETY
OF REMOVABLE NOSES, MOUTHS, AND STUFFED ACCESSORIES WHICH CAN BE PUT IN A STOMACH POUCH.

Fabric painting is also used in combination with other fabric decoration methods. Fabric painting can be used in connection with wood block prints, linoleum block prints, silkscreen, batik, and tie–dye. (Fig.176). Norma Rosen, a very exciting and talented artist, etches on fabric using zinc plates. Both intaglio and relief methods are used, and she also paints onto the fabric after the initial printing. (Figs.172–173)

COMBINING DIFFERENT IDEAS

Different ideas can be mixed together in a painting. Because fabric painting can use large amounts of space, it is possible to create various moods on different parts of the material. Unlike printed fabric, where the tone and mood pretty much remain the same over the fabric, painted fabric can express a variety of types of ideas. When you paint, open yourself up beyond the safe textile world of flowers and repeat motifs.

I see fabric painting as a bridge between the worlds of art and needlework. In this book, I have gone into detail in the areas of art history, the meaning of clothing, and technical aspects of painting in order to give you the tools to create more expressive, interesting, and varied clothes. Although there are many types of fabrics and designs on fabrics, there are limitations to what machines can do, as machines do not have human minds. The human personality and experience can be expressed through art and design, which then allows fashion design to expand beyond the time limitations of style. Fabric painting, when seen in this way and fully explored, becomes art: transcendent and universal.

THE END

• •

FIG. 176: **"LADY IN BLACK"**– BY CAROL RACKLIN. BATIK AND DIRECT APPLICATION OF PROCION DYE ON COTTON.

FIG. 177: "MAIN LOBBY # 2"– LINDA NELSON BRYAN. PAINTED AND STUFFED RELIEF (AIRBRUSH AND TRAPUNTO) ON ANTRON NYLON BLEND FABRIC WITH ACRYLIC PAINT.

APPENDIX A: LIST OF SUPPLIERS

PLEASE REFER TO MY COMPANION BOOK,1001 PRODUCTS AND RESOURCES FOR THE FABRIC PAINTER AND SURFACE DESIGNER, FOR A COMPLETE LISTING OF SUPPLIERS.

THESE ARE MAJOR DISTRIBUTORS AND SUPPLIERS OF FABRIC PAINTS, DYES, AND ACCESSORY ITEMS

COLOR CRAFT LTD.
14 AIRPORT PARK RD.
EAST GRANBY, CT 06026
(203) 653-6225
1-800-243-2712

Createx fabric paints, textile metallic, and fluorescent colors; Liquid fiber-reactive dyes; Iridescent fabric paints; chemicals thickeners for dyes

DHARMA TRADING COMPANY
P.O. BOX 916
SAN RAFAEL, CA 94915
(415) 456-7657
1-800-542-5227

Versatex textile paint,Deka metallic paint, Sennelier Texticolor Iridescent textile paint; Tinfix, Super Tinfix silk dyes; Seidercolor silk dyes and resists, brushes, gutta, resists, fabrics, printables,Dyehouse fiber-reactive dye,disperse dye, steamers

PROCHEMICAL AND DYE INC.
P.O. BOX 14
SOMERSET, MA 02726
(508) 676-3838
FAX: (508) 676-3980
Order #: 1-800-2-BUY-DYE

Procion-M, MX, and H fiber reactive dyes; acid dyes, disperse dyes, tex-tile inks; chemicals,Cibacron F dyes, respirator mask, liquid fiber–reactive dyes

RUBBERSTAMPEDE
P.O. BOX 246
BERKELEY, CA 94701
1-800-NEAT FUN

Rubber stamps & supplies

SOHO SOUTH
111 B1st St. NE
Cullman, AL 35055
1-205-737-9933
FAX: 1-205-737-9933

Fabric paints and dyes; silk fabric and scarves

BRITIAN

PEBEO, ART GRAPHIQUE, UNIT 2
POULTON CLOSE,COOMBE VALLEY ROAD
DOVER, ENGLAND CT17 0HL

Various fabric paints,including Pebeo fabric and silk paints;

HAYS CHEMICALS
55-57 GLENGALL ROAD
LONDON, ENGLAND SE15 6NQ

Procion dyes;other fabric paints (Helizarin fabric colors),metallic (bronze)powders and binder

BIBLIOGRAPHY

indicates booklets rather than books

FABRIC PAINTING

Ball, Kazz and Janitch, Valerie. **HAND PAINTED TEXTILES FOR THE HOME.** Devon, England: David & Charles ,1991.160 pages, $29.95

Campbell-Harding, Valerie. **FABRIC PAINTING FOR EMBROIDERY.** London: Batsford, Ltd., 1990.144 pages, $29.95

Johnston, Ann. **DYE PAINTING!** Paducah, KY: American Quilt Society, 1992. 87 pages, $ 19.95

Moyer, Susan Louise. **SILK PAINTING: THE ARTIST'S GUIDE TO GUTTA AND WAX RESIST TECHNIQUES.** NY: Watson-Guptill,1991. 144 pages, $24.95

*Nelson, Teresa. **HOW TO FABRIC PAINT IF YOU THINK YOU CAN'T.** Canby, OR: Hot Off The Press, 1991. 8 pages, $5.49

Peverill, Sue. **THE FABRIC DECORATOR: PAINTING, PRINTING, AND DYEING FABRICS FOR THE HOME.** Boston: Little,Brown, 1986. 160 pages, $29.95

Tuckman, Diane and Janas, Jan. **THE COMPLETE BOOK OF SILK PAINTING.** Cincinnati, OH: North Light Books,1992. 122 pages, $24.95

OTHER FABRIC DECORATION METHODS

Cohen, Daniel and Paula. **MARBLING ON FABRIC.** Loveland, CO: Interweave Press, 1990. 94 pages, $12.95

Drucker, Mindy and Finkelstein, Pierre. **RECIPES FOR SURFACES: DECORATIVE PAINT FINISHES MADE SIMPLE.** NY: Simon and Schuster, 1990. 255 pages, $19.95

Laury, Jean Ray. **IMAGERY ON FABRIC.** Martinez, CA: C & T Publishing, 1992. 160 pages, $24.95

Proctor, Richard and Lew, Jennifer F. **SURFACE DESIGN FOR FABRIC.** Seattle: University of Washington Press,1984.

Shipman, Wanda. **STENCILING MADE EASY.** Blue Ridge Summit, PA: Tab Books, Inc. 1989.

WEARABLE ART

Orban, Nancy. **FIBERARTS DESIGN BOOK IV.** Asheville, NC: Lark Books, 1992, 207 pages, $29.95

*Paulin, Lynn. **LYNN PAULIN'S WEARABLE ART 2.** Santa Maria, CA: LP Publishing, 1989.10 pages, $6.98

Rhodes, Zandra and Knight, Anne. **THE ART OF ZANDRA RHODES.** Boston: Houghton Mifflin, 1985. 240 pages.

Taylor, Carol. **THE GREAT T-SHIRT BOOK.** NY/NC: Sterling/Lark, 1992.112 pages, $12.95

Schafler-Dale, Julie. **ART TO WEAR.** NY: Abbeville Press,1986. 320 pages. $95.00

TEXTILE DESIGN

Fisher, Richard and Wolfthal, Dorothy. **TEXTILE PRINT DESIGN.** NY: Fairchild Publications,1987. 214 pages, $18.00

Jerstorp, Karin, and Kohlmark, Eva. **THE TEXTILE DESIGN BOOK.** Asheville, NC: Lark Books, 1990. 160 pages, $22.95

TEXTILES AND FASHION

Colchester, Chloe. **THE NEW TEXTILES: TRENDS AND TRADITIONS.** NY: Rizzoli, 1991.
Gillow, John and Barnard, Nicholas. **TRADITIONAL INDIAN TEXTILES.** London: Thames and Hudson, 1991.160 pages, $35.00
Meller, Susan and Elffers, Joost. **TEXTILE DESIGNS.** NY: Harry Abrams,1991.464 pages, $65.00
Singer, Margo and Spryou, Mary. **TEXTILE TRADITIONS.** Radnor, PA: Chilton Books, 1990. 128 pages, $16.95.
Sokolov, Joel. **TEXTILE DESIGNS-IDEAS AND APPRECIATIONS.** NY: PBC International Inc., 1991. 237 pages, $60.00

ABOUT DYES AND DYEING

Blumenthal, Betsy and Kreider, Kathryn. **HANDS ON DYEING.** Loveland, Co: Interweave Press, 1988
Walter, Judy Anne. **CREATING COLOR: A DYER'S HANDBOOK.** 1990.119 pages. $12.95

MAGAZINES, PERIODICALS

FIBERARTS, THE MAGAZINE OF TEXTILES (Asheville, NC))
SURFACE DESIGN JOURNAL (Fayetteville, TN))
THREADS MAGAZINE (Newtown, CT)

PHOTO CREDITS

Fig. 21: Chatham Press, Old Greenwich, CT.
Fig. 27: 1964.31.2, The Textile Museum,Washington
Fig. 28: Richard A. Pohrt, Flint, MI.
Figs. 37, 38, 42, 44, 45, 49,50: Dover Publications,
Fig. 51: Charles Uht, Heeramaneck Gallery, New York
Fig. 112,115: Dover Publications, New York.
Fig. 119: Harvard University Press, Cambridge, MA.
Fig. 123 Rainbird Publishing Group, London.
Figs. 144, 145: Verlag Ernst Wlasmuth,Tubingen, Germany
Fig. 151: Rizzoli International Publications. Inc. New York

Barbara, Dave: Figs.,69,98
Bryan, Ray: Fig. 177
Bryan, Steve: Fig. 160
Chandler, Sarah: Figs. 15,91,92, 114,117
Galgiani, Phillip: Figs. 62,80
Hartzel, Herman: Figs. 103, 9,11, 164
Kanzinger, Linda: Figs. 23, 24, 29,
74, 76,105, 122, 96, 14
Larsen, Rob: Figs. 6, 20,58,82,106
Nickolson, Anne McKenzie: Fig. 104
Richardson, Phyllis: Figs. 17,18
Roizen, Donna: Fig. 83
Ross, Ellen Essig: Figs. 1, 31,32,99, 102
Small,Perry: Figs. 84, 101
Straton, Jack: Figs. 8, 16,67,
109,110,121, 97
Thompson, Sue: Figs. 30, 140

GENERAL INDEX

ABOUT THE AUTHOR

I have always loved color, fiber, and texture. After 15 years, working with fabrics is still one of my greatest pleasures in life. I balance this intuitive work of designing and creating with the "thinking" work of writing books and running a business, The Alcott Press.

*I am presently working on several books which will be published in the years ahead. A resource book to this book is **1001 PRODUCTS AND RESOURCES FOR FABRIC PAINTERS AND SURFACE DESIGNERS,** due out in late summer, 1993. Another major work is **CLOTHING AND FASHION DESIGN FOR LARGE WOMEN,** which will be out as soon as possible!*

THIS BOOK CAN BE ORDERED DIRECTLY FROM THE PUBLISHER FOR $32.95 PP.

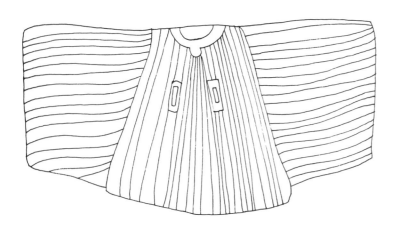

THE ALCOTT PRESS
2915 NE BROADWAY # C
PORTLAND, OR. 97232
(503) 287–3140